WHEN DREAMS CAME TRUE

WHEN DREAMS CAME TRUE

The GI Bill and the Making
of Modern America

MICHAEL J. BENNETT

BRASSEY'S
Washington

Copyright © 1996 by Brassey's, Inc.

First paperback edition 2000

Library of Congress Cataloging-in-Publication Data

Bennett, Michael J., 1936–
    When dreams came true : the GI Bill and the making of modern America / Michael J. Bennett.
       p.   cm.
    Includes bibliographical references and index.

    1. United States—Social conditions—1945– 2. Social change—United States—History—20th century. 3. Veterans—Education—United States—History. 4. Veterans—Education—Law and legislation—United States—History. I. Title.
HN58.B56   1996
306'.0973—dc20   96-27804
                                                CIP

ISBN 1-57488-218-X

10 9 8 7 6 5 4 3 2 1

Printed in Canada

For Mary and Michael, my mother and father,
who came to America from Ireland seeking their
fortunes only to find each other instead
and make a family.

CONTENTS

PREFACE

THE STORY OF the GI Bill of Rights is an American saga. But it is also, even more significantly, the personal and unique tale of each of the millions of individuals and families whose lives and futures were changed utterly through a law that worked.

In 1954, the tenth anniversary of the bill's passage, *Time* magazine observed that veterans, with their families, "come to nearly one-half of the nation's population." Unlike a generation before, when Franklin Delano Roosevelt had so memorably pointed to a third of the nation being in need, this one half of the nation was well fed, well clothed, and well housed. They were launched on lives unimaginable to their parents. Consider where they and the country had come from and where they were headed.

Most of these veterans had been born in city tenements or isolated farms around 1922, the year the Lincoln Memorial was opened. America was just becoming a predominantly urban rather than rural nation. Less than a quarter of those eligible went to high school, and of those, less than 20 percent graduated. In 1943, when these young soldiers, sailors, and airmen were privates and corporals or lieutenants and captains in Europe or the Pacific, the Jefferson Memorial was being dedicated. Slightly more than half the students in high school were graduating, and probably fewer than one hundred thousand Americans had been up in an airplane. Even fewer had seen a television program. In 1952, when General Eisenhower was elected president and called for a national highway system, the census results had been compiled by a new machine called a computer. Mothers were warning their sons that education beyond high school was becoming the passport to a new way of life called suburbia. In 1960, when the voters had a choice between two World War II veterans under fifty for president, the number of women in college was approaching 50 percent of enrollment. Blacks were demanding an end to segregation, and a walk on the moon was less than a decade away.

All this, and most World War II veterans were still less than forty years old.

They and America, this still very new country, had been growing up together, building monuments that seemed to have been there forever the moment they opened, creating inventions and marvels that seemed commonplace almost the next day, changing ways of living that had seemed impregnable just a few years before. Beginnings were made almost every morning by families in the postwar era, many of which would not have been possible without the GI Bill. And this may be the most extraordinary thing about this unique piece of legislation: It is the thread that runs through the personal and family memories of how lives changed after World War II.

After spending more than four years researching and writing this book, I feel I cannot overstate the value and meaning of the GI Bill. Its sweep was so vast, its impact so particular, that only one conclusion seems self-evident: The bill made a reality of Jefferson's concept of creating independent yeomen. Suburbia emerged when rural America—the setting in which the ideal of the yeoman started—was disappearing. I doubt whether those responsible for the bill's passage had any notion that they were creating a new way of life. All those who played a role in the bill's passage are dead, and during their lifetime, no one—as far as I could find out—thought to ask them what they thought they were doing during the legislative battles and whether they realized later what they had accomplished. The history of the recent past must be reexamined in light of what the bill accomplished.

I had two goals in writing this book: to make scholars realize how significant the GI Bill was in shaping American society over the past fifty years, and to tell a great story for not only those who benefited from the bill but also for their children and grandchildren. I hope this book will encourage readers to think about how the bill affected their daily lives.

I became aware of the story behind the GI Bill in the shabby

precincts of J. J. Foley's Saloon in Boston almost a quarter century
ago. Foley's was like the American Legion post bars where ideas that
became the GI Bill were first discussed in the twenties and thirties.
J. J. Foley's, like American Legion posts, served as a social crossroads
where printers and reporters, lawyers and police officers, residents
from the neighboring South End, even the occasional social worker
and stockbroker, celebrated, groused, gossiped, and sometimes actually learned something about the way other people lived, thought, and
dreamed. Throughout the sixties and early seventies, I was a reporter
for *The Boston Herald* and *The Boston Record-American,* covering
the poverty and protest beat, a catchall phrase for the tides of social
unrest sweeping through the "Athens of America" and the rest of the
country, making headlines but little positive change. That particular
day I was working on a story about Vietnam veterans with readjustment problems (including drugs) and about some efforts being made
to help them by the local NAACP. "Hell, what those guys need is a
52-20 Club," someone said. "You know, a year to soak their heads in a
bucket of beer if they need to, like we had after World War II. You
ought to talk to Frank Reilly about it. He covers the statehouse for
The Record-American. You know the Hearst people, Walter Howey
and all them, they helped pass the GI Bill. That was the greatest bill
ever passed, not like this War on Poverty crap. That really worked."

I knew very little about the GI Bill, but all too much about the War
on Poverty, which was presumably going to make Boston and every
other American community a "City on a Hill," as the Puritans had
called for long ago. For a long time, I had dutifully reported and often
believed the always-confident prescriptions for social change dictated
by academic and government experts. Time and experience had, however, made me almost terminally cynical. The cynicism had been compounded by two years spent as public relations director of the city's
antipoverty agency and six months running the state's first effort—
under federal mandate—to come up with a comprehensive plan for
employment training. I had come away from both with the sure
and certain knowledge—only suspected as a reporter—that the statistics so confidently trotted out by the experts were, as a British
economist said, "set down by the night watchman, and he puts down
whatever he damn well pleases." I had been one of the night watch-
men, replicating in the poverty program's planning, programming,
and budgeting what the best and brightest had done in Vietnam with
body counts.

My cynicism was sometimes allayed, even occasionally dispelled, by reporting how a few social work professionals and individuals from the community tried, despite impossible odds, to make a difference. Yet I knew any success would be limited to individuals and only rarely translated into institutional accomplishments.

In my work within these antipoverty agencies I learned that the bureaucracy ran everything, and we really didn't know what we were doing. It was not possible to determine if anything was being accomplished. We defined success with our domestic "body count"—number of people seen, interviewed, enrolled in a program, graduated, dropped out, placed, and so forth. We didn't have any sales record to point to, or collect commissions on, but by the same token, no one demanded real results. Even when less than 5 percent of the people eligible to vote in community elections showed up, despite massive publicity efforts, no one blamed us.

By contrast, I knew that while the GI Bill hadn't paid for the education of most of my childhood or college friends, most of us went to college because of the GI Bill. Growing up in a suburban area of Boston during and after the war, I became aware of the bill when an older boy from the neighborhood came back from the service and enrolled in college. Most of my playmates' fathers had been too old for the draft in World War II, and we were too young to be drafted for the Korean War. Our fathers, as skilled workmen, bookkeepers, and store managers, owned their own homes; they had not gone to college and saw no need for their sons to do so. But when that older boy came back and exchanged his combat boots for white bucks, every mother in the neighborhood began to say, "Well, if . . . can go to college, my kid can."

And we all did, just about. Somehow the money for tuition, which hadn't been in the budget, was found, because our parents thought it would be better to put off military service until we were older. Besides, with a college degree, we could become officers, not that anyone in the neighborhood had any idea what an officer did. But college graduates and engineers and doctors and teachers and social workers, even journalists, were being produced routinely by those neighborhoods by the middle of the 1950s. The results were not always salutary. As more than one of my editors groused, "You college guys are ruining this business with all your theories out of books. You just don't know how ordinary people think."

In retrospect, those editors were probably more right than wrong.

Despite some interest, I never looked up Frank Reilly to ask him about his role in passing the GI Bill. I certainly realized the bill had been far more successful than the War on Poverty legislation. But although I was a *Record-American* reporter covering major social issues, I still couldn't quite believe anything so important had been the product of people I associated with the raffish journalism of the movie *The Front Page*. Besides, soon thereafter, I came to Washington as a congressional fellow of the American Political Science Association, sure that under the tutelage of those wise in the ways of Capitol Hill, I would learn how government could really improve people's lives. Instead, I learned that, although Congress's ability to write bad laws is limited, when the executive branch develops the rules and regulations carrying out those laws, their joint capacity to exacerbate social, cultural, and economic problems and divisions is virtually infinite.

Other than writing a memorial tribute on the fortieth anniversary of the GI Bill for the *Congressional Record* in 1984 and doing some more research on it as a press secretary for a member of Congress, I had largely forgotten about it. Then I read a book by a Boston University professor, Howard Zinn, that both infuriated and dismayed me. I was infuriated because I didn't believe he was right, dismayed because I was afraid he might be. Zinn's book, *A People's History of the United States,* was an all-out attack on "the pretense . . . that there really is such a thing as 'a United States,' subject to occasional conflicts and quarrels but fundamentally a community of people with common interests. Nations are not communities and never have been. The history of any country, presented as the history of a family, conceals fierce conflicts of interest (sometimes exploding, sometimes repressed) between conquered and conquerors, masters and slaves, dominators and dominated in race and sex." We live in "a world of victims and executioners," he concluded.

That's nonsense, I thought then and now, but it's nonsense that has too much truth in it to be ignored. It's also particularly pernicious nonsense because it provides perverse justification for turning individual human concerns into social problems, treating people as abstract groups. But, except for the grace of God and the GI Bill, might not many who have done so well had lives all too unpleasantly like those Zinn described? Certainly any people's history of the United States should have an account of the GI Bill if it were to be complete. I went looking through all the history books, as well as the biographies and memoirs of people key to passage of the bill, such as William Randolph Hearst, James Conant, and Robert Maynard Hutchins. I found only fleeting references, at best. I wasn't a historian, but as a reporter, I sensed a story here, an important story, a news story despite its being half a century old. This is a story about something that profoundly influenced the lives of three generations of Americans for the better. This is a story that, if properly understood, could provide ideas for the next century. Nevertheless, three years later, I don't claim to understand fully how the GI Bill of Rights came about or why it worked so well. Maybe I'm finally learning the lesson my old editors tried to pound into me: You're only supposed to report what happened. Leave it to others to figure out what—if anything—it means.

I do know that, somehow, out of thousands of conversations in American Legion posts, not unlike the one I had in J. J. Foley's, those responsible for the GI Bill tapped into positive forces within Americans, both as individuals and as a people, that enabled them, with the resources provided by the government, to transform their lives and to pay back the investment many times over.

I am also certain that, despite the bill's indispensable financial resources, it would never have worked if the veteran beneficiaries hadn't had the basic skills, discipline, and determination to take advantage of them. This wasn't largess handed down to the multitudes by planners or bureaucrats but something they earned—and had the resolve to take advantage of.

When I started writing this book, I did so with only one clear conviction. It was my firm belief that whatever was distinctively American about the GI Bill, it was reflected in the grain of the poet Robert Frost's line, "Good fences make good neighbors," the idea that people respond better when they have a garden of their own to tend. As I was finishing this book, I came across this comment by Frost about the Harvard president who opposed the GI Bill's passage: "Conant was a very 'proper' individual, a Puritan and a prude if not a prig. He tried to regulate the lives of all his faculty—a task even a New Deal bureaucrat would have found strenuous. He tried to interfere with their mores. I have always felt that we should allow to every man his own manners. For myself I won't be shoved around. What's more to the point I refuse to be directed. My propulsion has got to come from inside myself. I'm a gyroscope, not a string top."

Maybe that's why no book about the GI Bill has been written

before. Many who write books, including myself, can be very proper, if not Puritan prudes and prigs, who find it difficult to believe that very improper people, such as Walter Howey and William Randolph Hearst and, above all, John Rankin, could liberate the best that's in people while allowing us our own manners. Many people and all governments really prefer to tell others what to do rather than exercising the kind of leadership I associate with Gen. Theodore Roosevelt Jr. He took people as they were but got the best out of them.

Perhaps the ultimate irony behind this story filled with ironies was best expressed by Zinn when he wrote: "If history is to be creative, to anticipate a possible future, it should, I believe, emphasize such possibilities by disclosing those hidden episodes of the past, when even if in brief flashes, people showed their ability to resist, to join together, occasionally to win."

Where Zinn and I differ is that I think people can make their own path, not just resist what others do, that they can join together without being tied together, that their propulsion has to come from within, not outside. The GI Bill turned loose forces that quietly but dramatically transformed America. It originated in the blurred vision of a handful of legislators, journalists, and veterans who could not foresee the results. The GI Bill made modern America because of the ambition, maturity, and energy of millions of ordinary Americans who used the GI Bill to make their dreams come true. I can only hope that the story of the law that worked won't be just a nostalgic tale, but will stimulate creative thinking about how the government and citizenry can work together and improve America.

It would not have been possible to do a book of this length and breadth without the able assistance of many people. While it is not possible to list them all there, I would be remiss if I did not name several. First, my agent, Ed Knappman of New England Publishing Associates. Much support came from—and much gratitude goes out to—colleagues Leigh Tripoli, Jack Finnegan, Jim Breagy, John Chaffee, John McLean, Arnita Mongiovi; my brothers, Paul, Tom, and particularly Fred; as well as Mary Tierney, Jim Murphy, Jim Doyle, the Garritys, Bob and Joanne, Jack Cannon, Fred Brady, and above all, Herself.

The assistance provided by Dr. Reginald Wilson of the American Council on Education, Phil Budahn of the American Legion, Darryl W. Kehrer of the Department of Veterans Affairs, and Jill Cochran of the House Veterans Committee was indispensable. Let me mention

Carolyn McCormick as representing all the librarians in the Library of Congress and the Washington, D.C., public library who helped so much in my research.

Finally, I must acknowledge the considerable efforts of two more people. Frank Margiotta, Brassey's publisher, instantly realized how much his own family's life had been improved by the GI Bill and that America had not yet recognized the revolution caused by this remarkable legislation. His enthusiasm and willingness to provide sound advice on several drafts was invaluable. The final book was made possible only by the skillful, diligent, and caring editorial efforts of Lois Baron, one of Brassey's finest editors.

CHAPTER 1

A NEW LIFE

I T WAS AS IF THE earth stood still for a moment.
The time for dying was about to end. The time for living was yet
to begin.

Americans awoke the morning of August 14, 1945, as they had for
1,322 days, still fearing World War II would last another year, perhaps
two, perhaps three, even though atomic bombs had fallen on two
Japanese cities August 6 and 9. On December 8, 1941, Franklin
Delano Roosevelt had promised the American people inevitable victory. Yet no one had counted on peace until it was actually announced
from the White House on August 14, 1945, a few seconds after 7 P.M.
The message of victory, delivered in a flat, Midwestern accent still
unfamiliar to Americans after thirteen years of the mellifluous FDR,
was clear, and on hearing the news, every heart lifted. The war in
which more than fifty-five million had died was finally over. Marines
on Iwo Jima, Seabees on Okinawa, soldiers in the Philippines, and
sailors delivering reinforcements to the Pacific started chanting,
"Home Alive in '45!"[1]

But the jubilation didn't last long. Doubts about the bearer of the
good news, President Harry S Truman, and the peace he would preside over quickly multiplied. Within a year, a freshman Democratic
senator from Arkansas, J. William Fulbright, was advocating that
Truman appoint a Republican senator, Arthur Vandenberg of Michigan, as vice president and resign, allowing Vandenberg to become
president.

1

Demobilization came much more slowly than the public wanted, and it speeded up only after servicemen staged demonstrations overseas and wives, girlfriends, and mothers threatened members of Congress with retaliation at the polls. In the winter of 1945–46, massive strikes in the coal and railroad industries paralyzed transportation, forced factories to cut hours and pay, and chilled homes without fuel for furnaces. The prices of everything, from food to clothing, soared. The new consumer goods everyone had been promised—automobiles, refrigerators, and above all, homes—could be found only in the glossy advertisements in magazines. Peace had come, but prosperity had not.

In the fall of 1946, however, there were signs of the silent revolution that would first transform college campuses and then create a new suburban society. America was about to become a predominantly middle-class nation.

For the fall semester in 1946, enrollment in colleges and universities was up, predictably enough, from 1945's 1.6 million to 2.1 million. But the number and percentage of veterans enrolled was astonishing. Slightly more than 1 million—48.7 percent of the 2,078,095 students and 71.5 percent of all the males—were veterans. That same fall, an advertisement in *The New York Times* proclaimed: "This is Levittown. All yours for $58. You're a lucky fellow, Mr. Veteran. Uncle Sam and the world's largest builder have made it possible for you to live in a charming house in a delightful community without having to pay for it through your eye teeth." The ad ran on a Monday. By the end of the next day, fourteen hundred sales agreements were signed before the door of the model home was closed. People were beginning to get comfortable in the sun's warmth. Only leaves were burning now. The only sharp cracks heard came from new textbooks being opened. Some began to think that by Christmas 1946, for the first time in years, almost everyone would be home for Christmas.

A generation that had grown up under the Depression and the New Deal was about to get a new life, and the lives of all Americans would be transformed as a result. By 1948, a time many once feared the country would still be at war with Japan, everyone was going to see a movie called *The Best Years of Our Lives,* a movie about returning veterans and their families. Many were even beginning to think Harry Truman might not be so bad after all. Yet there was nothing foreordained about those years between the end of the war and 1948, nothing that Truman or FDR or the New Deal could claim credit for. Instead, three other converging forces were responsible for the change. The great untold story of World War II is the tale of those forces and the America they created after World War II.

One was the revival of the old belief that Americans should be yeomen, as Thomas Jefferson called them. These ideal Americans were educated citizens and independent property owners, neither rich nor poor, neither powerful nor wealthy, but self-sustaining, self-respecting people who took care of themselves and could be counted on by neighbors when trouble came calling. This concept was as old as the Revolution, but it was one that had faded as the United States became industrialized and urbanized. The second force was a sense of common American values, which had been forged among members of the American Legion who had fought in World War I, transcending their ethnic, religious, economic, and class backgrounds. Whether they descended from colonial settlers or more recent immigrant stock, they were determined that their children should have the same opportunities in civilian life as any other nephew—or niece—of Uncle Sam. They felt the government owed war veterans the financial resources to make them yeomen. The third force was a coalition of Republicans and conservative Democrats looking for a way to help veterans without making them clients of big government, minions of big unions, or wage slaves of big business.

These three complementary principles underlie the GI Bill of Rights, a bill that was forged in a singularly independent way. None of the bill's provisions was hammered out in ideological conferences or debated by political platform committees. Few precedents existed to look to for guidance. Chance, circumstance, even the "Superintending Providence" invoked by the Founding Fathers played crucial roles in getting the bill signed. Early defeats transformed into stunning victories were as much a part of the drafting and passage of the GI Bill as in the fortunes of battle. This law, written hurriedly in a hotel room by a former American Legion national commander, supported editorially by the most widely circulated—but least respectable—newspaper chain in the country, and sponsored primarily by an isolationist senator from the Midwest, a racist congressman from the South, and a patrician Republican congresswoman from a tough industrial town in the Northeast, created this silent revolution.

The GI Bill of Rights, officially called the Servicemen's Readjustment Act of 1944, was in place to help the nation reabsorb those who had been fighting in World War II. After the conclusion of World War I, the United States went through almost three years of ethnic, racial, and labor-management strife before normalcy returned. The prospects for an easy transition to peace after World War II were dim, based on the greater numbers of those in service. Four million had fought in World War I; sixteen million were under arms for World War II—12 million were still serving when Japan surrendered. Although everyone publicly celebrated after Hirohito bowed in surrender, beneath the euphoria, the nation's best informed businessmen, economists, and educators privately feared another depression was coming. Skeptics noted that even on the day of surrender, the most famous of all the many acronyms coined during the war, SNAFU, standing for Situation Normal, All F—— Up, was still standard operational procedure. Delivery of the official Japanese surrender telegram to the White House was delayed because the two Radio Corporation of America messengers, Earl Allison and Thomas Jones, got a ticket for making an illegal U turn at Connecticut Avenue and N Street. "We showed the police officer the radiogram," Allison said, "but he said we couldn't feed him those horsefeathers."[2]

The reaction was just as suspicious outside Marseilles, France, where eight thousand GIs were sullenly waiting for the famous singing Andrews sisters to entertain them. Maxine Andrews was thinking the audience was the unhappiest she had ever seen as her sister Patty was handed a message from offstage. "A big joke is going on here," Patty announced. "I have a note *supposedly* from the CO," she said and then quickly rattled off words saying the war was ended. None of the GIs moved; not a sound could be heard from any of them. Patty looked at the message again and said, "No, fellas—this *is* from the CO. This is an announcement that"—and she screamed—*"the war with Japan is over.* You don't have to go to the Pacific." She, Maxine, and Laverne began to cry. "This is the end," she screamed. "This is the end."[3]

It was the beginning.

Bright lights were coming back on. The blackout curtains that had parted after the May 7 surrender of the Germans were a precursor to the bonfires that blazed on August 14 on the rocky coast of Maine, the barrens of the Carolinas, the sandy shores of the Gulf coast and that glowed dimly through the fog of Oregon and Washington State. Startled pilots flying west with the sunset saw a diamond quilt of lights gleaming up from towns and villages that had been blanketed for more than thirteen hundred nights. A pile of now-surplus explosives was set off at Alamogordo Air Base by George Kistiakowsky, one of the scientists who had helped detonate the first atomic bomb nearby on July 16. In Hawaii, the sky was lit up by harmless flares, rather than lethal torpedoes. Ships returning from England and France and New Guinea to New York, Boston, Philadelphia, New Orleans, San Diego, and San Francisco saw the stars disappear in glowing clouds on the horizon.

Everyone celebrated, publicly and privately. Fifty years later, a woman didn't recall seeing either cops or drunks in Times Square, although both were there. "My clearest visual memory is the brightness of Broadway's lights shining down on a wall-to-wall carpet of human beings," Naomi Bliven remembered. "The emotional effect that stays with me is of serenity, security. I'd never seen a crowd like that, and it didn't occur to me that I'd never see another one like it again. How often does anyone see two million happy people?"[4]

Many happy people were to be seen during the next year, coming home, marching in Main Street parades, pinning "ruptured duck" discharge emblems on suits to be worn to interviews or just for Sunday. Within a month after Truman declared victory, GIs were being mustered out at the rate of one hundred thousand a month. By the end of 1946, only 3 million of the 12 million Americans who had been in uniform were still saluting. The army air corps went from 2,385,000 officers and men to 165,000. By 1948, the army, once 8 million strong, was down to 545,030. Those who returned from World War II and those who joined them to build new lives were the children of the first baby boom, 1919–25. They were the children of the soldiers and sailors who came home from the war to save democracy overseas only to find a country economically crippled by strikes in 1919–20, psychologically paralyzed by a Red Scare, and traumatized by the need to assimilate the millions of immigrants who had flooded the country between 1900 and 1917. In their early years their parents had reveled in being members of the first consumer generation, buying products *their* parents couldn't afford or had never heard of— automobiles, refrigerators, washing machines, cigarettes, hair permanents. Not all was rosy, however. All too often, the grammar schools those first baby boomers attended were wooden shacks or crumbling with age. The urban and rural villages most people lived in were more like ghettos than neighborhoods, in which the Irish lived only with the Irish; the Italians, Poles, Croats, and Jews only with Italian, Poles, Croats, and Jews. Even the Yankee Methodists,

Disciples of Christ, and Episcopalians clustered in their own communities on the other side of the railroad tracks, divided from the others by barriers of class and ethnic origin. A few community programs had helped create common bonds, notably the Boy and Girl Scouts and particularly the baseball teams sponsored by American Legion posts. They gave the boys who would fight in World War II their first real sense of an American identity, playing the national pastime.

By 1929, the flappers' party was over, and by 1932 only one in four men had a job. Economic necessity forced all too many students to disappear from the classroom as soon as they got into long pants or started using bobby pins. Those who stayed in school in cities were fortunate to have able teachers recruited during the prosperous '20s who stayed on and even more able ones who were lured into the profession by steady paychecks in the '30s. That was the extent of the good fortune. Everyone, no matter what their finances, knew families who were worse off, where the breadwinner had committed suicide, become a Communist, or fled in the night. Even before the Depression, the American dream had all too often seemed as insubstantial as the celluloid dreams flickering on the neighborhood silver screen. The old dream of the American yeoman idealized by Thomas Jefferson had been fading ever since the closing of the old western frontier in 1890. By the 1930s, the opening lines of a poem, "The Man with a Hoe," written by Edwin Markham, a high school principal in Berkeley, California, and first published in William Randolph Hearst's *San Francisco Examiner* in 1896, were being recited everywhere.

> Bowed by the weight of centuries he leans
> Upon his hoe and gazes on the ground,
>   The emptiness of ages in his face,
> And on his back the burden of the world.[5]

That the burden had become heavier, everyone agreed, from Hearst, whose tabloids were widely read by working-class people despite his regular denunciation of what he called the Raw Deal, to FDR's most ardent supporters. But even those who arose with hangovers on August 15, 1945, felt the burden was gone—at least for the moment. They opened their eyes with a sense of hope that the promises and boasts of the night before could come true. Men set out to do what they had said they were going to. They were going to school, starting their own businesses, even buying their own homes with their own backyards. Of course, that's what all the veterans of previous wars had said they would do—and usually didn't. If they had done so, it had been without help from the government they had fought for. Revolutionary War soldiers had lost their farms to back taxes, and when they did receive a pension, it was thirty years too late to start again. Civil War veterans had mobilized a powerful lobby and started getting pensions within 15 years, but had aroused so much resentment that World War I soldiers and sailors were discharged with only $60. Ultimately, the World War I veterans collected about $700 in bonus money, but only after they had marched on and been routed from Washington and twice had seen FDR veto congressional legislation authorizing payment.

This time, for the first time, the federal government, having carefully selected and trained its most intelligent and vigorous young people to kill in war, would give them the tools to make new lives in peacetime. The result was a revolution of changing expectations, which swiftly became rising ones. For the first time in history, a social revolution was being made, not by storming barricades, but by leaping over them. People were doing it on their own, as individuals, not as members of a class or race or ethnic group or political party— and certainly not as a mob. They would do it each in their own way, in their own time, in their own lives.

The GI Bill was the catalyst creating our present postcapitalist society, in which the computer has replaced the dynamo as the symbol of progress. Indeed, Peter F. Drucker, writing in *Post-Capitalist Society,* compares 1945, the year veterans began taking advantage of the bill, to 1776, the year in which the American Revolution began, James Watt perfected the steam engine, and Adam Smith published *Wealth of Nations.*[6] "The GI Bill of Rights—and the enthusiastic response to it on the part of America's veterans—signaled the shift to the knowledge society," Drucker writes. "Future historians may consider it the most important event of the 20th century. We are clearly in the middle of this transformation [in 1993]; indeed, if history is any guide, it will not be completed until 2010 or 2020. But already it has changed the political, economic and moral landscape of the world." This transformation of America has been so sweeping and yet so much a part of everyday life that young people cannot imagine the world in which their grandparents lived, he observed: "And the grandparents themselves have difficulty remembering how they lived then."

The GI Bill was a Marshall Plan for America, but one that encouraged innovation and change rather than rebuilding on old foundations. Without anyone being fully aware of it, the GI Bill was stimulating decentralized market and individual incentive approaches to economic and social problem solving, while its much more closely studied historical equivalent, British socialized medicine, was taking the opposite approach. Quite literally, the GI Bill changed the way we live, the way we house ourselves, the way we are educated, how we work and at what, even how we eat and transport ourselves. It was both the catalyst for and the central driving force behind most of ordinary life over the past half century. To understand what the bill did, however, it is necessary first to understand the way we were, back then, fifty years ago.

Most Americans, except for those on the farm or in the small towns of rural America, lived in what is now called the inner city. Home was usually a three- or four-story tenement or apartment house; a two-, three-, or four-decker for as many families; or a single-family shotgun house with tiny rooms off a single corridor, so called because a shotgun could be fired down the corridor without hitting anyone. Only the better-off lived in fairly spacious houses on the outskirts of town. Even those houses, however, had tiny front lawns and were separated from each other by little more than a hedge between gravel or partially paved driveways.

No one took showers in the morning except for the very rich. They were the only ones with showers. The fortunate had their own bathroom—with a tub—but it was only used for baths on Saturday night. The water had to be specially heated in the boiler tank that dominated most kitchens. Many families had to share toilets and sinks as well as tubs with people living on the same floor. Coal was used for heat, and its dusty grit got into everything. Spring cleaning, consequently, was a backbreaking necessity. Heavy draperies that stanched the drafts from leaky casements had to be taken down and sent out to be dry-cleaned. Fathers and sons were dragooned into beating clouds of dust out of rugs spread over straining clotheslines. Windows had to be sluiced clean from the outside with garden hoses and scrubbed down with ammonia and old newspapers from the inside. During the winter, groaning fathers or oldest boys had to get up in the night to stoke the furnaces and, in the morning, haul the ashes out into the alleys.

Kids played stoopball, stickball (variations of baseball), and touch football on the street or in the alleys. In the city there were few lawns or fields. Even if a scraggly tree or telephone pole was available to put up a basketball backboard, few had played the game. *A Tree Grows in Brooklyn* was the title of a popular postwar novel; it was also news to many. Most clothes were washed with scrub boards in sinks, but the some had washers in which clothes were churned by electric power. The washing ladies of really well-off women squeezed the water out of the clothes through electrically powered rollers. Most women used rollers that called for muscle power to turn the crank. In the winter, clothes had to be hung in the basement, as far away from the coal bin as possible, and if anything fell on the floor, it automatically was thrown right back in the washer as dirty.

Rooms were small and dark, sealed off from each other by doors to keep in the heat, and painted in blues and browns dark enough so the dirt didn't show. The garbage went out with the trash and, all too often, was left on the street behind the trucks supposed to pick it up. Refrigerators were literally iceboxes, and the pans to collect the drip had to be emptied often or the water would further crack already-brittle linoleum. The old and the single living alone nailed a box to a window sill and kept milk and butter and bread there in cold weather. Milk was delivered to doorsteps daily, sometimes still by horse-drawn wagons leaving organic deposits behind.

In the summer, the wealthy had sleeping porches; the luckier residents of tenements had a fire escape big enough to use on hot nights. Flies and mosquitos were everywhere in hot weather. The flypaper that hung from ceiling lights in the kitchen was the same color as the yellow packets squeezed through oleomargarine to make it look like butter. War needs consumed metal for window and porch screens. What little was left went into fly swatters, which didn't kill many flies but helped let off human steam. There wasn't enough gasoline for those who did have cars to take a drive in the country, even though the country was only a few miles away then. People picnicked in cemeteries instead. Farmers got barely enough gas for their tractors, if they had them, and even by the end of the war, electricity hadn't come to most of the nation's 40 million farm families.

No home was more than a few blocks away from a grocery store. That was convenient but also a necessity because everything had to be carried by hand. Groceries had to be carried, not only from the store to the kitchen, but also from the shelf to the counter in the store. Push carts weren't supplied, and a child's wagon was the only alternative to lugging groceries in your arms. All food, even that which no one wanted to eat, was rationed. When sugar was available, kids spread it on white bread as a substitute for candy. Fresh fruits and vegetables were moldy, canned goods usually came in only one brand, and housewives seemed to get the meat-ration coupons the day after the last roast was sold and a week before the next shipment came in. Soup bones were usually available, but even those ran out when cold weather came.

The rivers were clean enough in most cities for kids to swim in, but the threat of polio, presumably spread by contaminated water, had mothers almost hysterically fearful in July and August. Only the rich ate in restaurants. Office workers went to diners, and factory and shipyard workers made do with lunch-cart specials. Dances were the most popular entertainment, but many of the best dance bands were overseas. In bars, the aroma of spilt beer and Lysol provided the only ambience. A big treat was an ice cream soda after a double feature at one of the few air-conditioned movie theaters in town—and even that was rationed. After the war, ice cream became the first big consumption item, leaping from 15.7 pounds per person in 1945 to 23.7 before slacking off to 20.1 in 1947. In the '30s, people had eaten less than 10 pounds annually.

In the cities, where political power had moved along with the majority of the population (as reflected in the 1920 census), the New Deal had been of little or no help in enabling people to own their own homes. The housing projects built before the war were far superior to many tenements, but could accommodate only a small—and politically connected—percentage of those in need of decent, affordable housing. People had money—more than they'd ever had in their lives—but nothing to spend it on. Taxes were high, as much as 90 percent on personal incomes over $50,000 a year. Taxes weren't enough to run the most expensive war in history, however, unless working people in the lower brackets were either hit with equally confiscatory rates or encouraged to save. Encouraged to save they were through war bond drives whose best salesmen and women were Hollywood actors and actresses. "This decision, combined with strictures on wartime spending and the dearth of consumer goods, enabled Americans to accumulate enormous sums of readily available cash," Joseph Goulden wrote in *The Best Years: 1945–1950,* the only social history of the period. "For the last two years of the war, citizens socked away about 25 percent of their take home pay, and by midsummer 1945, their liquid assets totalled an astounding $140 billion in savings and war bonds—three times the entire national income in 1932. Add in the individual incomes of $120-plus billion for 1945, and Americans had a quarter of a trillion dollars to spend during the first year of peace—a mountain of wealth sufficient to make an economist blink."[7] Moreover, the wealth was evenly and widely distributed. According to the Federal Reserve Board, about 60 percent was in savings accounts of people with less than $5,000 in savings. Almost 84 percent of a sample of adult New Yorkers surveyed owned war bonds. Only 7.9 percent of those surveyed had no savings.

When World War II ended, America was the most powerful nation in the world. Almost half of the world's goods came from its factories, fields, mines, and forests. Those production levels wouldn't last long, however. Economists expected—and business leaders hoped that accumulated savings would spur domestic consumption, but many would have been more inclined to keep on saving rather than buying if the GI Bill hadn't tided them over with unemployment compensation or with stipends for education. With the wartime boom over, factories closing down, and jobs disappearing, consumer confidence couldn't be expected to be high. The arsenal of democracy had produced 296,000 warplanes, 107,351 tanks, 87,620 warships, 5,475 cargo ships, and 20 million rifles, machine guns, and pistols between 1940 and 1945.[8] But the goods needed to provide a cornucopia of democracy would take months, if not years to produce. What had survived the war, however, was a spirit of confidence never experienced before and almost impossible to imagine now. Americans felt they could literally do anything. The wartime production figures were "all so astronomical they cease to mean much," observed Bruce Catton, who worked for the War Production Board before writing several Civil War histories. "Say that we performed the equivalent of building two Panama Canals every month with a fat surplus to boot; that's an understatement, it still doesn't begin to express it all, the total is simply beyond the compass of one's understanding. Here was displayed a strength greater than cocky Americans in the old days of unlimited self-confidence had supposed; strength to which nothing—literally nothing in the physical sense—was any longer impossible."[9]

That self-confidence, that cockiness, was needed. The backlog of domestic needs was also so astronomical as to be beyond the compass of one's understanding. For example, every adult American—and almost every adolescent—wanted a new car to drive. An even more pressing need, however, was modern roads to drive on. It seemed axiomatic that government planning, the kind of planning that had produced the largest and most powerful military force in history, was essential to convert the wartime economy into a peacetime one. One advocate for such a scenario was Walter Reuther, the president of the United Auto Workers, who had been more prescient than management executives in seeing before the war that automobile assembly lines could be used to produce airplanes and tanks. He recommended after the war that the assembly lines be turned over to the production of factory-made, prefabricated housing with a Peace Production Board overseeing, if not directing, postwar conversion through unified government planning. The proposal was enthusiastically supported by New Deal planners. FDR's first priority, however, was holding down prices. Calling it the toughest domestic job in Washington, FDR appointed Bernard M. Baruch, the financier who had headed the World War I price control program, to a similar post in 1943. FDR and Baruch feared a repetition of the recession after World War I when 110,000 businesses failed, 400,000 farmers lost their land, and 8 million were unemployed. Their worries were shared by a number of business leaders, including members of the National Association of Manufacturers (NAM), who were in a good position to speculate on what might happen. But such worries didn't always make it into common public forums, such as newspapers.

Fresh out of Columbia Journalism School, *New York Times Magazine* staffer Edith Efron was assigned to write a piece in 1945 about what could be expected with the veterans coming home. "It was my first lesson in what happens when you discover something that's really new. It can upset the front office. We and all the other papers and magazines had been running stories quoting business leaders as confidently predicting there'd be little or no difficulty in absorbing veterans back into the economy," she said. When she spoke with leading members at a NAM convention, however—after they had extracted promises that she wouldn't quote them by name—she discovered something quite different. "They were scared stiff," she said. "Once the war was over, they knew the production lines producing war goods would shut down. They weren't sure when or even if the lines could be converted to provide the consumer goods people had gone without for years. They also knew the 1940 draft law required

employers to give returning veterans back their jobs even if that
meant kicking out men and women who had been holding the jobs for
years. When I talked to these business leaders privately, that's what
they told me."[10]

Efron turned her first draft in to Lester Markel, the legendarily
independent editor of the Sunday sections of *The Times*. This was
one piece, however, he consulted his superiors about. "I knew Markel
discussed the piece with the people in the front office," Efron said. "I
never found out what was said. All I did know was I was taken off
the story until assigned to do a piece in 1946 about veterans on the
college campus. In my innocence, I thought perhaps the paper didn't
want to run the piece because, of course, I had to agree to attribute
what was said to anonymous sources. . . . Instead, I'm sure all my
superiors were just scared stiff by this story turned in by a neophyte
that just confirmed all the fears they themselves were afraid to
openly acknowledge."

The worry was logical. The total workforce in 1945 was 65.2 million, and women were almost 20 million of those workers. Even if all
those women quit—and it turned out that 2.5 million did between
1945 and 1947—that didn't leave that many vacancies for almost 12
million veterans coming home to fill.

Businesses were worried, and they did not want price controls to
hem them in once the war was over. They launched a massive attack
on the Office of Price Administration (OPA) in 1945 demanding to be
freed from the shackles of price controls on more than eight million
commodities and services. In protest, housewives by the thousand
marched on Capitol Hill in a consumers' crusade, but other consumers, sick and tired of rationing, were prepared to accept higher
prices in return for new products, not to mention the meat, milk, eggs,
fruit, and vegetables that had been so scarce during the war. The battle "reached proportions of bitterness, stridency and obfuscation which
have not been matched in years," *The New York Times* declared. Truman appointed a pro-business friend, John Snyder, as head of a new
Office of War Mobilization and Reconversion. Snyder promptly
plunged into internecine political warfare with Chester Bowles, the
pro-consumer head of OPA. Truman, determined to make price controls "click," told all his top appointees to quit if they couldn't go along
with his policies. The policies were moot, however, when a new Republican Congress, sworn in January 1946, reenacted the wartime price
control act but without adequate enforcement authority for OPA.

Prices took off; milk went from sixteen cents to twenty a quart, veal cutlets from fifty to ninety-five cents. *The New York News* published a classic headline:

PRICES SOAR, BUYERS SORE
STEERS JUMP OVER THE MOON[11]

The battle over price controls dominated the headlines at the time, and small forests were sacrificed to print arguments, pro and con, of economists over the efficacy—or insanity—of price controls. Prices did go up from June 1946 to December 1948 from a base of 132 to 170, a 22 percent increase.[12] Missing in all the arguments then and since was the fact that wages also went up correspondingly, and above all, the unemployment rate remained below 4½ percent. The price controls were designed to avoid a repeat of the recession of 1919–20, but that had really been caused, largely if not primarily, by the dumping of 4 million veterans on the economy. By contrast, in 1945–46, the GI Bill of Rights painlessly reabsorbed 12 million veterans into the economy, 7.8 million through educational programs and 8.5 million—many of them the same individuals at different times—through the 52-20 Club, the unemployment provision worth $20 a week for up to a year.

The market was at work, but it was a market neither liberal nor conservative economists recognized then or now. It was not dominated by private demand or public intervention through public works projects such as the Work Progress Administration. Instead, it was shaped by direct infusions of cash into the pockets of individuals through bonuses of $300 to $500 paid by many states and the 52-20 Club; vouchers for education and training at schools chosen by the individuals, subject only to the requirements of the educational institutions; and long-term loans for home buying and establishing businesses—often with no money down. That gave people the confidence to spend accumulated savings they otherwise might have hoarded against a new depression. An entire generation of Yankee Doodle Dandies, real live nephews (and some nieces) of their Uncle Sam, was getting what amounted to a small inheritance, and with it the kind of opportunities that before then only the sons and daughters of the well-to-do could have expected. Moreover, these were opportunities that could be adjusted to every individual veteran's needs and preferences. Those veterans who already had trades and skills could get jobs and buy houses immediately. Others had to go to school for years before they could afford to buy a house, but their tuition was paid for and a stipend for living costs provided. Savings and a part-time job could provide whatever else was needed. Above all, they had choices. They had the luxury of not being forced to accept the first opportunity that came along. That meant the enormous pent-up demand for housing could be phased in over the next few years as some families put off buying homes until college or training was completed.

The World War II generation, despite having endured the most destructive war in history, had come into a legacy of hope that enabled them to believe they could live new lives with the expectation that things would get better. The housing shortage, for example, became part of the adventure of going to college, although not without grumbling. To GIs, dormitories weren't much different from barracks. Often, in fact, the bunk beds came with Quonset huts, both right out of military surplus. "It was almost like being back in the army," Senator Dale Bumpers recalled of his undergraduate days at the University of Arkansas. "There was very little privacy."

That lack was more keenly felt by the young couples who started married lives in attics, basements, even partially weatherproofed outbuildings. Ninety-five percent of all dwellings were occupied, and 1.7 million families were doubled up, sharing accommodations with another family. *Fortune* magazine reported in April 1946: "In Norwood, Ohio, within 24 hours after the arrest of a man who strangled his wife, police received five telephone calls from people who wanted his house." The Republicans' successful campaign for control of Congress in 1946 featured two billboard signs. The first read, "Have You Had Enough?—Then Vote Republican." The second read, "Under Truman: Two Families in Every Garage." That sign convinced Arthur Krock, the Washington bureau chief of *The New York Times,* "Confident GOP Knows It Must Win Out in 1946."[13]

While the statistics can't convey the claustrophobia felt by people desperately looking for a place of their own, they do provide, at least, a measure of the demand. In 1936, the worst year of the Depression, only 304,000 houses were started. In 1941, the last year of the prewar peace, the number had doubled to 620,000. Starts plunged to 184,000 in 1943 before hitting an all-time low of 136,000 in 1944. By 1945, the last year of the war, starts had come back up, but still numbered only 325,000, just 21,000 more than in 1936 and about half the 1941 figure. In 1946, the first full year of peace, housing starts more than trebled, to 1,015,000, climbed steadily to 1,265,000 in 1947;

1,314,000 in 1948; 1,430,000 in 1949; and then zoomed again to 1,908,000 in 1950.[14]

While people wanted housing, that did not necessarily mean they wanted houses to buy. Until the GI Bill came along, most working-class people, particularly in the large cities, didn't think of themselves as homeowners. The development and expansion of suburbia, not only as a form of housing but also as a way of life that would be adopted by most Americans by 1970, meant changing the way people thought about themselves. The difference in mind-set involved is summed up in a simple question Reginald Dunne's father hurled at him: "Who are you to own a home?"[15]

Dunne, a young ex-Coast Guardsman, was living with his wife, whom he had married in Puerto Rico, in a furnished room. He had no credit history and hadn't even been on his new job long enough to acquire any seniority protection in the event of layoffs. Ordinary working people didn't own their own homes, not in the cities, any-way—and didn't expect to. Besides, for the first year or so after the war, there were no homes available for purchase by people in working-class circumstances. While many veterans—through their own savings and wives' wartime earnings—had saved enough for a down payment on a house, memories of Depression-era stories about people losing their homes when banks foreclosed made them leery of buying.

Almost everyone was afraid, with millions of people losing their wartime jobs, that the Great Depression would come right back. It wasn't hard to believe that what happened after World War I could easily repeat itself. Within days after the formal surrender papers were signed aboard the U.S.S. *Missouri* in Tokyo Bay on September 2, the country was seized by paralyzing strikes that gave every sign of reproducing the violent conflicts between right and left known as the Red Scare after World War I.

First, workers for Ford Motor Company suppliers went out in September 1945, followed by General Motors workers. The GM strike was settled quickly, but not before newspapers began writing about revolt and rebellion among workers. After that 750,000 steelworkers hit the bricks for almost eighty days, and as soon as they returned, 400,000 soft-coal workers in twenty-one states went out. In April 1946, two railroad brotherhoods announced they would close down the rail system, which, at the time, transported almost every product made in the country, not to mention most of the traveling public. On May 17, 1946, President Truman stopped that by signing an executive order seizing the railroads and threatening to draft the railroad workers into the army.

Conservatives, as well as liberals, were appalled by Truman's threat, not to mention the labor unions. John Lewis, president of the defiant United Mine Workers, threatened to shut down the country in retaliation. He could have, too. Coal provided 62 percent of the nation's electricity, 55 percent of its industrial power, and ran nineteen out of twenty railroad locomotives. When another strike began that fall, Truman hauled Lewis into court, a $3.5 million fine was imposed on Lewis, and Lewis was forced to order his miners back to work. Two years later the Taft-Hartley Act was passed—over President Truman's veto—and the power of the union movement, for good or for ill, was curtailed.[16]

Without the GI Bill, if the veterans hadn't been absorbed in getting on with their lives, drawing unemployment while applying for school, looking for a job, or starting a business or profession, the automobile, rail, and coal strikes might well have had cataclysmic effects. Idle, without money or prospects, the veterans would have inevitably been drawn into the rail and coal strikes on one side or the other. "After the last war, except for England, this is the only country where the men who wore uniforms did not overthrow the government on either side of the conflict," Henry Colmery, the American Legion national commander who wrote the GI Bill, had warned Congress when the bill was under consideration.[17]

It was a touchy time, and it could have been far worse than the Red Scare. Russia in 1919 was a backward, third-rate nation whose new Communist rulers were barely holding on to power. In 1945, the Soviet Union had emerged as a rival to the United States in military power, and a significant number of Americans believed its system was economically, politically, and morally superior to capitalism. If the twelve million veterans of World War II had been dumped off the boats like the nearly four million from the previous war and given only $60 and a train ticket home with neither educational nor economic opportunity waiting when they got back, violent revolution might have easily been sparked.

Instead, a silent revolution would begin, unexpectedly, on the college campuses and quickly spread to the emerging suburbs. Initial projections of GI enrollment in colleges and universities had been quite limited. Six months after signing the GI Bill, FDR estimated enrollment would be "in the hundreds of thousands." The total might be 700,000 "distributed over several years," Frank T. Hines, the VA administrator, calculated about the same time. Earl J. McGrath, an education adviser to the chief of naval personnel who later became U.S. commissioner of education, was equally cautious. "In no academic year will more than 150,000 veterans be full-time students in colleges and universities," he said in March 1945. He figured enrollment increases would average no more than 10 to 15 percent a year, and he thought total GI enrollment would be 600,000.

All these projections were proven too low as soon as GIs started mustering out in strength. The 88,000 veterans among the 1,676,095 students in 1945 had multiplied to 1,013,000 by the fall of 1946, almost twice the number of GI enrollees expected by Education Commissioner McGrath. By 1947, total enrollment was 2,338,226, with 1,150,000 veterans accounting for 49.2 percent of the total. The falloff didn't come until 1948 when total enrollment was 2,403,396, with veterans making up 975,000, or 40.5 percent of the total. In 1949, veteran enrollment was 34.4 percent of the total; 25.2 percent in 1950; 18.7 percent in 1951; 10.8 percent in 1952; and 6.1 percent in 1953. After that, the numbers reflected both the relatively few men and women in military service and the reduced benefits available under the Korean War Bill of Rights.

These figures would probably never have been so high if it weren't for the literally first-class education benefits afforded under the original bill. The World War II bill, unlike the subsequent Korean, Vietnam, and cold war bills, paid full tuition up to $500 a year, and Harvard and other top schools were charging $400 when the war ended. That meant the veterans could—and did—try to get into the best schools. "Veterans flocked to the Ivy League schools, the state universities, and the better liberal arts colleges and technical schools," according to Keith W. Olson, author of the only academic study of the bill's impact on higher education. "They enrolled only as a last resort in junior colleges, teachers' colleges, and lesser-known, small liberal arts colleges." Harvard's enrollment almost doubled in 1946—from 2,750 in February to 5,000 in September. By comparison, teachers' colleges only had "an enrollment of 150,000 compared to 143,000 in 1940," observed Benjamin Fine, the education editor of *The New York Times,* in February 1947. Even that figure was deceptively high. The University of Minnesota, for example, made 2,500 students take freshman and sophomore classes in the school of education before they were allowed to transfer to the liberal arts program.

"Why Go to Podunk College?, When the Government Will Send You to Yale?" *Time* magazine asked. Why not, indeed, when veterans were proving to be the best scholars on campus. "Here is the most astonishing fact in American higher education," Fine wrote for *The Times* in November of 1947. "The G.I.'s are hogging the honor rolls and the Deans' lists; they are walking away with the top marks in all their courses. . . . Far from being an educational problem, the veteran has become an asset to higher education."[18] The major private colleges quickly realized it, despite initial opposition to the bill from such leading educators as James Conant, the president of Harvard, and Robert Maynard Hutchins, president of the University of Chicago. Indeed the private institutions enrolled 52 percent of all World War II college students, in comparison to the 80 percent who attended public facilities under the Korean and Vietnam bills.[19]

The phrase "upward mobility" had not been coined yet, but GI Joe obviously didn't need vocational counselors to tell him how to get the best out of the educational opportunities offered through the GI Bill. Perhaps serving under officers with degrees from good colleges—and not being terribly impressed—had given the veterans confidence to apply for the top schools, despite the enormous chasm separating the social classes. Articles in national magazines must have encouraged many, particularly "GIs at Harvard: They Are the Best Students in College's History," in *Life,* which was then the largest circulation publication in the country with an impact comparable to perhaps two TV networks today.

"Were he alive today, Harvard's late distinguished president, Abbott Lawrence Lowell, could hardly be comforted by what is going on at the university, over whose affairs he presided for 24 well-regulated years," wrote Charles J. V. Murphy in *Life.* Murphy reported that the fastidious Lowell would be appalled at the "slums" occupied by student-veterans, their wives, and children where once his "young gentlemen" disported themselves. Indeed, even the "fine Houses Mr. Lowell caused to be built in the hope of inculcating taste" were having double-decker beds installed while "chow lines" were being installed in the elegant dining halls, giving them an "an unwonted cafeterian clatter." Those Harvard used to call the "poor boys" were taking over from the young gentlemen. Dormitory space, in fact, was so tight that before long, house masters simply stopped asking young gentlemen if they minded sharing rooms with Jews and Catholics.

Had Lowell, "a squire who had made Harvard over in his own

image," looked a little deeper, though, Murphy suggested, he would
have found much to be impressed by. What the veteran students
lacked in academic credentials, they more than made up for by war
records that had to pass muster by a jury of their peers. All applica-
tions for admission had to be approved by a committee of six veterans drawn from the Harvard faculty. Those admitted, as the dean of
the business school put it, had "demonstrated capacity and character." No one discovered that faster than faculty members. "You've
got to be awfully careful," Murphy quoted one as saying. "These kids
have been everywhere; they've stored up an enormous amount of
information." Another observed, "The window watchers and hiberna-
tors have vanished. This crowd never takes its eyes off you."[20]

GI Joe, in fact, was remaking the colleges and universities of the
country in his image even though Joe College didn't like it, as Efron
wrote in the GI Bill article that was published in *The New York
Times Magazine* the same month Murphy's article appeared in *Life*.
"Here it is spring, yet all we do is go to class and study," she quoted a
Lehigh University sophomore as sighing amid the rolling hills of
Bethlehem, Pennsylvania. The sophomore pointed with disdain to
three young men in flight jackets hurrying toward the chemistry
building. "But those guys don't even know it's spring," the sophomore
groaned. "They're vets. . . . All they care about is their school work.
They're grinds."[21]

Worse, the veterans refused to wear beanie caps, pledge fraterni-
ties, light upperclassmen's cigarettes, even try out for sports. These
were all rituals freshmen had observed for decades, without question
and with considerable pleasure in becoming part of a privileged society most Americans could experience only through the novels of
F. Scott Fitzgerald. That was when college was reserved for only a
few, primarily wealthy young men more interested in attending football games clad in raccoon coats and carrying hip flasks full of boot-
leg booze than in going to class. In 1920, the total number of degrees
awarded was 53,516—hardly enough bodies to fill a Big Ten football
stadium in the '50s. Twenty-five years later, most veteran students
weren't that interested in sports, although those veterans who did go
out for teams played tougher and harder ball than the Dink Stovers
of earlier decades. "They have no school spirit," was Joe College's
complaint. Worst of all, the coeds admired the GIs' attitude as well
as other attributes more manly than those of Joe College. "They

think just because they've been in the service, they have a right to feel superior, to run things," complained one junior to Efron.

Most faculty members disagreed with Joe College. Indeed, an element of satisfaction and pleasure crept into teachers' evaluations of the situation. "The civilian kids consider most of us doddering imbeciles," one professor confided in Efron. "But the veterans seem impressed by our knowledge. They are old enough to realize they know very little. And that helps a great deal in teaching them. They are the most receptive and responsive students Lehigh has ever had." The assessment was hardly unique to Lehigh. Neither was another effect of veterans on campus: a marked improvement in overall performance as the nonveterans tried to keep up with the veterans. "The level of performance is steadily increasing," another faculty member told Efron. "Because of government funds, the college doesn't have to kowtow to idiots anymore to make money. We actually have the privilege of flunking the poor students without getting reprimanded."

Some traditionalists on the faculty disagreed, and Efron summarized their minority view as follows: "The G.I. Bill was a political weapon and as such would eventually destroy the college; that the very concept of mass higher education was anomalous, that men were being admitted to college who instead should be hod carriers; that the veterans, because of their intense interest in careers were 'vocationalizing' the school and intensifying an already dangerous trend; that the G.I. Bill was being interpreted to mean that every veteran was entitled to go to college—bringing about a 'nonsensical' situation in which every empty grocery store was soon to be converted into a 'college' to satisfy the demand."

The Lehigh University educators preferred to remain anonymous. By contrast, Hutchins, president of the University of Chicago, and Conant, the president of Harvard, were outspoken in their initial opposition to the educational provisions of the GI Bill. They saw it as a misguided substitute for a public works program that would far more effectively deal with the massive unemployment they and business leaders expected after the war. Most veterans would simply be unable to meet academic standards, the two educators felt. They were proven wrong.

No one fully understood what was going on. No one really cared. They just knew they had a chance to do things no one they knew had done and be people more successful than anyone from their old neighborhood. Those young ex-GIs were in their early or midtwenties, a little brash on the outside, insecure on the inside, anxious to make up for years lost to the gods of war, tedium, and terror—with similar stories they soon wanted to forget. Life was waiting; the days of dying were over.

"It was time to face up to whether I was serious about attending school," recalled one, the famous satirist Art Buchwald, almost a half century later.

> My decision was to go down to the University of Southern California and find out what I should study at night to get into the place. There were at least 4,000 ex-GIs waiting to register. I stood in line with them. Hours later, I arrived at the counter and said, "I would like to—" The clerk said, "Fill this out."
> "Yes, Ma'am," I said.
> "What do you want to take?"
> "It doesn't matter."
> "Math?"
> "Sure."
> "English?"
> "Why not?"
> "History?"
> "Of course."
> "Have it stamped over there."
> A man stamped it and I was in college.
> It was a miracle.[22]

The real miracle might have been that Congress actually passed a law that worked well, one that changed America. It was called the GI Bill of Rights because "GI" was the catchall name for enlisted men and women in the American military forces of World War II, an abbreviation of "general issue," the name for all standard equipment, clothing, and weapons. The name fit because World War II was the first great modern war of the Industrial Revolution; human beings had become in this war an interchangeable part in a factory system whose product was death. Yet, in a marvelous irony, individual opportunity on a scale unknown in history and unlikely to be repeated was the reward for victory on August 14, 1945. The GI Bill was in place to benefit all veterans—immigrant or native-born Americans, black and white.

Reginald Wilson had been trained as a pilot thanks to his high IQ scores and grades at Cass Technical High School in Detroit, the

equivalent of the Bronx High School of Science. His training, however, had been at the rigidly segregated Tuskegee Air Base. He was
sent to Italy as a pilot as the war was ending and flew fighter escort
for bombers manned by whites. He could fight and, if need be, die for
them, but he could still live only among his fellow Americans of colored skin. And when he got back home, the only job he could get was
shoveling coal at a Ford Motor Company steam plant. "My dad got
me the job," he remembered a half century later in his Washington,
D.C., office at the American Council on Education (ACE), which rep-
resents all the college and university presidents in the country.
"Man, it was hot. The other guys said, 'Pace yourself,' but, of course, I
couldn't. I wanted to prove how tough I was. At the end of the first
day, I got on the subway, sat down, and fell asleep. When I woke up I
was at the end of the line. I took the train back and fell asleep again.
This time when I woke up I said to myself, 'There's got to be a better
way.'" There was, through the GI Bill at Wayne State University,
where a Ph.D. in educational psychology eventually led Wilson to
become the senior scholar at ACE.

Efforts in the era right after the war to explain the success of the
veterans proved largely fruitless. The most sophisticated study, conducted by the Carnegie Foundation for the Advancement of Teaching,
found no significant correlation or difference between two groups of
five thousand veterans and nonveterans who completed an elaborate
questionnaire in the spring semester of 1946–47. The researchers
could only conclude the superior performance was "due to a process
of self-selection growing out of a complex of circumstances which
included the educational benefits of the G.I. Bill of Rights and the
delaying of college matriculation on the part of veterans. Those
veterans who decided to go to college included a larger *proportion*
[emphasis researchers'] of strongly motivated and academically-
motivated men than would otherwise have gone to college."[23] In other
words, the GI Bill was an earned opportunity—and its beneficiaries
made the most of it.

Ambiguous as that finding was, what was obvious during this
time was that America was producing a record number of babies. It
was obvious, at least, to the one man who would be responsible for
building the first suburban community that would become the model
for all other suburban communities, William J. Levitt. The social
scientists and economists weren't fully aware of the phenomenon
until the data were compiled, but the birth rate, which had been as

low as 2,315 per 10,000 of population in 1936, had jumped to 3,104 by 1943 and 3,817 in 1947. The first rush slackened down to 3,637 in 1948 before climbing to 3,823 in 1952 and reaching an all-time peak of 4,308 in 1957.[24] The demographic figures were quickly reflected in housing production statistics as the GI Bill changed *where* and *how* Americans lived. Suburbs sprang up like mushrooms around every sizable city, creating a new frontier in which cars replaced trolleys and subways; clean cellars with oil and gas furnaces became recreation rooms and home fix-it shops; and the traditional "night out with the boys" became a neighborhood barbecue. As surely as the Homestead Act of 1862 filled the prairies of the Far West, the GI Bill created and filled the suburbs. Veterans Administration mortgages paid for well over one third of those new homes, almost five million in all. The number of VA mortgages approved went from 43,000 in 1945 to 412,000 in 1946; 542,000 in 1947; 350,000 in 1948; 277,000 in 1949; and 498,000 in 1950.[25]

Much of that construction and the rapidity with which it went up would not have occurred, however, without the insight of one man, William J. Levitt. Levitt knew not only how to build houses faster and cheaper but how to provide the neighborhood amenities people wanted. He also understood how the GI Bill would provide effective one-stop mortgage financing. VA mortgages took the fear out of buying a home, both for the buyer and for the lender. No money down was needed, but the bank had the assurance that the mortgage was backed by the full faith and credit of the U.S. government. The home buyer could also hold on to his wartime savings as a hedge against another depression. Even with nothing down, mortgage payments rarely exceeded $89 a month, well within the common pay scales at the time. The GI Bill made possible the development of housing as an industry on a scale comparable to automobiles, but Levitt got it going. In doing so, he identified the demographic market of young families who would become the customers for the franchise operations that would transform American retailing over the subsequent decades. "If the first great business figure of the 20th century was Henry Ford, the second, arguably, was William J. Levitt," wrote David Halberstam in *The Fifties*.[26] If Levitt were given credit for anticipating the franchising methods that now dominate American marketing, he might, more justifiably, be given first place.

By 1955, Levitt-style subdivisions accounted for 75 percent of all housing starts. Almost all of those houses were being built by 10 percent of the builders, assembly-line builders like Levitt rather than the old-time, small builder. There were critics, of course. The "inferior type of small house being provided by speculative builders to meet the veterans' demands [were] doll houses that out-slum the slummiest of our prewar slums," Dr. Charles Winslow, professor emeritus of public health at Yale University, told an American Institute of Architects forum. He predicted families "living in these houses might suffer serious mental and physical ills."[27]

Yet despite these problems, the home building made possible by the GI Bill produced a social revolution even greater than Henry Ford's. Whereas Ford put millions of cars on the road and spawned one of the nation's biggest industries, Levitt put people in homes and spawned an even bigger one, while indirectly spawning ancillary industries in furniture and appliance making and sales, supermarketing of food, franchising of restaurants for young families, even expansion of schools. The results were quickly apparent. One year after President Truman announced Japan's surrender, 11 million World War II veterans had been discharged, leaving less than 1 million in service. Seventy percent of the veterans were employed, the majority in jobs other than those they held before the war. Almost 1 million veterans were in school, another 1 million drawing checks to supplement farm work, 403,000 employed in on-the-job training, and 318,000 being helped to establish businesses or professional practices. As of September 1946, only 13 percent were drawing unemployment benefits. During the previous year, 4.9 million had collected unemployment, but, of those, 86 percent were on unemployment for less than twenty weeks. One percent had exhausted the fifty-two weeks of benefits they were entitled to. Of the remainder, 396,000 were on vacation, taking rehabilitation training, or just resting up, and 86,000 were hospitalized.[28]

Because Congress listened to almost unknown people like Henry Colmery, who had written the bill, and followed the lead of the relatively obscure members who sponsored the bill, rather than notable figures like Hutchins and Conant—and FDR's planners—millions went to school who otherwise might not have done so, suburbia was created, and an entirely new economic and social infrastructure was put in place. Moreover, beyond its specific education and housing accomplishments, the GI Bill did something more. It created a new way of thinking about and dealing with social problems by harnessing private entrepreneurial skills to the financial incentives and security afforded by federal funds. Levitt wasn't only building houses; he was demonstrating that a product could be built and sold to a select demographic market, young families, without government intervention. Levitt proved homes could be built to standardized specifications without factory assembly and sold through mass merchandising techniques by local and regional developers. Other entrepreneurs quickly saw opportunities in discount stores, motels, restaurants, supermarkets, even schools, and churches.

When John Kennedy took office as president in 1960, the New Frontier he talked about had already been created in the suburbs. In that new life, almost exclusively for whites then, were the seeds of a new life for blacks and other minorities as well. The GI Bill was America's first color-blind social legislation. Social Security had excluded farm workers and domestics from coverage, the jobs employing most blacks. The bill enabled many blacks to go to college, educating many of the middle-class leaders of the 1960s' civil rights movement. The GI Bill opened opportunities for blacks, which once extended, could only be expanded. Eighty-three percent of the nation's growth occurred in the suburbs during the forty years after World War II. Starting in 1950, almost all the nation's cities lost population while the suburbs gained sixty million new residents. The bill, like all laws, had unexpected consequences; in this instance, it helped accelerate the concentration of blacks and minorities in the cities. If people were leaving the cities to find a better life, they were also fleeing them to avoid shadows cast by urban blight—and people of darker skin. At the same time, the GI Bill was creating a far larger black middle class than the past's cadre of preachers and teachers confined to the old Strivers' Rows of segregated communities. Wartime service, then the GI Bill helped make Martin Luther King's hope that black children would be judged by "the content of their character rather than the color of their skin" practical. The standard by which all Americans were inducted into the military; the standard on which the GI Bill was built; the standard by which the military became the first social institution integrated in American society was a simple one: If someone was good enough to die for America, he or she was good enough to enjoy all the rights of an American. In the first years after World War II, that was not enough to get a black veteran into a segregated college or university or to get a nisei—a first-generation Japanese— who had fought with the army's most decorated unit into a whites-only development, or a Mexican-American buried in an Anglo ceme-

tery. It was enough, however, to enable Oliver Brown, the plaintiff in
Brown vs. the Board of Education of Topeka, Kansas—the hometown
of Colmery, the author of the GI Bill—to buy his own home; it was
enough to pay for the law school education of Edward W. Brooke, the
first black to serve in the Senate since Reconstruction; it was enough
to provide the training Harry Belafonte needed to become the first
entertainer Americans thought of first as an actor and singer and second as a black. It was enough to make a beginning, to let the sun start
shining on everyone.

The GI Bill of Rights, in a very fundamental sense, put real, practical meaning into the Declaration of Independence's boast that
Americans had a right to the pursuit of happiness. By extending
opportunities and opening possibilities never before contemplated
and not even demanded by Americans, the GI Bill created social
options and expectations far beyond the purely legal rights granted
under the original Bill of Rights. In so doing, the bill laid the foundations for the later civil rights campaigns of blacks in the '60s, women
in the '70s, and the disabled in the '80s. By making a middle-class
life, rooted in education and homes, the norm for a majority of Americans, it created the demand for its extension to all Americans.

Above all, it changed the way the veteran and his family and all
their neighbors—regardless of their ethnic, religious, and racial backgrounds—began to think about themselves. They owned their own
homes now, taxpayers, not wards of political machines. Their education, rather than union membership, was both the source and the best
guarantee of their income. Thomas Jefferson's dream of the independent yeoman, self-sufficient on his own farm, had come true in a way
he didn't anticipate. Soon, veterans became the principal element in a
fundamental breakup of the political coalition that had kept the
White House in Franklin Delano Roosevelt's command for more than
twelve years. Harry Truman's upset victory in 1948 proved that the
New Deal coalition was still alive and well, but its temporary eclipse
in the 1952 election and a restoration of effective competition within
the two-party system would come soon enough—influenced by the
GI Bill.

Even as Republican politicians were puzzling over how to get blue-
collar, rent-paying workers to vote for the Grand Old Party, the GI
Bill was turning these voters into white-collar, home-owning taxpayers. Paradoxically, a government program could and did encourage
people to become more independent of government. Government fund-

ing could be invested in human potential rather than dissipated in a pension such as veterans of earlier wars had received, one that just kept them alive.

The economic prosperity, in itself, could be called a silent revolution, a revolution "in the American grain—it was nonideological," as Geoffery Perrett, the author of the only social history of the war, *Days of Sadness, Years of Triumph,* observed. "No mass movement was behind it, nurtured it, sought recruits for it, elected candidates or defeated them as they helped or hindered. . . . [The New Deal] was a triumph of appearances over reality. The triumph of reality came . . . with the war."[29]

The GI Bill made modern America. Yet the story of the GI Bill, despite being perhaps the most extraordinary one of twentieth-century America, has never been fully told. That may be because it doesn't lend itself to a conventional plot line, that is, as the saga of a great hero—FDR—or as a morality tale pitting the forces of good against evil—liberals versus conservatives, the oppressed against their oppressors, or wisdom against folly. The fault may also lie in the way we think about history. When we look back to discover why things turned out the way they did, we like a simple, black-and-white version. We prefer the guys in white hats to be the good guys the whole time.

The story of the GI Bill instead is a tale of ironies, paradoxes, ambiguities, unexpected events, role reversals by extraordinary—but very real—people. The narrative often reads as if it were a screenplay written by Frank Capra and featuring characters from some bad novel. Yet if there is a moral, perhaps it's simply that sometimes democracy does work, that miraculously the worst of systems except for all the others can produce the best results.

Gen. Theodore Roosevelt Jr., the cofounder of the American Legion, inspired the Legion to become the primary sponsor of the bill. Once FDR's rival to succeed his father, Theodore Roosevelt Sr., as president, if the younger Roosevelt is remembered now, it is more likely because he led the breakout of American forces into France from Normandy Beach.

In Congress, all the GI Bill's founding fathers—and one mother— were white, middle-class, small-town Republicans or conservative Democrats. Perhaps the greatest accidental catalyst for the bill's enactment was Representative Andrew Jackson May, a congressman from Kentucky who slipped out of town before Christmas of 1943 without reporting out a bonus bill for a House vote and, afterwards, threatened a couple of Hearst newspaper reporters with a visit with the undertaker.

If William Randolph Hearst's writers hadn't been threatened, perhaps Hearst would not have thrown the full resources of his enormous newspaper empire into the battle for the bill. Hearst, a one-time liberal who became the favorite villain of liberals in the '30s and '40s, is remembered best as his movie caricature, *Citizen Kane*. Coincidentally, his editor, Walter Howey, himself the prototype of a character in a play (the unscrupulous managing editor in the classic newspaper play, *The Front Page*), urged Hearst to make the GI Bill his greatest crusade.

Among the members of Congress who played starring roles in this social drama were Representative John Rankin of Mississippi. A notorious racist and anti-Semite, Rankin nonetheless stood up to Harvard's President Conant and other educators during the principal House debate to insist that historically black colleges be covered by the bill—before later becoming the biggest stumbling block to passage of the legislation.

Senator Bennett Clark, another key player, was the senior senator from Missouri. He had nominated Truman for the vice presidency at the Democratic national convention in 1944, but he had been an isolationist and a consistent opponent of the New Deal, even briefly opposing Social Security. Before she helped with the GI Bill, Representative Edith Nourse Rogers was responsible for legislation creating the Women's Army Corps, and she also spoke out against Hitler's persecution of the Jews. But she was also a Republican Brahmin who, inexplicably, represented Lowell, Massachusetts, a quintessential textile mill town. Perhaps the most nail-biting moment of the bill's passage came when Representative John Gibson of Georgia had to be summoned back to Washington to cast a tie-breaking vote; Rankin had arranged a stalemate to kill the bill because it provided the same unemployment benefits to blacks as to whites.

Aside from William Randolph Hearst, these names are footnotes in history books. Yet, obscure and unheralded, they nonetheless created a revolution in American life. Those who made the GI Bill of Rights were wonderful characters, and the new life they made possible for World War II veterans and all of us since then has been, with all its faults, a wonderful life. A quarter of a century before the GI Bill passed, General Roosevelt, as a former World War I American

Expeditionary Force colonel just elected to the New York Assembly, told his fellow legislators, "Unless you base your social and governmental reforms on human nature, they cannot be permanent."

It's doubtful those who passed the GI Bill had any more profound sociological or philosophical or economic principles than that in mind. But by just thinking of what the veterans would want for themselves and sharing their human—and specifically American—desires, they helped make Americans what they have always wanted to be: middle-class citizens. That's why this story isn't just about those who made the GI Bill. That's why it's about us, about what they believed Americans are and ought to be—and what we have become largely because of them.

This book tells their story and describes that silent revolution—a miracle of democracy—wrought by fallible human beings who had, nevertheless, enough sense to have learned from the mistakes of the past. So, for the first time in American history, veterans were treated generously and wisely, rather than callously and foolishly. Both they and the nation have benefited ever since.

CHAPTER 2

PATTERNS OF ABUSE

T HEY ALL HAD the same dream, those who fought in the nation's wars, to come back and begin a life as self-sufficient farmers, independent businessmen, educated professionals, or skilled workers. But the dream was betrayed by civilians or corrupted by the nation's leaders. Somehow they had to figure out for themselves how to make the dream come true. First, however, they had to decide what they had been and what they had become as veterans and, above all, as Americans.

In all the nation's conflicts, war was the blast furnace in which men of every origin, color, and religion were shaped, toughened and sometimes warped—but, inexorably, tempered into something new on earth, the modern American.

From the Revolution through World War I, however, victory had come with a price, one that grew steeper after peace was won. When the men came marching home, bands played, firecrackers popped, small boys and girls waved flags, and the oratory flowed as copiously as the whisky and beer. But almost before the last echoes of jubilation faded—and long before the dully gleaming medals were tucked away in dresser drawers—despairing sighs were heard, punctuated by the harsh staccato of recrimination. Heroes of the Revolutionary War, the War of 1812, the Civil War, the Spanish-American War, and World War I quickly became dispossessed farmers, factory workers without factory jobs to go to, even unemployed bums. The whisky and the beer were used to relieve pain rather than celebrate. Before long, even the desperate days of war seemed better than the even more desperate days of peace. During the war, the enemies had been just the enemy and easy to fight; at home, they were the employer who wouldn't hire, the banker who wouldn't extend credit, even the government that couldn't or wouldn't help those who had suffered and nearly died in its service. At home, both the government and the ungrateful citizens it represented were the enemies of those who had fought to preserve both. Veterans became victims—and predators.

After the Revolutionary War, many veterans lost their homes and were thrown into debtors' prison because of overdue taxes. After the Civil War, veterans organized perhaps the most powerful special interest lobby in history and plundered the treasury. Yet, veterans exerted a beneficial influence on the evolving democracy, spurring the 1783 Constitutional Convention in Philadelphia that restructured government power and later forcing a reluctant federal government to accept responsibility for the needy by the Bonus March of 1932. Above all, they did so by being the primary moving force behind the GI Bill of Rights and a silent revolution that transformed America into a predominantly middle-class country.

Veterans are a "replica of the country itself," Theodore Roosevelt Jr., the principal founder of the American Legion, wrote almost a decade after World War I. "Our army in France was more representative of the United States than is the national Congress." Of course, that didn't make veterans any wiser or more visionary than Congress. But after World War I, the uniquely representative character of those who served as members of the nation's first multicultural army helped them to become the architects of the GI Bill. But bitter lessons had to be learned first.

Wars are marvelously effective full-employment programs, but until the end of World War II, no government had devised a postwar replacement for the economic productivity of a fully mobilized people making and using weapons to kill their enemies. Peace can be bad for business. Forging swords into plowshares is a poetic image, not a conversion program from wartime to a peacetime economy. And a peacetime economy cannot redress the inevitable economic and social injustice war produces. Those who stay home and reap the bounty of harvest and factory production sold to the government at top dollar are far more able to weather economic downturns when peace comes than yesterday's heroes. Even the lowest-paid civilian worker in wartime usually makes as much as an officer and several times more than an enlisted man. That was particularly true in the revolution against England. The Continental soldiers and sailors of the victorious United States of America couldn't collect the $6 million they were owed in back pay as the war ended. The Continental Congress couldn't pay up. It had run out of silver and gold long before the final battle at Yorktown, and the paper money it had been passing off to settle its debts was, as one officer wrote, "fit for little else but to make the tail of a kite."

Without money to either pay their way home or to satisfy their creditors once they got there, most Continental soldiers remained encamped at Newburgh, New York. George Washington, fearing mutiny, remained with his troops while pleading with Congress by mail to provide them with at least three months of accumulated back pay. That was the minimum necessary, Washington thought, for the men to return home, fend off their creditors, and get back to work. "To be disbanded at last, without this little pittance," he wrote, "like a Sett of Beggars, Needy, Distressed, and without Prospect will not only blast the Expectations of their Creditors, and expose the Officers to the utmost Indignity and Worst of Consequences, but will drive every man of Honor and Sensibility to the extremist Horrors of Despair." Eventually, Robert Morris, the congressional superintendent of finance, raised enough money in anticipation of a loan from Holland to give the soldiers a few months' wages. But there were delays in getting the money to Newburgh, and some impatient soldiers struck off for home penniless.

Victory was particularly hollow for those veterans who returned to their farms in the Connecticut Valley of western Massachusetts. Their fields were returning to brush and bramble, and local authorities were threatening foreclosure for unpaid taxes. Evictions spawned a new rebellion led by Capt. Daniel Shays, a veteran of the Revolutionary War battles of Bunker Hill, Fort Ticonderoga, and Stony Point. Shays, who had to sell a ceremonial sword given to him by the Marquis de Lafayette to satisfy debts, was elected chairman of a committee of armed and angry farmers. James Bowdoin, the governor of Massachusetts, after seeking unsuccessfully to raise $530,000 from Congress for a special force to disperse these new rebels, got enough private funds to field a militia. It scattered eleven hundred farmers who attacked the Springfield Arsenal seeking weapons on January 25, 1787. After a few more skirmishes, Shays's main force was routed at Petersham on February 4, 1787. While Shays fled to Vermont, fourteen other leaders of the revolt were captured and sentenced to be hung. New members more sympathetic to the farmers were elected to the legislature, however, and a conciliatory John Hancock succeeded Bowdoin as governor. The death sentences were either dismissed or reduced to brief prison terms. Shays himself was pardoned in 1788 and moved to New York.[1]

The rebels weren't protesting just unfair taxes, but betrayal of the promise regarding the pursuit of happiness in the Declaration of Independence, defined by Americans at that time as independent ownership of property. When Jefferson wrote the Declaration, he was putting into his own words the fundamental premise of John Locke's *Second Treatise on Government:* "The great and chief end . . . of men's uniting into commonwealths and placing themselves under government is the preservation of their own property." Jefferson's first draft of the Declaration of Independence is reported to have concluded all men are entitled to "the pursuit of property"—rather than happiness. Thomas Paine had argued in *Common Sense* that western lands, closed to settlement by the Crown in 1763, were a common domain all Americans should be able to share in and benefit by. "They seem made by our benevolent creator to reward our efforts," Paine wrote, "a common stock . . . purchased by the joint blood and Treasury of the Confederacy."

Both the states and Congress had promised land to soldiers as a bounty after the war. Consequently, Washington's officers at Newburgh, with his approval, demanded that Congress honor the promises. They recommended that distribution should range from eleven hundred acres for major generals down to one hundred acres for privates. With 288 officers approving the plan, Washington forwarded it to Congress. As an alternative, officers said they would take half-pay for themselves for seven years, with the enlisted ranks to get full pay. Congress rejected the plan because several states, particularly Virginia, claimed all the land westward to the Pacific under their original seventeenth-century charters from the king of England. Indeed, such charter claims were safeguarded by the Articles of Confederation, which explicitly withheld jurisdiction over the West from Congress. Congress could not substitute money because it was broke.

Eventually, New York and Connecticut surrendered their western claims, and Virginia's position was undermined by a secessionist movement. But before then, Washington's officers lost patience with the squabbling. Maj. John Armstrong Jr. drafted what were called the Newburgh Addresses, urging the officers to turn their bayonets against a Congress that "tramples on your rights, disdains your cries and insults your distresses." Washington was asked to assume the dictatorship of the country. The general, convinced that would be "the greatest mischief that could befall my country," disarmed his officers by saying first, "Gentlemen, you will permit me to put on my spectacles, for I have not only gone gray but almost blind in the service of my country." Many of the assembled officers cried openly as he denounced those who would "open the flood Gates of civil discord, and deluge our rising Empire in blood."[2]

The mutiny was headed off. But the officers and men were still unpaid and didn't even have a promise of western lands. Yet another petition was sent to Congress. This time it arrived in Philadelphia in June 1783 along with troops of the Maryland Line passing through on their way home. "An enraged Soldiery" surrounded the statehouse where Congress was in session, but after three hours, the members were allowed to leave without being molested, and they fled the city. During the next year, Congress wandered from Trenton to Princeton to New York while soldiers drifted back to their homes with the pittance Morris had provided.

During that year, Jefferson drafted the Territorial Ordinance of 1784, which became the Northwest Ordinance when it was enacted three years later. Although not directed at veterans, this first piece of federal legislation was the real-world expression of Jefferson's yeoman ideal. It set a precedent for government to encourage both home ownership and education, using one to help finance the other. "I am now entirely absorbed in endeavors to effect the establishment of a general system of education," Jefferson wrote at the time, "placing a college within a day's ride of every individual and adding a provision for the full education at public expense of select subjects from among the children of the poor." The land in ten territories that are now the Midwest states was divided into townships containing thirty-six sections of forty-four acres, with section number sixteen reserved for public schools.

"I think by far the most important bill is that for the diffusion of knowledge," Jefferson wrote to Madison on August 13, 1786, when the Continental Congress had the Northwest Ordinance under consideration. "No other sure foundation can be devised for the preservation of freedom and happiness. . . . Preach, my dear sir, a crusade against ignorance; establish and improve the law for educating the common people. Let our countrymen know the people alone can protect us from these evils, and that the tax that will be paid for this purpose is not more than one part of what will be paid to kings, priests and nobles who will rise up among us if we keep our people ignorant."

Shays's rebellion in 1787 may have done nothing for the cause of the veterans when it took place, but it made the states realize a more powerful federal government was needed. The Continental Congress's failure to help Massachusetts put down the rebellion, even after the federal arsenal in Springfield was attacked, "was the final argument to sway many Americans in favor of a strong central government," wrote historian Samuel Eliot Morison.[3]

It was the "news from Massachusetts," John Dos Passos wrote in *Men Who Made the Nation,* that persuaded George Washington to preside over what became the Constitutional Convention. Dos Passos observed, "Washington's correspondents feared that the Massachusetts rebellion might be the prelude to 'some awful crisis' in which the advocates of paper money and the distribution of lands and of levelling generally would seize the state governments."[4]

The veterans had little influence in the deliberations at Philadelphia. But the adoption of the Constitution and the establishment of Washington, D.C., as the capital meant the new federal government now, at least, could be asked to help those who had suffered in its service, particularly the disabled. Most of the pension requests went to Henry Knox, the secretary of war, who usually rejected them if the disability wasn't proven to "be the immediate effect of some exertion or suffering in the line of duty." He recommended that Congress approve all valid claims "in one general act to be passed towards the close of each session." That, he argued, would avoid "the perplexity arising from a multiplicity of acts of the same nature"—and avoid the appearance of favoritism.

Favoritism nevertheless occurred. Baron von Steuben, the Prussian martinet who had helped whip Washington's "rabble in arms" into disciplined troops, was given $7,000 in addition to a gold-hilted sword. The Society of Cincinnatus, founded by Knox himself, gave its members, Revolutionary War officers, the right to confer membership on their oldest sons. That apparent attempt to produce a hereditary aristocracy produced resentment, especially since Lucius Quinicus Cincinnatus, the Roman counsel for whom it was named, had decreed one law for the aristocratic patricians and another for common plebeians. Benjamin Franklin, James Jay, and John Adams denounced the society as "the first step to deface the beauty of our temple of liberty." Other veterans, led by Tom Paine, were infuriated by the society's demand for lifetime pensions based on half their pay while on active duty. Paine himself was denied a pension, and his earlier words were given new and bitter meaning: "I know not who the Committee of Claims are," Paine wrote in March 1808, "but if they are men of younger standing than 'the times that try men's souls,' and consequently, too young to know what the condition of the country was when I published *Common Sense, . . .* they are not capable of judging the whole of the services of Thomas Paine."[5]

The claims of the Revolutionary War veterans, both officers and enlisted men, weren't settled until 1817. With the War of 1812 over and America fully recognized as an independent nation, President James Monroe had proclaimed "an era of good feeling"—with the feeling extended to veterans. Acting on Monroe's initiative, Representative Joseph Bloomfield of New Jersey introduced a bill for a pension program, estimated as costing no more than $500,000 annually at $20 a month for officers and $8 for enlisted men. All veterans were entitled to benefits, without regard to income. Within a year the cost was six times Bloomfield's estimate, almost $3 million. By 1820, the law was amended to make veterans declare themselves indigent before they could qualify. The secretary of war was also given the power to wield a "scythe of retrenchment" against those already on the rolls. The number was duly cut from 18,880 who were receiving benefits in 1818 to 12,233 in 1820. But when better economic times returned in 1823, many whose benefits had been cut were restored to the rolls.

In 1829, President Andrew Jackson proposed an increase in benefits, but he was opposed by Senator Robert Haynes of South Carolina, who inveighed against "mere sunshine and holiday soldiers, the hangers-on of the camp, men of straw, substitutes, who never enlisted until after the preliminaries of peace were signed." The bill was defeated. Too much was already being paid, Congress felt, and too much of that fraudulently.

In 1833, efforts were made to expand pension benefits to veterans of the frontier Indian wars. This time, Representative Thomas T. Bouldin asked for an inquiry "into the moral and political effects of the pension laws of the United States." The practical effect of the pension system, Bouldin declared, was "to discourage private industry, and lead a large portion of the people of the United States to look to the Treasury as the unfailing spring from which they were to receive every good." Other members of Congress agreed pensions should be limited to those in need, those who declared themselves paupers. Representative Edward Colston of Virginia eloquently disagreed. "Let not the soldier by whose bravery and sufferings we are entitled to hold seats on this floor be required to expose his poverty to the world," he said, "and exhibit the proof of it to entitle him to relief." Senator William Smith, also of Virginia, was equally eloquent in protesting the burdens the pension program placed on the children and grandchildren of the Revolutionary generation. "Posterity will writhe beneath the [fiscal] yoke . . . of a military pension," he said.

Smith did point out the fundamental flaw in the pension program: it was unfunded. All payments for pensions had to come either out of current revenues or from borrowing against future revenue. The ultimate—and inevitable—result was a monumental increase in government debt. The problem was resolved only when all the Revolutionary War veterans died off, and with them the pension program. At least before that, Daniel Shays was able to become a property owner once again, buying a twelve-acre farm in Livingston County, New York, with his pension.

It took some time for the Revolutionary War veterans to die off, especially on paper. In 1834, the House Committee on Revolutionary Pensions charged: "Men in the highest walks of life, of the most honorable pretensions are drawing money from the Treasury, by means of false papers, the grossest acts of forgery, and the most willful and corrupt perjury." Bloomfield had estimated in 1817 that only 10,000 veterans of the war were still living; the House Committee reported that in 1832 the number of applicants for pensions already exceeded 32,900. Average life expectancy at the time was only about fifty, and almost fifty years had passed since the Treaty of Paris was signed in 1783. The congressional report wondered, "Can so many Revolutionary officers and soldiers now be living?"

In the aftermath of the next great conflict, the American Civil War, the nation's first large veterans' organization pushed through a scandalous pension system—helped by the lawyer-lobbyists who began to dominate Washington after the Civil War. In the process, the Grand Army of the Republic (GAR), the first veterans' organization, deliberately unseated one president, looted the treasury, was reviled as a greedy lobby cloaking itself in public virtue, and indirectly contributed to the limited bonus program afforded World War I veterans.

What was provided Civil War veterans initially was modest enough and was designed only to correct some indisputable abuses in the Civil War draft. On January 25, 1879, President Rutherford B. Hayes signed an "arrears" and "bounty equalization" bill. Arrears were claims for disabilities filed after a five-year cutoff date had passed in 1870. Bounties had been paid to encourage enlistments by the poor as substitutes for the wealthy, an inequitable response to an inequitable draft system. The nation's first conscription act, enacted on March 3, 1863, required all men between twenty and forty-five to register, and quotas of draftees were imposed on the states in proportion to population. No exemptions were allowed for married fathers, ministers, or essential civilian workers, and no efforts were made to take younger men or bachelors first. Names were simply chosen by lot from those on the registered list. Those chosen had only one out—if they were wealthy.

Substitutes paid up to $300 were retained, primarily from among the sons of poor Irish workingmen. They took the money, but resented wealthy abolitionists who wanted to do away with black slavery in the South, but were unwilling to pay a living wage to white workingmen in the North. Rage boiled over when blacks, freed under the recently announced Emancipation Proclamation, were imported into New York to break a strike by stevedores. On July 13, 1863, the federal provost marshal was attacked as names of draftees were being drawn from urns. The homes of antislavery leaders were sacked, stores plundered, saloons liberated, and hundreds killed. Gen. George G. Meade, victorious in battle at Gettysburg, had to detach so many troops to New York to put down the uprising that he could not pursue and cut off retreating Confederate troops.

The vast majority of the 2.2 million who served in the Union Army were volunteers; only 200,921 were paid bounties.[6] Nevertheless, many of the volunteers felt they were due an amount equal to a bounty retroactively as a matter of simple justice. Senator John T. Ingalls of Kansas was persuaded in 1878 to introduce a bill both for them and for veterans disabled by wounds during the war. Ingalls estimated the cost at between $18 million and $20 million, but when asked to be more specific, he declined, saying, "What would be required . . . could be no more calculated or estimated than one could calculate the number of birds that will fly through the sky next year." His demands were supported by the GAR, which had been formed by Dr. Benjamin Stephenson of Decatur, Illinois, a former soldier turned obstetrician. The GAR was enormously powerful, incorporating within itself many of the functions and membership now divided, for example, among the American Legion, the AFL-CIO, the National Association of Retired Persons, and the National Rifle Association. This national soldiers' mutual benefit society, as it described itself, was also secret, with rituals comparable to the Ku Klux Klan. Recruits were initiated kneeling before an open coffin as a mock firing squad cried out, "The penalty of treason is death." The GAR's real strength, however, as one letter writer to *The Boston Advertiser* put it, was as "a political power to be known as 'the soldier's vote.'"

That vote encouraged President Hayes to sign Ingalls's bill despite a warning from John Sherman, the secretary of the treasury, that the actual cost would be closer to $150 million than the $18 million to $20 million Ingalls estimated. In 1881 alone, in fact, expenditures by the newly established Pension Bureau were estimated to be $200 million. The bureau soon had fifteen hundred clerks and its own headquarters, the Pension Building, a red brick structure with soaring Corinthian columns inside and a terra-cotta frieze inspired by the Parthenon girdling its exterior. By 1885, when Grover Cleveland was inaugurated as the first Democratic president since the Civil War, 520,000 veterans were receiving pensions and the number of GAR members had quadrupled from 61,000 to 270,000, out of the approximately 1.5 million veterans living. Then, in 1887, Cleveland vetoed a new piece of legislation, the Dependent Pension Bill, which would have granted pensions to all veterans who claimed disabilities—even if those disabilities were not service connected. Cleveland's political virtue had to be its own reward. Outraged veterans cast their votes for Benjamin Harrison in 1888, narrowly defeating Cleveland. Harrison's victory was "unquestionably due to the veterans," *The National Tribune,* the GAR's official newspaper, gloated. Pensions, which by that time consumed almost 20 percent of the national budget, went from $88.4 million to $95 million just between 1889 and 1890. As *The Nation* magazine pointed out, "This is a greater amount than the cost of the entire military establishment of Germany, under which the people of that nation groan so loudly. The regular expenditures of the Pension Bureau now far exceed the total cost of the federal government before the war." The federal budget had been $56 million in 1860 and only reached $112.6 million in 1863 at the height of the war. The Dependent Pension Act signed by Harrison in 1890 was the fiscal equivalent of General Sherman's march through Georgia. By the end of 1893, 1 million survivors out of 2.2 million who had served during the 1861–65 war were drawing $150 million annually in pensions from the government. The total federal budget for 1893 was $385.6 million. The veterans had proved they were the most powerful political bloc in the country. They profited from that, but lost much of their fellow citizens' respect.

This feeling was changed when the Spanish-American War, declared in response to tales of Spanish atrocities in Cuba drummed up by the newspapers of Joseph Pulitzer and William Randolph Hearst, produced a surge of patriotic feeling and sympathy for returning veterans. Few American soldiers were killed in "the splendid little war." Tropical disease, however, left the survivors "ripe to dying like rotten sheep," as Theodore Roosevelt put it when he cabled his superiors, having resigned as assistant secretary of the navy to charge up San Juan Hill. Several shiploads of soldiers, weakened by malaria, dysentery, typhoid, and yellow fever, were dumped on Montauk Point on Long Island without adequate hospital facilities. Their only food was hardtack biscuits filled with worms and canned meat so spoiled the men called it embalmed beef. When members of New York's 71st Regiment marched down Broadway in a victory parade, *The New York Times* described them as "pathetic . . . emaciated, hollow-eyed and enfeebled."[7]

During the following years, American public opinion toward military service seesawed as war loomed in Europe. Neither native-born Americans nor the almost 20 million immigrants who flooded into the country between the turn of the century and 1917 wanted war. Immigration was producing other social strains, making the proverbial melting pot leak from every seam. But when war did come, the armed services became a crucible shaped of bullets, bayonets, and rifles, in which the modern American was forged. Out of the 4 million called to service, 1,390,000 saw combat, 290,000 were wounded, 49,000 were killed, and 57,000 died from disease. By contrast, 8 million European men died in military service, including 1 million from Germany; 1.4 million from France; and 947,000 from Great Britain.[8]

Europe lost a generation; America lost its innocence. But the Americans who marched off to war singing George M. Cohan's "The Yanks Are Coming" gained a new identity. Once the most brutal war in history was "over, over there," veterans came back thinking of themselves as Yanks—not as northerners or southerners, easterners or westerners. All were Americans now—not Irish or Italian or Polish or German, not even Catholic, Protestant, or Jewish. Yet they were treated worse than veterans of any previous war. "The Keys to the City had turned out only to be a pass to the flophouse," as one historian wrote.[9] They marched off to "save the world for democracy" in President Woodrow Wilson's words, but came home to a nation disillusioned by a futile and useless war.

They came back, however, with a sense of common purpose as Americans. "The commonness of death in war . . . makes a more effective preachment of immortality than ever was made from a pulpit," President Roosevelt's son, Theodore, who emerged from the war as a colonel, wrote in the introduction to his 1928 book of profiles of World War I heroes, *Rank and File*. Colonel Roosevelt had been among the young professional men who had joined a private military training program at Plattsburgh, New York, in 1915 well before war was declared. The war was a transforming experience for him, like many of his upper-class contemporaries, enabling them to transcend the ethnic and religious differences between them and their enlisted men as fellow soldiers. Having shared the horrors of war, they became bound together in peace as patriotic, if not social equals. Having served together would indissolubly link the four million for the rest of their lives and help shape America for the rest of the century.

World War I also began to make a mass consumer society in America, as recruits lined up to get machine-made clothing and boots, marched to see silent-picture training films, and were trained to drive and repair cars and trucks. These and other products would provide the revenues for radio and mass-circulation magazines in the '20s, but they would be test-marketed first on World War I soldiers and sailors. Cigarettes and safety razors, toothbrushes and tooth powder, bars of soap and hair preparations, the paraphernalia of modern mass armies, became the consumer products of a new culture in which military men, wearing trench coats and caps, set new styles of what was distinctively American. The men of the American Expeditionary Force, in fighting in a common cause, had also started a common culture "over there," which quickly took root back home.

Back home, meanwhile, there was little to be proud of in the record of the American government both during and after the war. Hundreds were sent to jail for protesting the war; newspapers ranging from

The Gaelic-American to *The Masses* were suppressed; government-sponsored vigilantes were encouraged to spy on neighbors; playing music by Mozart and Beethoven was forbidden in the schools; sauerkraut became liberty cabbage; even the conductor of the Boston Symphony Orchestra was deported for allegedly failing to play "The Star-Spangled Banner" at concerts—a song that wasn't even declared the national anthem until 1931. As the war came to an end, bombs ripped through Wall Street; the steel, coal, and automobile industries were crippled by strikes; police walked off the job in Boston; Seattle was closed down by a general strike; federal agents rounded up thousands of suspected Reds in simultaneous raids all over the country, and the Ku Klux Klan began to recruit hundreds of thousands of members. Usually remembered as the Red Scare period, that label actually applied only from after the war until 1921. Yet from the declaration of World War I in 1917 to the "return of normalcy" in 1922, the country had a national nervous breakdown.

The strains of the war, added to the tensions created by unrestricted immigration, ripped the country apart. President Wilson had predicted what would happen in a conversation the night before he declared war. "Once lead this people into war and they'll forget there ever was such a thing as tolerance," Wilson told Frank Cobb, the editor of *The New York World*. "To fight, you must be brutal and ruthless, and the spirit of ruthless brutality will enter into the very fiber of our national life, infecting Congress, the courts, the policeman on the beat, the man in the street."[10]

Social fissures created by native-born Americans' suspicions of foreigners soon turned into yawning crevasses. About 1 million people had immigrated into the country every year since 1900, and the number kept going up. In 1910 alone, 1,041,570 immigrants were counted; 1,197,892 in 1913, and 1,218,480 in 1914.[11] The war also exposed the nation's domestic social problems. Twenty-four percent of the 10 million who registered for the draft, 2.5 million in all, were found to be illiterate. Twelve million of the 27 million children of school age weren't going to school.[12] Only 14.5 percent of all seventeen-year-olds were high school graduates. Most immigrants were illiterate in English, if not their native language. There were thirteen hundred foreign language newspapers in the United States during the 1920s with a circulation between seven million and ten million. Among the *daily* foreign language papers published in 1920 were twenty-nine in German, eleven in Italian, and others in Ukrainian, Spanish, Russian, Albanian, Bulgarian, Serbian, Romanian, Finnish, Arabic, Croatian, Chinese, Greek, Japanese, Slovenian, Lithuanian, and Hungarian.[13]

American popular culture, in the modern sense, didn't exist. The small native-born American middle class sang Stephen Foster songs, went to ice cream parlors, and played baseball. A larger class of poor and working-class native-born Americans were miners, loggers, fishermen, and hardscrabble farmers whose only indulgence away from work was raw whisky on Saturday night and church on Sunday. The traditional America of both was being eclipsed by a new America that was predominantly urban rather than rural, as documented by the 1920 census. Millions of European-Americans dominated the cities that by then housed most of the people in America. Those immigrants and their children provided labor for an economy that was largely industrial rather than small town and rural. Yet they lived in urban villages very similar to the ones they had left in Ireland, Italy, Germany, and Russia. Nevertheless, their "hyphenated-American" loyalties worried the capitalists who profited from their labor, the politicians who vied for their votes, and the radicals who wanted their bodies for barricades. Other Americans mingled with them only at work, if then. Entire industries were taken over by ethnic groups: Jews in the garment trades, Germans in brewing, the Irish among carpenters and longshoremen, for instance. The immigrants' homes were in America, but they lived very much as they had in the old country, eating the same food, following the same customs—and avoiding American authorities. The most popular textbook in American schools, *An American History* by David Saville Muzzey published in 1911, asked, "Can we assimilate and mold into citizenship the millions who are coming to our shores, or will they remain an ever increasing body of aliens, an undigested and undigestible menace to our free institutions?"[14]

While the war was going on, before the troops brought home their new sense of unified Americanism, America was being rocked by working-class anarchists who were influenced by Socialist theories and who drew strength from opposition to the war. Some were unabashed revolutionaries. Daniel De Leon, an American Socialist whom Vladimir Lenin read admiringly after the Bolshevik Revolution of 1917, called on the working class to take over and destroy the government. He and the International Workers of the World (IWW), native radicals who had organized a general strike in Lawrence,

Massachusetts, in 1912, believed the workers could come to power through elections. Once elected, however, the Wobblies, as they were called, would resign in favor of a network of industrial unions, and government would be abolished.[15] While relatively few, the Wobblies were fervent, dedicated, and determined, and they had adherents among eastern textile mill workers, loggers in Oregon, cowboys in Texas, and fishermen in California. They also had socially prominent members—and propagandists—such as Jack London, the famous novelist, and Jack Reed, the journalist who would write *Ten Days That Shook the World* and be buried within the Kremlin walls.

To the Wobblies, strikes were just tactics in a strategy to bring down government itself. Wilson's signing of the Selective Service Act on May 18, 1917, six weeks after the declaration of war, seemed to open the curtain on what one Socialist thinker called the Götterdämmerung of the capitalist world. America was the country "in which the Marxian theory of evolution has been most minutely fulfilled," proclaimed Werner Sombat, one theorist, and events seemed to bear him out.[16] Protests erupted everywhere. In Wichita Falls, Texas, farmers were hauled off to jail as were other protesters in Wisconsin and Kansas, many of them German-American. Police broke up mass meetings of the Anti-Conscription League in Manhattan and the Bronx attended largely by Irish Americans. The IWW newspaper, *The Industrial Worker,* declared: "Capitalists of the World, we will fight against you, not for you. Conscription! There is not a power on earth that can make the working class fight if they refuse." One hundred and one members of the IWW were convicted of sedition, and a fine of $2.5 million broke the IWW's treasury—and the Wobblies as a union although they remained a political force.

The limits of free speech were tested with contradictory results. Charles Schenk, a Socialist, was jailed under the speech provisions of the Espionage Act for passing out pamphlets opposing the war, but released by the Supreme Court in a decision written by Justice Oliver Wendell Holmes: "The most stringent protection of free speech would not protect a man in falsely shouting fire in a crowded theater. . . . The question . . . is whether the words are of such a nature to create a clear and present danger." Schenk's pamphleteering didn't constitute such a danger, the Court decided.[17]

But Eugene Debs, the Socialist candidate for president in 1912, later went to jail for denouncing the war as promoting "enslaving and degrading capitalist institutions." The Supreme Court upheld his conviction in a decision that focused on Debs's assertion that working men were not concerned with the war. The "natural and intended effect" of that argument was obstruction of recruitment, wrote Holmes for the majority. Debs was pardoned only after the war by President Warren G. Harding.[18]

On June 1, 1918, an appalled Theodore Roosevelt, the former president, wrote his son, who was commanding an infantry battalion near Paris: "The last five years have made me bitterly conscious of the shortcomings of our national character, but we Roosevelts are Americans . . . it is the business of each of us to play the part of a good American and try to make things as much better as possible."[19] Earlier, the younger Roosevelt had had little time for philosophical contemplation of such shortcomings. However, that summer, having won the Croix de Guerre in the trench fighting, the younger Roosevelt was thinking about forming a veterans' organization as a way of "doing something better" for America.

The idea of a veterans' association, which became the American Legion, apparently originated from a casual conversation between Roosevelt and Sgt. William Patterson while both were convalescing at a base hospital in the summer of 1918, according to a 1919 account.[20]

The two men, both limping from wounds, stopped to rest against a shade tree. The sergeant's hand rose in quick salute.

"Eager to get back soon, Sergeant?" asked the officer.

"Yes, sir. Anxious to go back and get the whole job done, sir."

"So am I, but what will we all do when the Germans really are licked?"

"Go home and start a veterans' association for the benefit of the country," the sergeant said.

Patterson was later killed in action, but on February 16, 1919, Colonel Roosevelt, acting on his idea, hosted a dinner for twenty officers in Paris. He thought such an organization should contain all those in the U.S. Army during the war, a sort of GAR that should be in the "forefront to do good things," according to a letter to his wife, Eleanor, dated January 21, 1919.[21] Those good things unquestionably included opposition to communism and the IWW. "There was a general concern about the postwar attitude of the average soldier," Richard Sellye Jones, a Legion publicist, wrote in 1945. Officers, in particular, "worried about rumors and reports from America on radical, Communistic movements of soldier's and sailor's councils among men who had been discharged quickly after the Armistice. . . . Even the restless lack of discipline in the army itself was vaguely attributed by some to Soviet ideas. A safe and sound association of veterans might be the best insurance against their spread."[22] Such an association would also be the seedbed from which the GI Bill would grow and create a real revolution.

The officers Roosevelt invited to dinner were already in Paris as frontline commanders ordered there by headquarters to provide ideas for keeping the troops out of trouble until they could be shipped home. Although forming a veterans' association was an idea junior officers were far more likely to be reprimanded for than commended, the group established a temporary committee, with Roosevelt and Maj. Bennett Clark, the son of House Speaker Champ Clark, as cochairmen. The officers agreed that the organization should be entirely democratic, with enlisted men playing leadership roles at every level. That meant delegates of the enlisted men had to be brought to Paris for another organizational meeting, despite army regulations and the expenses involved. "The enlisted personnel, by devious means, were ordered to Paris under one guise or another," recounted Colonel Roosevelt's widow, Eleanor, in her autobiography, *Day Before Yesterday*.[23] One sergeant had orders stating he was carrying important documents when his dispatch case was just stuffed with wadded waste paper. Another noncom had orders to report to Paris to obtain a supply of rat poison. Several privates had "diseases of so peculiar a character that only Paris physicians could treat them," according to Mrs. Roosevelt. By various means, nearly two hundred delegates reached Paris for the Legion's first caucus March 15–17.

Once assembled, an old American tradition was revived, the town meeting: "A few moments after the caucus convened a high-ranking officer moved that rank be forgotten while in the conference hall and should be resumed only when the delegates had resumed the street," Mrs. Roosevelt wrote. "From then on generals argued with corporals, and everyone talked with everyone else in complete equality."[24] Two months later, one thousand delegates met in St. Louis, Missouri, on May 8–10 for the first public convention of the association. As Colonel Roosevelt, acting as temporary chairman, called for nominations for permanent chairman, several delegates began to cry out, "We want Teddy. We want Teddy." The call swept through the hall, and Roosevelt's name was placed in nomination over his objections. "Gentlemen, I would like to speak in regard to the nomination," Roosevelt declared and went on speaking over continued shouts of "We want Teddy; we want Teddy."

"Gentlemen, I wish to withdraw my name," said Roosevelt. He was shouted down with cries of "No, no," as a tide of acclamation began to sweep through the hall. "The temporary chairman's features suddenly became stern," an account in *The American Legion Weekly* of July 4, 1919, reported. "He strode to the front of the stage with all the vigor and determination which had personified his father. 'I wish to withdraw my name,' young Roosevelt began, and after a long disturbance, continued, 'I want the country at large to get the correct impression of this meeting. We are gathered for a very high purpose. I want every American through the length and breadth of the land to realize there is not a man in this caucus who is asking anything for himself personally, but that he is simply working for the good of the entire situation . . . now, gentlemen, it is my absolute determination to withdraw myself.'"

Nevertheless, the motion to nominate was seconded, moved, and voted unanimously. "Gentlemen, I resign," Roosevelt shouted over cries of "No, no," walking around the stage until the disturbance subsided. "I want quiet for a moment," he said. ". . . This is something I have thought of and given my earnest consideration to, and I am positive I am right in it . . . I am going to stick by [my decision] because we have got to . . . create an impression on which this organization will carry on and serve a great purpose for many years to come."

"It seemed almost a superhuman feat for a young man to refuse the honor tendered him in such a manner," *The New York Evening Mail* commented on May 11, 1919. William Slavens McNutt, the author of a lengthy article on the convention in *Collier's Magazine,* concurred: "He was distinctly a dramatic figure during that hour-long demonstration, that slim young soldier with the air of his heritage about him, holding stubbornly to his purpose in evident agony of mind. But he stepped to the footlights and said no in a characteristically emphatic way that got across to the mob on the floor. In spite of the unanimous demand for him, his firm and persistent refusal did wonders in relaxing the tensity of suspicion that existed when the caucus opened. . . . On the last day of the meeting one heard on all sides the expression, 'Why this is the biggest thing ever.' It is! It is because it is the perpetuation of the sane, common sense, honest best of America in its greatest hour. . . . Potentially, it is all of the good that was in the army with none of the bad." [25]

Roosevelt's refusal to serve was followed by the election of another colonel as chairman; a sergeant, a seaman, and a private as vice chairmen; and a lieutenant colonel as secretary. The next issue on the agenda lifted the curtain on a drama that would end six months later with a confrontation in a small logging town in Washington State. Four American Legion members and a Wobblie would die in a shootout that became symbolically significant in American social and political history. The incident, in Centralia, Washington, would color liberals' perception of the American Legion. Because of its anticommunist activities in the 1950s, the Legion has been considered right wing, antilabor, and generally unprogressive. This perception began with the Centralia incident, which had its real beginning at the Legion's first caucus. The first act of the drama began when the Soldiers' and Sailors' Council of Washington State, composed largely of IWW members who were also veterans, asked to be accepted into the Legion as a state affiliate. A credentials committee recommended exclusion because the IWW played a central role in the general strike in Seattle four months before.

The strike, which had polarized public opinion all across the country, started with a shipyard walkout by thirty-five thousand workers, primarily IWW members, and quickly spread to one hundred thousand workers when 110 union locals, mostly from the moderate American Federation of Labor, joined in. The entire city was closed down. Although firefighters agreed to stay on the job, the police went out on the picket lines. A Labor War Veterans' Guard claimed it would preserve "law and order without the use of force. No volunteer will have any police power or be allowed to carry weapons of any sort, but use persuasion only." Very little violence occurred, and the strike lasted only five days. Nevertheless, Ole Hansen, the mayor, claimed that the very lack of violence was, itself, proof of revolution: "Revolution, I repeat, needs no violence," he said. "The general strike, as practiced in Seattle, is itself the weapon of revolution, all the more dangerous because it is quiet. To succeed, it must stop everything; stop the entire life stream of the community. . . . That is to say, it puts the government out of operation. And that is all there is to revolt—no matter how achieved."

A letter bomb was found in Hansen's mail in April 1919, a month before the Legion convention. It didn't explode, but the next day, a similar bomb blew off the hands of a black maid employed by Senator Thomas Hardwick of Georgia. Sixteen other packages containing bombs and addressed to prominent citizens were intercepted at the New York Post Office. A month later, in early June, a bomb exploded in the home of Mitchell A. Palmer, the U.S. attorney general, and blew

out the windows of the house next door rented by Franklin Delano
Roosevelt, former President Roosevelt's nephew, who was then assistant secretary of the navy. Franklin and his wife, coming home from
a party, discovered their son, James, eleven, stunned but otherwise
unharmed in his bedroom. The next morning, James, "rummaging in
the debris outside the house, found an unusual object and brought it
for his father to see," according to a biographer. "Eating breakfast,
Franklin paled when he saw what James had placed on the table-
cloth. It was a piece of the collarbone of the anarchist who had set
the bomb and been blown up in the explosion."[26]

These atrocities were fresh in the memories of the assembled Legion delegates as Sherman H. Curtin, the delegate of the Washington
State Soldiers' and Sailors' Council rose to speak. He was shouted
down, but Henry D. Lindsley, the Texas colonel who had just been
elected permanent chairman, rose and declared, "We are for a fair
deal, and without a motion I ask you to hear this delegate." Roosevelt
shouted, "Give him a hearing." Roosevelt's voice was echoed by others.
Curtin said he and others wanted to rid the Soldiers' and Sailors'
Council of IWW influence and bring the organization in line with
Legion principles. Then a key question was asked from the floor.
"Sgt. George H. H. Pratt raised his voice, asking Curtin if the constitution he had rewritten excluded officers," according to a semi-
official American Legion history.[27] "Curtin was shaken and the caucus
became noisy." The reason was obvious to those present. Officers were
excluded from membership in the IWW as they also were in Soldiers'
and Sailors' Councils established in Russia. In rallying to the dictatorship of the proletariat two years before, the councils in Sevastopol
and Kronshtadt had killed most of their officers as representatives of
the ruling class.

Pratt demanded the flustered Curtin answer yes or no, according
to the Legion's history: "Curtin eluded the question. An intelligence
officer from an Army camp near Seattle told the assembly Curtin
was 'personally all right but he is here as the official representative
of that organization. If he wants to be admitted, let him cut loose
from it and come into this organization.'" Curtin vowed to clean out
the council, but the caucus affirmed the committee's recommendation
to exclude the Soldiers' and Sailors' Council.

At the next encounter between the Legion and the IWW, rifle bullets killed three Legionnaires outright. On November 11, 1919, the
first Armistice Day after the war, parading Legionnaires were fired

upon from the IWW Hall in the little logging town of Centralia, Washington. Another Legionnaire died later trying to arrest a fleeing Wobblie, and the Wobblie was later lynched. The Legion claimed the attack was unprovoked, while IWW members asserted they were just trying to defend their hall. In popular legend, the Wobblies were portrayed as martyrs and the Legion members as tools of reactionary business interests, an image that may have helped deny the Legion credit for its role in the passage of the GI Bill years later.

The Legion's reputation among liberals was tarnished, if not irredeemably blackened by the incident. An editorial the week of December 26 in *The Legion Weekly* was clear in its attitude: "The Legion is committed to the principle that violence does not beget law and order. Things are entirely in the public hands in America. Normal processes provide a cure for every evil, political, industrial and social. The American Legion is interested in seeing that the orderly processes whereby equality, justice and democracy are vouchsafed do not languish through the indifference of the public and its servants. American ideals need no improvements, but their attainment requires stimulation." Another article added historical perspective: "Each great war of the past was followed by a period of great social unrest," with labor and management blaming each other for their mutual misdeeds: "Capital charges labor with reduced production through strikes; labor charges capital with profiteering."

The Centralia incident was the only significant clash between the Legion and the labor movement. It seems unlikely, in any event, that an organization with almost one million members at the time, most of them working men, would have been antilabor. A December 19, 1919, editorial in *The Weekly* probably summed up the reality: "The American Legion has no quarrel with either capital or labor. It is for the average American."

The convulsions of the labor movement, however, would later encourage conservative Democrats and Republicans to support the GI Bill of Rights as a middle-class alternative to class warfare. Throughout 1919 and well into 1920, four million workers walked off the job—more than at any time in history. A strike by the Boston police had Governor Calvin Coolidge calling out the state national guard and asking the secretary of war for federal troops. Less than two weeks later, 280,000 steelworkers shut down mills in New York, Pennsylvania, Ohio, and Illinois. Martial law was enforced by federal troops in Gary, Indiana, after four people were killed. William Z.

Foster, an alleged Communist, was blamed, and for another three decades some Americans would see communist influence, if not control, behind all union activity. But the most powerful—and hated—labor leader of the first half of the twentieth century was a registered Republican. In 1919 John L. Lewis was elected president of the United Mine Workers (UMW), and his first act was to shut down the coal fields, demanding a 60 percent increase in wages and a thirty-hour week. When the attorney general got an injunction against the UMW, Lewis backed down, ordering the miners back after a week. "We cannot fight the government," he said. In 1946, however, emboldened by New Deal support for union organizing in the '30s, he would try to shut down the country, arousing once again many of the fears generated by the Red Scare.

The Red Scare climaxed on September 16, 1920, almost a year after the Centralia shootout, when a bomb killed thirty-eight people on Wall Street, injured hundreds, and caused $2 million in property damage. The anarchy in the streets was reflected in state legislatures and Congress, which displayed a contempt for democracy, freedom of speech, and due process. Victor Berger, for example, a Wisconsin Socialist, was denied his seat in Congress three times because he had been convicted under the Espionage Act, despite the fact that the Supreme Court had set aside the conviction.

A convulsive sea change occurred in America after World War I. The Progressive movement peaked with the ratification of the Nineteenth Amendment in 1920 giving women the right to vote, followed soon thereafter by the Twentieth Amendment taking away the right to drink alcohol. Both were largely the product of the same constituencies, upper-middle-class native-born Americans and Protestants. They were the upper-class guardians of the social and cultural values of America as a white Anglo-Saxon Protestant nation rooted in an essentially rural society and, other than their preoccupation with the evils of drink, usually sensible and compassionate reformers. Republicans in the North and populist Jeffersonian Democrats in the South, they believed in local—but strong—government, leaving to the federal government responsibility for controlling and, if need be, breaking up big-business trusts and monopolies. They also strongly supported liberal programs such as slum-clearance projects and child labor laws. And, of course, as leading members of what amounted to a native-born American aristocracy, their patriotism and loyalty were unquestioned.

This upper-class Protestant leadership changed as America become, as certified by the 1920 census, a predominantly urban nation. Both urban politics and popular culture were defined by people who were Catholic, Jewish, and Negro. The street-corner political leaders of these people were ward bosses, usually Irish and Italian, and their political strategists, Eastern Europeans, often Jewish, were heavily influenced by socialist thinking. When FDR came to power with their aid and began centralizing power in Washington, the old Progressives and Populists supported his goals but deplored his means—big government and, later, big unions—fearing an alliance with big business. At the same time, the more reactionary all too often identified liberal causes with left-wing, Socialist, if not Communist, Eastern Europeans. Politics in the 1930s was largely defined by class considerations, and the ideal of a common Americanism—with civil rights for all, regardless of political views—receded.

These class and ethnic divisions had been submerged in the '20s as radio, advertising, automobiles, mass-circulation magazines, and records started creating a new common culture. Movie stars, singers, even novelists replaced the minister, college president, suffragist, and politician as trendsetters. Cultural and social standards were much less exalted. Public virtue was no longer in vogue, while pursuit of money, booze, sex, and personal comfort was. But it was a more realistic and, for most, a far more comfortable, even reasonable age.

By 1920, the soaring passions—and overblown rhetoric—that accompanied World War 1 were subsiding. President Wilson urged James M. Cox, the Democratic presidential candidate, and his vice presidential running mate, Franklin Delano Roosevelt, to make the 1920 election a solemn referendum on the League of Nations. But even hard-core Democrats such as Artillery Capt. Harry Truman had lost interest in saving the world. "For my part, and every A.E.F. man feels the same way," Truman wrote his wife-to-be, Bess, from France, "I don't give a whoop (to put it mildly) whether there's a League of Nations or whether Russia has a Red government or a Purple one or if the President of Czecho-Slovakia wants to pry the throne from under the King of Bohemia, let him pry but send us home."[28] Warren G. Harding, campaigning from his front porch in Marion, Ohio, caught the nation's mood exactly when he proclaimed: "America's present need is not for heroics, but for healing, not nostrums but normalcy, not revolution but restoration . . . not surgery but serenity." Harding and Coolidge won 61 percent of the vote—sixteen million

votes against nine million for Cox. The Republicans swept the Senate
with a twenty-two member majority and came up with a 167-vote
margin in the House. Frederick Lewis Allen explained it pithily in
Only Yesterday: "Whereas Wilson wanted America to exert itself
nobly, Harding wanted to give it a rest."[29]

That was the atmosphere in which the American Legion was
created and began to make itself felt. While in many fundamental
respects the Legion was rooted in the older, rural America of white
Anglo-Saxon Protestants, Legion posts also sprang up in all the
urban villages of America, the predominantly Irish, Italian, Polish,
Greek, German, and Russian-Jewish neighborhoods where city dwell-
ers lived between the world wars. There, the Legion's members, along
with their neighbors, sought the kind of normalcy defined by mass
media. The Legion's rallying cry, "The community takes care of its
own," wasn't that different from Voltaire's advice in the conclusion of
Candide: "What you say is very well, and may be true, but let's tend
our garden." Tending gardens, of course, meant the prosaic work of
making families and raising children and creating communities.
That's what the veterans of World War I wanted, and it's what their
sons and nephews would want after World War II. And that was what
the Legion, in its twelve thousand autonomous posts, was all about
in the next two decades, the prosaic and the revolutionary.

It was revolutionary because the Legion provided both America's
rural and urban villages, for the first time, with social, cultural, and
political clubs that welcomed laborers as well as bankers, assembly-
line workers and factory managers, the wealthy and workers, without regard for ethnic origin or religion. In a society in which class
differences largely dictated whom people socialized with, the posts
were perhaps the only places where mill owners, bankers, butchers,
newspaper editors, and millhands could meet, drink, and talk as
equals. Contributing to the leveling influence was the fact that during Prohibition and in dry counties for many years thereafter, the
posts were often one of the few places where beer and whiskey flowed
without interference from the authorities. Each post also had its own
welfare and youth programs, along with women's auxiliaries, which
made the posts far more than drinking clubs.

Proud members of the local American Legion post, many of them
immigrants or the sons of immigrants, actively worked to remedy the
educational deficiencies exposed by the war through campaigns to
improve schools and teachers' pay, and pass compulsory education and

anti–child labor laws. Posts also started and supported 4-H Clubs, Boy Scout troops, oratorical contests, and mock legislative sessions through Boys' and later Girls' State conventions. None of these simple activities received much public attention, but posts became community centers helping care for their own, whether through employment and health care programs, rehabilitation services for adults, or baseball leagues for youngsters, all the prosaic, everyday tasks of making a democracy live in real life. "I believe that a nation is mirrored in war by the rank and file of its soldiers, not by any individual strategist," Colonel Roosevelt wrote in the introduction to *Rank and File,* "just as I believe that it is mirrored in peace by its ordinary citizens rather than by some brilliant statesman." That philosophy lived in the posts' activities.

It was grassroots democracy, although to some that could seem threatening. Thorstein Veblen, the author of *The Theory of the Leisure Class,* complained of "this era of spiritual dilapidation" in which the nation was saddled with "a Legion of veterans organized for a draft on public funds and the cultivation of a warlike distemper." The Legion would, he was sure, perpetuate "the puerile mentality" of the military "in such organizations as the Boy Scouts . . . and the doings and aspirations, individual and collective, of the type of the YMCA." All these organizations were bound to the Legion, Veblen was convinced, in "systematized delusions of dementia praecox."[30]

Where dementia praecox was alive and well, however, was in the Ku Klux Klan, which had been originally formed as the southern equivalent of the GAR. In 1920, the Klan had only 5,000 to 6,000 members, but between 1922 and 1925, membership ballooned to between 4 million and 5 million, largely in response to exaggerated fear of radical organizations on the left. Yet Communist Party membership from 1918 to 1929 was estimated as no more than 30,000 to 60,000, that of the Communist Labor Party 10,000 to 30,000. Another 39,000 Socialists advocated law-abiding methods of securing the "dictatorship of the proletariat."[31] The Klan was far more dangerous than the Communists. But the "hooded empire" disintegrated soon after a 1924 massive march on Washington, D.C.; David C. Stephenson, the king kleagle of Indiana, was convicted of raping a young girl who later committed suicide.[32]

Nevertheless, Veblen and his fellow intellectuals were convinced the small towns of America were cultural deserts and havens of bigotry. Consequently, the rural and ethnic villages were best ignored.

That was the premise behind the founding of a sassy new magazine called *The New Yorker,* edited by Harold Ross, who had been the first editor of *The American Legion Weekly.* He and the writers of the period liberated themselves from "the little old lady from Dubuque." H. L. Mencken lampooned the "booboisie" in *The Smart Set* as Sinclair Lewis did in *Main Street* and Sherwood Anderson in *Winesburg, Ohio.* But the villages, and their mind-sets, were still there in both the small towns and the ethnic neighborhoods of the cities, whose principal social center was often the American Legion hall. It was in those villages where the great changes that would transform America after World War II were being germinated.

The veterans of World War I enjoyed, for only one decade, the prosaic peace found in education, family, work, and community before being dumped into the Depression. After World War II, they were determined to help their sons secure that peace for a lifetime, but they had learned not to trust the grandiose promises of statesmen. They knew what had worked in the past and what could work in the future. One of the Legion's first national commanders, Alwin Ownsley, had said it all in speaking about the Roman legions:

> They pacified whole peoples and subdued the civilized world. And yet today the very localities of most of their battles are unknown, and the nations they conquered are free and have forgotten them. The work of their swords is undone. It is the work of their spades that survives. The work of the humble entrenching tool that has outlasted that of the spear and the terrible short Roman sword. . . . Where a legion was encamped, there came peace and order and security. Farmers and tradespeople sought the shelter of the Roman law within those sanctuaries. . . . These ordered camps were the origins of some of the proudest cities of the Europe of today. It is a curious thought, that the works of war have gone down while the less considerable labors of the soldiers in time of peace have endured wonderfully. . . . The sword casts a glamour over men's minds.[33]

But veterans of the World War I generation had to suffer, once again, the neglect and abuse that had typified American treatment of those it sent to war before they could embark on the labor of peace that produced the GI Bill. Two veterans and two children would die, and a great march on Washington, D.C., take place before World War I veterans were paid a bonus they had been promised in legislation passed by Congress in 1924. The Bonus March of 1932 would also help depose one president, Herbert Hoover, and elect another, Franklin Delano Roosevelt. Yet FDR would twice veto bills authorizing payment of the bonus.

The first of the four to die was William Hruska, an unemployed butcher from Chicago. He was among a group of jobless men who had been camping outside the Treasury Building on Pennsylvania Avenue. "They were from the American yeomanry, if the term had been in use then; they would have been called members of the lower middle class now," William Manchester wrote in *The Glory and the Dream*.[34] Some twenty-five thousand penniless World War I veterans had been straggling into Washington since May 1932, some with their wives and children, camping in parks, dumps, and abandoned buildings. They had come to Washington looking for a bonus, authorized by the Adjusted Compensation Act of 1924. The bonus wasn't payable until 1945 under the law, but veterans wanted the money, and some powerful members of Congress were willing to oblige them. The 1924 bill provided a paid-up "adjusted compensation" policy—a deferred bonus or annuity—into which the government had paid amounts for individuals computed at the rate of $1.25 per day of overseas service and $1.00 for home duty. The bonus was intended to make up to veterans the large increases in wages given workers during the war. Most veterans had been issued certificates worth, on average $1,500; in 1945, after twenty years of 4 percent compound interest, the certificates would be worth $3,287.

Passage of the 1924 bill had not been easy. Despite support from the Legion, opposition came from some veterans, including an Ex-Servicemen's Anti-Bonus League formed in 1922 with support from Colonel Roosevelt, while he was assistant secretary of the navy in the Harding administration. The league declared veterans would be "pauperized in spirit and body" by a bonus and also noted veterans had already received $60 as a bonus on their discharge in 1919, above and beyond service pay. Nevertheless, the bill had solid political momentum behind it—despite resolute opposition from the Republican White House. A bonus bill introduced in 1920 had passed the House 289 to 92, but had been buried in the Senate Finance Committee. It came up again in 1922, passed the House 333 to 70 and the Senate 47 to 22, only to run into a veto from President Harding.[35] Andrew Mellon, the secretary of the treasury, warned Harding the bill would deplete a treasury already staggering under the costs of World War I. Mellon, who had made millions out of the war, said: "War service should be

performed as the highest duty of citizenship and is a sacrifice that can
never be measured in money."[36] Mellon, although accused of hypocrisy,
was fiscally correct. The government was in sad financial shape, and
newly elected President Harding has been credited by historians for
trying to put its financial affairs in order. As one of his first acts, he
secured the passage of legislation creating the Office of the Budget—
a measure President Wilson had unsuccessfully sought. Until then,
the appropriations process had been completely uncoordinated. Each
department and agency cut its own deal with Congress without any
coordination, never mind control, by the Office of the President.[37]

Harding agreed "the avowed purpose of the bill to give expression
to a nation's gratitude," while pointing out the cost, $3 billion, would
amount to one sixth the national debt and "would undermine the
confidence in which our public debt is built [because] it is politically
appealing to do so." His veto was rejected overwhelmingly by the
House, 258 to 54, but sustained by the Senate, 44 to 28, four votes
shy of the two-thirds majority needed to overturn the veto. The bill
was reintroduced in 1924 and vetoed again, this time by President
Coolidge with a new argument, one that would dog every effort to
pass veterans' benefit legislation until 1944. Coolidge contended the
bill violated principles of equity by singling out one class of citizens,
that is, veterans, for benefits. In other words, no citizen should receive financial benefits from the government not given any other citizen, an idealistic principle that, if ever enforced, would close down
the Capitol. Congress overrode the veto despite Coolidge's claim that
"we must stop this bill or revise our definition of patriotism."

The bonus was far from the only fiscal obligation the government
incurred on behalf of veterans. The Veterans Bureau, precursor of
the Veterans Administration, had been created in 1921 and by 1931
was providing compensation and disability payments to 530,000 veterans and 100,000 widows as well as hospital treatment for 500,000.
By 1931, the bureau was paying out $14 billion, three-and-a-half
times the $3 billion estimated by Harding for the bonus bill and
more than half, rather than one sixth, of the nation's total debt
burden.

The American Legion wasn't concerned about national finances
during the prosperous '20s, but took them much more seriously when
the Depression hit. Those larger considerations aligned the organization with President Herbert Hoover against the Bonus Army. Legion
leaders feared the only way the bonuses could be paid would be with

paper currency, unsecured by gold deposits, as advocated by Representative Wright Patman of Texas. That would deliberately increase inflation, a strategy advocated by rural Populists for years to effectively reduce the indebtedness of borrowers, primarily farmers. The strategy was vehemently opposed by bankers and other financial interests whose sentiments were shared by FDR, running for president against Hoover. FDR was even critical of Hoover for not exercising greater budgetary restraint, arguing he could reduce government expenses by 25 percent while simultaneously balancing the budget and enacting unemployment relief, public works projects to provide jobs, and old-age pensions. Legion leaders' fears about the deficit would disappear after Gen. Douglas MacArthur routed the Bonus Army, but the mind of the newly elected FDR did not change. He called, as his first act of office in March 1933, for cuts in already existing veterans' compensation programs and also refused early payment of the bonus.

The politics were confusing, but eventually the Bonus March would have much the same impact on Washington as Shays's Rebellion had on those gathered in Philadelphia. The plight of veterans dramatized the nation's economic and political situation. First Hoover, then FDR would find abstract economic arguments weren't so persuasive any more. Government statistics, moreover, although relatively simple then, provide insight into the enormous dimensions of the human problem. The first federal estimates of unemployment during the Depression, between three million and four and a half million, came out of the 1930 census. In 1931, the Legion, in cooperation with the AFL, conducted an unemployment survey of its ten thousand posts. That showed 6 million out of work, 710,000 of them veterans. By 1933, the newly established Bureau of Labor Statistics (BLS) provided more exact figures, 12 million. But no one had any real idea of what to do about the appalling reality behind the statistics.[38]

The phenomenon was worldwide and had brought Adolf Hitler to power in Germany with his Brown Shirts, primarily unemployed World War I veterans. No such charismatic figure arose in the United States, but a former sergeant in the Idaho National Guard by the name of Walter W. Waters started talking to other veterans in Portland, Oregon, about stories he had read in newspapers recovered from trash cans. Waters had spent time in several hospitals after World War I and drifted around through the '20s as a mechanic, salesman, and baker. He married and got a job in a Portland cannery, but Waters lost the position because of the Depression in 1930. Looking for work to support his wife and two children, he started thinking about news stories describing federal loans being given to railroads and large corporations. "The 'Bonus' in men's minds became a substitute for that long dreamt of new start," he wrote later. "These men had nothing to look forward to except to the shiny shoulders of the man in front of him in the breadline."

Waters soon began giving speeches that inspired others—among them members of the long-shattered IWW—to remember Coxey's Army. The army was a ragtag collection of twenty thousand men who had marched on Washington after the financial panic of 1893 under the leadership of Jacob S. Coxey urging public works projects for employment. President Cleveland sent federal troops to Montana to throw them off freight trains. Tales of those days became hobo folklore as a failed, but still inspiring crusade to IWW members. In early May of 1932, Waters and three hundred other men turned folklore into news by hopping cattle cars to Council Bluffs, Iowa, stopping long enough to volunteer blood for a little girl having an operation and picking up favorable publicity. From there, they were reluctantly given free freight car rides by the Wabash Railroad to East St. Louis, Illinois. When Baltimore & Ohio Railroad officials refused further free passage, the State Guard and private citizens provided truck and auto rides to the state line. Hitchhiking and hopping the rails brought the little band of marchers to Washington on May 29. Soon thousands more from other parts of the country, inspired by the news stories, drifted into town until the total was variously estimated at twenty-five thousand to forty thousand. Accompanying some unemployed husbands and fathers were women and children with no place else to go.[39]

The newspapers started to give the march some of the attention they had been lavishing earlier on the kidnapping of the Lindbergh baby. But true to the old journalistic tradition of never letting the facts stand in the way of a good story, *The New York Times* reported the marchers were veterans who were "not content with their pensions, although they were seven or eight times those of other countries." In fact, only a relatively few disabled veterans were getting pensions; the mistakes of the Civil War pension system weren't being repeated. The bonus, as a form of deferred compensation invested for future payment, was specifically designed to avoid the treasury raids of the Civil War and Revolutionary War pension programs. Indeed, the word "compensation" had deliberately been written into the 1919 disabled veterans legislation to "denote indemnity for loss, rather than 'pension' to denote gratuity," as one historian wrote, thereby forestalling "repetition of the Civil War pensions system." The principle of compensation, within definable limits and only for service-connected disability, although it was stretched somewhat to include tuberculosis and neuropsychiatric disease, had been established and would remain.[40]

Fortunately, the retired brigadier general who commanded the District of Columbia police wasn't influenced by *The Times*. Gen. Pelham D. Glassford had been, at thirty-five, the youngest general in World War I, and he still drove himself around on a motorcycle. He refused to panic over the invasion of the marchers, and he tried to get surplus tents and cots from the War Department as shelter for at least the women and children. Failing that, he donated $120 of his own money for food. Unfortunately, the hitherto imperturbable President Hoover, who had organized massive relief efforts in Western Europe and Russia after World War I, got nervous. Hoover wrote an American Legion post in Boston that he suspected "less than half" of the bonus marchers had "ever served under the American flag." In fact, a Veterans Bureau survey had already found 94 percent of the marchers had service records, 67 percent had served overseas, and 20 percent were disabled. Nevertheless, *The Washington Post* joined other newspapers in calling the marchers Reds "who had double-crossed the nation." Hoover communicated his nervousness to General MacArthur who, despite the advice of his aide-de-camp, Maj. Dwight D. Eisenhower, told reporters the marchers could be easily dispersed. *The Washington Star* wondered editorially why District policemen hadn't put "a healthy sock into the nose of a bonus marcher with all the strength of healthy emotions?" MacArthur was prepared to use guns instead.

Hruska and other marchers were camped out in what one reporter called a "conglomeration of tented huts made out of tattered cloth" on Pennsylvania Avenue a few blocks away from the White House. Most of the other bonus marchers were living in a tarpaper village in Anacostia several miles away across the Eleventh Avenue Bridge. The camp of Hruska and his friends was an eyesore, all the more blatant because none of the great buildings that now line Pennsylvania Avenue—including the National Gallery, the Federal Trade Commission, the Labor Department, Customs Service, and the Commerce

Department Building—had been erected. What is now the Old Post Office was the only major landmark on the avenue. The bonus marchers, sprawled in and around small, ugly, abandoned red brick buildings scheduled for demolition, were easily seen—and the aromas from their cooking fires smelled on nearby Capitol Hill.

The morning of July 28, two unidentified men, sweating in coats and ties, told Hruska and his friends to leave. When the marchers refused, the pair left. An hour later, Glassford pulled up on his motorcycle and told the veterans he had orders to clear the area. By then, other veterans, responding to rumors of an attack, were rushing over the Eleventh Street Bridge from Anacostia. Bricks started flying. One hit Glassford in the cheek, and as he staggered back, he found himself facing one of his own men, also hit, pointing a pistol at him. Ducking behind a column, Glassford heart a voice shout, "Let's get him," and heard a shot. Glassford emerged and saw a policeman who had gone wild-eyed shoot Hruska. The unemployed butcher fell dead, a bullet in his heart. Bullets also struck three other veterans. One, Eric Carlson of Oakland, California, who had survived gassing and shell shock in the trenches of France, was mortally wounded. "Stop the shooting," Glassford shouted, restoring control, but a riot report had already reached Attorney General William D. Mitchell. Mitchell promptly issued orders to General MacArthur to disperse the veterans from all government property.

When the orders reached MacArthur, he was seated at a desk placed in front of a fifteen-foot mirror that reflected his image back at him. Flourishing a cigarette holder even longer than FDR's, the general declared in the third-person imperative: "MacArthur has decided to go into active command in the field. There is incipient revolution in the air." He was driven to the marchers' encampment in a limousine just as Maj. George S. Patton rode up on horseback leading mounted troopers flourishing sabers. They were followed by a machine gun detachment and two regiments of infantry with fixed bayonets. Their arrival coincided with the quitting time of twenty thousand civil service workers who spilled into the street. Veterans and government workers alike assumed at first that a parade was being staged. Then the calvary charged "without the slightest warning," according to J. F. Essary, bureau chief of *The (Baltimore) Sun,* "into thousands of unoffending people . . . ridden down indiscriminately." The mounted men shouted, "Clear out!" In response, veterans and government workers cried, "Shame." The soldiers spurred their mounts back up Pennsylvania Avenue, re-formed ranks, and charged again. Infantry troops behind the charging calvarymen donned gas masks and threw gas grenades. Civilians and veterans scattered, and troopers and infantry soldiers, under Patton's urging, pushed forward, scattering the government workers and charging into the Bonus Army reinforcements now pouring down Pennsylvania Avenue from Anacostia. The disciplined troops pushed back the Bonus Army. The marchers, with choking and gagging women and children among them, poured back over the Eleventh Street Bridge into Anacostia. By 9 P.M., the Bonus Army had been routed.

MacArthur wasn't going to be satisfied with anything less than the total destruction of the veterans. A message from President Hoover, according to Eisenhower, "forbade any troops to cross the bridge into the largest encampment of veterans on open ground." MacArthur told Eisenhower, however, he "did not want either himself or his staff bothered by people coming down and pretending to bring orders." Ordering that machine guns be placed along the bridge to ward off a possible counterattack, MacArthur personally led a troop of infantry into the marchers' camp, which had been turned into a swirling melee. Men, women, and children were scrambling to save a few scraps of clothing and food from lean-to shelters and disabled automobiles. Troopers' boots trampled down tomato and bean plants in scrawny vegetable patches. At 10:14 P.M., the Associated Press reported, torches were thrown into the jumbled collection of impromptu shacks. The ramshackle Hooverville—the first of thousands of similar tarpaper villages to deface the countryside during the Depression— exploded into flames fifty feet high fed by gasoline poured on the shambles by the soldiers. "The whole scene was pitiful," Eisenhower wrote later. "The veterans, whether they were mistaken or not in marching on Washington, were ragged, ill-fed and felt themselves badly abused. To suddenly see the whole encampment go up in flames just added to the pity one had to feel for them." Two babies died from gas fumes, and the editor of a paper put out by the marchers suggested as the epitaph for one, "Here lies Bernard Myers, aged three months, gassed to death by President Hoover."

The editor may have been "unfair," as Manchester wrote, but he reflected a growing shift in public opinion. On his way to the Olympics in Los Angeles, Vice President Charles Curtis got into a shouting match with hecklers who cursed MacArthur and hailed FDR. "If you wait for Roosevelt to be elected, you'll be an old man," Curtis shouted back. Four months later, however, Roosevelt was the elected president, due, in part, to public revulsion over the armed dispersal of the veterans.[41] The newspapers initially had taken the side of Hoover and MacArthur, especially after MacArthur said at a press conference that only one out of ten marchers was a real war veteran. "The misguided men have refused to listen to persuasion," *The New York Times* editorialized. "Now they must submit to compulsion." The Hoover administration in September once again claimed many of the marchers weren't veterans. That drew a double-edged barb from H. L. Mencken: "Hoover had to defame the poor idiots he gassed," Mencken wrote in *The (Baltimore) Sun*. The newspaper consensus was reflected in a *Washington Evening Star* editorial that declared, "The end of tolerant dealing with itinerant tramps and idlers, as well as bonus marchers, has come."[42]

The Legion, despite the fact that many of its members had been reduced to being "tramps and idlers," was still sympathetic to Hoover. The year before, 1931, Congress had passed a law, over Hoover's veto, allowing veterans to borrow up to 50 percent of the value of their certificates rather than the 22 percent allowed under the original law. Supporters of the bill estimated that 30 percent of the certificate holders would borrow against them. "The beneficial results of this were soon apparent," the semiofficial *American Legion Story* reported. "Distress among veterans subsided." But 90 percent rather than the anticipated 30 percent borrowed the 50 percent—and wanted to borrow up to the full amount. Early in 1932, even before the marchers began to throng the capital, a bill to allow 100 percent redemption of the certificates was introduced and passed in the House but was stalled that June in the Senate at Hoover's intercession. Prominent members of the Legion who shared Hoover's concerns quietly rounded up support at the 1932 Legion convention for a resolution opposing prepayment. Hoover made a personal appearance at the convention to argue that money was needed instead for public works to spur employment. The Legion's legislative committee reported out a resolution opposing prepayment, which the convention delegates approved 902 to 507. The committee resolution, as read aloud by Henry Colmery, who would actually write the GI Bill of Rights thirteen years later, stated: "That the American Legion in full possession of its limitless faith in the destiny of the nation we fought to preserve, calls upon the able-bodied men of America, rich and poor, veteran, civilian and statesman to refrain from placing unnecessary financial burdens upon the nation, state or municipal governments and to unite their efforts as they did in 1917 to the end that the war against the depression be victoriously concluded, prosperity and happiness restored."[43]

The Legion never endorsed the Bonus March. *The American Legion Story,* published thirty years later, described the march as a "deplorable and futile odyssey, accompanied by certain excesses. While the whole incident did not affect [payment of] the bonus," it concluded, "it took its toll in the declining popularity of President Hoover." The official reaction of other veterans' organizations was similarly unsympathetic. The Bonus Army "is doing all veterans all over the country a great harm," Oscar Hollingsworth, deputy commander of the Veterans of Foreign Wars (VFW), was quoted as saying. "The Bonus Army has in no way been sponsored or encouraged by the DAV," said Richard O. Melton, national commander of the Disabled American Veterans. As the battered and bleeding survivors of the Bonus Army streamed out of Washington, the American Legion's national commander, Henry Stevenson Jr., reached in Spokane, had no comment. On the other hand, the military eviction of the marchers was criticized as "unwarranted and un-American" by Norman Landreau, the newly elected district commander of the Legion in Washington, D.C. He also attacked Hoover and his associates for having "no sympathy in their hearts for the American people, no desire to aid the common man, but their whole aim is to care for Wall Street."[44]

Wall Street still had more allies than the marchers and the common man. Ironically, the most preeminent among them was none other than the soon-to-be-elected FDR. When he took office in March 1933, eight months after the rout of the marchers, he was determined to be an even tougher fiscal conservative than Hoover. As one of the new administration's first acts, Lewis Douglas, Roosevelt's budget director, wrote "An Act to Maintain the Credit of the United States Government," introduced on March 10 and passed on March 20, 1933. This act was supposed to save the government $750 million—$470 million, or 69 percent, of that in veterans' benefits. Roosevelt argued, along with his equally unlikely allies, the Chamber of Commerce and the National Economy League, that Hoover had been a spendthrift who had accumulated a $5 billion deficit between 1929 and 1932 that was hurtling the nation toward bankruptcy. "Too often in recent history liberal governments have been wrecked on the rocks of loose fiscal policy," Roosevelt said. A historian observed that "the words might have been Mellon's."[45] FDR's credit bill swept through the House but encountered strong rearguard opposition in the Senate from a few members, notably the newly elected Senator Bennett Clark. Clark, faithful to his past as cofounder of the American Legion, said he wanted his vote against the measure, especially the provisions cutting assistance to veterans with war wounds, tuberculosis, and neuropsychiatric illnesses, inscribed on his tombstone.[46]

Eventually, most of the provisions in the economy bill affecting veterans were knocked out. By that time, the Legion had also formally changed its mind on the bonus. A 1935 bill introduced by Representative Patman was passed by Congress with Legion support, after some inflationary provisions were excised. The bill authorized payment of the bonus with newly issued treasury notes or greenbacks. Now, it was Roosevelt's turn, following Hoover, Coolidge, and Harding, to refuse payment of the veterans' benefits. This time, Henry Morgenthau, the Democratic secretary of the treasury, echoed his Republican predecessor, Mellon, in declaring payments would be "an unsound, unwarranted, even immoral subsidy to a special interest group." Morgenthau also told FDR a veto would be politically profitable. Roosevelt responded to Morgenthau with "a great smile. He raised his fists in the air and shook them and said, 'My God, if I win I would be on the crest of a wave.'" Roosevelt was so convinced he would ride the crest, he went to Capitol Hill and read the veto message directly to Congress on May 22, 1935, the first time a president had done so—and linked the veto to passage of Social Security legislation: "Able-bodied veterans should be accorded no treatment different from that accorded to other citizens who did not wear the uniform during the war. . . . There is before this Congress legislation providing old-age benefits and a greater measure of security for all workers against the hazards of unemployment. We are also meeting the . . . need of immediate relief. In all of this the veteran shares."[47]

Although a strong element of political calculation was involved, Roosevelt was also hewing to egalitarian political principles that were more consistent with the New Deal's philosophy than the rugged individualism of the previous Republican administrations. Veterans had argued the bonus bill was designed as compensation for income from lost civilian work, not as a gratuity. But FDR wasn't buying that and took his case to the 1933 American Legion convention in Chicago. Despite advance warning from Mayor Edward Joseph Kelly of Chicago that the police force might not be able to protect him, Roosevelt told the assembled Legionnaires, "no person, because he wore a uniform must thereafter be placed in a special class of beneficiaries over and above all other citizens."[48] While Roosevelt's veto was overwhelmingly overturned, 322 to 98, in the House, it was sustained in the Senate, 54 against 40—two votes under the two-thirds rule. The next year, 1934, a compromise measure drafted by the Legion that allowed bonds to be either cashed immediately or held to maturity in 1945 was passed. Roosevelt vetoed the bill, but he knew the fight was over. Even before the final override vote was taken, the Veterans Bureau was told to start getting bond certificates ready for mailing. FDR's veto lost by more than five to one, 325 to 61, in the House, and four to one, 76 to 19, in the Senate.[49] About $1.2 billion was paid out to the veterans in the next few months out of a total obligation of 1.4 billion.[50] Most of the bonds were cashed in within the year.

The Bonus March broke new ground in American history. It was the first instance in which ordinary Americans marched into Washington to demand benefits to which they thought they were entitled. Its success unquestionably inspired A. Philip Randolph, the head of the Sleeping Car Porters, when he threatened FDR with a civil rights march on Washington on Independence Day 1941. The march was called off when the president signed an executive order creating the Committee on Fair Employment Practices. Twenty-two years later, 250,000 Negroes and white supporters actually did march on Washington on August 28, 1963, and, through the new instrument of television, "subpoenaed the conscience of the nation," in Martin Luther King Jr.'s phrase. Since then, every group with a claim on the conscience of the nation has characterized its demands as a fiscally sound, historically warranted, and moral investment in American values, rather than special benefits. Congress's agreement to pay the veterans' bonus set a social and political precedent that would go unchallenged almost until the end of the century.

There was and is a difference, however, between veterans and groups with other special claims on the government. The claims of such groups as workers, African-Americans, women, homosexuals and the handicapped stem from what they *are,* from the problems and disabilities inherent in their social condition as a consequence of being workers, African-Americans, women, homosexuals, or handicapped. The claims of veterans, by contrast, were rooted in what they had *done* and *become* as a consequence of their military service. Those who had worn a uniform had, in fact, done something more, something over and above all other citizens, whether risking one's life in the trenches or even working as an underpaid laborer, as most black soldiers had done during World War I. Moreover, the veteran, simply by serving his country wherever he was sent and in whatever he was ordered to do, had become, regardless of his racial, ethnic, or religious background, a new American in the blast furnace of war.

To some Americans, FDR's social experiments didn't seem that different from those of the great social experimenters of the times, Adolf Hitler, Benito Mussolini, and Joseph Stalin. FDR's New Deal measures, however, would stoke other fires of protest—as well as impassioned support. Historian James MacGregor Burns had two explanations for the passion, one psychological, the other economic—but both rooted in the presumption of class hatred. "Roosevelt had robbed the capitalists of something more important than some of their money and power," the psychological interpretation went. "He had threatened their self-esteem. The men who had been the economic lords of creation now inhabited a world in which political leaders were masters of headlines and recipients of deference, even adulation. . . . Roosevelt, said a French observer, had exploded one of the most popular of American myths—he had disassociated the concept of wealth from the concept of virtue."

The economic argument went: "What had come to gall these conservatives more than anything was that a lot of bureaucrats were sitting in Washington offices dreaming up codes and tax laws that would tell businessmen who might or might not run *their* factories, *their* mills, *their* banks, *their* shops or slaughterhouses—as though their hold on that property—*their* right had no basis to it other than the sufferance of government.[51] Those who believed FDR was subverting, if not overturning, the American ideal of limited government while throwing gasoline on the fires of social class, ethnic, and class hatreds, banked after the Red Scare, were assumed to be without ideals and to have only selfish motives.

The Supreme Court's overturn of some New Deal programs, notably the National Recovery Administration (NRA)—and FDR's highhanded reaction—did change the political equation, placing in office many of those who would later pass the GI Bill. Nevertheless, even the fiercest critics of the New Deal recognized there were certain things the government could—and should—do that benefited not only individuals, but the economy as a whole. Several federal programs, although bitterly resisted at first, eventually became so widely accepted and uncontroversial that they became an integral part of the social, financial, and political landscape. The most significant were those that enabled individuals to acquire and hold on to their property. The Farm Mortgage Foreclosure and the Frazier-Lemke Bankruptcy Acts of 1934, for example, put a peaceful end to massive evictions of farmers that had the potential for making Daniel Shays's rebellion a tea party.

Another program was, in some respects, the most successful of the New Deal and the direct precursor of the GI Bill's home mortgage provisions. The Home Owners Loan Corporation (HOLC) saved almost one million families from being evicted from their homes. When the agency, which refinanced almost one out of five home mortgages, came into existence in 1933, almost one thousand homes were being foreclosed daily. HOLC refinanced more than $3.1 billion in mortgage loans for borrowers who, on average, were delinquent more than two years on mortgages and almost three years in arrears for real estate taxes. In the process, HOLC, as the precursor of the Federal Housing Administration and the Federal Home Loan Bank Board, completely modernized mortgage lending practices. Previously, homes had been financed under a crazy quilt of multiple short-term loans. HOLC created the long-term, twenty year mortgage and demonstrated how the federal government could stabilize markets, protect individual investors, and actually help private business institutions as well as consumers without direct government intervention. People were provided the resources to act for themselves in a private, but unobtrusively regulated market without the need of placating either labor bosses or bureaucrats.

"By enabling thousands of Americans to save their homes, it [HOLC] strengthened their stake both in the existing order and the New Deal," Arthur Schlesinger Jr. wrote in *The Coming of the New Deal*. "Probably no other single measure consolidated so much middle-class support for the administration." In 1939, the National Association of Real Estate Boards was invoking HOLC principles when it criticized legislation that was establishing public housing authorities: "If the federal government is going to give subsidies, let it subsidize people and not brick and mortar. Let the federal government go directly to its object instead of going into the real estate business and elaborating grandiose plans which often seem to fail of their objective."[52] More than fifty years later, the Department of Housing

and Urban Development would use almost identical words in acknowledging the failure of public housing while referring to the GI Bill
to support its new efforts to find housing for the poor in the private
market. HOLC, like the Northwest Ordinance and the Homestead
Act, helped Americans to become the independent yeomen Jefferson
envisioned.

By 1938, the New Deal was largely in place, and arguments about
its programs, whether they were HOLC, Social Security, the Tennessee Valley Authority, or others, were largely irrelevant. Whether
these laws were socialistic or had actually saved capitalism from
itself had become polemic and academic issues for the ideologues and
the historians. The vast majority of Americans could not care less.
Unemployment was still high but within manageable limits, and the
transcendent concern was the looming threat of war in Europe. On
that issue unanimity prevailed among Americans across the political spectrum from the Liberty League to the Communists: They
demanded, in the words of Samuel Goldwyn, the movie producer,
"Include me out."

FDR, who would eventually lead the United States into war along-
side the Allies, spoke for the vast majority in a 1938 fireside chat in
which he blamed the approaching war on the failure of European
governments to address both the economic needs and democratic aspirations of their peoples. "We in America know our democratic institutions can be preserved and made to work," he said. "The only sure
bulwark of continuing liberty is a government strong enough to protect the interests of the people and a people well enough informed to
maintain its sovereign control over the government." If that meant
Americans had to accommodate themselves to "the ambit of the regulatory state," as Christopher Tomlin, a scholar of the era, observed,
so be it.[53] The government could go toward war only as far as the
Gallup polls allowed—and no one knew it more than FDR.

The threat of war dampened enthusiasm for grandiose social
planning. But the military and big corporations such as General
Motors, United Steel, and the emerging airplane companies were
busily engaged in another kind of planning—for war—and the profits that war provides to those who don't have to do the actual fighting. Political leaders, such as Senators Clark and William Edgar
Borah, reflected the public's determined isolationism. Some were
reluctantly beginning, however, to believe America had no choice but
to become, in FDR's phrase, the arsenal of democracy.

One was Colonel Roosevelt, who endorsed the Lend-Lease Act, which provided England with more than $50 billion worth of arms, food, and supplies. He had no objection to making the United States the arsenal of liberty, but he didn't want to make it a frontline combatant. His views were typical of most Americans' before Pearl Harbor. He wrote a friend:

> More than twenty years ago, with some two million other young Americans, I went to Europe to fight a war to end wars. At that time I thought I was fighting to make the world safe for democracy. Theoretically, we won the war. One glance at the world today is sufficient commentary on the value of the victory. . . .
>
> I dislike greatly the governments of Germany, Italy and Russia and do not believe in appeasing any of them. [But] I am convinced that, in spite of my great sympathy and liking for England, . . . my first duty is to the United States and her citizens. . . . I am sure they will be irrevocably damaged should we launch this country into war. As a strong neutral we would be of inestimable help at the peace table.
>
> The sober truth is no one wins a war. The victor loses as much as the vanquished. . . . By remaining strictly neutral we can best serve not only ourselves but the other people in the world as well. Our Ark of the Covenant is our representative self-government. It was badly shaken in the last war. It might not survive another. Our primary mission is to preserve it for future generations of Americans. . . . If we preserve it, it will be a beacon toward which other nations can struggle from the mire of dictatorship. If it perishes, the light will have gone out of the world.[54]

War did eventually come to America, on December 7, 1941. Almost a year before, Roosevelt had reactivated his commission and was in training in Fort Devens in Massachusetts. By that time, the country was better prepared socially and psychologically to fight a war initially opposed by both Roosevelt and Clark and many other members of the American Legion they had founded. Lines of communication, if not bridges, had been thrown over the deepest divisions between the ethnic and religious groups and the classes, with considerable help from the Legion. The necessity for unity within diversity made the emphasis on common qualities of Americanism pioneered by the Legion essential as the nation committed itself to defeating external enemies.

The media that created the American consumer during the '20s and '30s now turned to creating a new image of the American fighting man who would not only conquer the foe but also emerge from the war with a new sense of united purpose. Real tales of real heroes, such as Colin Kelly, who was initially credited with sinking the battleship *Haruna,* and Dorie Miller, an untrained black mess steward on the battleship *Arizona* who took over an ack-ack gun and shot down three Japanese planes at Pearl Harbor, were eagerly fed to the newspapers and magazines. The movies created the image of the average American platoon or ship's complement being composed of whites and minorities, Catholics, Jews, and Protestants, almost in direct proportion to their numbers in the population.

Blacks were then and for several decades to come, however, invisible people. But war, at least arming for war, could produce social benefits for everyone in the form of increased employment, including blacks. It also provided the best of all possible excuses for deficit spending, which FDR had taken a keen interest in since John Maynard Keynes published *The General Theory of Employment, Interest and Money* in 1936. "Spending offered the President a middle way between doctrinaire economizing (as in the case of the veterans) and doctrinaire socialism," Burns observed. Adopting that course also entailed "an unprecedented degree of planning, not only in the fiscal areas of spending, taxing, investment price policy and the like, but in physical planning of public works, housing transportation, urban rehabilitation, and much else."[55]

The rise of the conservative Democratic and Republican coalition in Congress stopped domestic government planning. Carl von Clausewitz, the German military theorist, wrote that war is the extension of politics by other means. War can also be the extension of planning. War contracts, even though financed by deficit spending, encouraged corporate executives to put aside their distaste for government dictates and labor unions. Even if the contracts called for obedience to federal planning requirements and acquiescence with closed union shops, businessmen were willing to sacrifice their principles for the common good—and profits. The liberal community also saw social merit in a bigger and more prosperous private sector. "Progressives should understand that programs which do not forward the war must be given up or drastically curtailed," David Lilienthal, then head of the TVA, told friends. "Where a social service doesn't serve to help to beat Hitler, it may have to be sacrificed."[56]

Even though comprehensive planning, for political reasons, was no longer fashionable in dealing with social and economic problems, however, it was "increasingly in vogue in business, education and planning," as Burns observed. Power was shifting to a managerial elite in both private industry and government, as evidenced by a book by James Burnham, which, despite its forbidding title, *The Managerial Revolution: What Is Happening in the World,* became a massive best-seller in 1941–42. The accomplishments of every society are the accomplishments of its elite, he wrote. "Its history is properly understood as the history of its elite; successful predictions of its future are based upon evidence drawn from the study and composition of its elite." [57] Elite rule, unacceptable in peace, was tolerable, even comforting, when the alternative was totalitarian victory.

First the Depression, then the war seemed to be placing the central government in Washington firmly—and inexorably—in charge of the nation's destiny for decades to come. Ordinary Americans were still congenitally suspicious of government, as Morison wrote, but the nation's elites, in business and education as well as government, had now accepted the idea that professional managers should run society. Nothing could stop the flow of power to Washington during the war, and the flow didn't seem likely to be reversed when peace did come. The unions had benefited from the federal government during the '30s. Business, especially big business, would profit from government orders during the war. Even the states themselves, already accustomed to central direction, would inevitably want more rather than less. The national-state Employment Service was taken over by the federal government to help feed workers into industry wherever they were needed in the country. Eleanor Roosevelt and others were beginning to talk about conscripting everyone into national service. Putting the government in charge of most of the nation's production during war would inevitably mean the government would control markets in peace. The old idea of limited government, so beloved of conservative Democrats and Republicans, was just that, an old idea whose time was swiftly passing.

Nevertheless, the administration's efforts to prepare for a return to peacetime—and the absorption of veterans back into society and the country—were fiercely resisted. Creation of the instrument FDR would use in planning for peace, the National Resources Planning Board (NRPB), "aroused more frenzied opposition" from Congress "than anything else in the New Deal," according to Morison. Senator Robert A. Taft of Ohio, the leader of the Republicans; Senator Millard Tydings of Maryland, whom Roosevelt tried to purge in 1938; and Senator Harry Byrd of Virginia, perhaps the most respected member of the Senate, were among those who apparently suspected Roosevelt of attempting to put over a Russian-style five-year plan through the NRPB, Morison wrote.[58]

The NRPB was, in fact, charged by Franklin Roosevelt with planning for the veterans' return home, but it only came up with an extremely modest readjustment plan, with no provision for housing. The NRPB plan, if adopted, would never have encouraged millions of Americans to move to the suburbs or provided them with the unprecedented and unfettered access to education available through the GI Bill.

The GI Bill would create a new—and largely unrecognized—mechanism through which the government would *regulate* and *provide* but not *do*. It would take almost another fifty years before the success of that mechanism, rather than the New Deal's creation of governmental, business, and union empires, would be recognized by social thinkers. The GI Bill wasn't even recognized as being, in fact, a major social program, unlike the British Health Service, which also came into existence as a response to the social demands after World War II. Yet the Health Service was, by contrast, perhaps the classic example of what happens when the government becomes the doer. "The part that pays physicians for patients on their list works extremely well," Peter Drucker observed. "But in the other part—where government manages hospitals and dispenses health care—there has been problem after problem." Costs are uncontrollable, even though care is rationed.

Here in the United States, Drucker calls Head Start the one success story of Lyndon Johnson's War on Poverty. Head Start "pays independent and locally managed organizations to teach disadvantaged preschool children. None of the programs government itself has run had results. . . . In other words, we are beginning to apply to elementary education what we learned forty years ago from the GI Bill of Rights with respect to higher education. Government sets the rules, government sets the standards, government provides. But government does not *do*."[59]

The authors of the GI Bill, while opposed to government planning, obviously thought government should help those who had served.

Unlike the New Dealers, however, they thought veterans could decide what was best for themselves. In many respects they were simply reacting against what they considered to be the abuses of the New Deal. The GI Bill was by and large accidental, born out of the circumstances that existed. Those who had been tempered by the blast furnace of war, however, were prepared to seize on the opportunity such circumstances presented to make sure there would never be another Shays's Rebellion or Bonus March.

CHAPTER 3

MAKERS OF A
SILENT REVOLUTION

T HEY WEREN'T the kind of people who make revolutions.
Neither did the times seem ripe for revolutionary change.
"Liberals meet in Washington these days if they meet at all to
discuss the tragic outlook for all liberal proposals, the collapse of all
liberal leadership and the inevitable defeat of all liberal aims." The
speaker was Archibald MacLeish, the poet and former librarian of
Congress who was then serving with the World War II Office of War
Information.[1]

Yet liberal proposals were actually being championed through conservative means and proving victorious. Strange encounters, unpre-
dictable turns of events, and, above all, the roles played by individuals
who would normally be considered too ordinary—or too nutty—to
affect society would all prove crucial in the passage of the GI Bill of
Rights. Indeed the event that got the ball rolling was, on a less cos-
mic scale, much like the "damn fool incident" that Otto von Bismarck
predicted would cause World War I. Instead of an actual assassination, though, a damn fool congressman threatened to send two newspaper reporters to the undertaker, infuriating a press lord with more
real power than any archduke.

The confrontation between Representative Andrew Jackson May
and Hearst reporters David Camelon of *The Chicago Herald-
American* and Frank Reilly of *The Boston Record-American* on January 21, 1944, fundamentally changed the political climate in which
the administration had offered only limited proposals to help return-

ing veterans and the American Legion had asked just for a $500 bonus. The incident made the Hearst newspapers the Legion's most determined and powerful ally in a six-month struggle, an ally whose support was indispensable. Hearst employees played crucial roles at crisis points in the struggle when the bill could have been lost. In addition, the newspaper chain's influence in building public pressure in support of the legislation was politically essential.

The press lord needed very little incentive to put the full resources of the chain behind the GI Bill. Hearst thought earlier administration plans for returning veterans were inadequate. He also vehemently opposed another proposal also pending in Congress, the funding of the United Nations Relief and Rehabilitation Administration (UNRRA). UNRRA was being established to provide economic assistance to liberated countries, and Hearst, an isolationist, was afraid the agency would be a precursor of a new League of Nations. By embracing the GI Bill, Hearst would have a popular cause with which to counter FDR's internationalist schemes, and his legendary editor, Walter Howey, would have the greatest human interest story of a career built on the motto "Humanity Is Wonderful." A little sense of humanity was surely needed. Every edition of every paper carried new casualty lists. The number of returning veterans, most wounded, many disabled, was steadily mounting, well over the half-million mark. In Italy, the Allied invasion had bogged down north of Rome in the snow and ice of the Apennine Mountains near Monte Cassino as the Germans slowly retreated, using demolition mines with murderous efficiency. In the Pacific, the Americans had taken Guadalcanal and New Guinea with heavy casualties and were now being met with banzai attacks on Tarawa.

The target of these converging interests was Representative Andrew Jackson May of Prestonburg, Kentucky. May would later have the dubious distinction of having the nation's two ranking military leaders, Gen. Dwight D. Eisenhower and Gen. George C. Marshall, as well as Secretary of Defense Robert Patterson, testify against him at his trial on unrelated bribery charges. At the time, however, May was the chairman of the House Military Affairs Committee. The committee had been charged in December 1943 by House Speaker Sam Rayburn of Texas and Majority Leader John McCormack of Massachusetts with writing a bonus bill to help the members of what was called "The Forgotten Battalion." The battalion was the name given by the American Legion to thousands of soldiers, sailors, and airmen whose bodies and minds had been broken in the defense of the nation. But their only reward was a discharge, with nothing more than back pay and a warning not to wear their uniforms for more than ninety days. If World War II veterans were going to sell apples on street corners as the World War I veterans had, the Pentagon wanted to make sure they did so in civilian clothes.

The American Legion had collected more than fifteen hundred stories of discharged veterans and presented them to Congress—and a horrified public—through dramatic stories, published in the Hearst newspapers that December. Warren Atherton, the national commander of the American Legion, after reciting the stories to Congress, had asked for mustering-out pay of up to $500, depending on length of service. The bill was referred to May's committee by Rayburn and McCormack to be acted on by Christmas. May seemed to accept the task eagerly, saying, "This is incredible. Shocking is the only word to describe it. The sick and wounded from the battlefields are the very men who are most entitled to expect every assistance the nation they have defended can give them." May then promptly drafted a bill paying no more than $300 and went home to Kentucky for Christmas, refusing to report the bill out of committee in time for action on the floor before the holiday.

Camelon of *The Chicago Herald-American,* who had covered the congressional hearings for the Hearst newspapers, wrote a column blistering May. The congressman had "slipped out of Washington back to his own Christmas in the mountain district that returned him to Congress with a scant 540 votes in 1942," he wrote. "In May's absence went all hope that decent mustering-out pay could be enacted this year; all hope there would be a little money, a little hope and cheer this Christmas for the veterans who have been mustered out of the Army without a cent in their pocket, without a suit of clothes."

After the story appeared in Hearst papers all over the country, the telephone circuits were soon buzzing from Washington to Kentucky and back again to Texas and Massachusetts. Rayburn, McCormack, and May were all aware of a Gallup poll showing overwhelming support for a bonus, although an unspecified one. Eighty-one percent of those polled were in favor of giving veterans "a certain amount of money"; only 8 percent disapproved. Some sort of a bonus bill was a political necessity. Rayburn personally assured Camelon that May had promised to report out the bill within two or three days after the House reconvened January 10, 1944, and Camelon duly reported that fact in the paper. May returned to Washington, "still seething from the lashing he had taken from public opinion," according to Camelon, and formally announced: "We are going to dispose of this matter in very short order. Our committee holds its first regular meeting on Tuesday, January 11, the day after Congress reconvenes. We will report out a mustering-out bill that day." So it did, but it was only for $300. The Senate bill authorized $500. Majority Leader McCormack urged House Democrats to vote in favor of the $300 bill, and so they did, defeating an opposing option 137 to 71 with less than half the members in the chamber. Then the May bill was unanimously approved. May, who had fasted during the long floor debate as a symbolic gesture, munched with satisfaction on a tangerine. The bill was sent to a House-Senate conference in which the Senate agreed to go along with the $300 limit.

Camelon and Reilly confronted May January 21 as he was emerging from the House-Senate conference in which his version of the bonus bill was adopted. May may well have felt flushed with success, confident his bill would take pressure off Congress to act on a bill Representative John Rankin, the chairman of the Committee on World War I Veterans, had filed on behalf of the American Legion January 10. That measure, which had been dubbed the "Bill of Rights for GI Joe and Jane" by the Legion, had been drafted in response to May's earlier refusal to act on the bonus bill, and it went far beyond readjustment plans offered earlier by the administration. The administration, however, had the power to effectively kill the bill; it could pressure House leadership to send the bill to May's committee, where he could bottle it up. A political chess game was being played, and the administration and the House leadership had the advantage.

The reporters were also playing in the game, although as pawns. Any story they got out of May, as long as it promised benefits to veterans, would be consistent with the long-standing pro-veteran, anti-FDR editorial policy of their boss, Hearst. Nonetheless, May must have been feeling very much in charge on that day. He had persuaded senators who had unanimously approved a $500 bonus bill just a month before to come down to $300.[2] He had prevailed over both the nation's largest veterans' organization and the country's biggest newspaper chain.

"Reilly and I went up to him to ask what progress had been made," Camelon recalled five years later in published reminiscences.

"What is your name?" he [May] asked Reilly. Reilly told him.
May then said, "I just wanted to know if David Camelon was
here."

I told him my name was Camelon.

"I'll give no more interviews to you," he said. "Why did you say
I sneaked out of Washington?"

"Because," I told him, "you left without notice, and because
you left the Military Affairs Committee without the authority
to function. Mr. May, you consider yourself a powerful man in
Washington—a big man who can deprive veterans of proper
mustering-out pay."

"I am a big man in Washington," May retorted. "I'm sufficiently big to tell you this.

*If you say any more about me sneaking out of Washington,
you make arrangements with the undertaker before you do*"
[italics Camelon's].

With that threat, May turned and strode off down the corridor. Twenty feet away, he turned and repeated:

"Remember—before you mention me again, you consult the
undertaker—because, brother, you'll need him."[3]

Camelon and Reilly consulted Howey, instead, and what had been
routine coverage of congressional hearings turned into a monumental
newspaper crusade. Until then, according to Camelon, he and Reilly
had "devoted all our time to the day-by-day developments," straight
news rather than advocacy reporting. "That coverage had been on
instructions from our chief, William Randolph Hearst," according to
Camelon, but May's threat made the battle "a personal fight and I
know Reilly felt the same way." With May's threat, the stakes more
than doubled—in addition to the inadequate $300 bonus, they now
included the GI Bill. The GI Bill was "the answer to the problem
of readjustment—and we knew it was urgently needed," Camelon
wrote. Hearst decided to throw the full resources of his media empire
into the legislative campaign for the bill. Through Howey, Camelon
reported, "Mr. Hearst offered all the facilities of his organization to
help the Legion insure passage of the G.I. bill." The offer was conveyed by Camelon to Warren H. Atherton, national commander of the
Legion, who promptly accepted it.

Up until this point in the war, almost two years since Pearl Harbor, plans for the eventual discharge of the millions in service were a
distinctly secondary concern both for the administration and Congress. Although a number of possibilities were being bandied about,

the Legion's dramatization of the problems encountered by thousands of wounded and disabled veterans already being discharged began to focus public attention on the issue. Now, May's fumbling response to the bonus proposal and his threat to Camelon and Reilly had precipitated an alliance between the Legion and the Hearst newspapers that would produce within six months one of the most sweeping pieces of legislation ever approved by Congress. By late January, administration officials, members of Congress, the Legion, other veterans' organizations, educators, and the Hearst newspapers would find themselves fighting on a legislative battleground as confused as any in the war zones. The result was a struggle in which political philosophies were turned upside down, conventional definitions of liberal and conservative took on entirely different meanings, a time when states' rights advocates were Progressives and a notorious southern racist became an eloquent advocate of federal control of education. The time had finally come, after two years of administration planning and legislative skirmishing, for attention to be paid regarding what would happen to American fighting men and women and the country they were serving when the fighting was over.

The first move in the political free-for-all had actually occurred more than eighteen months earlier, in May 1942. The Federal Security Agency (FSA), precursor of the Department of Health and Human Services (HHS), introduced legislation creating a Federal Rehabilitation Service to administer training programs for all the disabled—civilian as well as military. However, neither Paul V. McNutt, the head of FSA, nor Gen. Lewis B. Hershey, the director of Selective Service, was held in very high regard on Capitol Hill. The two were the "overlords of Washington's most confused situation—manpower," in the words of reporter Alan Drury, who later became a well-known novelist. Mentioning their names was sufficient "to provoke most people on the Hill to near apoplexy," he added. McNutt was an impressive man in appearance, but one noted for "orotund generalizations," in Drury's phrase, rather than substance.[4]

The rehabilitation legislation, which called for the VA to refer people to the proposed agency, was introduced in the House by Representative Graham A. Barden, a Democrat from South Carolina who was chairman of the House Education Committee, and in the Senate by Senator Robert M. La Follette of Wisconsin. Both would later try to sidetrack the GI Bill on behalf of the administration. The proposal embodied the "humanitarian notions of President Roosevelt and his

New Deal staff" that everyone in need should be treated equally, as Davis Ross wrote in *Preparing for Ulysses*.

Veterans' organizations, still mindful of FDR's vetoes of World War I bonus bills, were automatically opposed to the legislation. The bill would "destroy the identity of the veterans for special consideration," Omar Ketchum, the legislative director of Veterans of Foreign Wars (VFW), told a congressional hearing on February 12, 1943. McNutt, a former national commander of the Legion, argued fuzzily that the rehabilitation program would provide "social gains while addressing wartime necessity." To members of Congress, that meant veterans were being used for what Rankin referred to scornfully as "social uplifting." A Republican, Bertrand W. Gearhardt of California, a founding member of the Legion, echoed Rankin: "The thing we have got to fight down is the crafty effort of so many groups to use the war for reorganization of the world after the war; to capitalize upon the war sentiment to accomplish their objectives which have to do with social uplift."[5]

Rankin and Gearhardt were also members of what Ross described as "a wrecking team in Congress that hoped to demolish the remaining vestiges of the New Deal." In previous months, the team had done away with the Civilian Conservation Corps (CCC) and the Works Progress Administration (WPA). They were also taking aim at the National Resources Planning Board (NRPB), headed by FDR's uncle, Frederic A. Delano. FDR was notorious for assigning the same task to competing agencies. This tactic had involved the NRPB as well as McNutt's FSA in veterans' concerns. Having established the NRPB in 1939—over congressional opposition—as his planning arm, FDR had ordered it to begin postwar planning soon after Pearl Harbor. In January 1942, FDR widened its scope by ordering it to prepare a companion document to the annual budget ambitiously intended to add new principles to the Bill of Rights. "We must add new freedoms and restate our objectives in modern terms," a 1942 NRPB document, written with FDR's participation, stated. Those new freedoms were to include "the right to fair pay, . . . the right to adequate food, clothing, shelter and medical care, . . . the right to education, . . . and the right to equality before the law." Two years later, as Congress was beginning to consider the GI Bill of Rights, FDR used language from the old NRPB statement in calling for an economic bill of rights in his State of the Union address of 1944.

That new economic bill of rights for all citizens, however, would in fact be superseded by the GI Bill of Rights.

Having come up with the concept of an overall economic bill of rights, the NRPB began to plan for the reabsorption of veterans into the brave new world to be created after the war. In July 1942, FDR approved Delano's request for a small planning committee to study demobilization issues, but insisted the effort be limited for fear of "diverting people's attention from winning the war."[6] Delano established the Post-War Manpower Conference, composed of twelve representatives of government and education, which met twenty-seven times between July 1942 and April 1943, accomplishing very little.

During that time, the FSA rehabilitation bill ended up in a compromise. In response to Barden and La Follette's bill, a separate Senate bill had been introduced by Senator Clark on September 30, 1942. That marked his entrance in the process, which would result in his introducing the GI Bill in the Senate on January 11, 1944, one day after it was introduced by Rankin in the House. Clark's vocational rehabilitation bill, cosponsored by Senator David I. Walsh of Massachusetts, provided help for veterans exclusively. Walsh, who had pioneered university extension programs as governor of Massachusetts, had broken with FDR over court packing in 1937 and, like Clark, had been an isolationist, calling for "absolute, unequivocal, unconditioned and determined neutrality." Ostensibly, the administration held firm against the Clark-Walsh alternative. In an October 8, 1942, message to Congress, FDR said: "In order to secure the most effective utilization of the capabilities of the physically handicapped, it is important that a single Rehabilitation Service be established both for veterans and nonveterans." But he privately told Harold D. Smith, the director of the Budget Bureau, "I cannot send a [formal] bill up with the message," and advised him to provide the committee chairmen with draft language giving the VA a substantial role in the program. The veterans' organizations were also willing to compromise.[7]

Rankin obliged both by ramming a bill through the House on October 19, 1942, but the Senate didn't have time to act before Congress recessed for the year. When the Seventy-eighth Congress was called to order in January 1943, the previous political calculus no longer worked. Democrats were still in the majority, but their margin had fallen from 106 in the Seventy-seventh Congress to a mere 10 in the House and from 38 to 21 in the Senate. The Barden–La Follette

Bill was redrafted to vest all authority over veterans' rehabilitation in the VA, but still as part of an overall program for both veterans and civilians. Barden and La Follette tried to rally support from state commissions for the blind, Lions Clubs, and the state federations of Women's Clubs, but Senator Clark destroyed their hopes in a speech in which he said: "I have never seen the veterans' organizations of the United States so much wrought up, as unanimous, and as bitter about any proposition as they are about the proposal to take a simple matter of veterans' rehabilitation and pitchfork it into a general scheme of social rehabilitation affecting all of the people of the United States, which, whether it is justified or not, has nothing in common with the question of military rehabilitation."

Clark witheringly dismissed administration claims that Gen. Frank T. Hines, the VA administrator, supported the bill by saying the heat had been put on him and VA had been "boldly raped." Clark's colleagues voted for his bill rather than La Follette's, and the House followed unanimously on March 15, 1943. La Follette's bill, revised to provide vocational rehabilitation solely for civilians, passed as a separate bill July 8, 1943. The veterans' rehabilitation bill, signed by FDR four months earlier, on March 24, 1943, set several precedents for the GI Bill. The first and most significant was that veterans' programs would be separate from programs for civilians. The fundamental difference of opinion regarding whether veterans should be considered as just a part, albeit an important part, of the entire population had been resolved in favor of the veterans. FDR's earlier refusal, in vetoing World War I bonus legislation, to treat veterans as a special class of beneficiaries above and beyond all other citizens had been explicitly disavowed by Congress.[8] The veterans' rehabilitation bill also contained two provisos covering training that would be extended to the able-bodied in the GI Bill: (1) Training could last as long as four years; (2) All those in training would receive a monthly stipend equivalent to full disability payment. A third provision, requiring those qualified for training to be honorably discharged, would be modified, after a dramatic confrontation between the Legion and military brass. Every veteran with other than dishonorable discharge would be allowed benefits.

The passage of the vocational rehabilitation bill forced the administration to focus on servicemen as veterans, not just as disposable human cogs in a war machine. The change in emphasis took a while to sink in. The Post-War Manpower Conference convened by Delano

initially recommended holding veterans in the service after the war
as virtual prisoners of peace. General Hines, the VA administrator,
remembering how World War I veterans were reduced to begging on
street corners, argued: "In the long run it was better socially and
cheaper economically to keep the men in service than to create a
period of unemployment which would necessitate large expenditures
for relief and welfare." Failure to control the rate of demobilization
meant "surrendering the one possible, positive, control that may turn
the margin between economic equilibrium or unemployment crisis,"
warned Leonard Outhwaite, a member of the committee: "Would
we . . . trade the illusion of personal liberty for the certain hell of an
unemployment depression? Compared to this the restraints of army
life are child's play in a rosy garden."

Col. Francis T. Spaulding, a former dean of the School of Graduate
Education at Harvard, suggested giving veterans a three-month furlough. After that, if they were jobless, they could return to the military for a training program. But veterans would get only two weeks
of pay during the three-month furlough, much less than the unemployment compensation benefits for civilians. No one was thinking,
at this time, about paying veterans to go to school. As unrealistic as
Spaulding's plan was, it was discussed seriously, perhaps because, as
Drury recorded in his diary, Spaulding was a "perfect academic type,
smooth as butter, sharp as a knife, ingratiating, reasonable, courte-
ous and ambitious." Those qualities didn't, however, endear Spaulding to members of Congress—an augury of conflicts that would
arise over the GI Bill. The planners were obviously out of ideas, so
they punted the problem back to FDR. The president responded with
vague hopes for a report "which would indicate the scope of the problem and the type of questions that would have to be dealt with."

Perhaps the reason the plans were so vague was that the administration was preoccupied by the international rather than the domestic postwar situation. While FDR was suggesting to Delano an
off-the-record assessment of veterans' needs, Sumner Welles, the
undersecretary of state, was approving a State Department proposal
for an Advisory Committee on Post-War Foreign Policy. "The President has decided that vigorous and intensive work needs to be done
now in preparation for the country's effective participation in the
solutions of the vast and complicated problems of international relations which will confront us and the world after the defeat of the
forces of aggression," Welles wrote on February 9, 1942. Some liber-

als, however, feared focusing on international concerns while neglecting domestic problems would bring another rejection of the League of Nations. Vice President Henry Wallace, who would later be derided as a Communist sympathizer, was one of them. "You can't expect men who are losing their jobs, their farms and their businesses to respond with an altruistic glow to an international idea," Wallace wrote to FDR on February 4, 1943.

The international arena, however, was increasingly preoccupying FDR's thoughts. Consequently, the administration's formal proposal for demobilization submitted to Congress in June 1943 fell back on Spaulding's original prisoners of peace plan. Servicemen would be allowed—not forced—to remain in the service, unless they had jobs to go to. Men with special skills needed by industry could be released early, and those who wanted to look for jobs would be entitled to a three-month paid furlough. Veterans and their relatives at home "would be likely to view with patience any unavoidable delay," the planners hoped. In fairness, a similar proposal was adopted by the Legion at its national executive board meeting May 6–7, 1943. There was no public protest when Department of War Assistant Secretary Patterson, who habitually wore the belt of a German he had killed in World War I, announced the plan. In a speech at Northwestern University, Patterson said the War Department would "do its best to see [that] no man is mustered out into a bread line, and avoid the urge to dump men willy-nilly back into civilian life, to let them find a job as best they can and where they can. . . . But the Army will not take that easy way. Its responsibility is too great."[9] Eventually, however, the planning board gave up the prisoners of peace idea. Any serviceman "would be sore as a pup, if he could not get out of the armed forces and look for a job on his own," even Spaulding agreed by October 1943.

The planners improved the proposal slightly with an education program modeled on one provided World War I veterans under the Wisconsin Educational Bonus Law of 1919. That bill provided any veteran who had served for three months prior to November 1, 1918, $30 a month to attend any nonprofit elementary or high school, technical institution, college, or university in Wisconsin. If a program wasn't provided in Wisconsin, a veteran could go to a school in another state. While the program was administered by the state's board of education, admissions and instruction policies were left to the institutions. The planners also considered, but rejected as too expensive, a Canadian law passed in October 1941 that provided educational benefits up to the postgraduate level as well as unemployment benefits and business assistance.[10]

Under the NRPB proposal, all veterans would be entitled to one year's vocational training—but not college. College education would be available only to an extremely limited and carefully selected few. A competitive system of scholarships would be "structured to encourage the education of men for technical and professional occupations for which there are likely to be shortages of adequately trained personnel." IQ tests, which the military had pioneered in World War I and used even more extensively in World War II to select recruits for specialized training, would be used to determine who would go to college. Such tests would later be criticized for a strong cultural bias favoring the more affluent, but at the time they were considered unassailably scientific by educators as well as the military. The scholarships would be good for only three years and be restricted to training for occupations in which more jobs were available than candidates—teaching, for example. The committee implicitly acknowledged the huge gap between the problem and their proposed solution. Unemployment of eight million or nine million after the war was projected, with as many as three million expected to be out of work two years after the war. Nevertheless, the plan was approved despite the fact that its only improvement on Spaulding's original proposal, other than a year of vocational training, was that veterans would be paid for their three months' furlough, up to $100 per month.

The proposal, however, got lost in the uproar generated by a far more ambitious NRPB proposal released in March 1943, which advocated cradle-to-grave social security measures comparable to recommendations of the British Labour Party released earlier. In England, the so-called Beveridge Report was eagerly embraced by the public and provided the Labour Party with the platform for its election victory in 1945. The English report's principal recommendation was for the nation's socialized system of medicine. By contrast, the NRPB report produced a congressional uproar and led instead to the death of the NRPB in the summer of 1943. Also lost with the NRPB proposal was a plan maintaining the unemployment compensation program as a federal responsibility. The NRPB wanted to retain Washington's direct authority over the joint state-federal system after the war ended, ostensibly to help veterans. "Any proposals for special measures for veterans must be coordinated with the existing framework of security measures applicable to the civilian population as a whole, including members of the armed forces," the NRPB contended. Republicans in Congress, led by Everett M. Dirksen of Illinois in the House and Taft in the Senate, denounced the proposal as utopian, if not socialist. Others saw darker motives. Representative John M. Vorys (R-Ohio) thought the NRPB's planning was just a way of giving FDR maximum control over warring oligarchies. "The New Deal theory of planning seems to be to have a number of agencies covering the same ground," he said, "with a personal appeal to the President the only way to settle their differences."[11]

The stakes, consequently, were upped rather than lowered in a political struggle in which the big spenders turned out to be in Congress rather than the White House. By the spring of 1943, the White House had come up with little more than a rudimentary proposal for a three-month furlough and one year's vocational training for all veterans and three years of college education for a carefully selected few. By June of 1943, several members of Congress, responding to pressure from veterans' organizations, were already upping the ante with bills providing more extensive and varied benefits. Ultimately, 640 such bills were introduced—and the administration got nervous. Harry Hopkins, the president's closest adviser, warned Roosevelt that "unless something is done soon on the legislation of returning soldiers, the opposition may steal the thunder."[12] FDR decided to end run Congress with an appeal to the public. On July 28, 1943, in a fireside chat entitled "First Crack in the Axis," FDR, after first expressing cautious optimism about military progress in the war, said: "While concentrating on military victory, we are not neglecting the planning of things to come, the freedoms which we know will make for more decency and greater democracy in the world. Among many other things we are, today, laying plans for the return to civilian life of our gallant men and women in the armed services. They must not be demobilized into an environment of inflation and unemployment, to a place on the bread line or on a corner selling apples. We must, this time, have plans ready—instead of waiting to do a hasty, insufficient, and ill-considered job at the last minute."

After urging Congress to pass minimum education, unemployment, and social security benefits, the president concluded by saying: "The members of the armed forces have been compelled to make greater economic sacrifice than the rest of us, and they are entitled to definite action to help take care of their special needs."

Outside academics now joined the debate. Howard Mumford Jones, the dean of the Harvard Graduate School of Arts and Science, and the deans of four other prominent graduate schools urged that graduate as well as undergraduate education be included in any program. So did the unions. The CIO reprinted and distributed two hundred thousand copies of the speech under the title "A People's War . . . A People's Peace," along with comments of Vice President Wallace delivered at the CIO's annual convention. The nation had to avoid a future "of roving bands seeking food where there is no food, seeking jobs where there are no jobs, seeking shelter where there is no shelter," the vice president said. Harrison Spangler, the Republican Party chairman, complained that FDR's fireside speech had been broadcast overseas for partisan purposes. The complaint as well as the suggestions merely confirmed that FDR had effectively seized the initiative.

FDR's speech created the public impression that the administration had a comprehensive veterans' program and had cleared the first hurdle in getting a bill through Congress. In fact, no specific legislative proposals had been hammered out by the administration itself or real consideration given to guiding any proposals through the congressional labyrinth. If the administration were to effectively take charge, it had to somehow obtain "qualities found lacking in the struggle over job training for disabled veterans," as Ross observed.[19]

Those qualities were clearly lacking in the March 1943 proposal, although the NRPB had tried to improve its education package with advice from the American Council on Education (ACE). The ACE, an umbrella organization of all the college and university presidents in the country, circulated a questionnaire to six hundred colleges and universities and other educational associations. But it only came up, in October 1943, with a two-page memo approving the Wisconsin and Canadian programs as models. The ACE's vague language was echoed by an equally amorphous report issued by yet another government planning group FDR had set up, headed by Brig. Gen. Frederick C. Osborn along with John W. Studebaker, the U.S. commissioner of education. An amalgam of the NRPB and Osborn proposals was introduced in the Senate by Elbert D. Thomas, a Democrat from Utah who was a loyal New Dealer and former political science professor, on November 3, 1943, in his capacity as chairman of the Education and Labor Committee. Thomas duly held the hearings on December 13–15 on what was now considered the administration measure.

An encounter Spaulding had with Senator Claude Pepper of

Florida during the hearings on December 13 threw into sharp distinction conflicting social attitudes over education. Pepper, who, according to Drury, was very aware of his own experiences coming up "by his bootstraps through Harvard and Phi Beta Kappa," wanted to substantially improve training opportunities for veterans. Spaulding, "a typical Dean of the younger, pragmatic type," in Drury's words, "an interesting fusion, this combination of the army and the academic . . . gave Pepper as good as he got, with, of course, consistent suavity and courtesy and from time to time a gently acid irony, all in the best tradition of the little boy who didn't work his way through Harvard talking to the little boy who did."[14]

The bill was duly reported out of committee to the Senate floor on February 7, 1944, where it was promptly shuffled aside—as were the 639 other veterans' bills introduced by individual members.[15] The GI Bill, introduced in January by Clark and Rankin, simply preempted any serious considerations being given the Thomas bill and its administration counterpart in the House. In the House, the administration bill was referred to the education committee headed by Representative Barden, who had earlier cosponsored the administration's rehabilitation bill with La Follette. It remained in limbo there until months later when a coalition of educators and state governors, with the support of the administration, tried to use it to sabotage a key element of the GI Bill, freedom of veterans to choose the college they wanted to attend.

The initiative had not only been taken, but seized and gripped, by the American Legion between November 30, 1943, when a Legion committee was formed to develop a master plan, and January 9, 1944, when the Legion publicly announced its own plan, originally called "The Bill of Rights for GI Joe and Jane," one day before it was introduced in the House by Rankin. Both the dimensions of the legislation and the speed with which it was developed (a little over a month) were unprecedented and unparalleled in American history. The Legion at its twenty-fifth annual convention on September 23, 1943, had directed its national commander, Atherton, a lawyer from Stockton, California, to come up with a master plan encompassing education, medical care, unemployment compensation, home, business, and farm loans as well as a bonus or furlough plan. On November 30, Atherton appointed John Stelle, a Democrat who had been the former state treasurer, lieutenant governor, and governor—for three months—of Illinois as the head of a planning committee. "We didn't organize the American Legion to finance a last man's club," Atherton said. "The best way to use our treasury is in assistance of the veterans coming out of this war." On December 15, the committee began meeting with education, government, housing, and business leaders and then, over the next three weeks with time out for the Christmas holidays, assembled a first draft by January 6. Henry Colmery, the Legion's national commander in 1936, actually wrote the bill between the sixth and eighth. The Legion, not being a governmental agency, didn't leave behind the customary records of deliberations, and none of the participants was subsequently interviewed by historians. Consequently, the only contemporary account was a memoir written by David Camelon and published as a three-part series in *American Legion Magazine* in 1949. However, the series does have at least a semiofficial status. "It was really written to make sure appropriate credit was given for what was done by whom," according to Earle Cocke Jr., national commander in 1950–51, the only Legion official of the era still living in 1995.[16]

More than half a century later, those responsible for the bill's passage have been largely forgotten. Even William Randolph Hearst, one of the most flamboyant figures of twentieth-century America, has never been given public credit for his role in the passage of the bill, nor was Howey, an equally fabled figure. Rankin is remembered now as one of two particularly notorious southern racists from Mississippi in Congress at the time, the other being Senator Theodore Bilbo. Senator Clark's place in history is secured primarily on being Harry Truman's Senate colleague from Missouri who had to be sobered up at the 1944 convention long enough to nominate his junior colleague for the vice presidency. Hearst, Howey, Rankin, and Clark, along with Colmery, who wrote the bill, and Edith Nourse Rogers, the ranking Republican on the House veterans' committee, were the principal architects of the GI Bill. Understanding what produced the bill has to begin with understanding who the architects were and what motivated them.

After the clash with Camelon and Reilly, May's role in the drama that produced the GI Bill was little more than a walk-on part. An administration supporter, he could have blocked consideration of the bill in his role as military affairs chairman; he also had a personal reason for doing so. As an opponent of the Tennessee Valley Authority (TVA), he was a political enemy of Rankin, who had coauthored that legislation with Senator George Norris of Nebraska. May supported the private power companies that fought TVA.[17] That, in itself, provided Rankin with additional incentive to wrest jurisdiction over the GI Bill away from May's military affairs committee to his own veterans' committee.

For Howey, the editor, the curtain went up on the GI Bill news drama November 29, 1943. That was the day Atherton, who had joined the army as a private in World War I and won promotion to captain, brought the stories of 1,536 members of the Forgotten Battalion before Congress. Those tales, gathered from the files of local posts, took the concerns of veterans out of the province of planners and into the world of politics. "The report is a shocking indictment of lack of foresight and preparation for inevitable casualties already here, and those yet to come," Atherton bluntly warned members of Congress. "I should not like to face the wrath of eleven million veterans after this war if our treatment of their disabled has been as shabby, indifferent and lax as the story of the last two years would indicate."[18]

The words that would drive veterans' legislation would no longer be the abstract terminology of planners, but the specific, personal, sometimes sentimental, often angry words of news writers. The passage of many laws seems dramatic at the time; certainly contemporary news accounts convey that sense. With the passage of time, however, knowledge of the issues fades and the impassioned rhetoric of the debates seems exaggerated, even slightly absurd. But the GI Bill wasn't about issues as much as human beings, individuals, each with his or her own story of pain and loss, hope and triumph. As such, the Forgotten Battalion cases were perfect material for tabloid writers and editors, vulgar Shakespeares whose words, despite their sentimental excesses, can still evoke emotion years later. The stories were so powerful it didn't take an Ernie Pyle, the great combat writer of World War II, to turn the case histories into the material Camelon wrote for the Hearst newspapers that Christmas of 1943. The stories were a golden treasury of what Howey called "humanity is wonderful" journalism, the mixture of sentiment and cynicism other newspapermen called "sob sister" or "tear-jerker" stories.

Howey had started his career on his hometown paper, *The Fort Dodge (Iowa) Chronicle,* in 1901 with a worldwide scoop. He used the telephone—and $10—to break the news of President William McKinley's death from an assassin's bullet. A servant in the Buffalo, New York, home where the wounded president had been carried gave

him the news over the phone in return for the $10.[19] Later, as a re-
porter in Chicago, Howey literally stumbled over one of the city's
biggest stories, when he saw a knight and three elves climbing out of
a manhole. They were actors escaping from a fire in the Iroquois
Theater in which almost 600 people died on December 30, 1903. By
World War I, Howey, as a Hearst editor, was shaping modern newspaper content by developing the first movie, medical, and advice
columns. "A Soldier's Friend," a World War I column, for example,
helped returned soldiers with job, medical, and personal problems.

Howey was known not only for an uncanny sense for the human
interest angle, but also for the aplomb to exploit it without embarrassment even when it was mawkishly sentimental. Once he persuaded a prison warden to release two safecrackers to open a bank
vault with a little girl trapped inside—and the air running out. But
when the safe was opened, there was no child inside. Another editor
would have spiked the story, but not Howey. Instead, a front-page
story described how the hardened criminals sank to their knees in
thankful prayer that the girl was not inside the safe. The headline
was: "Humanity Is a Wonderful Thing."

In 1922, Hearst gave Howey six months to boost the circulation
of the moribund *Boston Record-American* by fifty thousand. He
persuaded a woman sentenced to the electric chair for killing a
policeman in a holdup to repent in detail exclusively for *The Record-
American*—in return for a cash settlement on her daughter. Circulation jumped by fifty-four thousand in six days. In 1948, Howey
made a housing shortage come alive by printing a letter from a little
girl that read: "Please help me find a home—I have never slept in a
bed." Photos of the girl looking at children's beds kept the story
going for days until one reader wired a check for $10,000. "Please
buy the little girl a home," the telegram read. "You're breaking my
heart." Telegram and check were signed by Hearst. "It's the simplest
thing in the world to create circulation, but it took me years to learn
it," Howey said in explaining his formula years later. "People are
more interested in the repentance of a lost soul than they are in
themselves."

Howey could also actually help people, not just exploit their problems for headlines. *The Record-American* sponsored a Buddies' Club
for enlisted men and their wives and girlfriends on Boston Common
during both World War II and Korea. Storrow Drive in Boston was
built when he used the paper to jam the proposal through city hall

and the state legislature. He didn't take any credit for altruism. "I got sick and tired of spending as much time getting home from the airport as the flight took," Howey told a copy boy who later became a Boston journalist.[20]

This was the editor who shepherded into print human interest stories written by Camelon, Reilly, and other Hearst reporters that influenced public opinion during the time the GI Bill was produced. None of these stories was included in anthologies of classic stories of the war, as were the sketches in almost studied stoicism written about combat soldiers by Ernie Pyle and Bill Mauldin. "They wish to hell the mud was dry and they wish to hell their coffee was hot," wrote Bill Mauldin, the cartoonist who created *Willy and Joe.* "They want to go home." Not being able to go home, they made even their foxholes ersatz homes. "The American soldier is a born housewife," Pyle wrote.

Camelon and Howey, on the other hand, weren't trying to buck up the folks back home by telling them how their brothers and uncles, fathers and sons were enduring the unendurable. They were writing about "the legion of the disabled, who had come home in mid-war to delay, neglect and disillusion," in Camelon's words. They were trying to rouse the folks at home to protest—and to do something about the complacency in Washington. "War and its harsh truths were far away," Camelon wrote five years later in a memoir. "Casualties were unpleasant—but we could accept them as necessary. They were statistics; part of the cost of war—and they happened to other people; people far away from the Pentagon Building, the Mayflower Cocktail Lounge or the House and Senate Office Buildings."

That comfortable complacency ended, as Camelon wrote, when Atherton gave the story of the Forgotten Battalion to Congress, which attached human faces to the statistics. Bill Smith, for example, had been paralyzed by a bomb on Guadalcanal. Troy Lucas had lost a leg in Tunisia. Lawrence Edward Mahoney had never been in combat, but was blinded in one eye and had both hands torn off in a training accident.

"It was a shocking, incredible story of disabled men—their minds twisted, bodies torn in battle—shunted out of hospitals, out of the armed forces into a world of callous delay and neglect—even, in far too many cases of actual distress," Camelon wrote. "Everybody was going to 'do something' for the veterans 'after the war.' It was a nice thought, but hazy. Meanwhile, soldiers, sailors, Marines were being shot and discharged. But the public had forgotten that before a war ends it has its veterans. It seems impossible to believe, now, that thousands of disabled men discharged during the war were forced to depend upon charity for their very existence for months before the country they had fought to defend got around to caring for them.

"Incredible, too, that no one but The American Legion spoke for them; that no one but The American Legion undertook to find out what was happening, and, having found out, to fight for them relentlessly and unceasingly until some measure of human justice was done."

Although Camelon's rhetoric more than fifty years later seems a little overheated, it was anchored in reality, as he observed in his next sentence: "But the facts forced belief—the cold, inescapable facts marshalled by the Legion."

The road to passage of the GI Bill had to be built over the broken bodies, and sometimes broken minds, of thousands of early casualties of the war. Mahoney, for example, had been a star basketball player and swimmer in high school who had joined the New York National Guard in 1940, "well, because I thought it would be a good thing to do." When the guard was federalized, he was sent to Texas, and two years later, in 1942, he was a master sergeant training recruits in demolition. "I was showing the operation of an offensive grenade," he remembered later. "It must have had a defective fuse. It went off in my hands. It didn't knock me unconscious—but it blinded me at first." Mahoney had both hands torn off and was blinded in one eye. After being patched up in a hospital, he was like many others who were just thrown out on the street without money, employment assistance, even help in filing for the disability payments veterans and their dependents were entitled to. He was one of the 14,648 servicemen who were left minus one or more limbs by the war; 10,405 lost one foot, and 3,322 one hand. In all, sixty-four lost two hands.

Another member of the Legion's Forgotten Battalion was Bill Smith, a Marine declared unfit for service after a grenade at Guadalcanal destroyed nerves in his brain and paralyzed his left side. Smith was discharged six and a half months after being evacuated from Guadalcanal, but no one helped him file for disability compensation. The day he was discharged, his pay and his allotment to his mother, her only source of income, stopped. He was entitled under the law to disability compensation of up to $100 a month, free hospitalization and medication, and vocational rehabilitation training. But the benefits weren't forthcoming because the paperwork hadn't been filed. Instead, he was turned out onto the street with a warning: Find civilian clothes to replace his military uniform within ninety days. Smith went home paralyzed and penniless, to wait four months before his disability claim was adjudicated and vocational rehabilitation recommended. "How did Bill and his mother live during those months?" Camelon asked. "No one seemed to know, or, apart from the Legion, to care. Perhaps he was able to drag his paralyzed body to his neighbor's door for a handout."

Smith's case was all too typical. "This is only a quick sampling, based on a telegraphic inquiry among Legion service officers in 34 states," Camelon quoted Atherton as saying. At the time Atherton addressed Congress, more than six hundred thousand veterans had been discharged from the services. Among them was Case No. 12, a totally blind veteran who was discharged on June 30, 1943, but whose service records didn't get to the VA until November 22. As of November 29, he still hadn't received the government pension he was entitled to. "As Atherton spoke," Camelon wrote, "you thought of the confused bewilderment that boy must have felt, blinded in action, left penniless for months with only eternal darkness to comfort him." Case No. 13 was a veteran discharged as insane. The discharge was in April, but the necessary paperwork still hadn't been filled out by December. "That was eight months," Camelon wrote, "eight months in which a boy whose mind was shattered by war was left alone, without help, money or encouragement from the government he served."

In fairness to the VA, Camelon pointed out delays were inevitable given the volume of work and the shortage of manpower. Nevertheless, as he wrote, "the situation itself was intolerable, and although there was a way to correct it, it was not being corrected until the Legion acted." Atherton and the Legion called for a program to cut red tape so disability claims could be filed and processed while veterans were still in the service. Atherton had a powerful argument to offer for bonus pay up to $500. "Even a convict who is discharged from prisons is given some money and a suit of clothes," Atherton said. "The veteran, when he is discharged from a hospital or separation center, gets neither. . . . There'll be no Merry Christmas for these veterans unless something is done immediately. Time is of the essence."

On December 1, Atherton repeated the request for mustering-out pay before the Senate Military Affairs Committee. That committee

was already considering a bill submitted by Senator Alben Barkley, the majority leader, calling for $300. Atherton insisted $300 was inadequate and again suggested $500. In the meantime, Jack Cejnar, the Legion's acting public affairs officer—the regular employee was in the service—sent out copies of the 1,536 case studies to newspapers all across the country. Many followed up with localized news stories. Hundreds of editorials in support of the bonus bill were printed, and letters rolled in to congressional offices. Some members of Congress reacted immediately. "I never realized anything approaching this situation existed," Senator Edwin Johnson of Colorado, chairman of a military affairs subcommittee studying veterans' legislation, said. "It is almost unbelievable that this nation should permit boys to go for months without food, without money or clothes, except what they can beg. You can't explain away a situation like this. You can't brush it off or forget it. We must act immediately to put money in the hands of every man who is discharged. I am informed that we are discharging as many as 75,000 men a month, and that the totals will steadily increase. All of them face an immediate problem on discharge when they feel lost and alone. And that, apparently, is just the time when we have been neglecting them—when their need is the greatest."

The speech was fine, but, despite the news stories and the fact that men and women were being wounded on fields and oceans all over the world, Washington was still preoccupied by its own battles. Camelon quoted one congressman as rising on the floor to declare: "America's boys didn't go to war for money—for dollars. They went out of patriotism. And America is grateful. Why, when a boy dies, America gives him a flag to drape over his coffin."

Other voices were heard in Congress. Representative May, of course, had declared on the House floor that "shocking" was the only word to describe the situation. Camelon thought the word "shocking" should be more appropriately applied to May himself. He described May as a member of a "hard core of opposition, within the Congress, opposed to doing anything for the veterans—an attitude beyond the comprehension of the ordinary citizen." The congressman who declared a flag over the coffin was the only reward veterans should expect was actually speaking for May as well as himself, wrote Camelon. Camelon believed an "incipient 'economy wave'—directed only at veterans" was brewing. Signs of such an economy wave at the expense of veterans did become evident as the battle of the bonus proceeded in the House and Senate.

The Senate Finance Committee, responding to Atherton's plea, revised and reported out a new version of the Barkley bill providing up to $500 rather than $300 on December 15. The bill, approved by the full Senate December 17, was considered by the administration as "diluting the basic principle of equal treatment of all" because it provided a sliding scale of payments ranging from $200 for those with less than twelve months of service to $500 for individuals who had served overseas for eighteen months or more. Apparently the administration thought compensation based on the length and potential danger of service violated principles of equity.

On the same day the Senate bill was being reported out, the House Military Affairs Committee was learning, firsthand, about veterans' fears from Technical Sgt. Buck Hendricks of Council Bluffs, Iowa. Hendricks, who had lost a leg when he stepped on a land mine in Tunisia, testified: "The boys I'm speaking for have been through battle. They have received wounds, just as thousands of other boys and girls will receive wounds. We've got to get word to the boys still over there that Congress is taking good care of their buddies who have been wounded. We must not let them think that their buddies who have been wounded have suffered delay and neglect."

Hendricks said $300 was inadequate; as a result, Representative Walter Ploeser introduced a new compensation bill. Ploeser, a thirty-six-year-old Republican from Missouri, had already attacked the Democratic leadership for failure to address the problems of veterans several weeks before Atherton appeared before Congress. "The Democratic leadership of the House of Representatives should commemorate this Armistice Day—in shame," he said in early November. With Ploeser's bill now in the hopper, it seemed the House would have to match, if not improve, the bill already reported out of committee on the Senate side. But there were signals that powerful House members, particularly Mays, were not listening to the veterans, the case of Troy Lucas, for example. Lucas had, like Hendricks, lost a leg in Tunisia, and he was also a constituent of May's from Kentucky. A veteran of several battlefields, Lucas had been discharged from Walter Reed Hospital without money, job, or place to go. But his story came to the attention of Congress through Ploeser, rather than May, in a speech on the House floor. "The postwar period for this [man]has started," Ploeser said.

It is here now. Not tomorrow, not next year, not after the war, but now. To Troy Lucas—and the millions of his buddies—I say that the Military Affairs Committee of this House, under its present leadership, is too busy to give consideration to the human affairs of the men who are fighting to keep America free.

What if our men in Italy were too busy to fight and kill the enemy?

What if our fighting men in New Guinea were too busy to fight the battle for the preservation of democracy in America?

Hendricks's testimony and Ploeser's speech evoking Lucas came too late to move May, Lucas's own congressman. On December 13, May made it clear Congress might well be too busy to vote on a bonus bill before Congress. He announced on the floor of the House: "I do not know if we will be able to draft a veterans' mustering-out pay bill and get it to the floor before Christmas." At the same time, he announced he was appointing a subcommittee headed by Representative John M. Costello of California to study and draft legislation. The amount under consideration in the committee was still $300.[21]

"That announcement, in itself, was a death sentence to any action prior to Christmas," as Camelon wrote. "The appointment of a subcommittee to study a proposal on which the evidence of need was so clear could only result in delay." Of course, it was also a political maneuver designed to test public sentiment and a challenge to the Legion to rally support—if it could—for what, after all, was an entirely new item on the nation's political agenda at a time when most people were focused on the war itself. The next day, December 14, the Legion put out a press release, and Commander Atherton spoke over a national radio hookup, saying, "There'll be no Merry Christmas for these men unless Congress moves speedily to help them. Some mustering-out pay must be paid immediately. It must be done before Congress adjourns before Christmas. Whether or not Congress does that will mean the difference between a Merry Christmas and no Christmas at all to the men who have returned, sick and wounded, from the war fronts where they have been fighting to preserve safe, free Christmas for every other American."

Two days later, on December 16, Hearst newspapers summed up what was happening in a cartoon. The cartoon showed a disabled veteran silhouetted in the snow in front of the Capitol, leaning on a crutch with an empty left sleeve suggesting an amputated hand. The word "Politics" was emblazoned on the Capitol dome.[22] The message was obvious and simple: "The fix is in." It was also accurate. The White House didn't want action taken on the bonus bill, and the Democratic leadership was obliging.

On December 20, May announced consideration of the bill would be held over until the next session, which began in January, and he returned to Prestonburg. He also had a personal reason for returning home; a nephew had been killed in a plane crash. But he was obviously unconcerned by the fact that he could be accused of betraying a constituent, Troy Lucas. The fact that such behavior was politically dangerous for someone who had won his previous election by only 540 votes didn't deter him. Other members of the House were outraged, notably Mrs. Rogers, but to no avail. Failure to act was cruel and inexcusable, she said, and although the death of May's nephew was regrettable, other veterans could die while Congress was out of session. In a desperate effort to keep the bill alive, she asked for unanimous consent to have the bill taken off the speaker's table for consideration out of order. Speaker Rayburn refused to recognize her for the purpose.

That's when Camelon, a relatively new correspondent for a big but not greatly respected news organization in Washington, began to sense the power the press rarely exerts but can use with great force when it does. He recalled five years later: "And in May's absence, I wrote for all the Hearst newspapers at the time, went all hope that decent mustering-out pay could be enacted this year, all hope that there would be a little money, a little hope and cheer, this Christmas, for the veterans who had been mustered out of the Army without a cent in their pockets, without a suit of clothes."

In May's absence, Camelon reported, no action could be taken on the bill despite Rogers's denunciation and Rankin's blustering that he would oppose adjournment until a vote was taken on a mustering-out bill. "Their efforts were futile," Camelon reported. He didn't record how his stories were being played in newspapers all across the country from Boston to San Francisco, Chicago to San Antonio, Seattle to Albany, wherever Hearst newspapers appeared with little red, white, and blue flags emblazoned on the front-page banner. Hearst himself saw championing veterans as a splendid way of attacking FDR. In a personal letter to the editor of *The New York Journal-American* published on Christmas Eve 1943, Hearst accused the administration of "waiting and debating and wondering whether paying a debt of honor is good politics. . . . Let us continue to urge our political leaders to think less about their personal 'place in history' and more about whose heroism and self-sacrifice made that place possible." On January 12, ten days before Camelon and Reilly had their run-in with May, *The Journal-American* editorialized: "The country will not tolerate further procrastination by Congress. . . . There is nothing to DEBATE about, nothing to BARGAIN about, nothing to justify a further WASTE OF TIME." The campaign for the GI Bill of Rights provided Hearst with an opportunity to harass the Roosevelt administration, according to historian Ross: "He had long dictated a rabid, anti–New Deal policy for his newspaper chain. Finally, Hearst consistently had championed 'Americanism'; stories of maltreatment of veterans was tailormade." The isolationist Hearst, of course, was also vehemently opposed to the UNRRA bill. Hearst's attitudes on both the plight of the veterans and FDR's efforts to create and lead a United Nations that would fulfill President Wilson's dream of a League of Nations were summed up in a cartoon that appeared in Hearst papers December 29, 1943. Under the title "Merely Our Son" is shown a disabled veteran, with one foot gone, supporting himself on crutches and looking into a store window with a sign, "Ye New Deal Globaloney Shoppe: Goodies for Good Neighbors."[23]

Hearst had borrowed the word "globaloney" from a former playwright and magazine editor who was now serving as a member of Congress from Connecticut, Clare Booth Luce. She was married to Henry Luce, whose *Time-Life* publications rivaled Hearst's in circulation. Luce was using his magazines at the time to call for an American Century, in which the United States would take the unabashed leadership of the new world to emerge after the war. The attitudes of both men were at sharp contrast with the fervent belief of many at the time in the necessity of a new order dominated by a world parliament. Those feelings had been crystallized by the publication in the fall of 1943 of *One World,* a book written by Wendell Willkie, a lawyer whose representation of private companies fighting the TVA had helped propel him into the Republican nomination for the presidency in 1940. The book, written after a trip to Russia, would sell more than two million copies in a year, a record number. Another book, also on the best-seller list at the time, was *U.S. Foreign Policy: Shield of the Republic* by Walter Lippman, which preached, more realistically, that the country must get ready for the "eventual but unavoidable next war." Lippman wasn't as persuasive to most Americans as Willkie and Henry Wallace, the vice president. Wallace's book *The Century of the Common Man,* written to counter Luce's concept of the American Century, assumed the enormous benefits of modern technology would be shared by everyone everywhere. As one example, he advocated milk be made available to everyone, every day. The response of the president of the National Association of Manufacturers (NAM) shocked some but delighted others: "I am not fighting for a quart of milk every day for every Hottentot, nor for a TVA on the Danube."[24]

The words might have been written by Hearst himself. In a life and a career filled with contradictions and inconsistencies, the publisher had always adamantly believed America should steer clear of what George Washington called "entangling alliances." That belief, plus an old grudge, persuaded him his one great political achievement, the nomination of FDR for president at the 1932 convention, had been a disastrous mistake. Coincidentally, Walter Howey had sparked Hearst's president-making through favors he had traded with Joseph Kennedy, the financier. Howey helped Kennedy's father-in-law, John F. "Honey Fitz" Fitzgerald, in his campaign for governor of Massachusetts in 1922. "Howey had barred political news in his paper, which to its Irish readers was like printing blank pages," Richard J. Whalen wrote in *Founding Father.* "Kennedy persuaded Howey to lift the embargo, a break for Honey Fitz; he added casually that Howey might call on him should he need advice on financial matters." Howey called on Kennedy when speculators in the unregulated 1920s stock market bid down the price on his stock in Yellow Cab from $85 to $50 a share. Kennedy ran a counteroffensive against the raiders on behalf of Howey and other investors.[25] Howey recovered his money, and Kennedy called in his favor, in turn, at the 1932 convention on behalf of FDR. Introduced to Hearst by Howey, the financier persuaded the press magnate to abandon his support for "Cactus Jack" Garner of Texas, the speaker of the House. Hearst had backed Garner as "another Champ Clark," the earlier speaker of the House and father of Senator Clark, he had unsuccessfully supported for the nomination against Wilson in 1912. In 1932, Kennedy persuaded Hearst that Garner couldn't prevail against FDR, and the convention might turn instead to either Al Smith (the Democratic candidate for president in 1928) or Newton D. Baker, President Wilson's secretary of war. Hearst hated both, Baker as an internationalist who had campaigned vigorously for the League of Nations and Smith as an old political enemy. When FDR agreed to accept Garner

as his running mate, Hearst released the forty-four votes he controlled in the California delegation, putting the delegate count over
the required two thirds for the ticket. Within months after the convention, Smith and Hearst became FDR's principal political critics in
the name of Jeffersonian democracy, with Hearst instructing his editorial writers to refer to the New Deal as the Raw Deal.

Although Hearst's break with FDR was over the National Recovery Administration specifically, a break probably would have come
anyway. Hearst was his own favorite candidate for president, but he
had to settle for being "The Chief" of the largest publishing conglom-
erate in the United States and the owner of enormous estates in
Wales and California as well as the largest private art collection
in the world. A mamma's boy who shared his mother's bed until he
was almost four, he asked her to buy him the Louvre for his tenth
birthday; was expelled from Harvard at twenty-one for giving his
professors chamber pots with their names ornamentally inscribed on
the bottom; published the first modern newspaper when he was
twenty-four; started a war when he was thirty-four; was reviled as
the instigator of President William McKinley's assassination when
he was thirty-six; and made his first determined effort to become
president when he was forty—and he was just starting. "He might
well have been the greatest man of his era," his biographer, W. A.
Swanberg, concluded: He had the "awesome vigor, industry, capability
and intellect," but his crippling weakness was "his inability to anchor
his thinking to a few basic, rocklike truths that were immovable
in his heart."[26]

That wasn't really accurate, since Hearst did have certain firm
beliefs, isolationism being perhaps the most rocklike. In one respect,
he was also very like FDR, a "kind of universal joint, or rather a
switchboard, a transformer," in the words of John Gunther, author of
Inside America. Hearst was at the center of American political life
for more than a half century, propelling forward and sometimes trying to block the careers of more notable men, particularly Theodore
Roosevelt and Champ Clark—whose offspring cofounded the American Legion—as well as FDR. His publicizing of Roosevelt's Rough
Rider exploits in Cuba helped make TR president, and his failure to
secure the Democratic nomination for Clark in 1912 made him a bitter enemy of President Wilson and his international policies, which
FDR took over.

Hearst's father, George, discovered the fabled Homestake Mine and backed his son as publisher of *The San Francisco Examiner* after he had been expelled from Harvard. The shy but determined young man had a simple editorial philosophy, according to Arthur McEwen, his editorial page editor: "What we're after is the gee-whiz emotion." That was too modest, Swanberg commented: "Any issue that did not cause its reader to rise out of his chair and cry, 'Great God,' was counted a failure."[27] Hearst built a reputation as a Populist by forcing the bankrupt but powerful Southern Pacific Railroad to repay federal loans. He then took on Joseph Pulitzer and *The New York World,* the nation's biggest mass-circulation newspaper, with $7.5 million raised by his mother through selling the Anaconda Mining Company. Buying the ailing *New York Journal,* he hired away many of Pulitzer's best reporters and editors and also stole away *The World*'s highly popular comic strip, "The Yellow Kid." The cartoon's name was the origin of the phrase "yellow journalism."

Hearst supported many liberal causes, child labor laws and the vote for women, for example, but became famous—or infamous—for instigating the Spanish-American War. When Frederick Remington, the famed artist, complained by telegram to Hearst he couldn't find any fighting to illustrate, Hearst fired back: "You furnish the pictures; I'll furnish the war." The war provided *The Journal* with the largest circulation in the world, 1.2 million daily. In addition, "Colonel Roosevelt was made famous by Hearst," according to Swanberg. "It was his enormous publicity as the intrepid leader of the Rough Riders—publicity which Roosevelt shrewdly exploited—that formed the basis of his brilliant career in politics. Since Hearst brought on the war, it can be said that he also put Roosevelt in Albany as governor and in the White House as President."[28]

Hearst's own political ambitions flowered with his election to Congress in 1902, where he introduced the legislation requiring election of senators by popular vote, rather than by state legislators. In 1904, making a determined effort to win the Democratic nomination for president, he allied himself with Tom Watson of Georgia, the leader of the southern Populists who were the political ancestors of southern conservatives such as Rankin. Watson dedicated his biography of Thomas Jefferson to Hearst. Hearst got only 263 delegate votes for president at the 1904 convention and in 1912 decided to become a president-maker, backing Clark, the first Democratic speaker in almost twenty years. Clark, with Hearst's support, got 440 delegate votes against 324 for Wilson, almost a 59 percent plurality but five points shy of the two-thirds majority needed to prevail under the party's rules at the time. Hearst tried to trade votes for Clark in return for support of Tammany Hall, but the effort was sabotaged by William Jennings Bryan, the party's three-time unsuccessful candidate. Support slipped away to the austere Wilson, who won nomination on the fortieth ballot and who rewarded Bryan by making him secretary of state.[29]

Perhaps partially out of resentment, Hearst was obdurately opposed to American intervention in World War I. "In what was known as the Great War, Hearst who yearned for high office and public acclaim, deliberately made himself the most hated man in America," Swanberg wrote. "He fought for American neutrality at a time when neutrality was considered little short of treason . . . Hearst sincerely believed America should stay out of the war. Years after the conflict, many who had attacked his anti-war stand came to regard him as right and to admire the stubborn courage with which he held his ground in the face of nationwide opprobrium." Hearst distrusted the British, but, above all, he hated Wilson. "Whatever Wilson did, Hearst instinctively felt that it was wrong," Swanberg wrote. A lifelong Democrat, Hearst urged Teddy Roosevelt to run for president in 1916, but Roosevelt stayed home in Oyster Bay.

After the war, Hearst fought against both the League of Nations and American participation in the World Court. He flirted with elective politics again as Tammany Hall's candidate for New York's senator in 1922, but Al Smith, the party's nominee for governor, refused to have him on the ticket. Smith referred to Hearst as a "pestilence."[30] Two years later, Smith was reelected governor against Theodore Roosevelt Jr. despite Hearst's covert support. Hearst's power in the state Democratic Party was over, and by 1933, he had become, in Swanberg's phrase, "a reactionary radical," denouncing the New Deal as not being "radical enough for his 'Jeffersonian democracy.'"

In 1937, the Depression and Hearst's out-of-control spending forced him into bankruptcy. Papers were closed or sold, radio stations disposed of, real estate ventures liquidated, even construction stopped at San Simeon, his fabled palace near San Clemente, the Shangri-la of *Citizen Kane*. His newspaper chain was still the largest in the country, however, and wartime prosperity meant his papers were soon filled with advertising. Hearst's influence over the working-class readers of his newspapers expanded during the war. Liberal Democrats and Republican internationalists feared him and suggested he was a

potential Fascist. An exclusive interview Hearst secured with Hitler
came back to haunt him when a photograph taken with Dr. Albert
Rosenberg and other Nazis was circulated in the United States along
with distorted quotations suggesting he approved of Hitler. "Doubtless
Hearst saw in fascism a useful bulwark against Communism which
terrified him with its threat to liberty and private property," Swanberg wrote. "If he had to choose between the two, he certainly would
have picked fascism but the evidence indicates that he preferred
traditional American democracy first of all. One gets the picture of
Hearst, his faith in Roosevelt lost, seeing the country foundering in
continued Depression, eying the horizon uneasily, fearful of collapse,
for once uncertain of the cure."

His uncertainty was widely shared. To most Americans, though,
including the vast majority of Hearst's readers, FDR was the one
leader they trusted, even if they didn't always agree with him. Ordinary people certainly didn't believe FDR had all or even most of the
answers to their problems. But they fervently hoped he would somehow sort out among all the proposed solutions those that had the best
chance of working and reject the ones that didn't. One of the agnos-
tics, however, and a persistent critic of FDR's judgment on both
domestic and foreign policy throughout the period, was yet another
Jeffersonian Democrat, Bennett Champ Clark, son of the one man
Hearst might have been happy with in the White House.[31]

Shepherding the GI Bill through the Senate was the greatest triumph of Clark's career; he took the bill through every legislative
hurdle in the Senate without stumbling once or losing a single vote.
"In effect, the bill had been passed before it reached the Senate floor,
as it bore the signatures of 81 members, with others complaining
today that they had not received an opportunity to be active sponsors," *The New York Times* reported in its March 25, 1944, story
recording the Senate floor vote on the bill. Debate had been nonexistent, the only questions perfunctory, a tribute to Clark's legislative
skills. "Most of the questions put to Senator Bennett Clark, Democrat, of Missouri, who introduced and handled the bill, were for the
purpose of clarifying its many provisions and of voicing approval of
the program," *The Times* reported.[32]

A few weeks later, Clark had his one great moment in the national
spotlight. He nominated Harry Truman, his fellow senator from Missouri and onetime political enemy, for the vice presidency at the 1944

Democratic convention. In November of that year, Clark's political career was over; he was defeated in his bid for a fourth term in the Senate. Clark's star was descending as Truman's rose. The failed haberdasher was in line for the presidency. The son of a former speaker of the House who had nearly won the Democratic nomination for president in 1912 and had himself been briefly pushed by Truman for the presidency in 1940 was a political has-been. Yet ten years before, in 1934, Clark had done his best to keep Truman out of the Senate. He had assailed Truman as a tool of the Kansas City political machine run by Tom Pendergast. Nevertheless, after several years, Truman, through hard, unobtrusive mastery of the legislative process and investigations of complex issues such as Wall Street juggling of railroad stock, emerged as Clark's equal in the Senate—and a friend.[33]

Truman, in announcing for reelection to the Senate in 1940, said he was opposed to a third term for President Roosevelt and proposed Clark for the presidency. That was, however, far from Truman's best moment, according to his biographer David McCullough. "Seldom had he seemed more the politician, in the least complimentary sense of the term," McCullough observed. "That he, Harry Truman, could honestly propose conservative, isolationist, alcoholic Bennett Clark for the presidency at the time, let alone now, with the world as it was, seemed so blatantly hypocritical and expedient as to be laughable. . . . Clearly it was Clark's support in eastern Missouri he was after." McCullough's later assessment failed to take into account Clark's considerable accomplishments in the Senate, particularly his stewardship of the GI Bill. Indeed, without that accomplishment, Truman's tenure in the White House would have been far more troubled, and the country would have been far worse off. The "gains in income, standards of living, education and housing since Truman took office were unparalleled in American history," McCullough himself wrote, adding: "As Truman would report in his final State of the Union address to Congress on Jan. 7, 1953 . . . the postwar economic collapse that everyone expected never happened, that through government support [the GI Bill] 8 million veterans had been to college, that Social Security benefits had been doubled, that the minimum wage increased."

Clark, after World War I, had deliberately chosen to stay out of politics and even Legion activities other than serving as a national committeeman from Missouri in 1922–23. Like Colonel Roosevelt, he was concerned their motives in founding the Legion would be suspect. On August 23, 1919, before the Legion's first convention in Minneapolis, Clark wrote Roosevelt a letter offering his support for the "Commander in Chiefship." If Roosevelt wasn't interested, he suggested an alternative candidate should be "to my mind, an enlisted man." Like Roosevelt, Clark was worried about "the impression which still prevails in some quarters—that a few of us got up the Legion for our own advantage and aggrandizement. Frankly, I am very tired of that sort of talk." Three days later, on August 26, Roosevelt wrote back saying he didn't intend "to stand for national commander" and agreed "heartily with what you say concerning the general policy. I want to talk this matter over with you so that we can quietly make up our minds where the proper head [leader] can be found."[34]

By the fall of 1921, both Clark and Roosevelt had bowed out of active Legion roles. Clark's first job out of law school had been parliamentarian of the House of Representatives from 1913 to 1917, in which he compiled a parliamentary manual in use for many years. His father's political career was one of the casualties of Wilson's demand that the election of 1920 be "a great and solemn referendum" on the League of Nations. But throughout the '20s, the son stayed out of politics, contentedly practiced corporate and trial law, and turned down an offer in 1928 to succeed James A. Reed in the Senate.[35]

In 1932, apparently appalled by growing Pendergast power in the state—the state capitol in Jefferson was called "Uncle Tom's Cabin"—Clark ran successfully for the Senate. Calling for the repeal of Prohibition and passage of social reform measures, Clark was the only congressional candidate to prevail against a Pendergast tide. In Washington, Clark, initially a Roosevelt supporter, turned strongly against him. He also aimed his formidable oratorical abilities against Truman, who ran for the Senate in 1934 as a fervent FDR supporter. Truman had initially wanted to run for the House, but had been passed over by Pendergast for Jasper Bell, who would go on to win election to the House six times. Then, very much to Truman's surprise, he was chosen to run for the Senate, after three other potential candidates turned Pendergast down. In the resulting three-way primary, Clark went after Truman, McCullough wrote, as a way of "challenging Tom Pendergast and gaining a second seat for himself." Truman countered by claiming Clark had political-boss aspirations of his own that he, Truman, if elected to the Senate, would frustrate.

Clark, like his father, "was a colorful, two-fisted stump speaker," McCullough wrote, "and he tore into Truman with, as they say in Missouri, 'the bark off'":

> "Harry fears that someone from the eastern part of the state may undertake to set up as boss," Clark declared. "Harry Truman fears a boss in Missouri—God save the mark! Harry places the intelligence of the Democrats of Missouri so low and estimates their credulity so high that he actually went to great length in promising people that if elected to the Senate he would not set up as a boss or undertake to dictate to anyone. Why, bless Harry's good, kind heart—no one has ever accused him of being a boss or wanting to be a boss and nobody will ever suspect him of trying to dictate to anybody as long as a certain eminent citizen of Jackson County remains alive and in possession of his health and faculties. . . . In view of the judge's record of subserviency in Jackson County it would seem that his assurances against any assumption of boss-ship are a trifle gratuitous to say the least."

Despite Clark's attacks, Truman won comfortably, and when he arrived in Washington the new junior and the incumbent senior senators from the "Show Me State" announced they were good friends. Beneath the surface amity, Clark, however, was referred to as the senator from Missouri and Truman as the senator from Pendergast. Federal patronage also went to the senior senator, although Clark was opposed to the New Deal and Truman was loyal to Roosevelt. Clark's appointments included a U.S. attorney who convicted 279 Pendergast allies of vote tampering and eventually sent Pendergast to jail for tax evasion. Truman denounced the U.S. attorney in a Senate floor speech in which he said, "A Jackson County Democrat has as much chance of a fair trial in the Federal District Court of Missouri as a Jew would have in a Hitler court or a Trotsky follower before Stalin." Nevertheless, Clark came to respect Truman as living up to a western saying Clark was fond of quoting, "He did his damndest." As for Truman, he recognized Clark was, as McCullough wrote, "a man with an extraordinary mind who knew the Constitution and parliamentary law as well as anyone in the Senate."

Clark took advantage of that skill as chairman of the rules committee at the 1936 Democratic convention to overturn "that undemocratic rule that deprived my father of the presidency." He abolished the two-thirds rule, and from 1936 on, because of Clark, a simple majority would be enough to nominate the presidential and vice presidential candidates of the Democratic Party and endorse the party's platform. Clark's "burning desire to avenge his father" was satisfied by the rule change, Senator Tom Connally of Texas recalled. As an unanticipated consequence, the simple majority rule would also mean that in the 1948 convention, the first one in a generation not dominated by FDR, the party would adopt a civil rights plank by a fraction of a vote, making the Democrats, rather than the Republicans, the political allies of blacks.

Clark's relationship with Roosevelt, already strained by his reluctant support of the Social Security Act, became acrimonious after the 1936 election. Clark was one of the first Democratic senators to oppose Roosevelt's attempt to pack the Supreme Court. Truman supported the president, but tried to stay out of the public debate. Nevertheless, he was denounced as being a "Roosevelt stooge"—an assessment the White House apparently shared, inadvertently giving Truman an opportunity to assert his independence of Pendergast. When Majority Leader Joseph Robinson, who had been carrying the Supreme Court fight for Roosevelt, died of a heart attack, Truman pledged his vote to Senator Pat Harrison of Mississippi despite FDR's open support of Senator Barkley. The White House telephoned Pendergast and asked him to tell Truman to vote for Barkley. An insulted Truman told Steve Early, the president's press secretary, he was tired of being pushed around and voted for Harrison. In the process, he won Barkley's respect by telling him, before the balloting, that he'd pledged his vote to Harrison. "I always admired him for the courage and character he displayed in coming to me as he did," Barkley said. "Too often, in politics the stiletto is slipped between your shoulder blades while its wielder continues to smile sweetly."

By 1939, Clark, already identified with the old Jeffersonian Democratic Party, turned his oratorical guns on the president's foreign policy as an outspoken advocate of "a flat, mandatory, automatic policy of neutrality." He opposed lend-lease munitions sales to all belligerent nations, including Great Britain, and supported an amendment to the Constitution making it necessary to conduct a popular referendum before declaring war. Along with many veterans of World War I, he believed the country had been drawn into the conflict by "the influence of big money lenders and money changers." Some critics claimed he was just using the neutrality debate to carry on his father's old quarrel with Wilson, but he claimed he was just continu-

ing the family—and old Jeffersonian—tradition of limiting the expanding power of the executive branch. "Clark had made himself a
favorite of the America First movement . . . and claimed, 'We have
everything to lose and nothing to gain in a war,'" McCullough wrote.
"Clark was destroying himself politically, Truman was certain."[36]

Clark, having been reelected to a second term in 1938, didn't have
to run again until 1944. He reluctantly backed FDR when he decided
to break the two-term tradition, but after Pearl Harbor, his isolationism, coupled with control of the Senate by Barkley, FDR's loyal
lieutenant, meant he was relegated to back-bench assignments. Truman, by contrast, was given the high-profile responsibility of probing
industry's role in the war effort. Clark seemed washed up. Yet he
would be largely responsible for passage of the law that would make
possible the successful transition of power from FDR to Truman and
the nation's transformation from economic cripple to world power.
Clark's leading—but circumspect—role in the passage of the bill and
FDR's awareness of his role in cofounding the Legion with Theodore
Roosevelt Jr. may have muted presidential opposition to the bill. FDR
was certainly aware of his own lack of veteran status. "I was told
later FDR had asked several times during discussions of the bill
whether his support meant he could now be allowed to join the
Legion," Cocke, the national commander in 1950–51, said, "but, of
course, he was told even being commander in chief didn't qualify him
as a veteran."[37]

On the House side, Rankin's reputation for being difficult to get
along with—especially for liberal New Dealers—probably had been
responsible for the original bonus bill being assigned to May's Military Affairs Committee. Whether that was dictated by the administration or by Speaker Rayburn and Majority Leader McCormack on
their own, once in charge, Rankin firmly rebuffed repeated efforts by
others to take control of the legislation. Rankin was acknowledged to
be a brilliant legislative tactician, as the coauthor of not only the
TVA but the Rural Electrification Authority (REA). He was also one
of the most openly bigoted racists and anti-Semites ever to serve
in the House of Representatives. He was a "wild-eyed Jew baiter,"
according to Russell Whelan, author of a contemporary biographical
profile published soon after the GI Bill had passed; "a prize anomaly
of Congress, . . . a ranting demagogue, . . . a bigot and a drawback and
a travesty of a true democrat." Yet that same Rankin had cosponsored the TVA with Senator Norris, to whom, as perhaps the greatest

progressive leader to serve in the Senate, Rankin's racial views were anathema. Indeed, they wouldn't have commended themselves to Hearst, who—while not being a notable champion of blacks—hired and promoted Catholics and Jews more than any other newspaper proprietor of the time.

Rankin's "Jeffersonian Democratic" connection to Hearst was an heir of the Populist movement through Tom Watson, the southern Populist elected to Congress in 1890 with the message to blacks and whites: "You are kept apart so that you may be separately fleeced of your earnings. You are made to hate each other because upon that hatred is rested the keystone of financial despotism which enslaves you both. You are deceived and blinded that you may not see how this race antagonism perpetuates the monetary systems which beggars both."[38]

C. Vann Woodward observed in 1972, "Never before or since have the two races in the South come so close together as they did during the Populist struggle." The closeness didn't last; the alliance couldn't hold. After an embittered Watson was defeated for reelection in 1892, he decided the only way the poor white could stand erect was on top of the black. "No matter what direction progress might like to take in the South," Watson wrote, "she is held back by the never failing cry of 'nigger.'" Southern Populism became a perverted form of democracy. Jeffersonian Democrats below the Mason-Dixon line became allies of upper-class planters and business interests, called Bourbons, rather than share political power with blacks. Any hope of creating, in the words of the Arkansas People's Party, a working alliance among "the disadvantaged, regardless of race," was doomed. The specter of race made liberalism schizophrenic in the South. The only question was whether the racism was expressed unabashedly and vulgarly or quietly and respectably. President Wilson, for example, had described *Birth of a Nation* as being "written by lightning." Rankin preached aloud what Wilson practiced quietly.

"There are four possible solutions," Rankin said to what was then called the race problem: "Extermination, deportation, amalgamation and segregation." Rankin discarded the first two, "with genial magnanimity" as 'impractical,'" biographer Whelan wrote. "Amalgamation is out, too; it would 'mongrelize' the white race. This leaves segregation as the only way"—preferably in Arizona and New Mexico with a passport needed for readmittance to the rest of the United States.

As crazy as Rankin was on race, he was also one of the most effective legislators in the history of the House; a master of parliamentary
procedure; a brilliant, if vicious, orator; a staunch proponent of public
electrical power for the poor; and a defender of both servicemen and
veterans, although not a veteran himself. He was not bashful about
making himself heard. Rankin "made more speeches devouring more
minutes than anyone in Congress," Whelan said. When he was in
full oratorical flight, "a bony arm is thrust upward the skylight,
the strands of the grey mop begin to wave like reeds in a gale, and the
chords of the Tupelo calliope are tweaking every solar plexus in
the place." Yet this autocratic demagogue had, ever since his freshman
days in 1920, Whelan acknowledged, worked effectively for veterans,
leading the fight to override the presidential veto of the 1935 bonus
bill. Rankin also "quietly slid" through legislation increasing base pay
for soldiers and sailors from $30 to $50 a month.[39]

Rankin was keenly aware that the people of his district, the First
Mississippi based in Tupelo, were desperately poor—white almost as
much as black—and needed government help. Fewer than 1 percent
of the adults in the district had ever attended college, according to
Whelan. "Less than a third went to high school and not more than
sixty percent finished grammar school. Fifteen percent of the whites
and twice as many Negroes have syphilis, [and] hookworm infests a
considerable percentage of every age group. It is a poor land of poor
people and a challenge to the United States. Its people simply cannot
help themselves."

Rankin had done well by his constituents. Only a few had electrical power in 1933, and they were paying "exorbitant rates to private
power companies," Whelan wrote. By 1940, everyone was "enjoying
the benefits of cheap electrical power. Thousands of Americans can
also thank Rankin for the work he accomplished behind his slogan,
'Let's electrify every American farm at rates the people can afford
to pay.'"

By simply cosponsoring the TVA with Norris, Rankin was placed
improbably in the ranks of John C. Calhoun, President Theodore
Roosevelt, and President Wilson. Its passage was the culmination of
their efforts over more than one hundred years and, along with the
GI Bill, is a classic demonstration of federal resources used successfully on behalf of ordinary people. Unlike most New Deal measures,
the TVA didn't just provide relief, "taxing the 'haves' for the benefit of
the 'have-nots,'" as Morison noted.[40] Instead, it used government capi-

tal to control a river, produce electricity, restore farm fertility, and improve the living standards not just for those living in the river valley but also for the millions within reach of its power grid. The Rural Electrification Administration (REA), also cosponsored by Norris and Rankin, brought electricity to millions of farm families. The most eloquent witness to that battle was Lyndon Johnson. "Those people are too poor; they won't pay their bills," was an argument used against REA, Johnson remembered in his 1948 Senate campaign. "We put light in 20,000 homes" in his Hill Country district, Johnson recalled. "And you know how many bills were delinquent? Not one." The REA's success also did more to liberate women from drudgery than any other action taken by government. No longer did they have to haul and pump water, cook with wood and coal, and sweat in midsummer over those hot "sad irons" that, as Johnson recalled, made the clothing of "[me] and my brothers and sisters neat like other kids."[41]

This was the environment Rankin—and many other Americans—came from at the time, one in which even the relatively well-off didn't have access to electricity, childhood diseases claimed lives on almost every block, college was an impossible dream for almost everyone, a life lived under nineteenth-century conditions well into the middle of the twentieth century. Whelan thought Rankin was a permanent "aginner, thinking in only two shades—black and white." He had warred against the Republicans "as unmitigated villains" in the '20s, pouring "his vitriol on them on every occasion." When FDR came to power and battled with Rankin and Norris, he "was a champion of righteousness until about 1935 when Rankin's 'black' phase returned and he began to rail and flail at 'New Deal' bureaucracy," Whelan wrote. "There never is any middle ground for the gentleman from Mississippi." Rankin also believed in the communist Jewish world plot, whose American leaders presumably included vehement Representative Vito Marcantonio of New York, a Republican with such strong Communist sympathies that the Republican Party of New York went to court to keep him from referring to himself as a Republican. "Yet, Marcantonio and Rankin, after a strong exchange, often would leave the House chambers arm-in-arm," another observer noted.[42]

This, then, was the man who led the fight for the passage of the GI Bill in the House—until, at the last minute, fearing it might indirectly help break down segregation—he tried to sabotage its passage in a joint House-Senate conference committee. This same man on the floor of the House said the Red Cross's refusal to label blood supplies by racial origin was a "scheme by crackpots, Communists and the parlor pinks . . . to mongrelize the nation."[43] Yet he would overcome much more hostility against the bill in the House than Clark would encounter in the Senate from fellow members, leading politicians in the states, and the massed force of the nation's educators. Whalen suggested the final verdict on Rankin would have to wait until that "Last Day when 'Silent John' trots noisily to a place near the Celestial 'mike' and squints belligerently at the Speaker. If he is not satisfied that he and the South are receiving a fair shake," Whelan concluded, "then heaven help heaven."

That pugnacity and tenacity would be needed as the Christmas of 1943 slipped into the New Year of 1944. So, too, would the unflagging support of Edith Nourse Rogers, the ranking Republican on the veterans committee, who would become the first woman to chair a major House committee when she succeeded Rankin. Rogers was an authentic codfish aristocrat from Massachusetts, a descendant of Priscilla Mullens of the Mayflower, known to generations of schoolchildren for having said, "Speak for yourself," to John Alden when he proposed to her on behalf of Miles Standish. The daughter of a textile mill executive, Rogers had been educated in France and was considered "a tearing beauty" when she accompanied her husband to Washington in 1912, after he was elected to Congress. Until war was declared, she was essentially a socialite preoccupied with entertaining, but she insisted on accompanying her husband as a member of the House Foreign Affairs Committee on a secret mission to France and England in 1917. In London, she volunteered at the YMCA working with wounded servicemen on leave. On her return to Washington, childless and nearing forty, she became a Gray Lady volunteer, quickly becoming known as an "angel of mercy of Walter Reed Hospital." President Harding subsequently appointed her a dollar-a-year inspector of veterans' hospitals, an appointment renewed by Presidents Coolidge and Hoover.

Her husband, John Jacob Rogers, a graduate of Harvard and Harvard Law School, died in 1924, noted for having sponsored the legislation making diplomats career foreign service officers. She eagerly agreed with Republican leaders that she should succeed him, but bowed to convention, as a new widow, by refusing to actively campaign and concealing her support of voting rights for women. "It was never revealed that both she and her husband were ardent suffragists," Barbara Sicherman and Carol Hurd Gich observed in *Notable American Women*. She won a special election with 72 percent of the vote against former Democratic governor Eugene N. Foss, and her winning margin never dropped below 60 percent during the New Deal years. From 1942 through her last campaign in 1960, she carried every city and town in the district with 72 percent or more of the vote.[44]

Mrs. Rogers was a very adroit politician who, despite being a Republican, represented for thirty-five years a city that by normal political standards should have been the bailiwick of a Democrat, if not a Socialist. Lowell and Lawrence, a few miles north on the Merrimack River, were America's first planned cities, but planned for work, not living amenities, taking advantage of, if not exploiting, women workers. Young women recruited off farms by the textile mills of the city started work at four in the morning and ended at 7:30 at night, often with only bread and gravy for supper. Their homes were bleak dormitories run like prisons, and pay could be and was cut arbitrarily. In 1834, the women of Lowell struck, proclaiming, "Union is power. Our present object is to have union and exertion, and we remain in possession of our own unquestionable rights." The strike failed, but another strike was called in 1836 and yet another in 1845, calling for a ten-hour day. This time, the strikers succeeded in getting the Massachusetts state legislature to conduct the first governmental investigation of working conditions in the country.[45]

Working conditions were still terrible a half century later when Mrs. Rogers was growing up. Her father's position, as the manager of the second-largest mill in Lowell, protected her from the realities of life among working women, but that didn't mean Mrs. Rogers was conservative when it came to government spending. She once told a colleague who disagreed with her over a social service bill: "I hope the vote did not disturb you. You know, I cannot refuse to spend mere money when I know that people need it."[46]

Another reason for Rogers's electoral success may have been the fact that Lowell was perhaps the most polyglot community in Massachusetts. Ethnic divisions made uniting on a single Democrat to oppose her impossible. A system of proportional representation in city elections ensured seats on the city council not only for the largest groups, the Irish, French-Canadians, and Greeks—the Greek community was perhaps the largest in the United States—but also Italians, Poles, and others. Lowell, on a small scale, was as mixed ethnically as New York and as far removed from the native-born American constituency of John Rankin as garlic is from grits. Moreover, it teemed with the union activists Rankin despised almost as much as Jews and blacks. During World War II as many strikes took place in Lowell in 1943 and 1944 as in 1937. "It might have been a 'people's war,'" as a historian observed, "but there was dissatisfaction at the fact that textile mill profits grew 600 percent, while wage increases in cotton goods industries went up 36 percent."[47]

The diplomatic skills Representative Rogers used in satisfying her constituency were equally useful in forging the coalition behind the GI Bill. She was also a powerful advocate for women's interests. The representative from the district where the Female Labor Association had conducted a successful strike in 1845 authored the bills creating both the Women's Auxiliary Army Corps (WAACs) and a permanent Nurses Corps in the VA. The WAAC bill carried only after a tough floor fight. "The logic of her argument . . . was inescapable," according to Hope Chamberlain, another biographer. "Thousands of able-bodied men were assigned to desk jobs that women could perform at least as well as they—but the idea that women should be officially introduced into the rough all-male domain of army camps was intolerable to many legislators."

She was the only architect of the GI Bill who had been an early supporter of American intervention in the war. She spoke out against Hitler's persecution of the Jews as early as 1933 and in 1940 cosponsored with Senator Robert Wagner of New York legislation allowing immigration visas to be issued to Jewish orphans fleeing fascist persecution. FDR vetoed the bill.

She scored her first great success in veterans' legislation early in her congressional career in a battle that foreshadowed the struggle over the GI Bill fourteen years later. "By the time she became chairman of the Veterans' Affairs Committee in 1947," Chamberlain wrote, "her legislative skill was legendary. The most impressive, though not the best known, bill bearing her name was for a $15 million appropriation to build a nationwide network of hospitals, which she guided through the House, over the opposition of the committee chairman, fewer than five years after arriving on Capitol Hill."[48] It was in that 1929–31 battle that Rogers and Henry Colmery, the man who actually wrote the GI Bill, became acquainted. The alliance formed in working on the hospital bill may very well have sown the seeds that produced the GI Bill years later.

Henry—"Harry"—Colmery, a Midwestern Republican and a lawyer, was also an outspoken civil libertarian, judging by a speech he gave the Legion after he was elected the national commander in 1936. The speech was described in a feature article, "Colmery of Kansas," by Alexander Gardiner in *The American Legion Monthly* of January 1937, the only source of detailed biographical information about the man who wrote the GI Bill in longhand in Room 570 of the Mayflower Hotel in Washington. "There has never been any doubt of Harry Colmery's courage," wrote Gardiner,

> but this trait rose to new heights when he told the delegates who had just named him National Commander by acclamation that in the past we of the Legion have had a tendency "to stick our nose into other people's business instead of keeping it within the confines of the Legion's program." He followed this up with a ringing declaration in the November *National Legionnaire* under the title of "Let's Be American," which set forth the fact that the Legion is pledged to uphold *all* [italics in the text] of the Constitution of the United States and not merely those sections of the Bill of Rights that happen to please it.
>
> "The guarantees of speech, free press, peaceable assembly and petition for redress of grievances," Colmery declared, "are the most American things in the Constitution, and interference with their operation plays into the hands of communists or fascists, or both."
>
> Read that Colmery declaration again. It is as fundamentally sound under the system of American democracy as the deathless words of Voltaire to Helvetius a hundred and fifty years ago today, "I wholly disapprove of what you say and will defend to the death your right to say it."

Colmery, a native of Braddock, Pennsylvania, may have come by his principles at Oberlin College in Ohio before earning his law degree at the University of Pittsburgh. Oberlin, founded in 1833 under the auspices of the Congregational Church, was, according to Gardiner, the "first college in the United States to accept women under exactly the same conditions as men." After graduating from Oberlin, an abolitionist stronghold and way station on the Underground Railroad for slaves escaping to Canada, Colmery worked his way through law school as a teacher at Carnegie Tech, now Carnegie-Mellon University. On graduation, he got a job at the Westinghouse Manufacturing Co., but when he asked what the pay would be, he was told: "Why, nothing, you ought to feel lucky to have a chance to get started here."

Colmery thrust a hand out toward the smoke and flames from the mill to be seen through a window, snapped, "I can get a job there," and stamped out.

He went into solo legal practice for a while in Utah litigating water rights claims on two million acres thrown open for settlement by the government. Joining the fledgling air corps as a pilot instructor in World War I, he soon learned that war breeds profiteering as well as patriotism. "His experience acquainted him with the terrific hazards imposed on wartime pilots, by the haphazard, criminal incompetence of those who furnished 'flying coffins' for the students in training," Gardiner wrote, "and as a result he became a thorough believer in adequate peacetime national defense."

After the war, he established a legal practice in Topeka, Kansas, primarily in corporate law, but also won two notable Supreme Court cases on appeal, one criminal, the other in an early environmental law dispute. In the first, he got a new trial for Charles A. Shepard, a regular army officer who had been found guilty of murdering his wife. Shepard was acquitted in the second trial. In the environmental law case, Colmery secured the Supreme Court's approval of an ordinance passed by the community of Marysville, Kansas, requiring underground storage of gasoline by oil companies.

Colmery met Representative Rogers when the hospital construction bill she originally introduced in 1929, as chairman of a subcommittee of the veterans' committee, was finally voted out of both houses into a joint House-Senate conference in February 1931. Mrs. Rogers was unable to get her colleagues from the House to go along with a more generous Senate version of the bill. Colmery had called Legion headquarters in Washington for a progress report and was urged to fly to Washington to lobby members directly. He did, and that night, according to a contemporary quoted in Gardiner's 1937 account, he and his fellow Legion lobbyists marched the 751-foot length of the Capitol arguing with conferees until 2 A.M. The following morning, with "fallen arches and aching corns," the march began anew until the House conferees gave in, and Mrs. Rogers "asked for Senate agreement which was immediately given." The bill was on Herbert Hoover's desk at 11:45 and signed ten minutes later.

"Harry was as cool as a cucumber during the whole trying row, never lost his head once," Gardiner's source commented. "This was probably his most interesting legislative experience, certainly the most beneficial and important." That year Colmery also played a role in the Legion's official support of President Hoover's opposition to prepayment of the veterans' bonus. Later, in Topeka, he supported Alf Landon as a faithful Republican, but his inaugural speech as national commander in 1936 indicated he hadn't succumbed to the bitterness of many who opposed FDR in that election year—or FDR's own retaliatory vehemence.

Eight years later, Rogers, Colmery, Rankin, and Clark would be the principal actors in the congressional debate over the GI Bill, with Howey, Hearst, Camelon, Reilly, Stelle, and Atherton playing supporting roles. Americans had been in the war since the holiday season of 1941, and in 1942, Bing Crosby had won an Academy Award for singing "White Christmas" in the film *Holiday Inn*. There were no outdoor holiday lights, of course, that Christmas of 1943 for the third year in a row. Those with a son or a brother or a cousin or a friend were getting misty-eyed every time they heard a snatch of Crosby singing, "I'll be home for Christmas, if only in my dreams." But that Christmas, everyone knew the long-awaited second front, the invasion of Europe, would probably take place that spring. Every day brought stories of new casualties among the soldiers slogging their way up the Italian peninsula, Marines wading through blood on Pacific islands with unpronounceable names, sailors blown apart by torpedoes and raked by machine-gun fire.

The battle to pass the GI Bill wouldn't be bloody in a physical sense; no one died, no one was injured. Nor did anyone who fought in this all-important home-front battle suffer politically because of his or her vote on the bill. By the same measure, they didn't get any credit either. Clark was defeated for reelection that November of 1944, not only by internationalists who couldn't forgive his isolationism but also by CIO members, many of whose sons would be among the principal beneficiaries of the bill. Passing the GI Bill was an intensely fought battle, nevertheless, one whose outcome was in doubt right to the last moment; a battle that aroused intense passions, exemplified by statements from two members of Congress, both, coincidentally, Republicans.

"Here we are a nation with wealth beyond the dreams of Midas," said Representative Thomas Rolph of California. "Here we are appropriating billions upon billions for people of other lands, still we are hesitating about our own."

"Have we gone completely crazy?" demanded Representative Dewey Short of Missouri. "Have we lost all sense of proportion? Who will have to pay this bill? You who think you are going to bribe the veterans and buy his vote, you who think you can win his support by coddling him and being a sob sister with a lot of silly, slushy, sentimentality are going to have a sad awakening."

In the end, the GI Bill passed and "eclipsed anything envisioned during the New Deal," as Geoffrey Perrett noted in just a few paragraphs of the 512-page *Days of Sadness, Years of Triumph,* the only full-scale social history of World War II: "What planning there was for the post-war world took for its object not something avowedly aimed at social welfare but the provision of veterans benefits for 16,000,000 veterans and their families. It was not thought of as a program of social welfare in the traditional mold. . . . The administration was not entirely blind to the potential of veterans benefits in advancing social welfare. Some of Roosevelt's staff tried to link the benefits to the entire nation. But Roosevelt would not fight for them. A handful of New Dealers fought against the principle of veterans' exclusiveness, without the support of the White House. The Legion was therefore under no serious pressure to compromise, and its bill passed almost intact. Liberals mourned it as a great opportunity lost."[49]

If they did, they did so quietly. Conservatives, on the other hand, have never taken credit for the bill, despite the fact it was, as Perrett observed, a product of a conservative revival. Both they and historians have also missed the opportunity it presents to see what government can do successfully. "The essence of the American experiment . . . would be discovered neither by the tough-minded people who live by the numbers nor the tender-minded who live by ideology," James MacGregor Burns has written in *The Crosswinds of Freedom,* "but rather by people who make their ideals explicit, are willing to test them out and experiment with them constantly."[50]

This experiment has remained as undiscovered as it was accidental.

Any arguments about the origins, liberal or conservative, of the GI Bill, of course, are irrelevant to most Americans. "To Americans the test of almost everything is how it works, not whether is it old, or divine or popular," Perrett wrote. "If they had the social substance, who cared about ideological dressing?"

But they are missing out on a story that does, incidentally, contain an ideological message: Sometimes democracy does work, but it may take the damndest people and the strangest turns of events to do so.

CHAPTER 4

SHOWDOWN ON
PENNSYLVANIA AVENUE

W ASHINGTON in the winter of 1944 was gripped by what amounted to a constitutional crisis. FDR's veto of a budget bill, accompanied by an insulting message, provoked a Senate rebellion led by Senator Alben Barkley, the Democratic majority leader, and an overturn of the veto. That produced headlines. So did other clashes between the administration and Congress over civil rights, a federal ballot for the military, and revelations of war profiteering. Bureaucrats and political appointees who were concealing information also aroused congressional ire. So did a proposal by FDR to conscript everyone into national service. In addition, FDR's call for a bill of economic rights in his State of the Union address that January was widely debated—and mocked. Big business and labor and their political allies were snarling at each other while small business was bewailing massive bankruptcies amid the prosperity of war. Amid all this turmoil, the press largely ignored the passage of the GI Bill. But it would hold the key to resolving the concerns preoccupying people in power at the time.

"It has been suggested by some," FDR had written in rejecting the tax bill, "that I should give my approval of this bill on the ground that having asked Congress for a loaf of bread to take care of this war for the sake of this and succeeding generations, I should be content with a small piece of crust. I might have done so if I had not noted that the small piece of crust had so many extraneous and inedible materials." FDR went on to describe the bill as having been written "for the greedy, not the needy."

Senator Barkley of Kentucky, who served in the House and Senate for thirty-two years, refuted FDR's tax veto message point by point, characterizing it as "a calculated and deliberate assault" on Congress. He then urged his fellow members to override it if they had "any self-respect left" and resigned as majority leader. His fellow Democrats unanimously reelected him before repassing the tax bill over the veto, 72–14. It was one of only nine times Congress repudiated FDR's 635 vetoes. Only one other president, Grover Cleveland, was in the same league with FDR in percentage of vetoes that stood; only 7 of his 584 vetoes were overridden.[1]

The overturn of FDR's veto on the budget bill in February 1944 meant the coalition of conservative Democrats and Republicans, formed in the aftermath of the court-packing battle, had become powerful enough to draw an unassailable line in front of the Capitol. FDR might still be the nation's undisputed political leader in the hearts of his countrymen, but not in the minds of a Congress reasserting its coequal power under the Constitution. Senator Elbert Thomas, the chairman of the Education and Labor Committee who was trying to shepherd the education provisions of the administration's readjustment plans for veterans through Congress, told Alan Drury later: "By his one-vote margin in the 1937 contest when he [Barkley] was first elected majority leader, the impression was given, and it has been the impression ever since, that he spoke to us for the President. Now that he has been unanimously elected, he speaks for us to the President."[2]

That was the atmosphere in which the GI Bill was wending its way through committee, having been introduced the month before. The New Deal and all its works had become anathema to the vast majority of members. Even FDR's few stalwart defenders, such as Senator Claude Pepper, had shown some suspicion about the administration's education plans for GIs. The overall feeling was perhaps best expressed by Senator Kenneth Wherry (R-Nebraska): "The New Deal and this Administration is having its wings clipped and from now on you can expect Congress to continue the clipping. I do think we have had quite an awakening and I think that the Senate realizes that we must cause a halt to government by Executive order."[3] Drury thought much more than a contest of will between political leaders was involved. He feared the stakes were nothing less than the future of the republic. "In the very nature of free government, the President in the long run *cannot* [emphasis Drury's] win over Congress," Drury wrote on February 26, a few days after Barkley's resignation. Congress should give the president as much help and cooperation as possible in addressing the country's problems, Drury felt. "But when the time comes—as Congress instinctively felt this week that it had—when he attempts to turn that power back upon its creators and use it deliberately to weaken Congress, then Congress has no higher duty than to crush the attempt," he wrote. "And this regardless of who, saint or sinner, sits at the other end of Pennsylvania Avenue."[4]

The man who sat at the other end of Pennsylvania was still regarded as a saint by most Americans, but even many of them were beginning to suspect he might be succumbing to the arrogance of being in office too long. On January 11, 1944, as the GI Bill was being introduced in Congress, FDR delivered the State of the Union address, in which he said, "If ever there was a time to subordinate individual or group selfishness to the national good, that time is now." He then proposed a massive tax increase, renegotiation of war contracts, a cost-of-food law, and, most radically, national service for everyone. A national service law would conscript every civilian of working age into federal service. Everyone would become an employee—and ward—of the government. In this debate over individual freedom and the need to secure national, and social, objectives, Eleanor Roosevelt had been advocating national service for some time, along with the military. "I've come to one very clear decision," she announced after a March 1942 White House conference on manpower needs, "namely that all of us—men in the services and women at home—should be drafted and told what is the job we are to do. So long as we are left to volunteer we are bound to waste our capacities and do things that are not necessary."

Opposition to national service, particularly conscription of women, came from both ends of the political spectrum. Both liberals and conservatives compared the proposal to Nazi forced-labor methods. But the military, as well as Mrs. Roosevelt, argued conscription was necessary to effectively marshal the nation's workforce of more than sixty million employed in fifteen hundred trades and occupations. Earlier in the war, FDR had instinctively shied away from conscription, preferring instead to nationalize the jointly administered state-federal Employment Service. That enabled war industries to recruit all over the country and gave skilled workers, with draft exemptions, freedom to work where they chose. Indeed, the war created the greatest internal migration in history as more than fifteen million Americans moved. Just as in World War I, the great automobile, steel, and food factories of Chicago, Detroit, and Cleveland drew millions from the south, but other millions headed west for the airplane factories of California, Washington State, and Oregon. The population of the three western states increased 34 percent during the war years, with almost two million settling in California alone.

By the fall of 1943, booming production lines were making as many tanks in a month, four thousand, as Germany did in a year. But FDR had been converted to the military's and Eleanor's viewpoint that the best prescription for even greater productivity was more government. When he returned to Washington from his home in Hyde Park, New York, after Christmas, he told reporters at a press conference on December 28 that he no longer intended to refer to his administration as the New Deal. Asked why, he compared the United States to a sick patient who had been successfully treated by an internal medicine specialist, Dr. New Deal, from 1932 to 1941. "Those ills, that illness of 10 years ago, were remedied," the president said. "But after [the patient] became pretty well, he had a very bad accident. . . . Two years ago, on the 7th of December, he got into a pretty bad smashup. . . . Some people didn't even think he would live. So Dr. New Deal got his partner, who was an orthopedic surgeon, 'Dr. Win-the-War,' to take care of this fellow. And the result is that the patient is back on his feet. He has given up his crutches. He has begun to strike back—on the offensive."

Now, in a new role as "Dr. Win-the-War," FDR was calling for a much bigger federal government through massive new taxes and conscription of the entire working population. He balanced that by a call for a second bill of rights, an economic one. "This Republic had its beginning under the protection of certain inalienable political rights—among them the rights of free speech, free press, free worship, trial by jury, freedom from unreasonable searches and seizures," he said in his State of the Union address. "They are our rights to life and liberty." With the growth of the nation and economy, however, those political rights had proven "inadequate to assure us of equality in the pursuit of happiness. . . . True individual freedom cannot exist without economic security and independence."

Under FDR's new economic bill of rights, the government would provide every American with a good education; a job that paid well; sufficient food, clothing, and recreation; decent housing; affordable medical care; unemployment compensation in bad times, and economic security in old age. "All these rights were implicit in the program of the New Deal," Doris Kearns Goodwin wrote in *No Ordinary Time, Franklin and Eleanor Roosevelt: The Homefront in World War II.* Now, FDR was making economic rights explicit, linking them to what Kearns Goodwin called "the negative liberty from government achieved in the old Bill of Rights to the positive liberty through government to be achieved through the New Bill of Rights." She quoted James MacGregor Burns as observing FDR had for the first time in American politics erased "the fatal and false dichotomy—liberty vs. security, freedom against equality—which had deranged American social thought and crippled the nation's capacity to subdue depression and poverty." FDR was declaring "individual political liberty and collective welfare were not only compatible, but they were mutually fortifying."

There was a price—an enormous one—attached to the second bill of rights, which had been initially proposed by the National Resources Planning Board (NRPB) several years before. The budget for fiscal 1944–45 sent by FDR to Congress called for $10.5 billion. The total budget Congress sent back raised only $2 billion in revenues, less than one fifth what FDR had asked. The $8 billion difference between what FDR wanted and Congress was willing to appropriate was staggering, a little more than half the total of $14 billion eventually spent on the World War II GI Bill. But that was only one measure of the chasm between the president and Congress. What was really exercising Congress during the period wasn't just the tax bill, Barkley's resignation, or the GI Bill. Congress felt the executive branch was out of control and dictating its own agenda, contemptuously ignoring the legislative branch of government. Specifically, the members were concerned about the refusal of executive branch agencies to supply information to Congress—as they pursued their own bureaucratic and "social uplift" goals. Congress was determined to reassert its authority and, in the process, roll back much of the centralized power ceded to the executive branch during FDR's first three terms. The upshot was, as Drury wrote, "the President's dander is up [and] Congress is in no mood to take it sitting down either."[5] Drury foresaw a constitutional smashup and predicted, "Congress will win. So long as it holds the purse, it always has one last recourse: it can cut off the funds and in that manner cripple the office." The result would be disastrous for FDR and the presidency rather than Congress, Drury felt. He predicted when FDR "finally leaves the White House the Presidency will have been reduced nearer impotency than it has been in years." As soon as the war ended, he feared, "Congress will begin systematically stripping the Presidency of one power or another until only the irreducible minimum remains."[6]

That was the political and social context in which Congress was considering the GI Bill, one in which any proposal advancing a big-government agenda and the bureaucracy that would inevitably accompany it would be suspect, if not rejected out of hand.

The fury aroused in congressional breasts by bureaucracy came in two varieties. One was obfuscation on the part of career civil servants, who didn't really testify before Congress, but rather "squirmed and evaded and procrastinated and equivocated and qualified and sidestepped and weaseled," Drury observed.[7] The second variety of bureaucratic weaseling came from dollar-a-year men from industry whose professional experience was made available to the government out of ostensibly patriotic but all-too-often profiteering motives. Senator Truman had been investigating the dollar-a-year men's exploitation of self-interest in the name of what he scornfully referred to as their "righteous integrity." The investigation was making him a national figure, a potential candidate for vice president. The object of Truman's ire and that of most members of Congress, in addition to excessive profits, was favoritism, the belief that the dollar-a-year men were benefiting big producers at the expense of small ones. The situation illustrated "the dilemma of democracy in wartime," Drury thought. If the well-intentioned who have no business experience are put in charge, chaos results. But using experts inevitably produces dirty work at the crossroads. The Truman Committee, he thought, would perhaps put "enough fingers in the dike to keep the flood in check, but there will apparently never be any lasting correction while the war is on."[8]

Congress was also preoccupied at the time with bills providing federal voting ballots for GIs and outlawing the poll tax. The Republicans opposed a federal ballot for troops; they feared troops would be marched to the polls and effectively intimidated into voting for their commander in chief. Ultimately the Democrats in Congress prevailed, but FDR allowed the bill to become law without his signature. In fact, only 111,000 military personnel used the federal ballot. Four million military people applied for and used state ballots. Other bills attempting to strike down the poll taxes in the South, which effectively disenfranchised blacks as well as many poor whites, were vehemently opposed by southern members of Congress, led by Representative Rankin and Senator James O. Eastland, also of Mississippi. The anti–poll tax legislation, sponsored by Republicans, then the party of civil rights but supported, sometimes secretly, by northern Democrats, had obvious fairness on its side, but was barred by the Constitution, which vested qualifications for voting in the states. The Supreme Court's constitutional "one man, one vote" decision a generation later would be needed to pave the way for the Voting Rights Act of 1964, which would abolish the poll tax. In the meantime, northern and southern Democrats were hopelessly divided— and embarrassed—on the issue of race, a breach the GI Bill would slowly begin to bridge.

But in 1944, Drury saw only the impact the GI Bill might have on Senator Clark's reelection chances. On March 17, 1944, St. Patrick's Day, Drury reported that Clark had gotten the legislation approved by the Finance Committee and planned to bring it to the Senate floor the following week. Drury noted Clark would introduce the bill, not only for himself, but for "as many as can get on board. The number to date is 80. It includes everything but the kitchen sink, and its effects on the portly B.C.'s chances for re-election is not overlooked on the Hill." Drury suspected Clark would lose, but noted Truman was supporting him and thought he could win.[9] While the election results would be another matter, there was no fight in the Senate over the GI Bill when it was brought to the floor for a vote. It sailed through with the only complaints registered by senators who, for one reason or another, weren't able to sign up as cosponsors.

Without anyone realizing it, the bill addressed the conflict between Congress and the White House. That was the clash between members of Congress, still faithful to the old idea of the supremacy of the individual, and an administration that, more and more, felt the government, in Mrs. Roosevelt's phrase, was better qualified to determine "the job we are to do." The combination of fairness and independence, the idea that people should be treated on their merits and encouraged to go as far as their talents allowed as individuals, not as members of classes or races, was becoming a political idea whose time had come. There was little difference between being a conscript and a convict, Speaker Clark said during World War I. Faced with FDR's proposal for national service, almost everyone would agree with him a quarter century later. The American Legion effectively argued for individual freedom in asserting that veterans should be aided in reaching that place, position, or status that they had normally expected to reach and probably would have achieved, had their war service not interrupted their careers. At the same time, if only as an unintended consequence, with black veterans entitled to the same benefits as whites, members of both races would be treated equally by their government for the first time.

Another argument used to promote the GI Bill was fear, fear of another depression, fear of what might happen to the country if the twelve million still serving in 1944 were dumped on an economy potentially on the edge of bankruptcy when the mills of war stopped grinding. Veterans "will be a potent force for good or evil in the years to come," National Commander Atherton said during a radio address on May 2. "They can make our country or break it. They can restore our democracy or scrap it." Eleanor Roosevelt had also foreseen the potential threat. As early as April 1942, she warned that veterans could "create a dangerous pressure group in our midst." The nation would have to "adjust our economic system so that opportunity is open to them, [or] we may reap the whirlwind," she said. Both ends of the political spectrum expressed such fears. Unless returning veterans could find jobs, the country could become "a dictatorship," Representative Maury Maverick, a liberal Democrat from Texas, said. If veterans were forced to beg, Representative Fish of New York, FDR's conservative Republican representative from Hyde Park, told his House colleagues, "I believe we would have chaotic and revolutionary conditions in America."[10] But not everyone was eager to make concessions to the veterans' situation. A union official was prescient enough to foresee all the arguments would be heard again, in a slightly different context. The only basic change would be in substituting the word "black" for "veteran." "If we give special status to the veterans today," said Robert J. Watt, international representative of the AFL in 1945, "we will be faced with the problem of special consideration for minority groups tomorrow."[11]

Congress also feared the power of big labor in addition to that of the executive branch and big business and its dollar-a-year men. No labor leader worried Congress more than Sidney Hillman of the Garment Workers Union, John L. Lewis's old colleague. Hillman, who came to testify before the Senate Campaign Expenditures Commit-

tee on June 13, 1944, was also head of the CIO's political action committee, the nation's first special interest group to systematically support candidates with both money and workers. Hillman, described by
Drury as having "a heavy accent that betrays his Russian birth," was
the target of Senator Joseph H. Ball (R-Minnesota), who accused the
CIO committee of engaging in illegal political action. Hillman's
lawyer argued that the committee's endorsements of FDR were
entirely legal, since the presidential campaign hadn't begun. The committee was only urging FDR to make himself available for the nomination. Presumably, Drury observed sardonically, the posters and
publications produced by the committee were just helping FDR with
the difficult task of making up his mind.[12]

Money was another major matter of concern. Everyone, except of
course those in the military, was making money. However, the division of what was increasingly being thought of as the spoils of war
was uneven, and labor and management were perhaps even more
unhappy with one another than they had been during the '30s. Big
business was doing very well indeed, and so was big labor, although
not enough to satisfy its members. Small business was very unhappy
and with good reason. Thanks largely to the influence of the dollar-a-
year men, two thirds of all wartime contracts had gone to no more
than one hundred firms. Ten corporations got almost one third of
government contracts; corporate profits rose from $6.4 billion in 1940
to $10.8 billion in 1944; and corporate assets almost doubled to $100
billion in the same period. During the same time, almost a half-
million small businesses went bankrupt. The unions, however, profited from more dues as membership almost doubled, from nine
million in 1940 to nearly fifteen million in 1945. The National War
Labor Board (NWLB) had helped unions build membership rolls by
maintaining a membership formula that supported closed shops. If a
union negotiated a closed-shop agreement, workers who didn't want
to participate had only fifteen days in which they could refuse union
membership and still keep their jobs. After that, they would have to
pay union dues for the rest of the contract. But individual workers
didn't benefit that much financially from union membership. Wages
rose only 15 percent during the war under the so-called Little Steel
formula, barely enough to keep up with inflation. The discontents of
the rank and file, working eleven- or twelve-hour days while living
in shacks and trailers and commuting to work several hours, were
aggravated by militant grassroots leaders. National union leaders

had difficulty in controlling the militants, and more than thirty-seven hundred work stoppages occurred in 1943 alone and more in 1944, despite a no-strike pledge signed by both the AFL and the CIO unions. Philip Murray, president of the CIO, was stating the obvious when he observed workers were showing "an attitude of rebellion."

While every special interest group was struggling with every other special interest group for advantage at home, those fighting in the war were getting fed up. Lewis, in particular, aroused their ire. He had resigned the presidency of the CIO in 1940, after turning violently against FDR and toward Wendell Willkie, the Republican candidate, over intervention in the war. After Pearl Harbor, Lewis pledged support for the war effort, but militant rank-and-file miners staged walkouts in January 1943 demanding a $2 per day pay increase. Lewis negotiated with the mine owners while ignoring FDR's threats to draft miners up to the age of sixty-five; Lewis himself was sixty-three. An agreement signed in November 1943 provided only a $2 per week increase, "but Lewis and his union had demonstrated that he and his union were prepared to arouse the public's wrath if necessary to make the Little Steel formula bend a little," historian Burns wrote.[13] The service newspaper, *Stars and Stripes,* responded by declaring, "Speaking for the soldiers, John Lewis, damn your coal black soul."[14]

Relations, already strained between big and small business, labor-management and government, Congress and the presidency, could come unraveled when the veterans came marching home. And at that point no one could really be said to speak for them, except, perhaps, the veterans' organizations. No one knew what the veterans would want when they came back home, but it was evident that they could become a powerful force, one used as chips in a game played by business, labor, and government with the cards being dealt by politicians exploiting everyone. Somehow a new game, not just a new deal, was needed. Reshuffling the cards wasn't going to be enough, but what *would* be enough wasn't clear.

The atmosphere in which the administration's legislative proposals for veterans were being considered in Congress was getting more and more bitter. A bill giving $1.3 billion to the United Nations Relief and Rehabilitation Administration (UNRRA) had passed the House in the spring of 1943 at the same time the House Military Affairs Committee slashed $1 billion out of a Senate-approved mustering-out bill. One member of Congress, Representative Lyle Boren, a Democrat from Oklahoma, accused the administration of conspiring to keep the mustering-out pay low so the UNRRA proposal would seem affordable.[15] That suspicion was undoubtedly shared by Hearst, one of the reasons he supported the GI Bill.

A major turf battle was also shaping up over who would administer the educational provisions of whatever veterans' legislation emerged from committee. The administration's bill was strongly supported by Senator Thomas, the chairman of the Senate education committee. But the committee's first hearings were marked primarily by admissions that the Veterans Administration and the U.S. Office of Education were battling over who would administer the program.[16] Just the prospect of placing the Office of Education in charge of a program for veterans would, as historian Ross acknowledged, "wave a red flag in front before an easily enraged bull. The vociferous champions of veterans organizations would bellow at any attempt to give a bureaucratic New Deal agency responsibility over veterans." Indeed, the executive branch planners had tried to avoid the issue. The administration bill drafted under the direction of Judge Samuel I. Rosenman, special counsel to the president and one of his chief speechwriters, omitted any specific reference to any agency. Instead, all administrative authority was vested in the president under the assumption that doing so would "remove any basis for jurisdictional disputes at this time," according to a memo to Rosenman from Philip Handler, the attorney who wrote the first draft.[17]

There was, however, yet another problem with the educational provisions, one symptomatic of the administration's passion for planning. The administration's proposal submitted to Senator Thomas's committee tried to link educational opportunity for veterans with a national employment policy. Under the proposal, aid to veterans was restricted to one year of study with the exception of "persons of exceptional ability or skill." They, and only they, could get an additional three years' assistance. But their selection would be predicated on filling shortages in "technical and professional occupations in which there are likely to be shortages of adequately trained personnel." Moreover, the total number of servicemen eligible for supplemental benefits would be allotted to the states in proportion to the states' contribution of military personnel to the war effort. That cumbersome mechanism irritated even such a staunch New Dealer as Claude Pepper, who objected at the initial education committee hearings in December 1943 both to the state quota system and to the limits on the number of veterans eligible for educational benefits.

At the same time, institutional higher education saw an opportunity to deal itself into the political game with the other big players—industry, labor, and government. Virtually every educational association testified at the December hearings, ranging from the National Education Association to the National Council of Technical Colleges. All wanted to see authority over the program vested in the Office of Education. Dr. George Zook, the president of the American Council on Education (ACE) representing college presidents, took issue with the administration on one significant point, however. He wanted to eliminate the state quota system as well as the mechanism for determining availability of employment opportunities. That would greatly increase the number of potential students. At the same time, Zook made it very clear the educational institutions should select the students, under regulations promulgated by the Office of Education with guidance from an advisory committee made up of representatives of educational institutions and governmental agencies. His suggestions were based on an ACE committee recommendation that had earlier advised the government planners—and protected the institutions' interest. James Conant was also making his concerns about "the least capable among the new generation . . . flooding" the college campus through his annual report as president of Harvard.[18] In time, Conant's name would be invoked by most of the major educational institutions in an effort to make sure the bill's benefits could be used only at state-certified institutions, excluding many historically black, church-related, and cooperative colleges.

That January, the Legion was emerging as the prime player in the battle over veterans' benefits as the GI Bill, the Servicemen's Readjustment Act of 1944, superseded the administration proposal. The Legion's role, however, was contested at every juncture, partially because the policies it was advocating were unfamiliar to most of the other players. Indeed, the sources of the ideas that went into the bill, other than the World War I Wisconsin education program and a housing program for veterans in California, remain essentially undocumented. Twenty-five years after the passage of the bill, Commander Atherton said in a letter than the material the G.I. Bill committee and he selected to include in the bill came largely from "the best rehabilitation ideas and procedures developed between 1918 and 1943. . . . The contents were not new. They were born of many decades of sacrifice, suffering, trial and error."[19] But he didn't go into more detail than that. Old—or revolutionary—as the ideas were, what was perhaps the most remarkable about them was that they were packaged and presented to Congress as an omnibus measure, so extensive and sweeping that it can be compared only to Lyndon Johnson's Great Society and civil rights legislation. Of course, the great difference was the GI Bill vested control directly in the hands of individuals rather than new federally sponsored community action programs established to supplement—and supplant—old-line state and local ones.

The basic facts about who participated in the development of the bill are known, but details about what went into the deliberations are sketchy. The American Legion committee appointed by Atherton on November 30, 1943, met between December 15 and December 31, over the Christmas holidays, with representatives of interested organizations. A rough sketch was received by Edward E. Odum, the Veterans Administration solicitor, on December 31. The committee was headed by Stelle, the former governor of Illinois, with Robert Sisson of Little Rock, Arkansas, chairman of the Legion's national rehabilitation committee, as the executive director. The members were Colmery; Sam Rorex, the U.S. attorney in Arkansas; W. B. Waldrip, a Detroit banker; R. M. McCurdy, assistant city manager of Pasadena, California, who was described by Camelon as having "in his own person defied the crippling effects of combat injury"; Maurice F. Devine of Manchester, New Hampshire, chairman of the national legislative committee; and Lawrence J. Fenlon of Chicago, chairman of the national employment committee. The full-time staff employees were Francis J. Sullivan, the acting legislative director; T. O. Kraabel, the national rehabilitation director; Bruce Stubblefield, executive secretary of the rehabilitation staff; Carl Brown, chief of claims in Washington; and Jack Cejnar, the acting national publicity officer. Sullivan and Cejnar were considered acting because they were replacing men in the service.[20]

"It was not a hastily prepared measure," Camelon wrote, although it was obviously put together in a very short time. "Before the educational provisions were written," he noted, "the Legion had conferred with representatives of the Association of Land Grant Colleges, the National Education Association and the American Council on Education." The provisions for loans for homes and businesses were drafted by McCurdy, the assistant city manager of Pasadena, in consultation with the Federal Housing Administration (FHA) as well as private banking interests. Although the mortgage program was largely based on FHA methods and experience, the agency apparently made no effort to retain control over it, ceding authority to the VA without protest. The details of what would become known as the 52-20 Club were worked out with Stan Rector, chairman of the legislative committee of the Interstate Conference of Employment Agencies, representing the states, and Bob Leach, president of Unemployment Benefit Advisors, an unofficial group associated with both the state agencies and private employers. Somehow, within the limited time available, the major elements of the bill—unemployment compensation, home ownership, job placement, and educational opportunities— were written to conform with existing state and federal systems and laws. The committee members were particularly concerned that "the veterans should not become entangled in new, costly and complicated federal bureaucracies and agencies," Camelon wrote. An enormous mass of material was assembled, analyzed, and integrated into a systematic program during that one month. Then the bill had to be written in the appropriate legal language.

"It was Henry Colmery, in the end, who did the seemingly superhuman task of taking the material selected by the committee, and drafting in the form of the bill," Camelon wrote. "As John Stelle said: 'Harry Colmery jelled all our ideas into words.'" Writing the bill, as Colmery did in Suite 570 of the Mayflower Hotel, was the first essential step toward passage. "No one alive knows how long it took him to write—in longhand and on hotel stationery—the first draft of what would be introduced as the Servicemen's Adjustment Act of 1944," *The American Legion Magazine* of June 1984 reported. That draft was finished January 6, according to Camelon; the one received by Odum was apparently a rough sketch. Colmery's mathematical and grammatical skills were well known long before he sat down to write the bill. Those skills "pretty well shaped his ability to arrange complicated masses of detail and dovetail them into a model of preparedness in the face of unexpected twistings and turnings," according to Gardiner, who profiled Colmery.

It would take more than grammatical and mathematical skills to navigate the twistings and turnings of the next half-dozen months. First, the formally titled Servicemen's Adjustment Act of 1944 had to be given another name, one that would not only be immediately recognizable but one that, its authors hoped, would be its own endorsement, a phrase catchy enough to grab public attention. Public attention, at the time, was focused almost exclusively on the opening of the second front, the long-awaited and demanded invasion of

Hitler's Fortress Europe from England via Normandy. The inspiration needed to focus attention on the home front came from Cejnar, an ex-newspaperman. Reading over what Colmery had written, Cejnar, either consciously or unconsciously, borrowed from FDR's evocation of an economic bill of rights. "It's a bill of rights," he said. "That's it, a Bill of Rights for GI Joe and Jane," quickly shortened to the GI Bill of Rights and later to the GI Bill.

The name was "something close to genius," as Camelon recalled. "It was short, punchy, easily grasped. It told the whole story—and it became a fighting slogan from coast to coast." Colmery, having written the basic bill, then provided the words with which the draft was sent marching into Congress. The statement that accompanied the presentation to Congress read:

> The American Legion proposed this bill first because we believed it to be the duty, the responsibility and the desire of our grateful people to see to it that those who served actively in the armed services in this war not only should not be penalized as a result of their war service, but also that upon their return, they should be aided in reaching that position which they might normally have expected had the war not interrupted their careers.
>
> And second, we urge its enactment as sound national policy, for the good of the nation.

"Opportunity was to be the keynote of the G.I. Bill," Camelon observed. "This was to be no 'treasury raid' on behalf of veterans." The phrase, of course, had been used to criticize the excesses associated with the Civil War pension program, which, in turn, was largely responsible for the niggardly assistance given World War I veterans. The use of the phrase "treasury raid," if nothing else, reflected both an awareness of past abuses and the value of helping veterans immediately after they returned from war, not decades later when their earning capacity was diminished, if not gone. The World War I veterans who put together the GI Bill for their children, nephews, and nieces may not have read history, but their collective memory of "many decades of sacrifice, suffering, trial and error" kept them from repeating history.

The bill was formally announced at a press conference held on January 8, 1944, at which Colmery said: "The burden of war falls on the citizen soldier who has gone forth, overnight, to become the armored hope of humanity." In return, these citizen-soldiers should be given an opportunity for a normal civilian life comparable to that enjoyed by those who had stayed at home. "Never again," Colmery said, "do we want to see the honor and glory of our nation fade to the extent that her men of arms, with despondent heart and palsied limb, totter from door to door, bowing their souls to the frozen bosom of reluctant charity." The Legion knew you couldn't eat medals and ribbons.

The New York Times story the day after the press conference, headlined "Legion Bill Asks Wide Veteran Aid," quoted Rankin as saying the bill's first objective was to "remedy chaotic conditions of bureaucracy and red tape under which divided authority and responsibility has already victimized thousands of already discharged veterans." Five specific provisions were cited: (1) mustering-out pay; (2) designation of the VA as a vital war agency; (3) unemployment compensation; (4) education allowances plus all educational expenses in established colleges and universities for up to four years; and (5) "adequate provision" for handicapped veterans. Five senators were announced as sponsors: Clark of Missouri; David I. Walsh, Democrat of Massachusetts; Scott W. Lucas, Democrat of Illinois; Hattie W. Caraway, Democrat of Arkansas; and Henry Cabot Lodge, Republican of Massachusetts. In the House, in addition to Rankin and Rogers, Representative Ploeser, a Republican from Missouri, was also named as a cosponsor.[21] Ploeser was the member of the House Military Committee who had defied May and submitted a $500 mustering-out pay bill after bringing his colleagues' attention to the plight of Troy Lucas, May's constituent, in a floor speech.

Even with a fighting slogan and cosponsors in both the House and Senate, any bill crossing so many turf lines, legislative and institutional, faced enormous hurdles on Capitol Hill. Camelon summed up the conventional wisdom the bill's proponents had to contend with: "'No such all-inclusive omnibus bill has ever passed Congress,' the Legion was told. 'Your bill will be lost in committee jealousies and jurisdictional strife. Tear it apart—submit it piece by piece, and you'll have a better chance of getting it through.'" The assessment— if not the advice—was correct. Normally, the education provisions should have gone to the House Committee on Education; home, farm, and business loans to the House Banking and Currency Committee (the significance of guaranteed home and business loans was apparently so little recognized, they were omitted in *The New York Times*'s news story); unemployment compensation to the Ways and Means

Committee; and the sections providing for review of discharges to the Military and Naval Affairs Committees. But the Legion had an unassailable answer to the parliamentary objections: "Every veteran was a single, living being," as Camelon wrote. "You couldn't tear him up and scatter him about Washington. And to permit a kaleidoscope of conflicting and confusing government bureaus to administer to his problems would have only repeated the fiasco that followed World War I."

Events were on the Legion's side. The administration's planning and legislative efforts were about to collapse. The Federal Security Agency (FSA), which had been responsible for the earlier vocational rehabilitation debacle, announced on January 17 that it was revising the administration bill under consideration in the Senate Education Committee. The FSA came up with a substitute proposal four days later, but by that time, only the Legion bill was receiving serious attention. Many hurdles loomed ahead, however, calling for the deployment of extraordinary political, legislative, media, and diplomatic talents. By the time the bill passed, Frank Sullivan, the Legion's chief lobbyist, could say, without the usual Washington hyperbole, "It's a wonder that the State Department didn't grab us all for their top-notch diplomats."[22]

Indeed, the Legion played a very astute diplomatic game, particularly with FDR. The Legion maintained that its action merely complemented the administration's own program. As it turned out, historian Ross observed, "the Administration did permit the Legion to carry the ball. Roosevelt did not attempt to wrest the banner from the veterans' organizations; federal agencies, moreover, played only a minor role."[23] It would be more accurate to say FDR and the administration didn't have much choice. Its own proposals were being ignored, and FDR, having endured a bruising defeat at the hands of Congress over the budget, did not want any disputes with representatives of the millions of American servicemen and women risking their lives daily in combat.

With casualty lists high and bound to get higher, it would have been easy for the Legion to raise the issue of FDR breaking his promise not to enter the war. In 1940, five days before his reelection to an unprecedented third term, FDR had told an audience in Boston, "And while I am talking to you fathers and mothers, I give you one more assurance. I have said this before and I will say it again and again and again. Your boys are not going to be sent into any foreign wars." The promise was protested at the time by Sam Rosenman, who later supervised the drafting of the administration's veterans' legislation. Although similar language appeared in the Democratic Party platform, there it contained a disclaimer: "except in the event of attack," as Rosenman pointed out. But the Legion wasn't interested in political debates. It was interested in getting the GI Bill passed by Congress and signed by FDR. Moreover, as the nation's wartime leader, FDR was still highly popular despite his clashes with Congress. Under the circumstances, prudence dictated political elbowing be eschewed in favor of bowing, and even Hearst was apparently dissuaded from rubbing old sores in public.

Indeed, the first parliamentary move made by Representative Rankin in Congress was procedural. On January 10, six new veterans' benefits bills were introduced into Congress, and the mustering-out pay bill was scheduled to be reported out of May's Military Affairs Committee the next day. The New York Times observed a distinct change of emphasis, if not mind, among members of Congress. "While committee members had been inclined to proceed cautiously in order to give full consideration to all proposals," The Times reported, "they were presumably prepared to act now as a result of urgings by Speaker Sam Rayburn and Majority Leader McCormack who pledged themselves just before the Christmas recess to bring legislation to the floor by Jan. 15." Rankin had introduced the Legion bill "in a skeleton form with provisions applying only to strengthening of the veterans' bureau in a parliamentary move," The Times reported. The move took the bill out of May's committee and put it into Rankin's. Rankin said other provisions would be added to the Legion bill at hearings the next day at which witnesses for the Legion and the Veterans of Foreign Wars would testify.[24]

Only Representative Graham A. Barden (D-North Carolina), the chairman of the Education and Labor Committee, which was still considering the original administration proposal, tried to object. "Even then his objection wasn't so much to the House Committee on Veterans Legislation taking jurisdiction," Camelon commented rather disingenuously, "as to an honest belief that the education provisions of a bill proposed by his committee were superior." Those provisions would, of course, have placed the Office of Education, rather than the Veterans Administration, in charge of the educational portions of the bill. Barden would later lead a remarkably long and vigorous debate on the House floor over that proviso—the next-to-last crisis the bill would weather on the way to passage. At this point, however, disagreement among members of Congress was muted, which was fortunate because war was about to break out among the veterans' organizations.

Other veterans' groups became far greater obstacles to the passage of the GI Bill than anyone or any group in the government. The opening gun was heard on January 12, the first day of hearings on the bonus bill in Mays's committee, when Omar B. Ketchum, the legislative director of the VFW, testified. Instead of focusing on the GI Bill before Rankin's Veterans Committee, he directed his comments to the issue of mustering-out pay, which was still under separate consideration in May's Military Affairs Committee. He complained, reported *The New York Times,* that the rates of mustering-out pay in the American Legion's omnibus bill were too high. He suggested a maximum $100 to $200 as reasonable. Then, Ketchum warned against "an excess of zeal" on behalf of the servicemen. "Do not think in terms of mustering-out pay," he advised, "if you are thinking of helping a man to get re-established in civilian life." Mustering-out pay, he suggested, would only cover a veteran's immediate needs, buy him a suit of clothes and a pair of shoes. Ketchum had another idea. He advocated, instead of an education bill, a program of demobilization pay and deferred compensation similar to the deferred compensation for World War I veterans under the 1924 bonus law. Part of the money would be paid on discharge and the rest in monthly installments. Compensation would be calculated at a rate of $1 a day for service in the United States up to $800, and $1.50 for service overseas for a maximum of $1,200. On discharge, $200 for domestic and $400 for foreign service would be paid immediately. Such an arrangement, based on the World War I bonus concept, Ketchum argued, would be far more helpful in "assimilating men back into civilian life." Of course, at the same time, it wouldn't point them in the direction of educational opportunities.[25] That was, however, only the first salvo. A full barrage of objections from the other veterans' organizations would be shot off over the next several weeks.

In the meantime, the Legion's next step was entirely diplomatic, a visit to the White House. Commander Atherton spent forty-five minutes discussing the provisions of the GI Bill of Rights with President Roosevelt. Atherton was accompanied by Senators Bennett Champ Clark and Scott Lucas and John Stelle, chairman of the Legion committee that assembled the sections of the bill drafted by Colmery.

The New York Times said Atherton pointed out during the conference that some of the points in the president's recent speech on rehabilitation and the Legion program were running almost parallel. Clark was described as saying the president had "expressed himself in favor of the legislation although he did not comment directly on the omnibus bill."[26]

Although the meeting with Roosevelt went well, yet another conflict was brewing, this one with the military. Confrontational, rather than diplomatic, tactics would be called for. Earlier on the same day he visited Roosevelt, Atherton had testified before Senator Clark's committee on an issue that would spark a dramatic meeting between the Legion, led by Stelle, and the brass. Atherton's testimony honed in on the growing number of "neuropsychiatric cases," veterans whose discharge papers carried the notation "Discharged for nervous instability" or "Not mentally competent to serve." Such discharges, of course, could severely limit job possibilities, and the issue was one Clark, particularly, felt strongly about. He had said earlier he wanted engraved on his tombstone his vote against FDR's efforts to limit medical treatment for veterans with neuropsychiatric problems as well as tuberculosis.

Stelle, whom Camelon described as "the driver who led the fight for the bill's passage," had a personal interest in the issue. He had prompted the Legion to set up the committee that ended up drafting the GI Bill "after I received a letter from my son who'd been through the African and Sicilian campaigns," Stelle recalled for Camelon in 1949. "His letter was based upon what the men he knew over there were saying. He wrote all they wanted from their government was an opportunity to make good when they returned home for war, an opportunity to get education or training and to find work." Obviously, the opportunities available to any veteran whose discharge papers referred to "nervous instability" or mental incompetence would be severely limited. Yet combat veterans such as Stelle's son knew such disabilities were common.

The Legion also was concerned about the many soldiers and sailors being given less than honorable, or "administrative" or "blue," discharges for trivial or essentially unfair reasons. While the Legion was aware of thousands of such cases, the story of an apprentice seaman named Ray was cited as a classic example. Ray's parents were informed by official telegram from a rear admiral on October 14, 1942, that Ray had been wounded in action aboard the U.S.S. *Quincy*

on August 9, 1942, two months earlier. However, the letter from Rear
Adm. Randall Jacobs, the chief of naval personnel, concluded their
son's "immediate whereabouts have not been determined." On January 25, 1943—four months after the telegram—someone from the
U.S. Naval Hospital in San Diego wrote the distraught parents to tell
them Ray had been found. Actually, he had never been really lost. He
had been in the naval hospital since October 14, 1942, coincidentally
the same day the admiral's letter had been signed. The parents were
advised Ray had been under "treatment for a nervous disability." The
same letter said a medical survey board recommended him for a discharge January 14, 1943. Knowing his discharge was pending, Ray
had gone AWOL to see his folks back home. Caught for going AWOL,
on February 23, 1943, Ray was given a "general discharge" as an
"undesirable."

The parents protested to Mrs. Rogers, who, in turn, wrote to Admiral Jacobs on congressional stationary. Admiral Jacobs responded,
explaining the navy's position reasonably, logically, sensibly, and
patiently, as bureaucrats always do: "This man is not entitled to an
honorable discharge certificate, which is given [as] a testimonial to
fidelity and obedience. The bureau is without authority to alter its
records to show that [Ray] served honorably and was discharged with
honor." The Legion intervened and argued that if Ray had been a
deserter, he would have at least been given a trial. Moreover, even
a man court-martialed for striking an officer, even a man dishonor-
ably discharged, could appeal. The army, navy, and the air force, however, were determined to reserve the right to deny, by fiat and without
appeal, honorable discharges to veterans such as Ray and so testified
before Congress. The Legion insisted that an independent board be
established to review all discharges and also inserted a provision in
the GI Bill that anyone with a "blue" or "other than dishonorable"
discharge be entitled to GI Bill benefits.

On March 9, after representatives of the War and Navy Departments testified against these provisions, Stelle, who had been wounded
and gassed during World War I, asked for a meeting at Legion headquarters. He specified, in advance, that the generals and admirals
should come with authority to reach agreement on the discharge issue
as well as others in dispute. Fifteen beribboned officers showed up.
After six hours of discussion, the fifteen officers rose, saluted, and
said, "We'll have to consult our superiors." Stelle, whom Camelon

described as "a big, fighting, bulk of a man," exploded: "Our under-standing was that you would come here with authority to reach a deci-sion. If I had known you hadn't the authority to reach that decision, I wouldn't have wasted the time of my committee tonight. The provi-sions we have been discussing tonight are important to the men who have been fighting our battles. The American Legion proposes to see this bill passed—and passed as it stands." The generals and the admirals promptly agreed on behalf of the Army and Navy Depart-ments, and the proviso that benefits would apply to those discharged under conditions other than dishonorable was written into the bill.[27]

When the bill came up for debate in the Senate, however, Admiral Jacobs, the same man who had advised Ray's parents that the navy had misplaced their son before kicking him out of the service, made a determined personal effort to derail the provision. His objections were the subject of the only extended discussion during Senate de-bate before the bill passed unanimously on March 24. The admiral had sent a letter to Senator Walsh, one of the bill's original sponsors, in which he argued that the provision "might have a detrimental effect on morale by removing the incentive to maintain a good service record." Senator Clark's response on the Senate floor was blunt; per-haps he compared notes with Mrs. Rogers about the admiral. "In my opinion, they are some of the most stupid, short-sighted objections which could be raised," the senator said. He went on to point out that blue discharges were "contrary to what occurred in the last war" and argued further, "The Army is giving blue discharges, namely, dis-charges without honor, to those who have had no fault other than they have not shown sufficient aptitude to military service. I say that when the government drafts a man from civil life and puts him in the military service . . . and, thereafter, because the man does not show sufficient aptitude gives him a blue discharge, or a discharge without honor, that fact should not be permitted to prevent the man from receiving the benefits to which soldiers are generally entitled." He also observed that many of those given blue discharges were boys who had lied about their age. "If his father and mother come to the Army, and say, 'You cannot keep this boy, he lied about his age in order to get into the Army,' the commanding officer . . . is bound to give him what is called a blue discharge." Moreover, Clark said, in response to a direct question from Walsh, the bill's language made it very clear the VA had not only the discretion but the obligation to disqualify those with dishonorable discharges. Admiral Jacob's letter suggested his "sentiments," using Senator Walsh's word, were shared by the Army and Navy Departments. On the contrary, however, "representatives of the Navy and Army were present when the matter was discussed," Senator Clark replied, "and they seemed to agree totally with the terms of the amendment. I think probably the higher authorities have not consulted their representatives who were present at the committee meeting in order to find out exactly what the language means." The admiral could consider himself—and his objections—dismissed.[28]

Unfortunately, Admiral Jacobs wasn't alone in being confused about both language and politics. The fight—and infighting—over the bill was becoming Balkan in complexity. Opposing forces in the other veterans' organizations were still maneuvering for advantage. On January 12, when Ketchum of the VFW testified before the Veterans Committee, Representative May, who also served on that committee as well as on Military Affairs, expressed general agreement with Ketchum's proposal for deferred compensation. May doubted, however, such a measure was realistic since the Military Affairs Committee would be reporting out a bonus bill within a few days. "They're pushing us so hard to get some sort of a bill up for action that I don't see much opportunity to try it," he said. Eventually, the $300 bonus bill, which had at one point been scaled back as low as $100 by May, was passed 387 to 0 by the House on January 19. Atherton said he was "particularly gratified that one section was acted upon because it indicates that Congress would also act on educational and job aid, unemployment and home and farm purchase aid."[29]

What that really meant was that Atherton was glad Representative May was finally and safely out of the way. For the moment, at least, all veterans' legislation was safely in the hands of Rankin's Veterans Affairs Committee in the House and Clark's veterans' subcommittee of the Finance Committee in the Senate. Legion officials hoped that Ketchum's opposition would be forgotten. Three weeks later, on February 15, their fears over passage must have disappeared when Dr. Zook of the ACE appeared before the Senate Finance Committee to reverse the position the organization had taken in December. Zook endorsed the bill down to the last detail. All earlier disagreements over jurisdiction being exercised by the Office of Education rather than the Veterans Administration were conveniently ignored. "The United States government has a grave responsibility to offer educational advantages to the members of the armed services after this war," Zook said. "This is the least we can do for those whose education has been so rudely disrupted. In this respect, we agree emphatically with the provisions of the bill. Each man should be permitted to select the type of education he desires. In that we agree with the bill too. It is important, too, that students be allowed to select their own educational institutions in accordance with their own requirements. We are emphatically in accord with that provision of the bill, too."

The educators' limited role in developing both the administration's plans and the Legion's bill was over—momentarily. Olson quoted Zook as often remarking "the educational community . . . supported the educational title almost to a man, with the exception of those who wanted the U.S. Office of Education, not the VA to administer the program. . . . [But] they proved successful in almost direct proportion to the degree that their desires matched that of the American Legion."[30] Those desires would run directly contrary to the Legion's, however, during the ensuing months as the chances for passage improved, and educators began to fear losing control over what could be either a bonanza or a disaster. Zook's endorsement of the Legion bill on February 15 just deferred organized opposition while support was being gathered outside Washington. In the spring, that opposition would come surging to the surface during floor debate in the House with the full force of much of the nation's political as well as educational establishment behind it.

That would be just another one of the crises that punctuated passage of the bill like bombing raids. But the first major crisis was generated by other veterans' groups and was described under the title "A Surprise Attack" in one of Camelon's articles, although it might have been anticipated by Ketchum's earlier testimony. The attack came the day after Zook testified. A joint open letter, signed by leaders of four other veterans' organizations, was sent to Senator Clark and every other member of Congress on February 16 that warned:

> All that glitters is not gold. . . . [do] not be stampeded into hasty and potentially unwise legislation. . . . There is a serious question in the minds of some veterans groups whether this so-called G.I. Bill of Rights, in its entirety, is a sound and equitable solution to the problems and needs of World War II veterans. Our nation's first responsibility should be to those [who] have suffered physical and/or mental handicap by reason of military or naval service. Any legislation which grants entitlement to four

years of college training at government expense to any able-
bodied veteran who had ninety days service should be carefully
examined in the light of our tremendous war debt and the ability
of the nation adequately to care for its war disabled. . . . Let us
not have another example of "act in haste and repent in leisure."

The authors of the letter, Ketchum of the VFW, Millard Rice of the
Disabled American Veterans, Frank Haley of the Military Order of
the Purple Heart, and W. M. Floyd of the Regular Veterans' Association, were particularly worried about the educational provisions of
the GI Bill. Reminding the members of Congress of their combined
membership of 550,000, they warned that the bill's educational
component was "so broad in scope and potential cost, that its enactment . . . would probably not only prevent any consideration of
several more equitable proposals to solve such problems, but might
also subsequently jeopardize the entire structure of veterans' benefits and provoke another Economy Act." They were referring, of
course, to President Roosevelt's Economy Act of 1933, the redemption
of his campaign pledge to cut budgets more deeply than President
Hoover had.

The four were not opposed to the education benefits as such. Rice of
the DAV in January had emphasized that his organization favored
"all of the benefits" in the Legion's bill and three weeks after the open
letter was released said the DAV did not object to the education title.
But the four were afraid, as Haley of the Order of the Purple Heart
testified before the Rankin committee, that the education title would
"have a tendency to go too far," cost too much, and be "the golden egg
that killed the goose." Historian Olson noted that the opposition had
its roots "not in any defects of the bill or its objectives, but in fear
that by carelessness disabled veterans might suffer, as they had in
the past."[31]

The four groups, joined by the Army and Navy Union, then came
up with a counterproposal. On March 6, several members of Congress
introduced legislation on their behalf proposing payment to veterans
of up to $3,500 for service at home and $4,500 for service abroad.
Entitled "The Veterans Adjustment Pay Act of 1944," the bill would
credit servicemen and women with $3 a day for home service and $4
for overseas duty with an extra $500 for the wounded. All compensa-
tion of more than $300 would be in the form of nonnegotiable, tax-free
bonds, based on the 1924 model, as sketched earlier in Ketchum's tes-

timony. Bondholders would be allowed to withdraw only one third of the face value of the bonds during the first five years after issuance. The interest rates paid would be 3 percent for the first five years and 3 percent, compounded, for the next five. "The purpose of the bill is to adjust, in a measure, the pay of those serving in the armed forces and civilians employed in a war industry," a joint statement from the veterans' groups said. That same day, perhaps coincidentally, perhaps not, Atherton announced a drive for signatures from the public in support of the GI Bill. One million would be obtained by the time the House of Representatives took up the bill for floor debate on May 11.[32]

Other behind-the-scenes activity was going on, never reported at the time because the principal activist, stepping out of his normal role, was a reporter, none other than Camelon. A council of war was convened at Legion headquarters on February 17, the day after the bombshell letter was sent to Senator Clark. Stelle reported on a conference he had just had with Clark and told the assembled Legion and Hearst task force members: "The letter is embarrassing to our friends in Congress. People don't know the relative strength of our various veterans organizations." Camelon noted parenthetically the Legion's membership was almost three times as large as the 550,000 claimed by the other four groups. "This letter can't beat the GI Bill," Stelle continued. "But Senator Clark asked me to get those other organizations off his neck, if we can. They offer a wonderful excuse for some members of Congress to oppose the bill." As Stelle looked around the table for suggestions, Camelon volunteered: "It would be difficult for a Legionnaire to approach these other organizations. But I'm an outsider and I know Omar Ketchum [of the VFW] and Millard Rice [of the DAV]. If you want me to, I'll see what I can do." Stelle replied, "Go ahead and see what you can do."

At the same time, the Legion had its own intelligence sources within the other groups. The day the council of war was meeting, a VFW member showed Legion officials an internal memo from Ketchum urging local and state VFW officers to ignore the GI Bill as "spout and fizzle, spout and fizzle." Also, Representative Pat Kearney of New York, who was both a Legion member and a past national commander of the VFW, kept the task force informed about internal politics in Congress. Kearney would later supply the tip that resolved the bill's final crisis before passage. That led to a midnight ride by automobile and airplane that has been compared, without too much of a stretch, to the ride of Paul Revere. At this point, however, the letter from the four organizations seemed an almost insurmountable problem. Camelon thought he saw an opening. "I was sure that the VFW leaders really wanted to share the credit," Camelon wrote. "In his internal memo, VFW legislative director Ketchum had dwelt upon 'prestige,' 'credit,' and 'the spotlight.'"[33]

Camelon went to see Ketchum, who told him: "My legislative committee is in town. Let's talk to them." A lunch was arranged between Stelle and the VFW legislative committee headed by Paul G. Wolman, a past national commander of the VFW. An agreement was reached after the VFW made several suggestions, the chief being the insertion of a specific figure, $500 million, for a VA hospitalization program. The Legion had avoided until then a specific number, preferring to seek adequate hospitalization regardless of cost. With the agreement settled, Wolman said, "I think that, in uniting these two great organizations, we have made history here." Ketchum went before both Senate and House committees to publicly support the bill. The crisis was surmounted, and the way to passage seemed clear, but again, it turned out to be only for the moment.

Yet another attack was launched by Rice of the DAV—one in which he would get great support later from Rankin—over the issue that nearly doomed the bill before the midnight ride sealed the bill's passage. On February 22, Rice wrote a letter to Senator Walter F. George of the Senate Finance Committee in which he said, "Your cautiousness in resisting the 'blitz' methods used by an ill-advised group in its efforts to put across the 'G.I. Bill of Rights' . . . is indeed appreciated by those—American's disabled war veterans—whose future welfare very probably would be unfavorably affected." George, a cosponsor of the bill, was hardly looking for such credit and had never resisted its passage. Nevertheless, Rice continued: "The bill, referred to as an Omnibus Bill, has been more appropriately described as 'ominous.'" Then, Rice bitterly attacked the unemployment compensation provision, the so-called 52-20 Club, saying, "The lazy and 'chiseley' types of veterans would get the most benefits, whereas the most resourceful, industrious and conscientious veterans would get the least."

"We read that sentence in amazement," Camelon reported. "We didn't know it would soon haunt us from other sources as well." Camelon and others tried to get Rice "to recede from his position, to no avail." He was firm. Even before signing the February 16 joint letter, Rice had taken a position that seemed so extreme that he angered even the most sympathetic members of Congress. On January 18, he had already said in testimony before the Rankin committee: "I do not believe the Veterans Administration should have any responsibility as to the post-war adjustment of able-bodied men." Then, on March 8, he and Senator Clark engaged in the following mutually uncomprehending exchange:

> Sen. Clark: There has never been a desire by anybody to put the rights of anybody ahead of the rights of disabled veterans. It is the able-bodied veterans of the last war who made the fight to take care of the disabled veterans, and here you come on behalf of the disabled veterans protesting against the rights for able-bodied veterans.
>
> Mr. Rice: I am not protesting against the rights for the able-bodied. I do not appreciate having my words twisted that way. I protested against the submerging [of] the activities on behalf of the disabled veterans of this country and probably jeopardizing those benefits.[34]

There was, admittedly, potential for abuse in the 52-20 Club. "The Legion had not the slightest doubt," Camelon wrote, "that some would, indeed, 'take a rest' on 52-20 by getting local authorities to wink at the 'you must be looking for work' provision. . . . But that wasn't the point. The 52-20 provision was tailored to see that the veteran who was out-of-work and looking for work wouldn't be reduced to beggardom—the old, old story"—still vivid in the memories of World War I veterans working on the bill. As events turned out, of course, veterans collected benefits under the club for an average of only seventeen weeks. No one could know that then, of course; a certain faith was needed and not everyone had it. As Camelon put it, "In 1944 the logic of 52-20 made not a dent in those who felt that the servicemen were heros overseas but bums at home."

Other things were, of course, occurring simultaneously. In the Senate, Senator Clark had been conferring with key senators and had revised the bill he had submitted in January to accommodate concerns of Senator Thomas, the chairman of the education committee, and Senator Robert La Follette of Wisconsin, the committee's ranking Republican-Progressive member. Clark's changes and the concurrence of Thomas and La Follette avoided a turf battle over jurisdiction by the Office of Education and the Veterans Committee on the Senate side. Also on the Senate side, Clark defused another potential conflict

arising from a separate bill covering the employment provisions introduced by Senator Robert Wagner of New York, author of the Wagner
Act, organized labor's Magna Carta. On March 13, Clark introduced a
new version of Wagner's bill—with the benefit of finishing touches by
Colmery—and it was reported out of committee four days later, St.
Patrick's Day, with a unanimous vote. By then Clark had rounded up
the unprecedented number of eighty-one cosponsors. It was a moment
of high excitement when Stelle came rushing back to Legion headquarters flourishing a copy of the bill and shouting, "By God, I got
Alben Barkley, the majority leader, to sign it in his own handwriting."

The bill passed the Senate on March 24, and Stelle hosted a victory
dinner at the Statler Hotel that night. But jubilation soon turned into
tension. Rankin had promised swift action on the House side, but as
the days passed, he began to make it very clear he was opposed to
the 52-20 Club. An unnamed member of the House Veterans Committee said, "This bill provides unemployment compensation which
will not only cost $5 billion to $6 billion, but will also drive a wedge
into the ranks of the men now in the service," Camelon reported. "It
will discriminate against those who go right back to work." Not-for-
attribution comments were drifting out of the committee that the provision would make loafers out of the veterans. "In some sections of
the country, at least, men would rather loaf than work," was another
observation floating around Congress.

Rankin openly associated himself with that viewpoint at a hearing on March 20. "There are two developments I see in it [the 52-20
Club provision]," Rankin said. "I see the most violent discrimination
against that strong, virile, patriotic, determined man who goes into
the Army to fight for his country and comes back and says, 'I don't
want anything. I am going back and going to work and that is what
the rest of you ought to do.' . . . At the same time, I see a tremendous
inducement to certain elements to try to get employment compensation. It is going to be very easy . . . to induce these people to get on
federal relief, what we call unemployment compensation, rather than
getting back into active employment."

In private, Rankin expressed fears that blacks would take undue
advantage of the club. In a letter written on April 25 to a constituent,
he said, "If every white serviceman in Mississippi . . . could read this
so-called 'G.I. Bill,' I don't believe there would be one in 20 who would
approve of it in its present form. We have 50,000 negroes in the service from our State, and, in my opinion, if the bill should pass in its

present form, a vast majority of them would remain unemployed for at least another year, and a great many white men would do the same."[35] No one mentioned publicly that providing the same $20-a-week stipend to black as well as white veterans would unquestionably weaken, if not entirely break down, pay scales determined by race—but everyone knew it. Such racially determined pay scales were not only sanctioned by custom, but were legal under the NRA.

By mid-April, a month after Senate passage, tension turned to fear when Representative Joseph Martin, the minority leader, asked on the floor of the House when the bill would be reported out of committee for a floor vote. Rankin rose and said, "This is the most far-reaching and most explosive bill ever to reach congress. The committee is not going to be stampeded into bringing out a half-baked bill." The Legion decided to apply a little heat to the other members of the committee, if not set off firecrackers under them. Frank Sullivan, the legislative director, sent a telegram to all state commanders of the Legion: "Delay has developed in the House World War I Veterans Committee on reporting out our G.I. Bill. Program has been before it since January 11. You have done magnificent work, but would appreciate numerous telephone calls, telegrams or airmail letters insisting committee cease delay and report bill without substantial change. House membership anxious to act on it."

If the House—and the Legion, of course—was anxious for a vote, the administration wasn't. Although the Legion had assiduously avoided offending FDR by insisting for public consumption that the bill just carried out his earlier proposals, administration officials knew better. Obviously, if the Legion bill already voted out of the Senate were matched by the same or essentially the same bill coming out of the House Veterans Committee, the administration bills languishing in the Senate and House education committee would be doomed. With the Legion bill appearing sidetracked, FDR "remained aloof, letting the Legion keep the initiative," Olson observed.[36]

The editorial pages of *The New York Times, Washington Post, Chicago Tribune, Los Angeles Times, Des Moines Register, San Francisco Chronicle,* and other papers also remained aloof. The editorial writers of the nation apparently thought the bill wasn't worth commenting on. Other than the Hearst papers, only *The Army Times,* a private newspaper, took cognizance long enough to comment: "Don't you think it's time to quit stalling? The G.I. Bill of Rights has been in committee since January." The reason given for the delay, the paper observed, was the feeling that the bill should be rewritten to prevent "encouragement of idleness through over-liberal unemployment compensation. What kind of people do you think are fighting and winning this war? The G.I. Bill is not charity. It merely provides an opportunity for service men and women to navigate under their own power. They have been taken from jobs, homes and futures to win a war. Certainly they deserve a little assistance in making their readjustments."

At American Legion headquarters in Washington, meanwhile, lobbying efforts for the bill revolved around a war room dominated by a huge chart bearing the name and telephone number of every representative and senator. Every day, Reilly of *The Boston Record-American,* whose biggest story before this was an exclusive interview with Gene Tunney after the heavyweight champion married an heiress, would sit before the chart telephoning members. "Hello, senator (or representative)," he'd say. "We're making a survey of opinion on the GI Bill of Rights. Want to tell me how you stand on it?" Once he had an answer, Reilly made a mark with crayon after the member's name on the chart under "Yes," "No," or "Doubtful." Every afternoon, Stelle, Atherton, and the other Legion members lobbying for the bill would hold a meeting clustered around Reilly. "I'm running into resistance," he'd say, naming a member. The others sometimes argued that the individual had been positive when they made their "Fuller Brush Man" calls. "I talked to Senator X. He's for us," Stelle, for example, would say. Reilly would just as often shake his head. "When I talked to him, he was hesitant," he would say. The name would go in the "Doubtful" column.

At the same time, press releases were pouring out to papers across the nation under Cejnar's direction. A series of one-minute radio announcements by wounded soldiers, sailors, and Marines was produced. Four hundred of these were distributed to local Legion posts whose members, in turn, persuaded stations to air them. More than 125 two-minute motion picture trailers, using recent photographs of the fighting at Salerno and Tarawa, were also put together and pitched to theater owners by local Legion members. "Let the members of Congress know that every one of the Legion's 1,250,000 members are behind this bill," urged *The National Legionnaire.* "Let every Congressman know that the Legion demands its passage, and the Legionnaires will not forget those who fail them in this vital issue."

The Hearst reporters at Legion headquarters also got on the phone and took to the mails to persuade their colleagues at hundreds of papers to print blank forms. Readers were urged to fill out the forms and send them back to members of Congress in the petition drive announced by Atherton in March. Small-town newspapers were provided prewritten editorials proclaiming, "The country is glad to see such a bill," "An enlightened approach to the veterans' problem," "It is built on fairness and need," and so forth. The techniques of mass media and ward politics were blended; the campaign was in many ways the precursor of every "beyond the beltway" political campaign since—almost a generation before Washington's outer periphery highway was built. "When the chips were down, it was the Legionnaires back home that supplied the drive for passage," Camelon observed.

But with the bill still being stalled in committee by Rankin, Cejnar came up with yet another tactic. He wrote local Legion leaders urging them to encourage the editors of their hometown papers to ask the wire services—the Associated Press, United Press, and International News Service (owned by Hearst)—to supply them with full coverage of developments. The "news hole," the amount of space in papers devoted to news rather than advertising, is always tight, and with wartime rationing of newsprint, the hole was even more constricted. Nevertheless, after James Boyle, a Legion officer in Maine, persuaded the Gannett newspapers the story deserved every available inch of space, wire editors across the country began to demand more complete coverage. In the meanwhile, the national executive committees of the Legion met in Washington with representatives of thirty other organizations from April 26 through May 2, planning to merge their efforts. Colmery, at the same time, was spending uncounted hours revising compromise drafts in a ceaseless effort to get the bill reported out of committee. Finally, the committee members "simply overrode Rankin, something committees seldom do," Camelon reported. "He apparently had been willing to sacrifice the whole bill rather than grant the new veterans unemployment compensation."[37]

There was a second act in this great American drama: the debate that led up to the vote. It was the act in which Rankin overcame serious doubts about his commitment to the bill he had introduced and shepherded it through committee and emerged as the hero—before turning into the villain in the third act.

CHAPTER 5

A SUPERINTENDING PROVIDENCE

I T WAS MAY 11, 1944, three weeks before the invasion of Normandy, and on the floor of the House of Representatives a southern congressman was making one of the most extraordinary speeches ever heard in that chamber.

"This is Federal money. This is the Congress of the United States. This is the Federal government. It is the Federal government that these boys are representing on the battlefields. . . . As far as the States' rights are concerned there is not a man in this House that has not fought harder to maintain the rights of the states, but we are representing now the Federal government. . . . Since this is Federal money that is being spent, some Federal agency must have the power to say whether or not that money is being spent wisely."[1]

What made the speech extraordinary was that it was made by none other than Representative John E. Rankin of Mississippi, speaking not only in opposition to the nation's leading educators but also "to protect the rights of smaller schools, including some Negro institutions." This was the same Rankin who, in mid-April, had to be forced by other members of the Veterans Committee, under pressure from American Legion members back home, to report out the GI Bill. The same Rankin would later try to sabotage the bill over the unemployment compensation provision that would give black veterans the same benefits as whites.

If this was an instance of the "special superintending Providence" the Founding Fathers thought would guide the United States, it was

154

manifesting itself in a very cantankerous man. Rankin may have been standing up for principle, but, as the chairman of a very important House committee, he was also determined not to be pushed around by a bunch of New Deal bureaucrats, college presidents, and governors. And he would get most of the other members of the House to agree with him over the course of an equally remarkable five-day debate.

What had aroused Rankin was a statement attributed to fifty-six educational institutions and ten governors calling the GI Bill "the most serious threat to the existing State and local control of education that has yet appeared in this country." The public inspiration for the statement was a comment of President Conant of Harvard, who had declared, according to *The New York Herald-Tribune*, "In education, as in all other matters, we must guard the doctrine of local responsibility."

The educators, whom *The Herald-Tribune* characterized as "guileless in their simplicity," specifically wanted to restrict enrollment of veterans under the GI Bill to colleges already accredited by the states. Rankin obviously believed their "guileless simplicity" was being orchestrated from the Oval Office by the nation's leading political science professor. "The Roosevelt school of political science said the way to run a government department was to put two mutually antagonistic people in charge of it," one historian wrote. "They would then act like two scorpions in a bottle and try to sting each other to death, leaving the real power in the President's hands."[1] What held true for government departments held true for Congress. The real issue was money and the power that came from control over that money. Rankin knew it, as did his opponents and, more important, the majority of members who rallied behind the master parliamentarian under the fighting cry of "This is a bill for veterans, not educators."

Of course, the rhetoric often cloaked the underlying reality. But when Rankin rose on the House floor that day, May 11, to introduce the GI Bill for debate and a vote, he was being candid in acknowledging the bill's most controversial feature was education of veterans. In this instance, his adamant opposition to the prevailing wisdom, as expressed by Conant, would have basic, long-term effects that would be understood only years later. As a bill for veterans, not educators, the GI Bill would become a permanent force in American society, as Clark Kerr, former president of the University of California, observed fifty years after the bill's passage. It did so by financing higher education *"through students"* rather than *"through institutions"* (emphasis Kerr's). That precedent, set in the original GI Bill at Rankin's insistence, would eventually take permanent form in the Higher Education Act of 1972, despite the opposition then of the Carnegie Commission on Higher Education and a committee of the Department of Health, Education, and Welfare headed by Alice Rivlin, who would later become director of the Office of Management and Budget (OMB) in the Clinton administration. By choosing to finance higher education by giving money directly to individuals and, therefore, markets rather than institutions, Kerr observed, Congress (1) discouraged states from reducing institutional financial support for their colleges and universities; (2) sidestepped problems of federal financial aid to church-supported colleges and universities; and (3) avoided "internecine warfare over competitive and changing formulas" for aid, that is, bills favoring small institutions or ones strong in science.[3]

In addition, the bill made ability the sole criterion for admission to colleges and universities. Tuition bills of veterans would be paid in full by the government through the Veterans Administration, acting alone as a fiscal agent. Consequently, potential students would be and were judged entirely upon merit rather than the prevailing social and political preferences of college administrators, state bureaucrats, or the U.S. Office of Education. As a direct result, the nation's colleges and universities that had been the almost exclusive preserve of white Anglo-Saxon Protestants (WASPs) became largely populated by people who were none of those things without anyone really noticing or, if they did, complaining too much. Moreover, the new students, regardless of their ethnic, racial, or religious background, were rarely regarded by their fellow-students, their teachers, or the general public as receiving any special benefits.

Many professional educators at the time probably suspected Rankin might well be in cahoots with the kind of "educational entrepreneur" that President Hutchins of the University of Chicago had warned would buy up the charters of half a dozen bankrupt colleges and make his fortune. But Rankin addressed that concern candidly. "Precaution has been taken and proper safeguards written into the bill against so-called fly-by-night schools which may spring up to cheat the Government and the veterans," Rankin said. "We have also guarded against the Federal Government assuming any control or supervision whatsoever over State educational institutions or agencies. As long as I am a member of Congress I shall never support any

bill that permits the government to encroach in the slightest upon
State control of education." At this point, he got to the key provision
of the bill, giving the veteran an unfettered choice among institutions to attend:

> Furthermore, under this bill no Federal agency or bureaucrat
> will have the authority to dictate the selection of the school or
> the course to be pursued. The veteran only is clothed with these
> privileges. If the veteran qualifies and wants to attend college,
> or the "little red schoolhouse" or the agricultural high school, or
> even a one-teacher school, then we in the committee felt that was
> his business and he should be so privileged. In other words, he
> may select, free from even the most infinitesimal dictation of any
> individual, a school of his own choice. No one should be empow-
> ered to force a selection upon him. . . . The veteran will thus be
> empowered to prepare himself for the pursuits of a normal life.
> The title will also be of tremendous aid to the schools of our land
> whose campuses have been deserted as a result of war.[4]

The open-ended right of the veteran to choose his own school and
course of study, with the government picking up the entire cost,
whether it was $500 for Harvard or $100 at a state university, lasted
only a few years. After that, veterans received only a stipend with
which—along with their earnings and loans—they had to pay their
own tuition and fees. The Korean War bill, however, also substantially reduced the number of veterans who benefited from the program. That right of student choice might have been eliminated from
the outset in the World War II bill, however, if the administration
view, supported by all of organized education, had prevailed. Instead,
the basic pattern of personal rather than institutional financing, first
adopted in the GI Bill, has been reaffirmed in subsequent federal
programs, such as Pell grants. "As a result, the intent of the GI Bill
lives on," as Kerr observed. "Federal support of students, with attention to need, would do more across the board for educational justice
than institutional support would." That assumption, however, wasn't
shared by either the Roosevelt administration or the educational
establishment and was the pivotal subject of debate from May 11
through May 18, with a break taken for the weekend.

As the leading figure in that debate, Rankin was prepared to put
states' rights second in this instance, but not because he thought the
federal government had higher right or could do the job more efficiently. He did it because he did not want to bow to outside influences,

which in this case meant the executive branch and its spokesman in Congress, Representative Graham Barden. Barden, a Democrat from North Carolina, was at the time chairman of the Committee on Education. Normally, any bill dealing with education, especially one as enormous as the GI Bill, would have gone through that committee. In fact, the committee had been studying an education bill since October 27, 1943, when President Roosevelt had sent it a report done by the Osborn committee.

The committee, headed by Brig. Gen. Frederick H. Osborn, had been appointed when FDR signed the Selective Service draft bill on November 13, 1942. It had been charged by Roosevelt with helping those "whose education has been interrupted" as well as "other young men of ability" to either resume schooling or be given equal opportunity for training and education after their service in the armed forces had ended. The Osborn committee's recommendations mirrored the proposal of the Post-War Manpower Committee (PMC), whose earlier attempt to fold veterans' benefits in among social security provisions for the entire population had incurred congressional ire. Historian Ross saw the incorporation of the PMC plans into the Osborn committee recommendations as an example of FDR's administrative genius that let him put forward the same plans "with the stigma cleverly removed . . . without incurring the certain resistance that would have ensued if he used the tarnished PMC's efforts."[5]

The House education committee under Barden had reworked the Osborn committee recommendations slightly and reported them out on May 4, 1994, a day after the Veterans Committee bill was sent to the House floor. Debate on the House version of the GI Bill, which had been passed by the Senate unanimously, began May 11. The real problem with the House education committee's bill wasn't timing, however. It was substance.

The Osborn committee recommended a top-down, planned approach in which national needs and the desires of "young men and women with clear-cut and feasible [educational] plan[s]" would have to pass muster with educators and bureaucrats. Similar provisions in the Senate version of the administration's education bill had been struck out in the final vote. When the bill came over to the House of Representatives, the ever-unpredictable Rankin initially ignored that fact. He feared what he called a trend toward "an overeducated and overtrained population" and wanted to make sure the nation's heroes weren't channeled exclusively into higher education. That, to him, mean tutelage by sociologists, one-worlders, race mixers, and

other purveyors of New Deal "globaloney." There was, after all, a
double edge to the sword being wielded by some supporters of the
bill, notably Hearst: pro-veteran but very much antiadministration.
The social philosophy was summed up in a Hearst cartoon showing
an academic in spectacles and mortarboard standing near the Capitol holding out a large money bag labeled "Bills for International
Rehabilitation." In a second panel, the same academic is dropping
three coins in the hands of a disabled veteran on crutches, saying,
"We promised to economize."[6]

"I'd rather send my child to a red school house than a red school
teacher," Rankin said at one hearing on the GI Bill. He was also far
from being alone in wanting to move carefully toward enactment of
a bill whose "novelty" concerned and perhaps even frightened some
committee members, as Ross noted.[7] Sixteen public hearings were
held, and the committee met nineteen times in executive session before the committee reported out its bill for consideration on the floor
in May. The bill unquestionably reflected Rankin's views. Members
of the committee, however, made it clear he had prevailed through
consensus rather than fiat. He "did not attempt in the least way" to
have the committee adopt his personal ideas, Representative Fred E.
Busbey (R-Ohio), who along with other committee members provided
unanimous support for Rankin in the debate, wrote later. "Politics at
no time entered our discussions," the Republican member stated.

After all the hearings and executive sessions, the bill Rankin
offered for debate on the House floor differed from the Senate version
in only one significant respect. Under the House bill, benefits would be
available to those whose education and training had been "impeded,
delayed, interrupted or interfered" with by the draft, rather than all
veterans with other than dishonorable discharges.[8] An administration
spokesman, Adolph Sabath (D-Illinois), chairman of the Rules Committee, opened the debate with an attack on the Rankin bill for reducing the benefits in the Senate bill. Rankin replied that he and his
committee had done a good job "with an awfully bad bill to start
with." Representative Barden seconded Sabath's comments, calling
Rankin's measure "a rich man's son" bill, because it excluded the poor
who hadn't been able to attend school before the war. Rankin back-
tracked, assuring critics that, in effect, almost any veteran would be
eligible under the provision. A man who had left school at sixteen to
farm, for example, would be covered even if he had been farming for
two years before induction as long as he intended to go back to school.

But Rankin's answers were too slippery even for some of his key supporters, including Mrs. Rogers, who, as the ranking minority member, controlled the time allowed Republican members to speak. She allotted time to Busbey to offer an amendment striking the interrupted schooling phrase, and Rankin, ever the astute parliamentary tactician, quickly offered substitute language. All individuals under twenty-four and in school two years before the time they were drafted would be assumed to have had their education interrupted. The provision wasn't quite as generous as Barden's since individuals over twenty-four, for example, would have to submit proof of interrupted education. As a substitute amendment, however, Rankin's substitute language had to be voted on first. It passed narrowly and, as was often customary with a procedural vote, with a relatively few members in the chamber, 87–77. But Barden's defeat in the first skirmish made possible victory in the much greater struggle ahead. "The vote on eligibility proved decisive," Ross wrote. "The education title as defined by Rankin had weathered the debate in the House." [9]

Stormy and sometimes misleading words, along with high-pressure tactics from the higher education community, accompanied the next debate over certification of institutions eligible to admit GIs under the bill. Everyone agreed certification was needed. The two questions that had to be addressed were these: (1) Should schools unaccredited by the states be automatically excluded? (2) If they could be rendered eligible, would that be done by the states or the Office of Education or the VA? The Rankin bill included some precautions to prevent fly-by-night schools from springing up to cheat both veterans and the government: Initially, the schools would have to be certified by the states. Since, however, a considerable number of colleges, many associated with churches as well as institutions for blacks, weren't state certified, the Veterans Administration would be authorized to add such institutions to its list of approved facilities.

That didn't make the professional educators happy, though, because it meant the veterans—not the educators—would be controlling the market for educational services. Putting vouchers into the hands of millions to go out and buy educational services in the open market would threaten, if not break, traditional patterns of control. If the professional educators' language in calling the provision "the most serious threat to the existing State and local control of education that has yet appeared in this country" was extreme, so was Rankin's reaction. It transfigured him into a champion of unrestricted access to education—even for blacks.

If the sight of Rankin, the archetypical southern conservative and racial bigot, arguing for federal control over the states wasn't remarkable enough, he became also, wonder of wonders, a protector of black colleges from "prejudice." The cause of this prejudice and the subject of Rankin's wrath was, by normal political criteria, even more extraordinary. It was none other than fifty-six educational organizations under the umbrella of the American Council on Education, which was now flip-flopping in its support of the bill almost as radically as Rankin. In December, Dr. Zook, the president of ACE, had appeared before Congress to endorse the very limited administration proposals. And on February 15, the same Dr. Zook had in the Senate endorsed the GI Bill's provisions that allowed individuals to select the type of education they wanted and where they wanted to get it.

In the ensuing weeks, the emphasis had unquestionably shifted, undoubtedly under the influence of Conant, the president of Harvard, who was close to FDR as an adviser on the Manhattan Project for developing the atomic bomb. Conant had earlier objected that the bill would lower both admission and performance standards, and he had argued for a screening process prior to giving veterans educational benefits. His arguments, which dovetailed with the Osborn committee recommendations, now took a new turn with his observations on the sanctity of local control of education, as reflected in a letter signed by the ten members of the executive committee of the Governor's Conference, among them Leverett Saltonstall of Massachusetts, the chairman, and Earl Warren of California. The letter requested the House veterans' committee bill be amended to make "clearly mandatory to the States and educational institutions, approved by the states, control of the actual education of our veterans. . . . We urge also that provision be made in the Rankin bill to pay fair tuition to publicly supported institutions as well as privately supported ones."[10]

The governors' conference kept the letter short because it was produced a week before education leaders were scheduled to meet in Washington to consider implications of the GI Bill. Consequently, it had to be distributed quickly to fifty-six educational organizations and ten governors. While the educators' and governors' complaints used words such as "fair" and "states rights," the arrangement they wanted would have been prejudicial to many institutions, including black schools. The provision regarding tuition would also prove contentious, allowing state colleges and universities to charge veterans—actually the federal government—private school tuition rates that were higher than those paid by nonveterans. *The New York Times* story about the first day of the debate summarized the reaction of Rankin and his supporters:

> Mr. Rankin and other members of his committee contended that many of a group of educational leaders who met here last week and criticized the bill as a menace to State control of schools hadn't even read it [the bill].
>
> "We are here in favor of maintaining the rights of the States and keeping out as many bureaucrats as possible," he said, adding that the committee intended that veterans be allowed to select their own schools and pursue any course they wanted.
>
> To protect the rights of smaller schools, including some Negro institutions, he said, the committee provided that the Veterans' Administrator be allowed to add to lists certified by state educational bodies. This, he said, was done because "we want to be dead sure" that a veteran may attend the school of his choice."[11]

The educators' and the governors' arguments were reprised in greater detail by *The New York Herald-Tribune* in an editorial read into the record by Representative Barden during the debate:

> That is what the Nation's educators, guileless in their simplicity, are asking. Almost with unanimous vote they approve the Barden bill . . . which provides for the administration through State educational agencies, provides for State advisory committees and counseling service for State selection of institutions and the use of existing institutions. It provides, in other words, that the veterans be allowed to deal with local people handling matters with which they alone are conversant.
>
> Representatives of 56 national educational institutions called together by the American Council on Education declared the Senate provision and the similar Rankin bill in the House to be "the most serious threat to the existing State and local control of education that has yet appeared in this country." James B. Conant of Harvard warns: "In education, above all other matters, we must guard the doctrine of local responsibility." Our own city [New York] board of education opposes the Rankin bill as "creating yet another Federal agency in competition with State and local agencies," and urges the Barden bill. These are voices to be heeded. The House should substitute the Barden bill.[12]

During the often-heated debate many legislators made it plain that they saw plenty of guile behind the views endorsed by *The Herald-*

Tribune, generally considered the voice of the establishment at the time. Specifically, the provision in the Rankin bill in dispute allowed any veteran to go to any institution provided that (1) it was on a list provided by the states or that (2) it was one of "such additional public or private schools or institutions as may be recognized by the VA Administrator." The amendment offered by Barden on behalf of the fifty-six educational organizations would vest the authority to approve all institutions exclusively in the states. Moreover, it would create a war service and education and training agency in the VA subject to a fourteen-member advisory board. Other fourteen-member advisory boards to the certifying agencies would be created in the states. Unspecified "war persons" would also be eligible for benefits under the bill, presumably at the discretion of the advisory boards.

The Barden amendment came under attack from several directions. To begin with, the provision was criticized as an additional layer of bureaucracy. Moreover, Representative Barden had committed a significant tactical error before the debate in making the following observation: "The average veteran is more interested in the little red schoolhouse than in a more powerful Veterans Administration." Administrator Frank T. Hines, a former brigadier general who had been running the VA since 1923, took the remark personally despite Barden's later half-hearted attempts at dissimulation: "Certainly no one is charging General Hines with seeking any power or authority or bureaucratic powers," Barden said the first day of the debate. "Nobody has ever thought of that in connection with that mild-mannered, modest, fine gentleman."[13] Barden would have been well advised to leave matters alone at that point, but he added, "But should he [Hines] ask for the passage of S. 1767 [the bill already passed by the Senate] with such provisions as are now in the bill, then I would say he was calling for too much power."

Rankin, who had been dealing with Hines since he came to Congress, took full advantage of Barden's blunder. He produced a remarkably blunt comparative analysis by Hines of the two bills. Hines was a career bureaucrat—and a cautious one who had been attacked by liberals, largely because of his close association with both the American Legion and politicians such as Rankin. *The New Republic* on March 4, 1944, had called Hines an "old-line bureaucrat of Harding's day, who is hostile to the New Deal and the sort of government that will be needed to cushion the shock of transfer from war to peace economy." I. F. Stone, writing in *The Nation* on March 25, 1944, had written that Hines "makes the [VA] job a cruel joke. On the other hand, Hines was defended by Charles G. Bolte, one of the founders of the American Veterans Committee, a new veterans' organization established as a liberal alternative to the Legion. Bolte regarded Hines as "a man of irreproachable character, honesty and integrity, an efficient administrator within certain limits."[14] Hines's comments on the respective bills before the House were:

> The [Rankin] veterans bill is based upon the principle of affording a direct benefit to veterans with no purpose whatsoever of controlling or building up educational machinery or educational institutions. Inevitably it may be assumed educational institutions may profit indirectly through the Federal government affording educational and training opportunities as a veterans' benefit.
>
> The principle of the Barden bill is one of building up tremendous educational machinery, both Federal and State, for the avowed purpose of affording educational aid to veterans, but it will be noted that the term used is "war-service person" and, as indicated by the title, this includes other than veterans.[15]
>
> The irreconcilable difference in the two bills in this respect inheres in the fact that the one approaches the question from the point of view of a benefit for veterans whereas the other is the educators' approach with the veterans and others as the immediate occasion for the proposal. . . .
>
> As indicated, the veterans' rights would be determined by a state board and the Federal government would pay the bills. Under such conditions there is no apparent reason for placing this matter in the Veterans' Administration as it cannot be held responsible for results. . . . The only authority the Administrator would have would be to pay the bills.[16]

Hines's reputation for candor and integrity made what he had to say all the more devastating. The administrative structure called for in the Barden bill also came in for trenchant criticism from Representative Glenn Cunningham (R-Iowa) during the debate. Cunningham, who was a member of the Veterans Committee, said, "You set up an agency in each of the states, and then you set up an agency here in Washington to determine whether or not the state has complied with the rules, regulations and provisions of your so-called bureau in Washington. You are getting into such a complicated mess that you will never get him [the veteran] out of it and he will never get to college."[17]

Political suspicion and fear were the principal reasons behind the educators' efforts. They regarded the American Legion as "the most powerful lobby in America," as a letter by Cloyd H. Marvin, the chairman of the Conference of Representatives of Educational Institutions on Post-War Education—the proper title of the fifty-six organizations—stated. He went on to say:

> The American Legion is insisting on setting up a complete scheme, as far as veterans are concerned, of Washington bureaucratic control. This, in most of our educational institutions, is likely not only to mean the control of veterans' education but, because we cannot maintain two systems, to interfere with regular educational policies. If the latter becomes true, it will mean the invasion of our regular state plans for education. . . .
>
> This extension of bureaucratic control over any education within the realm of state activities is a principle which has been ruled out by tradition as well as court decisions since the establishment of this Nation. . . .
>
> So do not think of this letter as an apology. It is a call to arms. Please use your telephones, your telegraph blanks, or better still, follow what the American Legion has done, and, if possible, have your members come to Washington and talk to your representatives in the House and your senators about this legislation.[18]

What the Legion and the veterans' committee saw as a pure education bill—the provision of funds to buy educational services from any qualified institution—educators saw in terms of political clout and turf. Representative Rogers not only disagreed with the educators' assessment of the American Legion as the most powerful lobby, but argued, as did her colleagues, that the only lobby being heard from was the American public—with a little encouragement, of course, from the presumably irresponsible yellow journalists of the Hearst empire. She said during the floor debate, "With reference to calling it a lobby, I think the American press is strongly behind this measure as is the American public. It seems to me it is an all-over-the-country lobby."

"You are absolutely right," said Representative Busbey, the Republican from Ohio. "The lobby is from the people; it is from the press; and it is from all those patriotic citizens who want something done in behalf of these veterans. I want to pay particular tribute to the press, and especially the very active cooperation and participation that the Hearst publications have put forward in behalf of this G.I. Bill of Rights."[19]

For their part, the members of Congress had their own suspicions of the educators. Busbey saw "planned education—[if] not Hitlerism" in a bill similar to the Barden proposal that had failed in the Senate. That bill would have allocated $300 million for screening "1,000,000 for the first year's training in courses of national importance, and one-fourth that number for extended training of the same nature— the selection to be in the hands of the educators," he observed. "May I stress here one fundamental point we all lose sight of. This is not a bill for the educators; this is a veterans' bill."[20]

Representative Errett Scrivner (R-Kansas) emphasized the point: "It is the purpose of this bill to place the veteran on his own. He is going to be able to take care of himself. He has taken care of himself in a lot hotter places. That is all we hope to do, with the least possible supervision and control."[21] Mrs. Rogers noted: "It seems to me the state board would very much retard the veteran receiving his education because he would have to go to the advisory board, probably, before he could go to school and it would involve endless red tape."[22] She also suspected state boards of education would be "tremendously influenced" by the advisers the Barden amendment called for. "That board [of advisers] would have tremendous influence in controlling the schools to be approved by the board of education. I think there is great opportunity for political activity here. . . . Under the Barden bill the board of advisers might use influence to approve schools that should not be approved, and that board could be extremely powerful."[23] The advisers would also be well paid, by the standards of their times, for their advice—and political activity. "The members of the advisory committee would be paid $15 a day plus $10 per diem. . . . It will be a tremendous cost [to pay] these men," Mrs. Rogers observed.[24] Finally, she doubted if the state boards would be as sympathetic to or as understanding of the veteran as the VA. "In the Barden bill powerful state bureaucracies or agencies can be built up and the veterans will constantly be interfered with by the State boards which are created under that bill. The veterans, in many instances, may not be well, may be nervous after their service and after their fighting and the Veterans' Administration knows how to handle these men. I fear very much also that these advisory boards might interfere with the veterans' welfare."[25]

Fear that educators might be prejudiced against certain private schools was expressed by Rankin and Rogers in this exchange:

> MR. RANKIN: There might be some private schools that the public authorities might not want to recognize. . . . For the reason probably that they are not patronized by the state.
> MRS. ROGERS: It might be a matter of prejudice also.
> MR. RANKIN: Certainly.
> MRS. ROGERS: You could debar some excellent schools where the boys could obtain some special kind of education they wanted to secure.[26]

The example provided by Rankin might appall the college, if only because the notorious John E. Rankin of Mississippi once defended it from possible prejudice. "You have in the state of Ohio one of the most unusual schools in America—Antioch College—which is headed by Dr. Arthur E. Morgan, formerly head of the Tennessee Valley Authority," he said. "Those students go to school for a few months and then go out for a few months. In my opinion it fits them as well as any institution in America. I am not sure it will be recognized by the educational authorities of Ohio, but if not, the Veterans' Administration then would be permitted to recognize it for any veteran who wanted to go there." Of course, Rankin wasn't defending its well-known liberalism, but rather its cooperative work-study program, which was then quite novel.

State boards might also discriminate against a veterinary school or a school of osteopathy or business school, Representative Cunningham also observed.[27] Osteopathy, of course, was frowned on by the medical profession at the time, and schools of business were relatively rare. Cunningham provided a specific, although unnamed, example: "In my state we have an excellent college. It is not an accredited college . . . for the simple and sole reason that it does not have a large enough endowment. Yet it was selected by the Navy for one of the best naval training schools in the state. It was so good that the Navy wanted it and made it practically No. 1. . . . My personal experience is that graduates from that school can pass the entrance examination to West Point and Annapolis much better than almost any school from my district. Yet it is not an accredited school."[28]

The Barden amendment would also bar new schools, as Representative John M. Vorys, an Ohio Republican, pointed out:

> We know that there may be new institutions that arise which
> would thoroughly qualify. . . . For instance, schools in television,
> in radar and other new subjects that may come up through the
> years will be barred by this amendment. As the years go on, if
> we find there are abuses involving fly-by-night schools, which are
> organized simply to get the veterans' money, they can be taken
> care of. . . . We might as well face this fact, however: Either the
> veteran gets his choice, with such guidance and advice as he will
> accept, or the Government and the States make his choice for
> him. If he has no choice, the Government may make mistakes,
> according to the veteran's opinion. I hope that many good advisory groups and committees will spring up to advise and counsel
> veterans on their educational programs, but I want no Government agency, State or Federal, dictating to veterans what education they shall receive. I want the legal limitations on schools,
> new or old, to be very broad so as to leave the veteran a wide
> choice, under such voluntary guidance as he will accept.[29]

Vorys's championship of the GI Bill provides a classic example of the pressure American Legion members "back home" were able to bring on members of Congress in the internecine warfare between congressional committees that preceded—and could have prevented—any deliberation of the GI Bill. Early maneuvering over committee jurisdiction on veterans' legislation pitted Rankin against John Lesinski (D-Michigan), chairman of the Invalid Pensions Committee. Shortly after the war began, Rankin had introduced a resolution to give his World War I Veterans Committee, as it was then named, total jurisdiction over all legislation affecting World War II veterans. The Rules Committee refused to report Rankin's resolution out for a vote on the House floor. A fearful Lesinski, realizing age was decimating the ranks of invalid pensioners within the domain of his committee, also counterattacked with a resolution to change the name—and writ—of his committee to the Committee on Veterans Affairs. By the winter of 1943, it had become obvious little or no action could be taken on any legislation to benefit World War II veterans as long as the jurisdictional issue remained unresolved. Both the Legion and the VFW decided to support Rankin, and on March 31, 1943, Martin V. Coffee, the Legion's department commander for Ohio, wrote Vorys asking him to support a discharge petition to force Rankin's resolution out of the Rules Committee. Vorys initially refused to sign the petition, which required 218 supporters, a simple majority of the 435 members. By May, however, so many aroused Legion supporters had contacted his office, he agreed. The petition effort failed, nevertheless, before Congress went out of session in December of 1943. That meant that when Rankin introduced the GI Bill on January 10, his committee did not have formal jurisdiction over the proposed legislation. As far as the Legion was concerned, the GI Bill might very well fail for that reason alone. The words of a letter written by Coffee to Vorys, although written on July 15, 1943, had particular urgency six months later as consideration was about to begin on the GI Bill: "We must have our house in order to take care of . . . [veterans'] legitimate requirements promptly and efficiently so that crack-pots, long-haired professors, and radicals will have as little ground as possible to work on in an effort they will undoubtedly make to influence the thinking of today's discharged army."[30]

Using that and other arguments, the Legion and the VFW brought enough pressure so that on January 24, 1944, enough members had signed the jurisdiction petition that the resolution was discharged for a vote. The language of the resolution, however, had to be changed—postdated, in effect—to apply to the session of the Seventy-eighth Congress already under way. But when Rankin so moved on the floor, he was opposed by Representative Vito Marcantonio of New York. Marcantonio was a Republican with strong ties to Communist organizations and one of the Tupelo terror's most avowed public enemies—although the two were often seen leaving the House floor arm-in-arm after publicly lambasting each other. The exchange with Marcantonio nettled the Mississippian enough to make remarks that Speaker Sam Rayburn took umbrage at. He ruled Rankin out of order. Rankin refiled his motion the next day with the Rules Committee, and although the committee didn't act on it, Rankin predicted correctly that Rayburn would send veterans' legislation to his committee. In fact, Rayburn did just that with the entire GI Bill, although technically it should have gone to Lesinski's Invalid Committee.

Perhaps the principal reason Rankin prevailed and Lesinski didn't was the fact that the Michigan Democrat had been imprudent enough to suggest publicly that the veterans of World War II would form their own association rather than join the Legion and the VFW. "The Legion, if that were true, would face inevitable demise," Ross wrote. "After all, the doughboys, although durable, were not immortal. Legionnaires had to decide to open their doors or to commit suicide." Certainly, Atherton, as the Legion's incoming chief executive, was "an advocate of aggressive recruiting," as Ross wrote. As such, Atherton tried unsuccessfully to have a provision removed from the Legion's constitution that barred membership for individuals still on active duty. Although he failed, his activism helped transform the Legion into a universal veterans' organization. Atherton was an "expansionist," in Ross's word, and his actions were "reflected in the Legion's area of influence in the legislative branch of the Federal government: Rankin's committee on World War Veterans' Legislation."[31]

The fear of "mushroom" schools cropping up to take advantage of veterans wasn't a matter of great concern to Rankin. They would be quickly recognized and dealt with by the VA, especially with "Congressmen and Senators protesting," he said during the House debate.[32] Other House members were more concerned about giving veterans as many choices as possible among institutions rather than worrying about the more remote possibility that some of the institutions might not be suitable.

Certainly, Rankin felt, to paraphrase Georges Clemenceau, the prime minister of France in World War I, that "education is too important to be left to the educators"—and, most assuredly, should not be limited to colleges and universities. He pointed out millions of veterans "never went to college and never will go to college. There are millions who will never go to high school. Some of these little schools that teach the boys how to make their livelihood . . . would probably be overlooked by some 'brass hats' in some of the higher-up educational institutions that dominate the states. So we have made it possible wherever there is a shop or a little school that a boy wants to go to—it may be the old agricultural school out in the country. . . . He does not want to go to the University of Mississippi or Harvard. . . . He may want to go down to this training shop where this man is teaching the boys how to be automobile mechanics." Rankin was obviously thinking primarily of blacks, but he did not, of course, anticipate that blacks who took advantage of the GI Bill, if only to go to one of those vocational schools, might want to see their sons and daughters go to the University of Mississippi or Harvard. Nor, of course, did he realize the GI Bill would create a small army of black lawyers, teachers, and ministers who would make a reality of Thurgood Marshall's words before the Supreme Court in arguing against school segregation in *Brown vs. the Board of Education* less than ten years later: "We have just fought a war to stop Fascist racism abroad. We think the time has come to end racism at home." During the debate on the GI Bill's educational benefits, Rankin showed his Populist side rather than his racist side, despite his focus on vocational rather than technical or professional education. "For that reason," Rankin said, "we have given the Veterans' Administration the power to recognize that [vocational] school for the purpose of allowing those boys to go there. That authority, in my opinion, will be most carefully exercised and there will be no abuse of it."[33]

Of course, there was; virtually every law passed by Congress is abused, and the more successful it is, the more likely it will be abused—especially by members of Congress. By 1950, more than $10 billion had been spent on education alone under the bill; Rankin had estimated the education cost to be $6.5 billion; the total for the World War II bill was $14.5 billion. Congress had, as *The Saturday Evening Post* observed in 1950, fallen all over itself after passage of the original bill "to liberalize the law by amendment. . . . The education and training section of the GI Bill became, in reality, a relief act or a bonus act." A cutoff was needed six years after the bill passed, according to *The Post,* because "more than 15 million veterans [were still] entitled to an average of forty months of schooling at Government expense, including subsistence."[34] In fact, the cutoff date for enrollments by World War II veterans wasn't far off, July 15, 1951. At the same time, the number of graduating college seniors had risen from approximately 160,000 in 1940 to almost 500,000 in 1950, and in 1947 veterans accounted for 49 percent of all college students.

Public educators had another concern at the time the bill was being debated: the payment of "fair tuition to publicly supported schools as well as private." However, the issue was only peripherally and vaguely referred to in the House debate. A veteran attending a state institution would presumably be getting the same class of instruction that would cost Uncle Sam $500 if he attended a private college, Representative John Murdock of Arizona pointed out. Yet the federal government would be paying up to $500 a year tuition for veterans attending such private colleges as Harvard, Yale, and Princeton. Since little or no tuition was charged by state institutions, veterans' education there would be "at the expense of the local taxpayers," Murdock said. "I cannot see any fairness in that, and I do feel that since the education of the veteran is a Federal responsibility, the Federal government ought to bear the actual cost—without any padding of profit to the local institution such as might be termed 'gouging' Uncle Sam." He then observed that public institutions were "meagerly supported by local taxation and are struggling hard to furnish the best educational facilities with the funds supplied." Presumably, he wanted the federal government to pay a surcharge higher than the tuition paid by nonveterans at state institutions and closer to the maximum of $500 paid on behalf of veterans at private colleges.

The other side of the argument was presented by Representative Zimmerman: "Why should any institution require higher tuition from a veteran [than] from your boy or my boy? . . . Why should not all stand on an equal footing in these institutions? . . . The fact that one boy is a veteran and one is not a veteran should not make any difference. They go and enjoy the same educational facilities. The only thing is, whatever expenses are incurred are paid for by the government in the case of the veteran. It is the payment of a debt which they owe to that veteran."[35]

The issue was one that apparently hadn't been thought out very thoroughly on either side of the debate, and it only came up again when the Korean War bill was addressed. By that time, of course, the public school educators had years rather than days to address their concerns, not only to the governors but directly to members of Congress. The result was the considerably less generous Korean War bill. Instead of having full tuition paid wherever veterans were admitted, plus a stipend, Korean veterans got a stipend out of which tuition had to be paid. More than twice as many veterans, on a percentage basis, attended public as compared with private colleges under the Korean and Vietnam bills as did under the World War II bill.

Ultimately, the educators' attempt to intervene in the passage of the World War II bill and wrest control from the VA foundered when a prominent signer of the original telegram from the governors defected. "I am against the Barden bill and am for the provisions of the measure as supported by the American Legion for education privileges for the veterans of this war," Governor Dwight Green of Illinois said in a letter read on the House floor May 16 by Representative James V. Heidinger (D-Illinois). Heidinger also released a statement by John Stelle. The letters of both Green and Stelle thundered against "federal czars" while insisting they were "upholding state control of education." The statement fuzzed the facts with rhetoric, but the bottom line was unquestionable. In Stelle's words,

"Governor Green has expressed the determination of the people of Illinois in taking a stand definitely for the GI Bill and against the bureaucratic Barden bill." Heidinger pointed out that Stelle, a Democrat, had been the immediate predecessor of Green, a Republican, as governor of Illinois. "Certainly, no one can accuse these men of playing politics," Heidinger said with perfect innocence.[36] Of course they were, and Rankin, probably on cue, promptly called for a recess, and that should have been the end of the debate.

But another highly significant debate immediately preceded the vote. In that debate, Rankin clashed head-on with Marcantonio of New York in a brouhaha that prefigured the passage four years later of the Taft-Hartley Act. The clash underlined the emerging anti-communism that would dominate the postwar period. It also highlighted the unexpressed but very real hope of many backers of the GI Bill that the legislation would undermine at least the more militant elements in the organized labor movement. Rankin's dislike of labor unions as a real political force was, if anything, more intense than that he felt for the potential of blacks as a political force. Marcantonio, on the other hand, was a radical who attacked liberals and conservatives with equal vigor. He had, for example, been opposed to the Social Security Act, as had Senator Clark. Although, like Clark, he ultimately voted for the act, his objections to it were quite different; he didn't want any payroll tax imposed on workers. Marcantonio had also been an isolationist before World War II, not as a member of America First, but as a congressional spokesman for Russia First. After Hitler and Stalin struck a deal to divide Poland, Communists and Communist sympathizers opposed American intervention on behalf of the Allies. That changed, of course, when Hitler turned around and invaded Russia.[37]

All of these political differences simmering below the surface erupted on the House floor after Marcantonio objected to provisions in the bill that would disqualify veterans participating in a strike from getting unemployment benefits under the 52-20 Club. Marcantonio, seconded by Howard J. McMurray (D-Wisconsin), also objected to a provision offered as an amendment by Howard W. Smith of Virginia that would effectively eliminate the closed shop by fining employers $1,000 if they made union membership a prerequisite for employment. The amendment was a direct attack on union membership as a condition of employment, concessions wrested out of employers under the illegal but successful sit-in strikes of the 1930s.

Such closed-shop agreements were outlawed under the Taft-Hartley Act passed four years later.

When Marcantonio spoke up on May 18 on unemployment compensation for veterans and the right to strike, he must have raised a worrisome specter among business interests and their sympathizers in Congress, desperately afraid of an outbreak of strikes after the war comparable to that after World War I. Some saw his new pro-strike position as a new twist in the Communist line. Before the war, Marcantonio had been an unflinching advocate of the workingman's absolute right to strike, but after Russia became an ally against Hitler, he had supported federally backed no-strike provisions in labor-management contracts. His position was consistent with the Communist Party line, which had led Earl Browder to denounce the 1943 coal miners' strikes led by John L. Lewis as "insurrection against war."

"I realized that the committee has been debating this bill for several days and the members are sort of tired," Marcantonio said by way of preface. "I assure you that I would not offer this amendment unless I felt that the consequences of the language I seek to strike out were very detrimental to the cause of veterans who have to work for a living. The language I seek to strike out on page 69 provides that no benefits shall be paid to any veteran who has ceased employment due to a strike or other labor dispute. . . . The effect of this language is to penalize the veteran who goes out on strike in defense of his rights. It is aimed at veterans who are members of, or who become members of labor organizations. It strikes at organized labor. This language is antilabor in intent, scope and practice. It is anti-veteran in practice. The sole purpose of this language is to dissuade veterans from joining labor unions."

He then attacked Smith for trying "to use the veterans' bill to tack on the open-shop amendment." Marcantonio derided Smith's arguments: "Freedom, he says, for the veteran to work. What he means is freedom to work under the open shop; freedom to be exploited; freedom to work for low wages and long hours. He seeks to deprive the veteran of that which assures him decent working conditions; which guarantees him a decent living in keeping with the American standards of life."[38] The amendment "would violate many contracts now in existence for closed shops and conditions and precipitate chaos wherever it became an issue," Marcantonio and his supporters were reported by *The New York Times* as saying.[39]

A vital subtext in the argument was the fact that the State Unemployment Service, established under the Wagner-Peyser Act of 1933, had been federalized as a war measure in 1942. Wagner-Peyser had also created a Veterans Employment Service (VES) within the United States Employment Service (USES). In effect, the measures created a single labor market throughout the country with a common wage scale. That, of course, was anathema to employers in the largely nonunion South and West who enjoyed a competitive edge in labor costs (which admittedly reflected lower living costs), while strongly supported by unions, which wanted to organize closed shops everywhere. The need for a federal VES presumably proved the need for a single federal employment service for all. Unions, federal officials, and New Deal Democrats traded on a "save the veterans" theme during the two-year congressional battle over defederalization, according to historian Ross, to justify continued federal control of USES. For example, James D. Carey, secretary-treasurer of the CIO, had testified during hearings on the bill: "The veteran can best be served, as the whole people can best be served by national administration." Carey also warned: "The GI Bill of Rights should not be misstated or garbled by those eager to trade on the veteran for justification of their position." In opposition, states rights advocates such as Representative Harold Knutson (R-Minnesota) cited the presumably pernicious influence exerted by the CIO. A vote in favor of continued federal control of the Employment Service, he said, meant members were "voting the way the CIO wants you to vote and the way many have been ordered to vote."

USES, however, was "hurt more by its friends than by its enemies," Ross observed. "Its close identification with labor unions (fostered both by its own actions and the zeal of its defenders in labor's ranks) was particularly strong." Nor was USES very effective in getting veterans jobs. Members of Congress suspected as much when the GI Bill was being debated—and time would prove them right. A special committee appointed to study the agency's effectiveness reported in 1946 that the alliance of VES and USES had created endless confusion and "can only lead to administrative chaos." Active antagonism, rather than effective cooperation, was the order of the day: "In some instances [VES] personnel have been expending their energies in 'policing' with excessive zeal, the operations of the [USES], whereas their time might better be utilized in selling the [USES] to employers and the public, including the veterans themselves." Charles Hurd, *The New York Times* veterans' affairs reporter, in a February 24, 1946, column, wrote: "One of the worst complaints this column has heard repeatedly of USES is that for the most part it offers to veterans only the lowest paid and the most undesirable jobs in the industry." Data compiled by the USES itself confirmed the accuracy of the complaints. In fiscal 1947, only sixty-one of every one hundred veterans who applied for jobs through USES were placed; the ratio for nonveterans was eighty-one.

In the battle over payment of unemployment compensation, Rankin proved correct because the laws prohibiting such payment were state laws: passage of Marcantonio's proposed amendment would have amounted to federal preemption of state prerogatives. The same constitutional arguments that were used in voting down both a federal ballot for the military and repeal of the poll tax in the same session of Congress applied as well in this dispute. Nevertheless, Marcantonio, in effect, threw Rankin's own language in defense of the educational provisions of the bill back at him. "We are legislating Federal legislation," he said. "The question is before us. Irrespective of what the several state Legislatures have done, I think we must meet our responsibility. Shall we use this veterans' legislation as antiunion legislation? Shall we penalize the American veterans who are workers, because they become members of labor unions, or because they participate in labor activities in defense of their own welfare? That is the question we must answer." Marcantonio's arguments were seconded by Representative Howard J. McMurray of Wisconsin, in more colorful and derisive language: "Just because some state legislatures have been stupid is [it] any reason why the Congress of the United States should be likewise[?] You should not, as a matter of practice, write into our laws, things that are discriminatory against manufacturers or against labor unions or any other legitimate organizations."

McMurray's comments provided Rankin with an opportunity to indulge his taste for sarcasm: "Mr. Chairman, we would never have known of the stupidity of the State legislatures if it had not been for the erudite gentleman from Wisconsin [Mr. McMurray], who presumes to be an expert on that subject. It is a great thing for some professors to come to Congress. . . . It remained for the verbose gentleman from Wisconsin to develop the fact that the ills of the nation are traceable to the stupidity prevailing among members of the various legislatures, and to enlighten the benighted members of this august body on this point; and I want to take the opportunity to express our gratitude." Rankin used the opportunity to point out Marcantonio's amendment "is highly recommended by Sidney Hillman," the head of the CIO's political action committee. He also mocked the amendment by asking the other members "to give me the consolation of acting as if you are as stupid as I am, and the State legislatures are reputed to be by the able gentleman from Wisconsin and vote this amendment down."[40]

What had been up until then an ill-tempered but essentially germane argument on the issues soon flared into a bitter Pier Six verbal brawl, which did, however, illuminate the ideological, political, and cultural divisions that plagued the country at the time and would continue to do so for years. The arguments and name-calling reflected the class and ethnic tensions, fears, and bitterness beneath the surface of unity created by the war. Representative Clare Hoffman (R-Michigan) threw an angry verbal punch when he accused Sidney Hillman, the labor leader, of intending to turn America "into a government for and by the CIO." He observed Hillman and his associates had boasted about their $2 million political fund and boldly announced that they will defeat all Congressmen who venture to oppose their wishes in the forthcoming election that November. The passionate antagonism between liberals and conservatives, concealed by surface unity during the war, was coming to a boil.. Less than a year later, Hoffman, called a "labor baiter" by *Time* magazine, precipitated a much-publicized physical brawl on the House floor between Rankin and Frank E. Hook (D-Michigan). Hoffman accused the CIO of being under Communist influence. Hook, a beneficiary of the CIO's political action committee, said the CIO was doing more to keep down the Communists than any other group in the United States. Rankin replied, "That's because they are tied around their necks." Fists flew.[41]

In the debate on the GI Bill, however, Rankin confined himself to seconding Hoffman's sentiments by comparing Hillman to Benedict Arnold and calling the labor leader a "communistic racketeer" out to dominate the Democratic Party. Marcantonio, reacting to Hoffman's barbs, jumped into the fray. He took particular exception to Hoffman's denunciation of Hillman as "foreign born," a "transplanted blossom, if it can be called that, carrying with it the odor of a foreign ideology, who has brought nothing but trouble [telling us] our system of government, our way of life is all wrong." Marcantonio declared "those who speak in the interest of the American worker and defend labor's rights do not fear the attacks of the doodlebugs on the reactionary side of Congress. Whether Mr. Hillman is foreign-born or native-born is immaterial. He is American. What is material is that Mr. Hillman is engaged in a perfectly sound political activity consistent with basic American principles."[42]

As the words and epithets flew back and forth, Majority Leader McCormack, both a staunch anti-Communist and an equally staunch union supporter, took the unusual action of stepping down from the speaker's platform, where he had been presiding in Rayburn's absence, to intervene. "I think it is unwise to refer to anyone as foreign-born," McCormack said. "I am only two generations from being foreign-born, and I will match my patriotism with that of anyone else. I know many people who are foreign-born who are wearing the uniform. . . . I am speaking in my individual capacity as an American citizen and as a member of the Congress of the United States of America. Whether or not a man is a foreign-born person is immaterial. . . . The question of whether anyone is foreign-born or not is not before us. I hope I will never, while I am a member of this body, hear any reference made again to anyone on the sole ground of being foreign-born."

Marcantonio's proposed amendment to the GI Bill was voted down, again with only a few members in the chamber, as customary for procedural votes, but the margin was overwhelming, 122 to 28. Smith's amendment lost by 119 to 12. The votes, however, were the first indications that the power of the unions was about to grow vulnerable to assault from the very big government that had fostered its growth. Until then, unions had seemed not only unassailable politically but morally as the principal means through which ordinary Americans could earn and enjoy "the good life." Within four years, the Taft-Hartley Act, based on the same constitutional principles that forced defederalization of the USES and the upholding of state laws that prohibited unemployment compensation for strikers, would be the law of the land. Two trajectories were about to intersect: the rise of an educated, home-owning middle class due largely to the GI Bill of Rights and the decline of union power, spurred—for good for ill, like it or not—by Taft-Hartley.

A fundamental change in both labor law and public attitudes toward labor had taken place during the debate over the GI Bill of Rights. The union movement had already reached the height of its influence during those months from January through June 1944 when the GI Bill was being debated in Congress. Its long, slow decline occurred because many Americans, among them strong union advocates in the '30s, began to doubt whether they needed the closed shop to maintain decent working and living conditions. An epidemic of strikes after World War II would also begin to turn the public cynical about unions. Strikes by John L. Lewis's coal miners would be slapped down by the courts, and the obdurate efforts of railroad unions to tie up the nation's transportation system would contribute to the near destruction of the coal and rail industries.

If the fight over the closed shop during the debate over the GI Bill marked the beginning of the decline of the organized labor movement, the struggle for its passage over the 52-20 Club provision marked the genesis of racial equality as the touchstone of the next great movement in American life. Up to that point, little attention had been paid to the unemployment compensation provision of the bill. Nor was there any discussion of the fact that it provided for equal payments of whites and blacks. Apparently, everyone—even Rankin—stopped giving the provision much thought during the debate, despite the potential effect it could have on segregation patterns in the South. Rankin obviously wasn't worried that the bill's education provisions would break down the color line. He assumed few, if any, blacks would take advantage of the educational benefits except perhaps to go to vocational schools. But all black veterans would get the same unemployment benefits as whites, and in Mississippi and the rest of the South, $20 a week would go quite a bit further than in New York and the rest of the North. Blacks would, therefore, be less likely to seek—or need—work at lower wage levels than whites. The result could easily be the destruction of the informal two-tier pay scale given legal sanction by the National Recovery Administration.

As early as March 20, Rankin had declared during a public hearing that he could see in the provision "a tremendous inducement to certain elements not to try to get employment. It is going to be very easy . . . to induce these people to get on Federal relief, what we called unemployment compensation, instead of getting back into active employment." The next day, Colmery commented at the set of hearings, "The man who has served his country and wants a job does not want to live on his country. My God, he has fought to defend it." Rankin never again publicly criticized the provision. But soon the man who had shepherded the bill from its introduction in January through complex jurisdictional maneuvering among committees, judicious consideration in his own veterans' committee, and vehement argument coupled with shrewd parliamentary maneuver in floor debate almost killed the measure at the last moment. The man who deserved credit for being perhaps the prime mover in the enactment of the GI Bill turned into a man determined to sabotage it—and he had the power to do so. The unanimous vote in the House, following the unanimous vote in the Senate, should have been the climax of a drama filled with tense moments. Instead, it became only the prelude to a final drama with a chase scene worthy of the silver screen.

"A tough fight was still ahead of us," Camelon wrote.

CHAPTER 6

RENDEZVOUS WITH DESTINY

WARS DON'T stop after the last cannon roars. Hatred isn't easily shut off when it has become a habit. Fighting can become a way of life even when the weapons have been put away.

Americans had lost their innocence in World War I. They returned to a country riddled with class, ethnic, racial, and religious animosity, much of it generated by the government itself through suppression of dissidents. They knew the crusade to "save the world for democracy" had, instead, helped clamp totalitarian rule on Germany, Russia, and Italy. That, rather than any illusions about the Nazis, Communists, and Fascists, led many World War I veterans to vehemently oppose American involvement in the Second World War before Pearl Harbor. Theodore Roosevelt Jr. reflected those feelings in a letter to a friend in early 1941. "I can remember the last war. I remember that I felt when I came back that no matter what we might have failed in doing, at least we stamped out intolerance in the United States, for our common service, shoulder to shoulder in the common cause, could not help but accomplish this. The [actual result] was the Ku Klux Klan and bigotry, hooded and rampant."[1]

A potentially far more rampant reign of class, racial, and ethnic conflict could have occurred after World War II than had taken place under the Red Scare of 1919–20. John Rankin, the Mississippi congressman, could have produced that conflict if he had been able to sabotage the bill in a House-Senate conference. Nothing is inevitable in human events, even when logic and common sense demand that faith be kept with those who are sent to fight a nation's wars. What happened after the country's earlier wars proved that. Common decency might insist there must be a return for sacrifice in war, a reason beyond patriotic words, beyond empty ideals, a realistic hope for life after war. Humanity and logic rarely govern political affairs, however, and the bargain fulfilled in the GI Bill might well have been broken if Rankin, for his own bigoted reasons, had his way.

The clear vision for the fulfillment of this bargain was largely inspired by Theodore Roosevelt Jr., who at the time the bill was pending in Congress was a brigadier general training a division for the D day invasion, and consummated by one other man. Neither had anything to do with actually writing the bill or debating it in Congress. Roosevelt had stepped down from the leadership of the American Legion, the principal sponsor of the bill, almost as soon as it was founded. The other man wasn't even a veteran, although he was called "Colonel." He was an obscure member of Congress who served only three terms and a colonel only because the honorific was bestowed on all members of the Georgia bar at the time.

Roosevelt's faith in an "Americanism" imbued in men of different backgrounds through common service inspired Senator Clark and the others who fought for the bill's passage. But that force could have been dissipated, worn itself out, if it weren't for one man's vote cast after an epic midnight ride by car from Georgia to Florida and by airplane from St. Augustine to Washington, D.C.

The six-month congressional battle—and the more than 160-year struggle to adequately compensate those who had fought for the nation—ended with John Gibson's vote. Just two days earlier, General Roosevelt had decided, while the main Allied attack force was pinned down on Omaha Beach, to drive inland with the 4th Division from Utah Beach across the only causeway in Normandy vulnerable to attack. "I'm going ahead with the troops," he told Col. Eugene Casey. "We're starting the war from here."[2]

There was no connection between the journeys of the two men three thousand miles apart, no direct link, but the two personified the two faces of the nation at that time, one fighting to end the war, the other to secure the peace. The two men were as different as the roles they played in a rendezvous with destiny, to borrow a phrase from FDR.

Roosevelt's life has been extensively documented, although his role in the landing at Normandy was obscured for fifteen years. A mysterious order issed by the British Ministry of Information under the authority of unidentified "U.S. Advisers" explicitly ordered censors to delete any reference to the name of Roosevelt from war zone news reports. None of the other sixty general officers in the African and European theaters was included in the ban. "Who was responsible for this strange edict and what was behind it will probably be never known," Mrs. Roosevelt wrote. "It was effective in keeping people at home from knowing the full story of Ted's war record. Because of it Ted has been called 'the hero America kept hidden.'"[3]

Very little is known about Gibson other than what his son, Marvin Gibson, a Washington, D.C., surgeon, remembers. "He held strong opinions and didn't hesitate to express them," Dr. Gibson said in an interview. "The education element in the bill would have been the most important to him. Having children in school was the measure of a family's respectability in the South then."[4] Gibson's life is summed up in a few paragraphs of the only feature article written about him, in *The Douglas Enterprise,* his hometown newspaper.[5] Gibson was born on January 3, 1893, attended Georgia Normal College and Business Institute, and acquired a law degree from LaSalle Correspondence College while working as a teacher and as a railroad hand. A successful trial practice led to appointment as justice of the peace in Douglas and then as solicitor (the equivalent of a district attorney) of the City Court, and solicitor-general of the Waycross Judicial District. When the incumbent congressman, Ben Gibbs, died in office in 1939, Gibson won the seat against three opponents, was reelected in 1942 and 1944, only to lose to W. M. (Don) Wheeler in 1946.

The activities *The Douglas Enterprise* cites as instrumental in Gibson's political success evoke a world that seems closer to a century ago, rather than almost half that. He had auctioned off box suppers at schoolhouses, led square dances, was well known among foxhunters in the district, was respected by county officials, and his father had been a well-known Primitive Baptist preacher. The only other elected position he had held was president of the State Fox Hunters Association of Georgia.

Although Representative Gibson was very much a product of the South of that time, he was a fortunate one—but only by reason of education. His own experience anticipated the changes the GI Bill would bring to the lives of many others. Before World War II, the entire South, white as well as black, was still suffering from the effects of the Civil War. "The South never had a Marshall Plan," Dr. Gibson said. "The diet was poor for everyone. We had eggs, chicken, smoked meat, corn, but few potatoes and less fruit. We had too much choles-terol and not enough vitamins. Vegetables and fruit, blackberries, mostly, were boiled first before being canned for eating out-of-season. The boiling also boiled much of the nutrients away." Both pellagra and rickets, diseases caused by vitamin deficiencies, were common. Light indoors came from kerosene lamps until the New Deal provided rural electrification, and there was no heat in the winter except from fire-places. "Every family had someone who died sleeping in front of a fire when their flannel nightclothes caught fire," Dr. Gibson remembered. Even the better homes were unpainted. "The first time I went to New England, I was surprised all the buildings were painted," Dr. Gibson recalled. "Almost none were in the South. We really didn't get any prosperity at all in the South until World War II through the defense industry."

Everyone who worked on farms, white or black, was poor. And everyone worked on farms except those with enough education to get the few jobs available in small market towns such as Douglas. Only a few landowners and professionals could aspire to a middle-class life common enough in the North. Representative Gibson was the thir-teenth child in his family. "He and another brother were the only ones who escaped from the farm," the doctor remembered. "The brother became an accountant and worked for the Internal Revenue Service. My father went to Douglas Business Normal School, became a sort of itinerant teacher, and studied law through the LaSalle Corre-spondence College." A photographic memory helped him pass the bar examination on his first try after reading law at home after work. Otherwise, he probably would have remained a railroad clerk, the position he held during World War I when the rail system was effec-tively nationalized and its employees exempted from the draft.

Campaigning was a day-to-day retail trade for Representative Gibson, as it was for most politicians of the era. "My father talked to everyone," Dr. Gibson said. "We couldn't go anywhere without his pick-ing up anyone who could use a ride. It was bad enough already for my mother that the car always smelled of foxhounds." Dr. Gibson said his father had probably been at home riding to the hounds rather than electioneering when he got the call to rush to Washington for the GI Bill vote. "Foxhunting was his real passion," Dr. Gibson said. Whatever political philosophy he formed was through the sidewalk seminar outside McCrae's Drugstore and in the nightly discussion group in the Elks Club, which focused on pieces of pasteboard while inspiration was sought in amber liquids. "When he went to Congress he was with the farm bloc which was opposed to FDR's attempt to pack the Supreme Court," Dr. Gibson said. His colleagues in the farm bloc included Rankin, of course, as well as other southern conservatives. But Representative Gibson was also friendly with Senator Pepper of Florida, one of the most liberal members of Congress for many years. "He'd often sit up talking to Pepper on the overnight train trip to and from Washington," Dr. Gibson said.

This, then, was the congressman who cast the crucial vote on the GI Bill, a correspondence school lawyer in a time when the American Bar Association (ABA) had only stopped prohibiting African-American membership in 1943.[6] He was a white southerner who did not question segregation, but did not display any prejudices. "We grew up with several Jewish families in town, and no one thought there was anything different about them other than they went to a different church," Dr. Gibson said. "Of course, there was always a discomfort knowing your black friends couldn't go places you could go. On the farm, they'd come to your house and you'd go to theirs and theirs were just as clean as yours.

"My father was opposed to much of the New Deal," Dr. Gibson recalled, "although he was in favor of TVA and rural electrification. I know the one man he couldn't abide in Congress, or in the whole United States for that matter, was Vito Marcantonio of New York." Marcantonio, of course, sparked Rankin's most colorful rhetoric during the House debate over the GI Bill. As for Rankin himself, Dr. Gibson couldn't recall his father saying anything adverse about him except, "that rascal, Rankin. He did say that, often." Representative Gibson didn't have a sharply articulated political philosophy. "I think what my father believed in, more than anything else," Dr. Gibson said, "was not having to tip your hat to anyone. He tipped his hat to everyone, of course; it was just not *having* to tip your hat to anyone."

It was the timing as well as the drama of Gibson's vote that made it epic. On the night of June 8, 1944, as some two hundred thousand Allied troops were breaking out of the beachhead they had secured on forty miles of Normandy beaches the day before, a House-Senate conference committee was meeting on Capitol Hill. Gibson was one of seven senators and seven representatives charged with resolving differences between two versions of the GI Bill, already approved without a dissenting vote in either house. The committee had agreed on the education and loan provisions of the bill, but were divided over the job placement and unemployment title.

The Senate wanted responsibility vested in the Labor Department's Employment Service overseen by a board headed by the VA administrator. The Senate proposal kept control entirely within the VA, "in keeping with the Legion's hard learned lesson that veterans suffer when their affairs are in many hands," as Camelon observed. The House conferees, without Gibson present, had divided evenly 3–3, blocking passage. Gibson had gone home several days before. "It was said that he was home because he was either sick or campaigning," Dr. Gibson said. "The fact is he just liked to go home as often as he could." On June 5, Rankin had telegraphed Gibson asking for the right to cast his proxy vote. Gibson replied the same day, giving the Mississippian "full authority to cast such ballot as you see fit." On the seventh, however, Gibson changed his mind and instructed Rankin to "vote me in favor . . . of the Senate's" unemployment version.[7]

Rankin refused to cast Gibson's proxy vote when the conferees met the next day, June 8. Failure to reach agreement meant deadlock—and the doom of the GI Bill—if the vote tally didn't change by the next morning, Saturday, when the conferees would meet again. "We can't hold this thing together," Representative Pat Kearney of New York, a former VFW national commander, told Stelle, the American Legion's chief lobbyist. "If we can't agree by ten o'clock tomorrow morning, the conferees will have to report back to each House they can't agree. The bill will be lost."

"What can we do?" Stelle asked.

"Get Gibson up here from Georgia," was the reply. "He'll vote the right way. He's the only one that can save the bill."

The maxim that no one is indispensable applies as much and even more in war than in politics. But, at this moment, just as events had dictated that Representative Gibson would be indispensable in passing the GI Bill, across the Atlantic, Brigadier General Roosevelt was becoming the indispensable element in the D day invasion. His division had been landed in the wrong place—fortunately—on Utah Beach: fortunately because the main American assault on nearby Omaha Beach was tied down by crossfire from concrete pill boxes. Enemy fire was light on Utah, and Roosevelt decided to bring thirty thousand men and thirty-five hundred vehicles over the beach. In that moment, separated by three thousand miles, General Roosevelt and Gibson, each in his own way, were helping produce not just victory but a true domestic peace, unlike the hollow victory of 1918. The "high and serious purpose" Roosevelt had invoked in turning down nomination as the first national commander of the American Legion was being realized. But just as the bill still had to pass the conference committee before it reached the president's desk, the war had to be won before those in the service could return home to take advantage of its benefits.

FDR said those who endured the Depression and fought World War II were members of a generation with a rendezvous with destiny. What happened to Roosevelt and Gibson in those few days in June of 1944 were two particular and specific tales. Each story, however, illustrated in its own way what was happening to millions of others, the subordination of personal considerations to winning victory and, at the same time, the preoccupation of every family with their own lives and the lives of their loved ones. This wasn't a war being fought for imperial goals or the even more lofty purpose of "saving the world for democracy," but, as was said at the time—both approvingly and disparagingly—for Mom, apple pie, and the girl next door. It was a war fought for the ordinary things of life, work, and family, which are, ultimately, the only things worth dying for because they're the only things worth living for. That was the philosophy of the GI memorialized by Ernie Pyle and other war writers: apple pie and the girl next door were what they wanted—and clean clothes.

Roosevelt, who was fifty-six and had a heart condition, had been forced to obtain a stack of dispensations and special orders and then plead for permission to go ashore with one of the first waves on D day. "He had finally got what he wanted," Stephen Ambrose wrote in *D-Day, June, 1944,* "He sat on the platform grinning." On the trip across the English Channel, he moved among the men speaking softly and reassuringly. He began singing and urged the men to join in "The Battle Hymn of the Republic" and "Onward Christian Soldiers." It was a very sobering time to sing the words, "As God died to make men holy, let us die to make men free."[8]

The division was dropped midway between heavy artillery batteries that could have decimated the assault troops, but directly opposite a lightly defended causeway. Shells burst among the heavily laden troops but the obstacles cluttering the beach weren't as numerous as expected. Roosevelt plodded back and forth with his cane over the dunes, rallying small groups, urging them forward while telling them "not to turn into targets." He decided to attack the causeway.

The men in the first wave were already moving in over the beach fast. "I"m going ahead with the troops," Roosevelt told the beachmaster. "You get word to the Navy to bring them in. We're starting the war from here." The roar of trucks, tanks, half-tracks and jeeps following Roosevelt off the beach was the noise of victory.[9]

On June 8 as General Roosevelt was directing traffic on a Normandy beach, Representative Kearney was telling John Stelle to get John Gibson back to Washington. The only record of the next frantic, confused, heartstopping sixteen hours was written by Camelon five years after the events, a record of a time in America when telephone calls were delayed for hours; automobiles often couldn't run for lack of gasoline, which was rationed; domestic airplane flights had to be booked weeks in advance; and the only people with the clout to cut through red tape were the military and the only ones with the savvy to manipulate the bureaucracy and the military, newspapermen.

After Kearney said Gibson was "the only one that can save the bill . . . we looked at our watches," Camelon wrote. "It was already past 6 o'clock in the evening. We dashed from the Capitol and raced back to Legion headquarters."

Stelle made the first of what turned out to be a series of nerve-racking telephone calls to Gibson's home in Douglas. "Sorry, sir," the long-distance operator said. "There is a delay of five to six hours on all calls to Georgia."

"*The Atlanta Constitution,*" Cejnar, the Legion's publicity officer, snapped in the crushing silence. "They've written editorials for us. They'll help."

Another call was placed, this time successfully to Dupont Wright, the night editor, and Rolfe Edmondson, a rewrite man and World War I veteran, at *The Constitution.* The paper had a telephone with an emergency priority. This was an emergency. Edmondson called Gibson's home again; no answer. Edmondson explained the urgency of the situation to the Douglas operator—all long-distance calls were placed then by operators. "I'll find him for you," she said, "one way or another."

"My husband just landed in Normandy," another operator said. "We'll get that bill passed for him."

The Douglas operator knew friends of Gibson and began calling them. Gibson was thought to be on the road between Douglas and Valdosta, seventy miles away, she reported back to the Legion, headed home. "I'll ring him every five minutes until I get him," she promised.

Other telephone calls went to radio stations WSB in Atlanta and WGOV in Valdosta, and an appeal went out over the air among news bulletins from Normandy. "Anyone knowing the whereabouts of Congressman John S. Gibson ask him to call operator 2 in Washington immediately." A lieutenant at Georgia state police headquarters heard this and thought, "Hell, I'm a GI myself," and soon other calls were going out by state police telephone and two-way radio to police cruisers.

State police cars roared over roads Gibson might be traveling on. A siren would scream, a car pull over, and a puzzled motorist ask, "What's wrong?" The trooper would cut the driver short. "You John Gibson? No? On your way."

Other telephones were hastily grabbed in Washington after quick, huddled consultations. Is there an air corps base near Douglas? Yes, at Waycross, forty miles away. Can we get a bomber? Do we know anyone there?

Camelon tried to get an old friend, Bill Westlake, chief of air force public relations, and heard he was in California. But whereabouts? No one knew. A call was placed to *The Los Angeles Examiner,* a Hearst newspaper. Like *The Atlanta Constitution,* it was also preoccupied, mesmerized by the news from Normandy, the invasion for which America, Britain, and most of the world had waited for four long years. Nevertheless, the reporters and editors at *The Examiner* quickly responded, huddled to compare notes, and got on the phone again. Within half an hour, *The Examiner* had tracked Westlake down and he was on the line.

"I'll do anything I can," he told an *Examiner* reporter. He hung up and called the base commander at Waycross.

Minutes later, a phone rang at Legion headquarters. "I haven't got a plane available," the Waycross air corps commander said, "but there's an Eastern Airlines flight ready to leave Jacksonville at 2:20."

"I've got it," Roane Waring, a past national commander, shouted. Robert Patterson, the undersecretary of war, was called. He agreed to give Gibson a necessary flight priority for the Eastern flight—if the word could be gotten to Jacksonville.

Now it was 11 P.M., long past the quitting time of the operator in Douglas and less than twelve hours until the conference committee was scheduled to meet at 10 A.M. The phone rang on the city desk of *The Atlanta Constitution.* "I've got Congressman Gibson," the operator said.

"I thought it was important," Gibson told the men on *The Consti-tution* desk. "I heard the phone ringing as I drove in the yard. You bet I'll go to Washington. They promised to vote my proxy."

"He'd probably been out with the foxhounds," his son, Dr. Gibson, thought fifty years later. "If he'd been down at McCrae's Drugstore, they would have called him in from the sidewalk."

Clark Luke, the Legion department commander at Ocila near Douglas, had been pulled out of bed a few minutes before by a tele-phone call from Pat Kelly, one of the team at Legion headquarters, and asked to drive Gibson to Jacksonville. He got dressed and started to drive over to Gibson's place.

In the meantime, another call had rousted Wiley Smith, the Hearst wire editor, in New York out of bed with an urgent request that the approved priority from Patterson be forwarded to Eastern officials. Smith called Walter Sternberg, Eastern Airlines's traffic manager, asking him to hold the plane.

"Don't worry," Sternberg said. "I'll do it." Sternberg called Jack-sonville with a simple message: "Bring Gibson to Washington on that plane if you have to wait all night."

The news that the plane was waiting was relayed to Legion head-quarters and relayed in turn to Gibson. Suddenly, Gibson said, "I just remembered. I haven't any cash on me."

Wright, in Washington, stuttered ineffectually. Gibson said, "Never mind. There's always a poker game at the Elks on Friday night. I'll get some money from the boys."

Even as he spoke, Gibson saw headlights sweeping over the yard. "This must be Clark Luke now," he said. "Goodbye, I'm on my way."

The two men sped to the Elks Club. "He got a couple of hundred dollars there," Dr. Gibson said. Then they streaked to the Waycross air base forty miles away with Georgia state police providing an escort. At Waycross, Gibson jumped into an army car driven by Corp. Jack Hunter, a former Notre Dame track star, and Pvt. First Class Nils Stevens of Warnock, Ohio, as the relief driver.

The road was open to Jacksonville, but it was almost two hundred miles away across the rain-slick humpback road. "They were called humpbacked because they sloped off on either side into sandy ditches," Dr. Gibson recalled. "They were asphalt so you could get up to seventy, eighty, ninety miles an hour. You'd get right in the center and you'd go, and if anyone passed you it probably would be a bootlegger. A lot of counties were dry then. The biggest danger was the humpbacked cen-ter would stay warm and cows would go to sleep on them. I think they had a motorcycle escort with them that night to give warning. That was a good thing; my father went off the road once trying to miss a cow, took down six trees." The bulky, olive-drab car lunged forward into the storm racing at up to ninety miles per hour, at one point swinging out past a truck into a sharp curve looming ahead. Corporal Hunter's hands tightened on the wheel, his foot stabbed for the brake, the car whipped into the turn, wheels spinning and screaming.

Two wheels left the road. The car lurched and tilted sickeningly. "I thought my feet would go through the floorboards," Gibson said later. Just when the car seemed ready to tip over, Hunter fought it back into control. The ride through a slashing thunderstorm was illuminated only by the wavering headlights and the occasional slash of lightning. The only sound was music of Glenn Miller and Jimmy and Tommy Dorsey coming over the air between bulletins about the landing in Normandy. Destiny was riding with that car as surely as it was with the tanks, weapons carriers, and jeeps streaming off Utah Beach under the command of General Roosevelt.

Florida state police were waiting at the state line to escort the car to the plane.

"At 6:37 A.M. the plane landed at Washington National Airport," Camelon recorded with a newspaperman's precision,

> and the Legion's special committee greeted Gibson. He was fighting mad.
>
> "There's supposed to be such as thing as congressional courtesy," he said. "I can't understand why my proxy wasn't voted."
>
> Sharply at 10 o'clock, as the conference committee went into session, Gibson strode in.
>
> "Hello, John," someone said. "Have you got the opposition licked down in Georgia?"
>
> "Yes," Gibson answered, "I've got it licked there. And now I've come here to lick anyone who tries to hold up the G.I. Bill of Rights.
>
> "Americans are dying in Normandy in the greatest invasion in all history—and anyone who dares to cast a vote against this bill should be publicized to all the world.
>
> "I'm going to hold a press conference after this meeting. And I'm going to expose anyone who doesn't vote for the G.I. Bill of Rights."

Rankin got the message. He voted for the conference report. The deadlock was broken; the vote was unanimous; and the six-month fight—"long" to Camelon, the newspaper reporter; historically, probably the fastest moving as well as one of the most important bills to pass Congress—was about to become the law of the land.

"The G.I. Bill was reported back to the House and Senate," Camelon wrote, "in the form the Legion wanted. The Senate approved it June 12, and the House on June 13, 1944.

"President Roosevelt signed it on June 22, in the presence of John Stelle, Harry Colmery and other Legion members who had made the G.I. Bill of Rights—the Legion's bill—the law of the land."

On those three days, June 6–9, an old world was dying in Europe and a new world was about to be created in the United States, a world not of "gold in the streets," "a full lunch pail," "a chicken in every pot," or even a car in every driveway. Instead, it was the reality of millions of people going to college from families where fathers and mothers had often never graduated from grammar school, never mind high school. It was a revolution, not of rising expectations but of rising realities, as first 40,000 married veterans in 1945 but almost 2.5 million by 1947–48 jammed somehow into garages, converted Quonset huts, anywhere they could live while earning a college degree.

The America those veterans returned to, however, was one threatened with social strains and tensions even greater than those after World War I. It was a nation in which labor and management, resentful over grievances accumulated during the war, were angrily poised to test one another's strength, regardless of the public consequences. It was a country in which the ruling New Deal coalition had, in the words of Bernard deVoto, writing in *Harper's* in June 1944, became "tired, cynical, shifty, strained in its inner contradictions, grown as doubtful of its original ends as it is confused about its means."[10] And it was a society in which the returning veteran was considered a threat, rather than an asset, a threat to the full employment that had lifted the heavy burden of the Depression. Above all, it was now the most powerful—and potentially threatened—nation in the world. But it was now no longer presided over by an urbane, supremely self-confident aristocrat. Instead, a failed haberdasher with unseemly links to a machine politician was bombastically demanding but seldom getting respect from Congress and the press. In all this conflict and turmoil the returning veterans, in all their millions, would become forgotten men—fortunately for everyone. They were able to quietly go about their own business, going to school, buying homes, getting jobs, starting businesses, even taking a little time off to recover from the war, without making headlines or even attracting attention from social scientists. They were a silent army making a silent revolution, building the foundations of a new and better American society. The inspiration a young colonel got from a long-dead sergeant, William Patterson, in World War I who "wanted to go home and start a veterans' association for the good of the country" had borne fruit.

CHAPTER 7

COMING HOME

I F ANY WAR CAN be good, World War II had been so good that many actually regretted its passing, not out of nostalgia, but out of fear of the future.

"When Demobilization Day comes we are going to suffer another Pearl Harbor, a Pearl Harbor perfectly foreseeable—now—a Pearl Harbor of peace, not war."

That was the gloomy forecast of Richard Strout of *The Christian Science Monitor,* writing as the quasi-anonymous columnist, TRB, in *The New Republic* in 1943. Max Lerner, another well-known political commentator, predicted that once the economic stimulus created by the war ended, the unemployment rate would be "one of the most serious in American history." Almost 50 percent of those interviewed in a Gallup poll taken in July 1944 estimated seven million to twenty million of the fifty-six million then in the civilian workforce—14.2 percent to 35.7 percent—would be thrown out of work by war's end. The Labor Department estimated twelve million to fifteen million would be unemployed, 21.4 percent to 26.7 percent.

The cause of all these calamities would presumably be the veterans who had saved the country from the twin scourges of Nazi and Japanese imperialism. Even among the soldiers, 56 percent of those interviewed in a government survey predicted another depression; only 29 percent thought one would be avoided. "The veteran is a threat to society" was the measured judgment of perhaps the country's most knowledgeable authority, Professor Willard Waller of

Barnard College, author of the book *The Veteran Comes Home*. Waller's book, published in 1944 while the GI Bill was still being debated and a full year before the war came to an end, predicted "the veteran who comes home is a social problem, and certainly the major social problem of the next few years." The industrialists of the National Association of Manufacturers quoted anonymously by Edith Efron for *The New York Times* may have been reading the professor, but obviously Lester Markel, her editor, and the powers that be on *The Times* felt his alarmist views shouldn't be endorsed by the respectable businessmen as "news fit to print."

Some statistics convey how the postwar reality turned out. The unemployment rate, at a phenomenal 1.9 percent in 1945 (the lowest in U.S. history), did climb but only to 4 percent from 1946 to 1948. When a recession came in 1949, the rate was 5.5 percent, considerably lower than levels since and a percentage many economists consider normal.[1]

Reality is conveyed better in individual terms, in stories about a few of the many millions whose lives were transformed during those years. One such story was that of Les Faulk of Turtle Creek, Pennsylvania. Faulk graduated from high school in May 1944 and celebrated the death of Hitler and the overthrow of the Nazi regime a year later as a Seventh Army infantryman in Germany. When Faulk had left Turtle Creek, he had a pretty clear notion of what his life would be like after the war—assuming he survived. He'd come back to the small town wrapped in industrial haze and get his old jobs back—if he was lucky—caddying at the local golf course and racking balls at Kindler's poolroom. In time, he could expect to get a "good" job stoking an open-hearth steel mill or winding copper armatures in the Westinghouse generator plant.

Faulk was one of twelve Turtle Creek High School graduates that Edwin Keister Jr. interviewed for an article in *Smithsonian Magazine* in 1994, a class that was a microcosm of hundreds of thousands of others.[2] The young man who left high school in 1944 expecting to become no more than a steel mill stoker or an armature winder instead spent thirty-eight years as a teacher and an elementary school principal. Les Faulk had not only gone to college, he also had acquired both a bachelor's and a master's degree and several credits toward his doctorate, even though the name on his high school diploma was "Falcocchio." That name—and his decision to change it—was significant. In those days, being the son of an Italian immigrant family with a "foreign" name could be almost as much a barrier to getting into college as a black skin. "College," as Faulk recalled fifty years later, "was for teachers' kids and the preacher's kids. For the rest of us, with names like Tarantini and Trkula, it was a distant dream."

Faulk and his classmates in Mrs. Whittum's American history class had been urged to believe that that dream, no matter how distant, could come true for them. But the hopes held out in school didn't stand up very well to the living and working conditions Faulk and his classmates grew up in. Turtle Creek was a factory town where half the male students dropped out of high school. Only 5 percent went on to any kind of postsecondary education, even barber or secretarial school, the latter being one of the few avenues to white-collar work then pursued by men as well as women. The war and the GI Bill changed everything. Faulk, like millions of other young Americans sent off to war, grew up fast in a foxhole. That alone might have made it difficult to accept what Turtle Creek had to offer when he came back home, even with a job awaiting him as an apprentice bricklayer, a job arranged by his father. That wasn't the reason he quit after one day, though, throwing away an opportunity for a skilled, well-paid, and prestigious job at the time. He had heard of the GI Bill, and he had made a decision. "I went to the poolroom and told my old boss, 'I'm going to college.' He said, 'I read that only one vet in 20 who enters college will finish.' I said, 'I'm going to be that one.'" The government had turned him into a soldier who had helped beat the best the German army had to offer; now the same government thought he had the makings of a college graduate. Who was he to argue?

Faulk wasn't alone. Among the eleven other graduates of Turtle Creek High School who joined him at the fiftieth reunion of the Class of '44 were an aerospace engineer, a federal judge, a microchip engineer, a professor of law who is also a research scientist, and an engineer specializing in military survival techniques. The title of one classic book about the war, *Catch-22,* has entered the language as a shorthand expression for the insanity of war; the title of another book by the same author, Joseph Heller, sums up what occurred to those who came back, *Something Happened.*

Something had happened to the economy and the workplace, although its nature could be sensed only vaguely at the time. The nation's two most dominant industries were still coal mining and railroads, the technologies created by the steam engine and the Industrial Revolution. Unions in both those industries called strikes after the war that threw the country into economic gridlock and, until President Truman intervened, threatened social chaos. The "arrogance and irresponsibility" union leaders were demonstrating was "a poor return for their favors from the New Deal," historian Morison observed.[3] Since the industries themselves and the technologies they depended upon were also becoming obsolete, the strikes may have inadvertently hastened the process of what is currently called reengineering or reinvention. Increased reliance on automobiles, trucks, and airplanes for transportation and oil for heating and energy was rapidly accelerating. The first phase of the Industrial Revolution, based on the coal-fired steam engine, was over by the mid-1950s, replaced by a second phase based on the combustion engine in which the auto and the airplane became the dominant and sometimes the only forms of transportation and oil, rather than coal, would fire furnaces. It was a classic, although unrecognized, example of what Joseph Schumpter, the Austro-American economist, called "constructive destruction," the abandonment of processes, methods, techniques, skills, even organizations that no longer met the needs of societies or individuals.

Prominent analysts, particularly Peter Drucker, have argued that Western society goes through clearly defined—at least in retrospect—transformations every few hundred years, which Drucker calls "divides." New cities, such as Paris, London, and Venice, emerged out of the feudal society of warring lords and manors in the thirteenth century, crowned by Gothic cathedrals. The education of the individual conscience and mind began two hundred years later with Johannes Gutenberg's invention of movable type. James Watt perfected the steam engine in 1776, the same year that marked the beginning of the American Revolution and the first democratic republic. The French Revolution ushered in the rise of the nation-state as well as the modern "isms" of capitalism, socialism, communism, and their variants, fascism and Nazism. By the early twentieth century, the engine, first powered by steam and later by gasoline, had totally transformed every manufacturing process, as well as transportation by sea, land, and air. Science and technology had enabled people to control their physical environment; political philosophy and economics had given them "fighting faiths" for ordering their societies.

Today, at the end of the cold war, the faiths no longer war with one another. Another great divide is occurring, one whose positive character is not fully understood and is inadequately described as post-capitalist or postsocialist societies. Several specific developments and events have been identified as marking this transformation: the fall of communism, the rise of Japan as the world's first great non-Western economic power, the spread of the computer. "My own candidate would be the American G.I. Bill of Rights after World War II," Drucker has written, "which gave every returning American soldier the money to attend a university—something that would have made absolutely no sense thirty years before. The G.I. Bill of Rights—and the enthusiastic response to it on the part of America's veterans—signaled the shift to the knowledge society. Future historians may consider it the most important event of the twentieth century."

When Drucker's analysis is laid over the events of 1946, a blueprint seems to emerge, a pattern of American life that mirrors Jefferson's vision. The enthusiastic use made of the GI Bill by the veterans; the extremely rapid demobilization of the military demanded by both the troops and the country; the egalitarianism and lack of self-consciousness with which returning GIs ignored class boundaries; even the fierce defiance with which Truman attacked the liberal internationalists and labor forces who were apparently impregnable bastions of the Democratic Party all seem part of the pattern. Seen in this light, Truman emerges as far more than the heir to FDR and the New Deal. He may be the first truly middle-class president of a nation that was about to become the predominantly middle-class nation it had always believed itself to be. Certainly the middle-class dream had been mostly a dream before 1946. Until then, America was essentially a two-class society, dominated by capitalists and managers who owned or controlled the means of production and served by workers who were described by Karl Marx as proletarians, alienated, exploited, and dependent.

Admittedly, the powers of the great individual men of capital, the Morgans, Rockefellers, and Fords in the United States, had begun to ebb by the end of World War I when the American Legion was formed "to combat the autocracy of both the classes and the masses." During the '20s, the impact of mass consumer markets and the welfare capitalism introduced by the professional managers who began to actually run industry had blurred the lines of class conflict. The Depression and the organization of blue-collar workers into organized labor under FDR's "Tory humanitarianism" continued making proletarians into, at least, members of the lower middle class. Organized labor, in fact, during the years right after World War I had made industrial workers, far from being underprivileged proletarians, the power base of every successful political party in the developed world. Beginning in the '50s, however, the numbers of blue-collar workers in industry began to rapidly decline. With that decline came a precipitous dropoff in union membership, from 35 percent to less than 15 percent of the total workforce. While white-collar workers have replaced blue-collar workers numerically, they have made little effort to assert themselves as a political or special interest group demanding special considerations. The assimilated hyphenated-Americans of the World War II generation have become the acculturated middle-class Americans of the post–cold war period. They are now middle-class people, and middle-class people, almost by definition, don't consider themselves in need of special favors. Instead, they resent having to pay for—or step aside for—those who do demand particular concessions.[4] The "revolution" of the 1994 congressional election may well represent the culmination of this trend.

There was, perhaps, a certain inevitability to the process, as Louis Hartz of Harvard suggested in the 1950s. The United States has never had aristocracies, peasantries, and proletariats in the Europe sense. Americans all share a desire to be independent property owners, if not entrepreneurs and, therefore, as Hartz wrote, two national impulses have been felt throughout the nation's history: "the impulse toward democracy and the impulse toward capitalism. The mass of the people, in other words, are bound to be capitalistic, and capitalism, with its spirit disseminated widely, is bound to be democratic." To be American is to be a disciple of John Locke—to feel entitled to be a property owner despite any odds in one's own circumstance against it.

This "irrational Lockianism," as Hartz called it, was satisfied in the early nineteenth century by Jefferson's Louisiana Purchase, but after the Civil War, property became concentrated in relatively few hands. The Republican Party tried to satisfy the need through the Homestead Act. That was the government's most expansive effort before the GI Bill to fulfill the American dream. By the time mass immigration begin in the 1890s, however, the frontier was closed and, with that, working-class people had little or no opportunity to acquire property. FDR's New Deal reforms ameliorated workers' conditions with labor laws, pension systems, accident compensation, and so forth but were denounced by radicals as efforts to stave off the inevitable proletarian revolution. The only effective alternative to such revolution was making working-class people middle class. Only owning their own homes would make Americans socially and, therefore, politically independent.

That was the political and cultural situation in which Harry Truman became president of the United States. No one could have been more different from FDR than Truman, the reader who never stepped foot in a college classroom; the farmer chained to a plow until released for a few brief months of excitement as a World War I artillery officer; the failed haberdasher; the personally honest protégé of a corrupt political machine; unsophisticated, tactless, totally lacking in charisma but also completely confident in his own judgment, artless and plain. He was exactly the kind of person Tocqueville had in mind when he wrote about the House of Representatives—but not the Senate in which Truman had actually served—as being occupied by "obscure individuals . . . even persons belonging in the lower classes of society." Here was a president whom General Root of New York, a Whig political writer, could have held forth as a model when he said, "We are all of the same estate—all commoners." If the American Legion was "one of the best expounders of the national spirit that Whiggery discovered," as Hartz declared, and the GI Bill had given concrete expression to that Americanism, Harry Truman was the president of both.

Truman's first two years as president, 1945–46, were a tumultuous transition period in which American society underwent a metamorphosis as stunning as the transformation of a caterpillar into a butterfly. The lives of millions improved forever after years of suffering and sacrifice. The toll, just calculated in lives, had been enormous. Among those who had gone off to fight in World War II, 292,131 had died in battles and 115,185 from noncombat injuries. Another 670,848 were wounded, many of them permanently disabled. On the home front, the carnage was almost as great. In the factories and shipyards where the weapons of war were forged, getting the job done had been the number one priority. Health and safety considerations took a distinctly second place. The lives of almost 300,000 workers were lost in accidents, almost 66,000 a year, compared with the current annual rate of 6,300 occupational deaths in 1994. Another million were permanently disabled.[5]

An enormous price had been paid for peace, but, for the survivors, there were great rewards. Never before had so many people been so free economically, educationally, and socially. Astonishing numbers of people were entering and leaving the workforce. Military enrollment plunged from 11.4 million in 1945 to 3.4 million in 1946. Another nearly 2 million were discharged between 1946 and 1947, bringing military strength down to 1.5 million in 1947. At the same time, civilian employment climbed from 53.8 million in 1945 to 57.5 million in 1946, and to 60.8 million in 1947. In other words, while 10 million were discharged from military service, civilian employment increased by 7 million. In the jargon of statisticians, the labor market was "churning." Amid all those zigzagging figures, in theory as many as 7 million to 8 million were out of work at all times during those two years. Indeed, almost 9 million veterans drew 52-20 benefits between 1944 and 1949, but presumably because they were counted as part of the civilian labor force, the unemployment rate was unaffected. On the other hand, they did so for an average of only seventeen weeks—less than a third of the fifty-two weeks they were entitled to.[6]

Where were those people who were out of work, but not apparently looking for jobs? A great many were in school. About 7.8 million World War II veterans, in all, enrolled in some sort of educational or training program under the GI Bill. Total college and university enrollment leaped from 1,676,856 in 1945, with 88,000 veterans attending, to 2,078,095 in 1946 with veterans accounting for 1,013,000, or 48.7 percent of the total. In 1947, veteran enrollment peaked at 2,338,226 with 1,150,000 veterans, or 49.2 percent, among them. The surge of veterans enrolled began to fall off in 1948, when total enrollment was 2,403,396, with veterans accounting for 975,000 (40.5 percent). Veteran enrollment was 34.4 percent by 1949; 25.2 percent in 1950; 18.7 percent in 1951; 10.8 percent in 1952, and 6.1 percent in 1953. After that, the actual numbers of veterans in college—78,000 in 1954 and 42,000 in 1955—reflected both the relatively few men and women in military service and the reduced benefits available under the Korean War Bill of Rights.[7] But the colleges and the universities had been changed forever.

Many women who had left wartime jobs to have children and stay home were also among those who weren't counted among the unemployed. They were producing babies rather than tanks and airplanes now. The number who left the workforce for full-time motherhood wasn't quite as many, however, as memory would suggest. The actual number dropped from 19.3 million in 1945 to 16.8 million in 1946—a 2.5 million drop—then fell a little more to 16.6 in 1947 and crept back up to 17.3 million in 1948. Only 13 percent of the female workforce, in other words, left the office or the assembly line for the nursery and kitchen. Moreover, contrary to popular imagination, women didn't lose out in opportunities for a college education after the war. On the contrary, both the percentage and actual numbers of women enrolled in college increased substantially. The GI Bill didn't directly benefit many women; only 2.9 percent, or 64,728, of the 2,232,000 World War II veterans who attended college under the GI Bill were women. The war contributed substantially, however, to the percentage of women enrolled in college. That went from 33 percent of the total in 1939 to 55 percent in 1945, largely because men were in the service. That high-point figure obviously could not be sustained once the war was over. Indeed, the percentage dropped 15 points, to 40 percent, in 1946, but that was still seven points higher than the 1939 mark. Moreover, the absolute number of college students, including women, more than doubled between 1941 and 1946. The 40 percent figure remained stable or increased slightly over the next fifteen years: 44 percent in 1950; 43 percent in 1954; and 42 percent in 1960.[8]

By the 1970s, the percentage of women enrolled was gaining again, and by 1992, 55 percent of the 14.4 million college students in the country were women. In a society in which income and status became more and more determined by college education, finishing school wasn't enough for upper-class young women. Neither were girls from working-class and middle-class families left behind by their brothers and boyfriends.[9]

The GI Bill set in motion inexorable forces, unforeseen at the time and unappreciated since. However, events could have turned out much differently—and much more disastrously—although probably not quite as badly as H. G. Wells predicted. Wells was the author of *War of the Worlds,* which Orson Welles had dramatized on radio in 1938 as a simulated news broadcast, throwing hundreds of thousands of Americans into panic. In 1945, a dying Wells concluded that mankind, having lost its faith in scientific progress, was already "at the end of its tether" and doomed to extinction.[10] Fiorello La Guardia, the mayor of New York, wasn't a prophet and would willingly admit, "When I make a mistake, it's a beaut." Where Wells was spectacularly wrong in the abstract, La Guardia was more so in the specific. He warned that a million unemployed would descend on New York after the war, workers deserting wartime boom towns in New Jersey, Connecticut, and Pennsylvania. They would be drawn to the Big Apple, La Guardia

blurted, because of its "reputation for being big-hearted." The depth
of the fear—and foolishness of the prognostication—was illustrated
by the sensational headline on *The New York Times*'s report of
La Guardia's comments: "Post-War Jobless Seen Invading City."[11] The
fears proved as fanciful as those of a Japanese invasion fleet that
gripped the West Coast soon after Pearl Harbor.

Nevertheless, the threat of a Pyrrhic victory was real. The nation
had consistently paid "veterans claims too much, too late, in the
wrong way and to the wrong person," Waller had observed in *The Veteran Comes Home,* and the nation had paid a penalty. This time, so
many had served, almost 9 percent of the total population as compared with 2 percent in World War I, the penalty might well be overwhelming, he warned: "Our traditional policy has been to neglect our
veterans for a period of years after the end of a major war." Only
when "they suddenly emerge as a political force . . . is ample provision made for the unfortunate veterans. But it is too late to do
justice, too late to help many who have died or been ruined beyond
reclamation."

Waller's analysis didn't go uncontested at the time. Dixon Wecter,
the author of another book on the subject, *When Johnny Comes
Marching Home,* also published in 1944, thought the returning GI
would be "friendly, generous, easy-going, brave, the citizen-soldier of
America" interested only "in his girl, his job and his little home." He
dismissed Waller's claims that special efforts would be needed to
"renaturalize" the veteran, claiming such programs would "combine
the worst vices of Columbia Teachers College with those of Yale's
Institute of Human Resources." Even Wecter had to concede, however, that "a citizen can be whipped into shape as a soldier by the
manual of arms and a drillmaster, but no manual has been written
for changing him back into a citizen."[12]

Events proved both Waller and Wecter right—and wrong. GI Joe
was friendly, generous, easy-going and brave, but he was also burning
with resentment at anyone, including officers, bureaucrats, politicians, and anyone else who was getting between him and his girl, his
job, and his little home. And he was fully prepared to mutiny if need
be to get back home. Ten days before the war officially ended with the
surrender of the Japanese, Senator Edwin C. Johnson of Colorado,
acting on behalf of other members of Congress, sent a letter to Secretary of War Henry L. Stimson. There was "a widespread feeling in
Congress and the country now that the War Department is tena-

ciously holding men it does not need and whom it cannot use," the
senator wrote. He was also reflecting the fears of many wives and
girlfriends in observing servicemen were also being "thrown into the
path of diseased prostitutes and lewd women in the foulest human
cesspools."

What made the situation worse, in the opinion of the Reverend
Renwick C. C. Kennedy, a former army chaplain writing in *The Christian Century,* was that the men might be enjoying their enforced
absence from home and hearth, cesspools or no. According to Kennedy,
the average GI had three primitive instincts. The first was "to find a
German woman and sleep with her." The second was "to buy or steal
a bottle of cognac and get stinking drunk." The third, in order of priority, was "to go home." The average GI certainly wasn't any conquer-
ing hero to Kennedy. "There he stands in his bulging clothes," he
wrote, "fat, overfed, lonely, a bit wistful, seeing little, understanding
less—the Conqueror with a chocolate bar in one hand and a package
of cigarettes in the other." Almost half of these overfed sex maniacs
were infected with venereal disease at a rate of 427 per 1,000 in certain sections of Germany, Kennedy claimed. The minister, who was
safely back among his flock in Camden, Alabama, reported the lust of
the American troops was so overwhelming that even the few American
women in Germany were threatened. "Army headquarters in Frankfurt had to prepare special armbands for U.S. wives to protect them
from wolves," he declared. Many American women shared Kennedy's
concerns. Seventy percent of American women under the age of thirty
polled by Gallup in mid-1945 didn't want GIs dating German girls.
The army agreed. For several months, consensual relationships with
German women were punished by a $65 fine, more than a month's pay
for most enlisted men.[13]

The troops, in fact, were coming home—fast. Demobilization was
occurring in remarkably high numbers and with, despite the military's reputation, considerable efficiency at first. Gen. George C.
Marshall, the army's chief of staff, had been determined that an
orderly, systematic process for discharging the troops be developed
before hostilities ended. He wanted to avoid the last-minute improvi-
sation that took place after World War I when demobilization planning began only days before the Armistice was signed. The only
advance notification then had been a communication from the army
chief of operations to the Army War College president, in which the
chief observed, "There are one or two questions which it seems to me

should be studied and worked out so that you can be ready for any contingency. The first of these is a plan for demobilization and musters out. . . . I do not want to advertise it too much at present as it might be considered peace propaganda."

In World War II, demobilization planning started in 1943 with a sophisticated poll of twenty thousand troops who were asked what, in their opinion, would be the fairest way of deciding who got out first. They all agreed upon a point system for individuals, rather than units, that is, regiments, tactical forces, ship's companies. A point was given for every month in service, another for each month overseas, five for campaign stars or decorations, and five for Purple Hearts. Fathers with children under eighteen received twelve points each for up to three children. With the maximum number of points set at eighty-five, and German surrender coming in the spring of 1945, almost all of those serving in Europe could expect to be out by that fall. Indeed, as early as May of 1945, shiploads of men were being sent back to the United States, but most of them were actually intended for what the army brass considered a far more urgent priority than a reunion with the home folks: the invasion of the Japanese home islands. Japanese surrender, however, upended the plan and turned efficiency into chaos and near-mutiny.

"The sudden surrender of Japan in August, 1945, just as the War Department mobilization plan got under way, wrecked the plan," observed one historian. "The troops who'd already returned to the United States weren't high-point men about to be discharged but low-point men who were being re-deployed to fight Japan. Sending them on to the Pacific, for occupation duty, would tie up shipping that should be used for bringing high-point men home. What had looked so sensible and right turned into an unholy mess."[14]

Actually, both high-point men scheduled to be discharged and low-pointers destined for the Pacific were coming back, and even the military had difficulty distinguishing one from the other. By that fall, the navy had 843 troop and combat ships, converted liners such as the *Queen Mary*, and freighters ferrying sailors and soldiers across the Atlantic. In July, the *Queen Mary* made its first crossing fully lighted since 1939, jammed to the gunwales with 15,278 troops happily squeezed into space designed for 2,000. Almost 6,000 men a day were being discharged starting on May 7, and by mid-September the rate was reaching upwards of 25,000 a day. "It took us three and a half years to get the men overseas, and it will take us only ten months to get them back," Adm. James M. Callaghan, the director of naval transportation, told a Senate committee. Robert Patterson, the undersecretary of war, assured the Senate Military Affairs Committee that discharges were running 30 to 45 percent ahead of schedule, as many as 10,000 a day. That wasn't good enough for waiting wives and others, though. "We are getting *10,000* letters a day," Senator Johnson shot back. Many letters also came from former combat troops "mowing lawns with bayonets" to kill time, according to Johnson. GIs were also being enrolled in British and French colleges, and thousands were taking correspondence courses offered at every level from grade school to graduate school through the U.S. Armed Forces Institute. Everyone, however, preferred to mow lawns and study at home.

The newspapers were also upset. "Has the Army heard of peace?" the *Chicago Tribune* demanded. It saw incompetence and selfishness as responsible for laggard demobilization. "It has often been pointed out that the more rapidly the army is reduced from its wartime strength the more rapidly its higher officers will be reduced in number, rank and influence," the self-proclaimed "Greatest Newspaper in the World" declared. "It would be hard to imagine a worse reason than this one for keeping millions of men in the army, but what else is there?" The equally conservative *Wall Street Journal* was more sympathetic. As a voice of the eastern establishment, unlike the isolationist *Chicago Tribune,* it supported President Truman's intention of having the United States assume international peacekeeping responsibilities. Nevertheless, taking note of the fact that the army would still have six million men under arms by the end of 1945, *The Journal* declared: "On the basis of any information available to the public, that is a policy that is perfectly idiotic. If the United States saw any other country pursuing a similar policy, it would be crying to high heaven about 'militarism' and what not." The newspaper was convinced the military was "deliberately pursuing a policy of 'gradual' demobilization. . . . We wonder if anyone in Washington has any adequate idea of the resentment that is building up in the country?"[15]

The War Department's careful planning probably compounded the turmoil. The troops and their loved ones at home had been led to believe demobilization would be an orderly and fair process. When it turned out to be disorderly and was suspected of being unfair, anger and resentment flared. As early as September 6, 1944—ten days after Paris was liberated and four days before the lights were turned on in London after 1,483 dark nights—the War Department had announced its demobilization policy. Soldiers would be mustered out as soon as the Germans surrendered. *Yank,* the army magazine, banner headlined the War Department announcement, "Plan for Demobilization," and revealed: "Demobilization is all set to go. X-Day, that is the day that resistance ends, has been officially designated as the starting gun. So it is possible that by the time some G.I.'s in outlying bases read this story, the process of discharging surplus soldiers and sending them home may already have begun." A cautionary note was sounded further on in the article, the possibility that some European ground troops, "even including those who have had combat, may have to be shipped to the Pacific." The caution was ignored, however, in the first flush of anticipation. GIs started to daydream about the delights of home when they weren't shooting Germans, maintaining tanks or airplanes, marching, or doing KP.

The first signs of trouble began back home where Maj. Gen. Lewis Hershey, head of the Selective Service system, made one of the provocative comments he would be noted for up to the Vietnam era: "We can keep people in the Army about as cheaply as we could create an agency for them," he said. Thomas Dewey, the Republican candidate for president, charged the Roosevelt administration planned on maintaining a big army just to keep the unemployment rate down. General Osborn, the head of the postwar manpower planning commission, also objected vigorously. If Hershey's advice were followed, the army would be "making itself into a preventive WPA," he said. General Hershey was ordered by a Pentagon directive to stop talking in public. Theoretical arguments about the system among political figures back home were soon overshadowed by practical concerns that made themselves apparent in the battle areas. The point policy had been based on the wishes of the soldiers themselves. The wishes of the soldiers, however, didn't coincide with military logic, and that gap would become apparent only after the Germans surrendered in May 1945.

No one had any problem counting points for time in service, personal combat decorations, Purple Hearts, and children, but the military had its own way of deciding who got campaign stars. In the army air corps, for example, everything depended on whether an individual was assigned to a service or a bombing group. The results didn't make much sense to ex-civilians such as this staff sergeant who wrote to his member of Congress: "A man who does the engine changes on our planes is in the service group and gets no stars, but the man who drives the gas truck is in the bombing group and gets stars. A man who keeps a 2½-ton truck of the service group in top condition to haul bombs and other vital needs rates no stars; a man who keeps a 2½-ton truck of the bomb group in top condition to haul these very same needs rates four. A bomb group man in headquarters is handed twenty points; a service group man, at the next desk, doing the same work, is handed, it would seem, a gold-braided tough shit ticket."

The ticket was really tough for combat troops, who having helped defeat the Nazis, found they were being rewarded with a second opportunity to get killed, this time fighting the Japanese. Individual complaints turned into mass criticism that came perilously close to "open sedition and mutiny." Those were the words of Maj. Gen. Harry L. Twaddle, commanding general of the 95th Infantry. He was responding to his men's complaints to Congress while they were in transit from Europe to the Pacific across the United States. "Why should we serve on two fronts when there are so many who never served on one?" they asked in telegrams sent from railroad stations along the line. Twaddle had to indirectly concede the men had a legitimate gripe. The principal disturbing elements in the 95th, Twaddle said, were high-point men who were transferred into the division prior to departure from Germany. Such men had expected to be discharged. The Pentagon insisted, however, that high-point men were, in fact, supposed to have been screened out of units headed for an invasion of Japan. That was brass-hat propaganda to soldiers in the 28th Division, who also peppered reporters and editors with telegrams during their transit across the United States toward Japan. Regular army officers just wanted to keep the ranks full to justify retention of their temporary wartime rank, they complained. The fact that substantial numbers of officers would also be needed—and endangered—in an invasion of the Japanese home islands was ignored. Nonetheless, the *Chicago Tribune* wondered why several million soldiers were being sent to fight a single enemy in the Pacific when only a million were needed to fight "six nations and their auxiliaries" in Europe. War Secretary Stimson pointed out that the Japanese still had almost five million men under arms, two and a half million in the home islands, and another two and a half scattered throughout occupied territories in the Pacific and Asia.

While 73 percent of the public thought the point system was fair, when the Japanese surrendered on August 14, impatience and irritation rose. With new peacetime priorities now uppermost, complaints couldn't be as easily dismissed as coming from discontented individuals or from special interests. Southern politicians, for example, such as Senator J. H. Bankhead of Alabama, who had been calling for the immediate release of farmers, had been deflected by obsequious telephone calls from Pentagon colonels. The demand of John L. Lewis and the militant United Mine Workers for the discharge of thirty thousand mine workers was just brushed aside before the war ended. Now, however, Lewis's demand was seconded by Harold L. Ickes, the equally curmudgeonly secretary of the interior. "Next winter will be the coldest winter of the war for the people of the United States," Ickes warned. Moreover, failure to supply Europe with coal would mean "rioting, bloodshed and the destruction of nearly all semblance of orderly government," he added.[16] Truman was caught in the middle. He was trying, at the time, to persuade all the members of Congress to unify the military services under a Department of Defense, while warding off complaints from individual members. "The services are carrying out demobilization with considerable efficiency and with justice for all concerned," the president said, knowing his words were beginning to ring hollow.[17]

Autumn weather brought a change in the public mood as well, this one coming from the home front, sometimes wistful, but often with a cutting edge. Two letters summed up the changing attitudes. The first, from the wife of a soldier, was printed in the *Wyoming State Tribune:* "He's fat, sway-backed—with a crick in the sway—chipped elbow, has several teeth missing and hobbles into age thirty-eight this month," wrote the wife. "But he has a nice smile—with what teeth he has left—and I love him. So, why don't you send him home?" The other, from a soldier to his member of Congress, went: "You put us in the military and you can get us out. Either demobilize us or, when given the next shot at the ballot box, we will demobilize you." The attitude was reinforced—and gloom spread through the Pentagon and the White House—when General MacArthur, for not the first or the last time, demonstrated his unique talent for the inappropriate comment. He said he would need only two hundred thousand rather than five hundred thousand to occupy Japan. Then in September 1945, the normally judicious General Marshall injudiciously told Congress all men with two years or more of military service would be discharged by late winter. He may have been listening to the Pentagon's chief representative to Capitol Hill, who had warned in early March that "the attitude of Congress is beginning to approach that which exists during normal times of peace. . . . Until recently, Congress has responded to the Army as the desperate householder whose home is in flames welcomes the fire department: Drive over the lawn, chop down the doors, throw the furniture out the window, but save the house. Now, with the flames under control, the Congress, like the householder, is noting for the first time the water damages and thinking if the fire department had acted differently, the lawn would not be torn up, the doors smashed and the furniture broken." [18]

Getting the servicemen home seemed as chaotic as the metaphors the Pentagon lobbyist used to describe Congress's attitude. Stranded GIs watched ships leave for home from Pacific ports with empty berths; one ship sailed from the Philippines with 620 spaces free, according to *The Daily Pacifican,* an army newspaper. Because of the need to pick up men scattered on atolls all over the Pacific, a trip from Manila to San Francisco that should have taken one month sometimes consumed three. All over the world, combat veterans were being forced to take basic training courses over and over just to keep them occupied. Often, when they looked up from stripping an M-2 for the millionth time, they saw ships just drifting at anchor.

A senator asked Adm. A. William Callaghan at a hearing of the Senate Naval Affairs Committee about the complaint of one soldier who counted two hundred ships sitting at anchorage. Admiral Callaghan responded that the ships the soldier was referring to were too small to carry troops home. Sailing a forty-thousand-ton vessel with a forty-member crew twelve thousand miles over two and a half months just to return twenty or thirty passengers didn't make sense, he said. What the brass did, however, often made as little sense as what it didn't do, as Col. J. M. Johnson, the chief of the Office of Defense Transportation, candidly admitted: "Nobody knows what's going to happen. You can't look deep into this redeployment. It is too big and complicated for the human mind. We will make a lot of mistakes. Doing things as fast as we are doing, you can't hit all the balls." That wasn't much consolation, however, to seventy-three GIs who shipped out from Naples aboard a ship carrying Brazilian troops to Rio de Janeiro. They were told the passage was just a detour to the ship's ultimate destination in New York. Once in Rio, however, the captain was ordered to return to Marseille to pick up a full load of American troops. The GIs telegraphed complaints to their members of Congress, and a plane was dispatched to pick them up. But the ship had left for France, with the GIs still on board by the time the plane arrived. [19]

Once veterans got back on shore and in the United States, conditions often seemed worse than on sea. The railroad system, already massively overstrained from wartime demands, was approaching collapse trying to accommodate both the returning soldiers and civilians eager to take long-delayed vacations. Summertime excursion trains were canceled, and civilian reservations prohibited so that troops could be accommodated. Rail officials who pleaded with the public to give the right of way to returning soldiers were ignored. The military expression SNAFU took on new civilian meaning. Five hundred GIs on an eight-day train hegira from Massachusetts to California rioted over false rumors that German POWs had been installed in Pullman berths. Clogged rest rooms aboard trains carried signs declaring, "Nothing's too good for the returning Yanks—oh, yeah?"[20] Chaos reigned over the Christmas holidays. GIs who had developed scrounging abilities overseas put them to work on the home front. Five sailors hired a cab at $55 a man to get them home to Atlanta from San Pedro, California, *Newsweek* reported in a December 24, 1945, story entitled, "Colossal Rail Snafu Holds Up G.I.'s in Christmas Rush to Home."[21]

The delays also brought out the worst elements in the military caste system. "The most abrasive issue, however, had nothing to do with mustering out," William Manchester, who had been a Marine in the South Pacific, recalled in *The Glory and the Dream*. "It was a universal grievance of enlisted men who felt they were being systematically mistreated by their superiors. Military precedence lay athwart the thrust of egalitarianism, twentieth century America's most powerful social force." The rough and ready comradeship of combat quickly disappeared in the disciplined—and blatantly hierarchical—life of the barracks after the guns stopped firing. Hanson Baldwin of *The New York Times* reported colonels and generals were feasting on champagne and caviar while GIs ate C rations. Junior officers requisitioned the best quarters, laid claim to the prettiest Red Cross women and nurses, got the best seats at the movies, had GI bartenders pour them top-shelf liquor in their clubs, and got chauffeured home. Baldwin, who, as Manchester noted, was "no enemy of privilege," wrote there was solid grounds for discontent.[22] Helen Gurley Flynn, the American Communist leader, wasn't spouting a propaganda line when she reported her own experiences aboard the *Edward M. Alexander,* a troop ship she returned from Europe on. The men were initially philosophical, she wrote, when they were given frankfurters and sauerkraut for breakfast while the officers had eggs and fresh fruit. On Christmas Eve, however, as they gathered for a USO show, the announcement came over the loudspeaker that the performance was for officers only. Enlisted men were ordered to return to their bunks. "They drowned out the voice in catcalls and boos," Flynn recorded in *The Daily Worker* on January 10, 1946. The next day, the captain ordered another show be held for the men. "Agitation pays even on board an army transport," Flynn concluded, "especially on the way home."[23]

There could be also something disgraceful, if not treasonous, about agitation by GIs wanting to go home. The GIs, in justification, could claim they had been provoked. In January 1946, the Pentagon, worried that demobilization was proceeding too rapidly, announced abruptly that no other servicemen would be discharged until July 1, 1946, six months later. Certainly, judging by the figures, demobilization had proceeded quickly. From a peak of almost twelve million men and women in uniform at the end of 1945, the armed forces were reduced to three million by the beginning of 1946. The army alone discharged six million. Representative James Wadsworth (R-New York) was undoubtedly right, from a technical and a historical perspective, when he observed in January 1946, "I think when this thing is all over the historians will say that for speed and thoroughness this demobilization beats all records." But no explanation was provided for the suspension of discharges. An internal army memo did say Secretary of War Robert Patterson, who had succeeded Stimson, "feels it would be better to admit we made a mistake than try to qualify any announcement." Normally, that would have been a good public relations strategy. Coming four months after General Marshall's promise that all two-year men would be discharged by January, however, the men and their families greeted the announcement as a betrayal.

Patterson's announcement was made shortly before he embarked on an inspection tour of Pacific bases. The tour provided GIs—and others with their own agenda—an opportunity to vent their anger in front of the reporters traveling with the secretary. The resulting uproar made front-page news all over the country. Patterson's inspection trip became a political death march for the Pentagon. In Guam, his first stop, Patterson was greeted with the sight of his own burning effigy. In Yokohama, an infuriated provost marshal, trying to break up what he called a mutiny, told GIs they were behaving "like a lot of goddam babies." In Manila, mobs of up to ten thousand soldiers and sailors besieged Patterson's quarters for several days. A banner headline in the Pacific edition of *Stars and Stripes* declared, "Patterson Declared Number One Enemy by Jeering Mob." Mobs of soldiers and sailors in Manila marched through the city with banners that read: "We want ships, we want to go home." A colonel, ordering them back to barracks, shouted, "You men forget you're not working for General Motors. You're still in the Army."[24]

Such comments didn't impress Earl Mazey, who had been the right-hand man of Walter Reuther, president of the United Auto Workers (UAW). The UAW was, coincidentally, striking General Motors at the time, although Mazey, now a sergeant in the army and one of the prime movers of the Manila riots, wasn't aware of what was happening in Detroit. He had been deprived of mail and visitors and kept under surveillance after he and other former CIO workers had put their picket-line experience to work organizing what became known as the "Wanna Go Home riots." The anger they were tapping into had been sparked anew while Patterson was flying from Guam to Manila. *The Daily Pacifican* reported the demobilization rate had been cut from eight hundred thousand to three hundred thousand a month because General Hershey had stopped the flow of new draftees as replacements. He had slashed the monthly draft quota from eighty-eight thousand to twenty-one thousand. *The Pacifican*, in a front-page editorial addressed to President Truman, argued that American soldiers weren't needed in the Philippines since the island common-wealth was scheduled to become independent on July 4. Echoing left-wing political agendas back home, some soldiers claimed the military was about to be used to suppress the aspirations of the Philippine people. One noncom testified at a subsequent hearing that the protests were prompted by reports that "the chief of staff of the 86th Division [had said] the division would undergo training along battle lines to exert . . . American influence on prospective disturbances in the Philippines." Other soldiers feared they would be pressed into the service of Chiang Kai-shek in his struggle against his erstwhile allies, the Communists under Mao Tse-tung.

The suspicions and rumors were turned into political protests by Mazey and his CIO comrades. They mimeographed and distributed leaflets, organized a cavalcade of trucks and jeeps "liberated" from official duties, and gathered followers who marched under banners proclaiming "When Do We Go Home?" and "We Don't Like This Deal." Initially, only 150 or so soldiers had joined Mazey and his allies on their first foray into Manila. But by the following evening, more than 2,500 gathered angrily in front of Manila City Hall. Donations were gathered to place an ad in *The New York Times* and send telegrams to newspaper columnists Walter Winchell and Drew Pearson. Then Lt. Gen. W. D. Styer, commander of the armed forces in the western Pacific, proved, once again, what experienced organizers such as Mazey quickly learn: Your opponent is often your best ally. Styer decided the men needed only to hear him to be shown the error of their ways. He arranged to address the assembled protesters over a public address system in Manila's huge Rizal stadium. The result was a much bigger crowd and a news headline in *The New York Times* the next day that read "20,000 G.I.'s Boo General; Urge Congress to Speed Sailings."

A chain reaction began as radio and other newspapers described the response of Styer's troops. Patterson was heckled in Yokohama. In Paris, GIs tacked up crayoned signs in Red Cross clubs that declared, "Back Up Your Manila Buddies. Meeting Tonight at the Arc de Triomphe." Gendarmes waved the GIs away from the arch because it was a French national shrine. The march continued down the Champs d'Elysees with the men waving flares and calling other servicemen who refused to join them "scabs." In Tokyo, men paraded with signs reading, "Service, yes, but serfdom never" and "Japs go home, why not us?" In Yokohama, Secretary Patterson was heckled. In London, thousands of GIs gathered under the windows of Mrs. Roosevelt's room in the Hotel Claridge, shouting "Eleanor, Eleanor, Eleanor!" They demanded to know why space was being allocated on returning ships for war brides, but not for the GIs they had married. Mrs. Roosevelt appeared briefly on a balcony and promised to find out. Manchester thought the most offensive of the Wanna Go Home riots occurred in Germany: "The Paris demonstrators at least knew how to keep step." By contrast, in Frankfurt, demonstrators were a mindless, howling rabble. Military police turned them away from the I. G. Farben Building, which had been commandeered as military headquarters. They retreated, shouting Gen. Joseph T. McNarney was too cowardly to meet them. McNarney, who had been in Berlin, was one of the few military commanders who called in the organizers of the protest and spoke candidly to them on his return. "We will get you home as quickly as we possibly can," he said, "but if your Congressman gets the impression from his mailbag that what the public wants is 'to get the boys home and to hell with international commitments,' then you'll go home regardless of what happens to . . . chores in Europe that the nation has accepted." The general was sarcastic, Manchester observed, but "he hit upon the key to the entire campaign. . . . The campaign was a test of Congressional courage and Congress flunked."[25]

The lack of courage was bipartisan. Representative Rankin, always the aginner, introduced legislation to immediately release any GI with eighteen months or more of service. "The war is over," Rankin declared. "We do not have an enemy on earth that would dare bat an eye at us today. Why should we have an army of occupation in the Philippines?" Representative Emmanuel Celler of New York, a liberal luminary in Congress for many years, wondered what U.S. troops were doing "in a place like India." Daniel Flood (D-Pennsylvania), a former actor for whom the House of Representatives would be a stage for decades, probably spoke for almost all the Democrats when he urged President Truman to appoint a "civilian demobilization czar" and added the following qualifications: the appointee "must not be a Democrat. He might fail; that would be fatal in 1946 [elections]. This man must not be a Republican. He might succeed; that would be fatal in 1946."

Demobilization of the armed services unquestionably encouraged Joseph Stalin. The Soviet leader had ignored his promises at Yalta and Potsdam to allow democratic elections in the Eastern European states. The breakdown of army discipline resulting from the riots was virtually an invitation to Soviet imperialism, *The New York Times* editorialized. The demonstrators' actions were "indefensible," the paper said, "and they must be made to realize this." Congress was also guilty of abetting "a bring-the-boys-home campaign which disregards our international responsibilities and encourages such exhibitions as those in Manila and LeHavre," *The Times* added. That message was echoed by military leaders—with the exception of MacArthur—but the American public wasn't listening. "After every war the United States has thoughtfully and deliberately done what no enemy could do," Adm. Chester Nimitz said, according to the March 4, 1946, *Newsweek*. "At the present moment [January 10, 1946], less than five months after the defeat of Japan, your Navy has not the strength in ships and personnel to carry on a major military operation."

Rapid discharge was a political imperative, military imperatives be damned. Demobilization was the key topic at Truman's cabinet meeting on January 11, 1946, and four days later General Eisenhower was recalled to Washington to explain the army's—and the administration's—position to Congress. He found himself trapped in a congressional corridor by irate wives and was forced to take refuge in the office of Representative May, whose remarks about undertakers had been, in many ways, the catalyst of the GI Bill. Emerging, Eisenhower braved angry women pickets on the way to a special assembly of senators and representatives in the Library of Congress, where he said: "I am frank to say I never anticipated this emotional wave [to get men out of the army] would reach proportions of hysteria." He argued demobilization had to be slowed because otherwise "we will literally run out of soldiers." The military simply couldn't fulfill the international responsibilities laid on it "by higher authority," he said, adding: "If we should take every father today, authorize his discharge, and start him home, the army simply cannot do its job." Members of Congress said they agreed with the highly popular general. Nevertheless, soon thereafter, Eisenhower ordered all men with two or more years of service to be placed in the pipeline for discharge by June 30. Congress, the president, and the military had capitulated. The United States Army, which had ranked fifteenth in the world behind Bulgaria's during the '30s, would never descend to that melancholy position again. But, as Truman recorded in his memoirs, "the program we were following was no longer demobilization—it was disintegration."[26]

The United States had solemnly pledged that, this time, after the carnage of a Second World War, it would not retreat from its solemn international obligations. The pledge was broken. In August 1945, Truman had written the House Military Affairs Committee giving it specific numbers of troops needed to "protect the fruits of victory," using General Marshall's words. Some 1.2 million men were needed for occupation duty in Germany and Japan, Truman wrote, based on estimates from General Eisenhower as well as General MacArthur. Another 1.3 million would be needed elsewhere, for a total of 2.5 million. In January, less than six months later, Truman told the Pentagon he wanted an overall total of 2 million. Congress slashed that figure almost in half to 1,070,000 effective July 1, 1947. For the next three years, the military power of the United States was all bluster and little brawn.

Career military officers saw danger, not only from the Soviets, but even from the thoroughly defeated and completely demoralized Japanese. "None of our divisions is up to strength," said Maj. Gen. Clovis E.

Byers, chief of staff of the occupation forces in Japan. "If any group of Japanese decided the time was right for revolt, they would certainly pick a time when they believed there was dissatisfaction in the American army. It appears there are subversive forces at work, for obscure reasons, attempting to undermine the morale of the Army." In Seoul, Lt. Gen. John R. Hodge, the American commander negotiating a division of Korea with the Russians, foresaw a war. The Russians "take great pleasure in our embarrassment and unwillingness to continue as soldiers," he said. The presumably invincible air force, armed with the atomic bomb, literally couldn't get off the ground reliably. "Airplanes were stranded in all parts of the world for lack of maintenance personnel to repair them," Gen. Carl Spaatz, the air force commander, said. "Serviceable and even new aircraft were left to deteriorate for lack of personnel to prepare them for storage." The most telling criticism came from General Marshall in a 1950 speech to a preparedness conference: "I remember, when I was secretary of state, I was being pressured constantly, particularly when in Moscow, by radio message after radio message to give the Russians hell. When I got back, I was given the same appeal in relation to the Far East and China. At that time, my facilities for giving them hell—and I am a soldier and I know something about giving them hell—was one and one-third divisions over the entire United States. This is quite a proposition when you deal with somebody with over 260 [divisions] and you have one and one-third. We had nothing in Alaska. We did not have enough to defend the airstrip in Fairbanks."[27]

There was, fortunately, no need to defend—by military means, anyway—either the United States or any ally for three years after the war ended. American influence in Europe did not go by default to some other country, as Eisenhower had told the representatives and senators assembled in the Library of Congress. Whether Russia was less aggressive than some feared or truly peace loving was debatable then and now. Such were the pieties of the time, however, that Russia wasn't even mentioned by name as a potential enemy until Winston Churchill gave his famous "Iron Curtain" speech at Westminster College in Fulton, Missouri, on March 6, 1946, under the approving gaze of Truman. Indeed, the very notion that Russia could possibly disrupt the peace, even as it was busily gobbling up the Eastern European countries occupied by the Red Army, sparked a revolt in the Democratic Party. Henry Wallace, when he was vice president, had warned FDR in 1943 that "men who are losing their jobs, their farms and the business couldn't be expected to warm to an altruistic idea" of a new League of Nations. With the GI Bill helping the nation to avoid a Pearl Harbor of peace, Wallace, now the secretary of commerce, was about to emerge as the leading apostle of "altruistic peace lovers" in America. That would make Wallace the foremost opponent of those, including Truman, who feared a cold war was already being waged—but only after the secretary of commerce made a public fool out of the president. Wallace delivered a speech that embarrassed Truman, raised profound questions about the president's grasp of foreign policy, and forced Truman to fire Wallace. The speech and Truman's bumbling also gave many reasons to vote for Republican majorities in the House and Senate in the 1946 elections. But it was also an ordeal by fire that steeled the new president, eighteen months into his unelected presidency, to take the first bold steps needed to contain the Union of Soviet Socialist Republics.

Wallace had shown Truman a copy of a speech he intended to deliver to a U.S.-Soviet friendship rally on September 11 in Madison Square Garden. Some attending would be pro-Soviet sympathizers; others would be supporters of Democratic congressional candidates in the upcoming elections. Wallace told Truman he would be critical, although not excessively, of Soviet actions in Eastern Europe. Truman didn't object to the speech; later, many wondered if he had read it. Perhaps he just assumed, in Dean Acheson's words, that Wallace, as a "responsible and experienced high officer of government" wouldn't say anything inflammatory. Acheson was being kind. Wallace, after all, had been replaced as vice president by Truman in 1944, because, as FDR himself had told Wallace, many people looked on Wallace as a Communist or worse. Truman, if he had read Wallace's speech, obviously didn't understand the impact of what he was about to say. Certainly, it couldn't have been said at a worse time. Secretary of State James "Jimmy" Byrnes was at a crucial meeting of foreign ministers in Paris trying to coordinate a common policy for dealing with the Soviets. Yet Wallace told a cheering crowd in Madison Square Garden that the United States had no right to interfere with the Soviets in Eastern Europe. That was Stalin's sphere of influence, said the secretary of commerce. Second, Wallace said, the United States should make the atomic bomb available to all other governments, whatever their political persuasion. Third, the United States should unilaterally disarm and not even consider collective security treaties with Great Britain and other Western European countries. "To make Great

Britain the key to our foreign policy would, in my judgment, be the height of folly," Wallace said. "Make no mistake about it: the British imperialist policy in the New East alone, combined with Russian retaliation, would lead the United States straight to war." Then Wallace added two sentences to the speech he'd written after seeing Truman. "I am neither anti-British nor pro-British; neither anti-Russian or pro-Russian. And two days ago, when President Truman read these words, he said they represented the policy of his administration."

Which Truman had indeed said. Drafts of the speech had been circulated in advance to reporters at a White House press conference on other subjects held at 4 P.M., three hours before it was scheduled for delivery. Truman, asked if he approved the speech and if it reflected administration policy, responded affirmatively. The first rumbles of an approaching disaster were felt only when Will Clayton, the acting secretary of state in Byrnes's absence, belatedly received a copy of the speech. He immediately telephoned Charles G. Ross, Truman's press secretary at the White House. "This will cut the ground right out from under Jimmy in Paris," Clayton told Ross, urging an immediate repudiation. It was too late, Ross said; the speech had already been approved, and besides, Truman was off at a stag party at Clark Clifford's house. The next day, the nation's apparent 180-degree turn in foreign affairs was headlined in 180-point type. Senator Arthur Vandenberg, the former Republican isolationist whose conversion to internationalism made a bipartisan foreign policy possible after World War II, was in Paris with Byrnes. His response when told the news was ominous: "I can cooperate with only one secretary of state at a time." Byrnes raged quietly to himself for four days before cabling Truman: "If it is not possible for you to keep Mr. Wallace, a member of your cabinet, from speaking on foreign affairs . . . I must ask you to accept my resignation immediately." Truman only made matters worse at a press conference he called to "clarify . . . a natural misunderstanding." The president said he had only approved Wallace's right to speak out, but had not endorsed his views as the foreign policy of the country. Under questioning, he contradicted himself—and the obvious facts— by saying Wallace's comments and Byrnes's foreign policy were "exactly in line."

Truman, considered by many since to be the most honest president of modern times, had committed a clumsy lie, which the press pointed out to the rest of the country. James Reston, perhaps the nation's most influential Washington correspondent, wrote in *The*

New York Times, "Mr. Truman seems to be the only person in the capital who thinks Mr. Wallace's proposals are 'in line' with either Mr. Truman's or Mr. Byrnes's." George Dixon, a Hearst columnist in Washington, was more cutting in explaining why Truman was late for the press conference: "He got up this morning a little stiff in the joints and has had trouble putting his foot in his mouth." Billy Rose, the showman, called on Americans to support W. C. Fields for president in 1948: "If we're going to have a comedian in the White House, let's have a good one." Wallace compounded the confusion—and growing outrage—by calling his own press conference, on the White House lawn no less, and saying, "I stand by my New York speech. Feeling as I do that most Americans are concerned about and willing to work for peace . . . I shall in the near future speak on this subject again."

Truman's temper was already strained by a Drew Pearson column in which Wallace was quoted as warning against a school of military thinking advocating "a 'preventive war' . . . *now* before Russia has atomic bombs." When he heard what Wallace said on the White House lawn, Truman's sulfurous vocabulary erupted. He wrote Wallace a note laced with every profanity and blasphemy he could think of and sent it by messenger to Wallace at the Commerce Department. Wallace immediately agreed to resign, but was so stunned by the language in the note he called press secretary Ross and warned the letter couldn't be allowed to get into the presidential archives. Ross agreed, asked that the note be returned, and promptly burned it. "Well, he's out now and the crackpots are having conniption fits," Truman wrote his wife about Wallace that night. "I'm glad they are. It convinces me I was right."

"He had been wrong, of course," as Manchester observed. "He had handled things badly." The blunder compounded public anger over the strikes, shortages, rocketing prices, and other frustrations of reconversion, tumbling Truman's popularity ratings.[28] Truman had begun his accidental presidency with a phenomenal approval rating of 87 percent, three points higher than FDR had ever scored. Liberals hoped he would continue New Deal policies; conservatives thought the machine politician from Kansas City was "safe." Now, however, Truman's popularity was well below 50 percent—heading south—and no one was happy, especially organized labor—and its critics. The unity created by war was being splintered apart by peace. The epithets used to describe the nation's enemies changed, from "Nip," "Kraut," and "Wop" to "labor barons," "finks," "goons," "Commies," and "scabs." The emotions, if anything, were even more heartfelt; domestic enemies are more hateful than foreign ones. The stage seemed set for a bloody rematch between labor and capital on a scale far surpassing the Red Scare. This time, however, Soviet Russia was a truly great power with infinitely more admirers in the United States than it had a generation before.

The price of civil discord was potentially far more severe than it had been after the Treaty of Versailles signed a quarter century before. If the United States, already poorly disposed to take international responsibilities, were riven by domestic conflict, the USSR might well come to dominate the world, almost by default. Indeed, Russia may already have been fomenting dissension in America. James V. Forrestal, the secretary of the navy, believed leftists had encouraged, if not inspired, many of the Wanna Go Home riots. "Considerable communistic influence" was behind the disturbances in Manila, the American high commissioner in the Philippines reported to Congress in 1947. The commissioner was none other than Paul V. McNutt, the former head of the Federal Security Agency, who had been FDR's point man on veterans' affairs. Truman had appointed him in 1945 to the position halfway around the world from Washington after McNutt called for the total extermination of the Japanese. John Brophy, a union official, observed "the most rabid in the CIO [for the return of troops] . . . the most articulate, were the Communist sympathizers." They were all right, as historian Ross observed. But so what? "Communists did 'want to bring the boys home,'" as Ross wrote. "Nevertheless it is clear that the American communists were but one voice among many in the cacophonous roar of 1945 and early 1946."[29]

Communists certainly had good reason, in accordance with Marxist-Leninist principles, to believe that America would soon be torn apart by the internal contradictions of capitalism. Veterans might very well do the tearing, just as they had in Italy, Germany, and Russia after World War I. Their exultation at being home from war would soon fade when jobs failed to materialize and wives and kids went without food and adequate shelter. Demobilization was already creating the conditions for Communist revolution. The idle and hopeless would be tinder only awaiting the flame. The capitalists, in their insensate drive to exploit the weakness of both workers and veterans for profit, could be counted on to supply the match. America was indeed stripped of effective ground forces, and Communists could reasonably believe the nation was rejecting its new status as a world power by the will of its own people. America, nevertheless, confounded all the Marxist prophets by remaining prosperous, as historian Morison observed.[30]

Communists were not the only ones predicting economic gloom. "There should be no mincing of words," wrote John W. Snyder, Truman's reconversion planner. The end of war spending would "cause an immediate and large dislocation of our economy" with the "severity of the shock . . . increased by the sudden ending of the war." August 1945 was called one of the most dangerous periods in our country's economic history by Chester Bowles, the director of the Office of Price Administration (OPA). Under Bowles's urging, Truman signed a "hold the line" order on August 18, 1945, effectively preventing Americans from buying a new car, refrigerator, or house—or even a steak for that matter—for another eighteen months, or until "economic conversion" took place.

Americans responded by reverting to what Finley Peter Dunne's Mr. Dooley, the Irish bartender-philosopher who was the most popular political columnist of the early twentieth century, called their "natchural state of illegal merriment"—the detested functionaries of OPA be damned. The OPA had become, as Manchester noted, a government within a government. With its seventy-three thousand full-time workers and two hundred thousand volunteers and offices in every town, it was "an intolerable tyranny, a mockery of freedom, and all that could be said for it was there was no alternative."[31] Once the war was over, however, that was no longer true, and even though the alternative wasn't legal, it was socially acceptable. A dealer would sell an automobile, for example, for the OPA-listed price, but only if the customer was also willing to pay $125 for an extra jack or $150 for an extra battery. Purchases of building supplies were often accompanied by side bets of $100 or more, with the customer always losing and happily paying. A whiskey drinker was often obliged to buy several additional bottles of wine, although he could trade the wine in for another bottle of Scotch.

Reston of *The Times* found Midwestern farmers openly flouting OPA regulations and contemptuous of people they thought were benefiting from price controls and rationing. "They do not think in terms of feeding starving human beings abroad," Reston wrote, "but in terms of 'feeding Europe' and 'feeding Asia,' and keeping prices down not for 'the people in the cities,' but 'for labor,' which, they assert caustically, goes on strike when it likes and forces up prices which the farmers have to pay." Manufacturers became as adept at inventing loopholes as at making goods. Textile plants allowed to return to full production turned out curtains and bedspreads rather than pajamas, shirts, and other clothing. Price controls had been taken off the former, not the latter.

The black marketer, regarded just a few months before as the moral equivalent of a draft dodger, began to become as popular and admired as the bootlegger of a generation before—especially when he came bearing beef. Almost 75 percent of the nation's meat was going to black market firms that ignored price ceilings, claimed James D. Cooney, a vice president of Wilson & Co., a big Chicago meat packer. "During the week ending July 16," Cooney wrote the White House, "36,604 head of cattle were received at the Chicago stockyards. We had fifteen active cattle buyers on this market and we were unable to buy a single head at legal compliance prices." Only horse meat was available for hospital patients in Boston, Majority Leader McCormack complained. By the fall of 1946, with the war over for more than a year, two out of three butcher shops in New York were closed. Armour's main plant in Chicago had only sixty-eight cows to slaughter one week in September rather than the customary nine thousand. Only 6 out of 139 cities surveyed by *Time* weren't experiencing acute meat shortages.

Labor unions, in giving voice to the legitimate anger of blue-collar workers, inadvertently drew upon themselves the frustrations of white-collar workers, who lacked collective bargaining agents. During the war, unions had faithfully, with the exception of two coal miners' strikes and a threatened walkout by railroad workers in 1943, observed the no-strike pledge Roosevelt called for after Pearl Harbor (although they hadn't been able to control strikes organized by militant members). In four and a half years, less than 0.0006 of 1 percent of total production time had been lost. The end of the war, however, meant militant union members were determined to catch up on wages that had lagged behind prices despite OPA controls. Union leaders, who had been patriotic Americans during the war, now had to prove their first loyalty was to their members. Some were also demonstrating an arrogance not unlike the "public be damned" industrialists they regularly condemned. For example, James C.—for "Caesar" many said—Petrillo, the head of the American Federation of Musicians, was demanding $10,400 for a ten-hour week for his members. Records weren't regularly played in radio broadcasts until 1945. Consequently, the demand for live music—and musicians—was enormous. From just a supply-and-demand perspective, Petrillo's demands weren't entirely outrageous. Nevertheless, this was at a time when most workers thought $5,000 a year, less than $100 a week, was beyond the dreams of avarice. Petrillo, however, was speaking for an entire generation fed up with economic deprivation when he asked, "Why the hell should musicians"—or anybody else—"be suckers?"[32]

After all, the "bloated capitalists" were apparently more bloated than ever. Accumulated steel industry profits, for example, had soared 113 percent, from $576 million in 1935–39 to $1.2 billion in 1940–44. While the wartime no-strike pledge kept unions from winning wage increases for their members, executive salaries had soared. Charles E. Wilson, the president of General Motors, for example, went from earning $288,178 in 1941 to $459,014 in 1944, while his two vice presidents saw their compensation increase from $235,000 and $250,000 to $350,000. At the same time, even in 1945, when the unemployment rate was only 1.9 percent, about one fifth of city families made less than $1,500 a year. An urban family of four needed an annual income of $2,700 to maintain a decent standard of living, according to Dr. Walter Heller, later the chairman of the Council of Economic Advisers under Presidents Kennedy and Johnson.

Now that overtime was slashed, however, many workers weren't earning enough maintain that decent standard. The weekly wage of the average factory worker was $40.98, according to the Labor Department's Bureau of Labor Statistics, with auto workers getting $44.80; steel workers, $45.60; electrical workers, $41.25; textile workers, $27.42, and garment workers, $23.75. It wasn't until 1949 that John L. Lewis, the nation's most flamboyant labor leader since World War I, made his mine workers the best paid in American industry at $76.94 a week. With the war's end, labor union members and their leaders most emphatically wanted more, and they wanted it *now*. So, with no laws to stop them, they went on strike to get it, 3.5 million of them during the last few months of 1945.

The economic and social realities, however, were considerably more complex than the statistics indicated. While executive salaries such as Wilson's were high, so were the taxes on them, up to 90 percent. So, too, were excess-profits taxes imposed on corporate profits, and the source of those profits was disappearing with the end of the war. General Motors lost $2 billion in defense contracts on V-J Day, and its assembly lines ground to a halt. Despite the slogan "from tanks to

Cadillacs in two months," GM wasn't going to be able to convert its 102 plants to peacetime production of cars that quickly. Even if it did, profits from new car sales weren't guaranteed. People had the money to buy cars—more than $140 billion in savings, three times the gross national product in 1932. But rationing was still in effect, including supplies needed for building everything from cars to homes. Wages were also beginning to plummet for workers. The reduction of the standard work week from forty-eight to forty hours meant the pay packets of 180,000 UAW workers shrank twenty-five percent when overtime was no longer paid. Another 140,000 GM workers lost their jobs completely. The UAW rank and file were scared—and militant. Walter Reuther, the UAW president, had been hailed as a visionary for advocating the conversion of automobile assembly lines to the production of tanks before World War II. People remembered that auto executives had pooh-poohed the idea, so he had credibility when he called for pay to be linked to the employers' "ability to pay." Nevertheless, GM flatly rejected the idea. It also turned down Reuther's call for public disclosure of its financial records—even though the information was available to OPA. "It's none of your damn business what the OPA does about prices," Harry Coen, a GM official, yelled at Reuther during one bargaining session.

"Unless we get a more realistic distribution of America's wealth, we don't get enough to keep this machinery going," countered Reuther.

"There it is again," Coen said. "You can't talk about this thing without exposing your socialistic desires."

"If fighting for equal and equitable distribution of the wealth of this country is socialistic, I stand guilty of being a Socialist," Reuther said.

The exchange summed up the basic conflict between labor and management—and within American society. So far as GM was concerned, Reuther might as well have declared class war and summoned the worker to the barricades. The company took out full-page ads in major newspapers entitled "This Is the Issue," which declared:

> Is American business to be based on free competition, or is it to become socialized, with all activities controlled and regimented? . . .
>
> America is at a crossroads! It must preserve the freedom of each unit of American business to determine its own destinies [sic]. Or it must transfer to some governmental bureaucracy or agency, or to a union, the responsibility of management that has been the very keystone of American business!

Reuther also sought to sway public opinion using veterans. He urged picket leaders to make special efforts to have veterans in prominent positions in picket lines wearing their service uniforms. Special picket banners should be prepared, he said, that read, "I did not fight over there to protect G.M.'s billions over here." Regardless of whether the contending public relations campaigns affected public opinion much one way or another, GM and other companies were in a better position to withstand strikes than unions were able to wage them. The tax laws were in their favor. Losses sustained in 1946, whether from strikes or any other cause, could be charged off against the excess-profits taxes imposed up until the end of 1945—and refunds cheerily demanded from the U.S. Treasury. "A strike might cost us production, but it won't cost us money," as one executive told a newspaper, *PM*. "Better let the union go out when it won't hurt us—and it will hurt them." A Georgia mill operator was even more explicit in writing shareholders: "We think it will take us four months before our strikers decide to come back to work. Any loss we sustain in 1946 will be made up to us out of our profits in 1944 and 1945." The business strategy paid off in the UAW strike, with an unintentional assist from Harry Truman. The president, whose nomination as vice president had to be first cleared with Sidney Hillman of the CIO, desperately needed the labor movement to maintain the coalition he had inherited from FDR. Nevertheless, he was about to become the most vigorous strikebreaker in the history of the White House.[33]

Truman tried to build a new social compact. On September 6, 1945, in a message of Congress, he announced his Fair Deal program based on full-employment legislation as the nation's "bedrock public responsibility." He called for "an immediate and substantial upward revision" of the 40-cents-an-hour minimum wage and a "national reassertion of the right to work for every American citizen able and willing to work—a declaration of the ultimate duty of Government to use its resources if all other measures should fail to prevent sustained unemployment. . . . Full employment means full opportunity for all under the American economic system—nothing more and nothing less." He urged the permanent establishment of the Fair Employment Practices Commission to fulfill the American ideal of removal of injustices based on race, religion, and color. At the same time, Truman warned, "This is not the time for short-sighted management to seize upon the chance to reduce wages and try to injure labor unions. Equally, it is not the time for labor leaders to shirk their responsibilities and permit widespread industrial strife."[34]

The Wall Street Journal denounced Truman's full-employment proposal as a halfway house to socialism. Paul G. Hoffman, chairman of the Council of Economic Development, was quoted in a National Association of Manufacturers' pamphlet as saying he didn't believe it is even socially desirable to have jobs for every man and woman who wants a job. The philosophical arguments quickly turned into real conflicts.

The first postwar strike begin in December 1945, five months after V-J Day, when 195,000 men walked off the job at ninety-five GM plants. In January 1946, strikes began to hit the steel mills, the meat packers, electrical equipment factories, and auto assembly lines, putting almost 2 million on the picket line. Truman urged business and labor to engage in free and collective bargaining. Management, however, felt the time had finally come to reassert rights lost under closed-shop agreements made in the '30s and early '40s. Veterans "must have the free right to join the union or, alternately, we must have complete open shop and no fooling," former President Herbert Hoover declared. Hoover's words resonated among many veterans. *Stars and Stripes,* after all, had said on its front page during the 1943 mine workers' strike, "Speaking for the American soldier, John L. Lewis, damn your coal black soul." At least some veterans silently cheered when the Atlantic Elevator Company of Philadelphia petitioned the Regional War Labor Board to modify its contract with the United Electrical Workers to allow the hiring of veterans without requiring them to join the union. "Word has come back from many sources," the company argued, "that soldiers and sailors on far-flung fronts have little sympathy for the methods used by some unions in this country in order to gain their purposes during wartime." Veterans were among those loudly cheering in the House gallery when Representative Paul Steward (D-Oklahoma) demanded that veterans be allowed to get jobs without being forced to pay union dues, fees, and tributes. The veterans' cheering was so loud Speaker Rayburn gaveled them into silence.[35]

"Plans are far advanced for a big-business drive to break the back of organized labor," using veterans as a "labor reserve," *The New Republic* warned. "Everybody knows how assiduously the commercial press has labored to drive a wedge between our fighting men and labor. Everyone knows, too, that the campaign has been at least partially successful and that labor has encountered serious obstacles whenever it has tried to get its own point of view across to the armed services. Big business now hopes to reap what it has sown." The provision of the 1940 Selective Service Act guaranteeing reemployment rights of draftees would be used, the magazine warned, to "knock into a cocked hat . . . the whole seniority structure so laboriously erected by the unions. . . . This is, of course, aimed squarely at union and closed shops, in which almost half of the 13.75 million workers now under union agreements are employed." The specter of veterans and workers pitted against one another on a scale far vaster than the occasional clashes between Legion members and Wobblies after World War I, was raised at a national UAW-CIO Veterans' Conference. The attendees issued a warning directed against those who "would like to see men and women, Negro and white, Catholic, Protestant and Jew, veteran and non-veteran pitted against each other in a wild and desperate scramble for jobs. In the chaos thus created, they hope to destroy organized labor and return to the business-as-usual days of high profits for the few and poverty and insecurity for the many."[36]

The outbreak of strikes and the ferocity exhibited on both sides forced Truman to abandon government neutrality and convene fact-finding panels in both the auto and steel disputes. The panels reported within a week that the cost of living had increased 33 percent since the war began but average industrial wage increases had amounted to only 15 percent. Consequently, a 33 percent wage boost, amounting to 19½ cents an hour in autos and 18½ in steel, was recommended. Benjamin Fairless, the president of United States Steel and the unofficial head of the industry, refused to accept the recommendation unless the price of steel was allowed to rise to $6.24 a ton rather than the $5 advocated by the administration. The press, which *The New Republic* had excoriated for driving fighting men and labor apart, now bedeviled management. *Life* declared: "Mr. Fairless should pay 18½ cents; right or wrong, the President picked it, and we've got to get on with the job." *The New York Daily News* headline on an editorial said it all: "Fairless Makes a Big Mistake."

The steel companies quickly settled, and workers' wages went up $32 a month, the largest wage boost in history. GM, however, refused to pay the additional one cent, and Reuther soon found himself trying to explain to his members why they should continue a "penny an hour" strike. Appeals to solidarity weren't enough, not when strikers were depleting their savings and borrowing to continue the strike. Reuther also faced pressure from a Communist faction in the UAW and the White House. He gave in, after negotiating a face-saving system for having union dues deducted automatically from paychecks, making management a fiscal partner of the union. In the long run, it didn't matter. Within four months the government allowed GM and the other automakers three price increases. The conclusion to *Time* was simple: "The plain fact was that people everywhere, not caring much who got what, sensing that both higher wages and higher prices were in the air, wanted labor and industry to get back into production on almost any terms."

But there were terms Truman could not accept. With the first round of strikes over, those terms were being laid down, this time not by management, but by labor. Facing down those intransigent terms, coming as they did from union leaders he regarded as allies rather than enemies, was certainly the first and perhaps the greatest challenge to Truman's political courage in a presidency hallmarked by decisions of great political courage. What was never asked at the time, and can only be speculated on now, is whether he could have made those decisions stick if millions of veterans hadn't been happily occupied rebuilding their own lives. If they had been without the jobs, educational opportunities, and unemployment compensation provided by the GI Bill, they might have plunged—or been pulled into—two strikes that challenged the authority of the presidency itself.

No sooner had the GM strikers returned to work in March 1946, after 113 days on the bricks, than four hundred thousand soft coal miners left their pits. Soon after, in April, a shutdown of the entire railroad system, which carried almost all interstate passengers at the time as well as almost all raw and finished materials, was threatened. Twenty unions, prodded by an arbitration panel, had been haggling with the railroads for weeks and had finally reached a tentative agreement. The two largest unions, however, the Brotherhood of Railroad Trainmen headed by A. F. Whitney and the Brotherhood of Locomotive Engineers, led by Alvaney Johnston, balked. Both men were personal friends of Truman, as well as political allies, and the president summoned them to the White House three days before a strike deadline expired. He offered a generous arbitration award, but both men refused it.

"If you think I'm going to sit here and let you tie up this whole country," an angry Truman told them, "you're crazier than hell."

"We've got to go through with it, Mr. President," Whitney said. "Our men are demanding it."

Truman stood, offered the two forty-eight hours to reach a settlement, and warned them: "If you don't, I'm going to take over the railroads in the name of the government."

The deadline was extended by five days, but the talks proved fruitless. The men went on strike May 24, 1946. That morning, Truman strode into the cabinet room and announced he would ask Congress for the power to draft all railroad workers into the military, regardless of age or the number of dependents they had. The idea was clearly unconstitutional, the attorney general said. "We'll draft them first and think about the law later," Truman snapped. He handed Ross, his press secretary, a handwritten statement he intended to deliver over the radio that night. "Here's what I've going to say," he said through clenched teeth. "Get it typed up. I'm going to take the hide right off those sons of bitches." A stunned Ross read possibly the most inflammatory statement ever committed to paper in the White House. While the nation's veterans "faced bullets, bombs and disease to win the victory," the dozen pages of ruled tablet paper began, "the leaders of the coal and railroad unions" had fired "bullets in the back of our soldiers" by "holding a gun at the head of the government." That was just the start. Truman went on to accuse some people of trying to sabotage the war effort entirely. John L. Lewis was singled out for calling "two strikes in wartime to satisfy his ego, two strikes that were worse than bullets in the backs of our soldiers." Truman accused Lewis, in concert with Philip Murray of the CIO and his Communist friends, of having a conniption fit and intimidating a weak-kneed Congress into "labor jitters." Having warmed up, the ex-haberdasher from Independence then proceeded to tell a few "home truths" as they call them in the Show Me State:

> Every single one of the strikers and their demigog [sic] leaders have been living in luxury, working when they pleased and drawing from four to forty times the pay of a fighting soldier.
>
> I'm tired of the government's being flouted, vilified and misrepresented.
>
> Now I want you men who are my comrades-in-arms, you men who fought the battles to save the nation just as I did twenty-five years ago, to come with me and eliminate the Lewises, the Whitneys and Johnstons; the Communist Bridges [Harry Bridges, head of the West Coast longshoremen and an alleged Communist], and the Russian Senators and Representatives and really make this a government of, by and for the people.

> I think no more of the Wall Street crowd than I do of Lewis and Whitney. Let's give the country back to the people. Let's put transportation and production back to work, hang a few traitors, and make our own country safe for democracy. Come on, boys, let's do the job.

Had Truman given the speech, his advisers feared, he might have been lynched himself—or nominated by acclamation on the first ballot at the next Republican convention. Calvin Coolidge's condemnation of the Boston police strike a quarter of a century earlier with the words, "There can be no strike against the public interest, anywhere, anytime" seemed pussy-footing vacillation by comparison. Ross and Clark Clifford persuaded Truman to adopt less inflammatory but nevertheless scathing language: "The crisis tonight is caused by a group of men within our country who place their private interests above the welfare of the nation. . . . This is no contest between labor and management. This is a contest between a small group of men and their government." While the language was being rewritten, John Steelman, Truman's chief labor adviser, alternately pleaded with and lectured Whitney and Johnston in a hotel room. Finally, Truman impatiently announced he was calling Congress into session the next afternoon, Sunday, at four o'clock. Five minutes after Truman mounted the podium in the House of Representatives to say he was asking for authority, as commander in chief, "to draft into the Armed Forces of the Unites States all workers who are on strike against their own government," the telephone rang in Speaker Rayburn's office. An anxious Clifford answered and was told by Steelman, "It's over. They've signed." Clifford scrawled a note to Truman, who broke off his somber address to announce with a grin, "Gentlemen, the strike has been settled." The House erupted in cheers, but Truman, still not satisfied, went on to demand legislation he could invoke in any future strike jeopardizing the public welfare. The House obliged that night with a 306–13 vote.

Truman, already unpopular among Progressives for firing Wallace, became a "Fascist" and "labor hater" to liberals and labor sympathizers. He was denounced in a mass Madison Garden rally in New York and made the subject of perhaps the longest headline ever to appear on the front page of a tabloid: "An Appeal to Reason: A Program to Save America from Truman's Plan for Military Fascism," *PM* declared. Under a 1930s picture showing uniformed German workers marching in military formation, *PM* offered a new recruiting slogan: "Join the Army! Your country needs you to defend the country and break strikes." Johnston of the Locomotive Engineers promised to spend every penny in the union's $47 million treasury to defeat Truman in '48. He had to back down when a reporter revealed the union's liquid assets were less than $2.5 million. The CIO branded Truman the country's number one strikebreaker. Labor meetings around the country labeled the bill repressive and un-American. Victor Riesel, the labor columnist, declared Truman "has just thrown away almost all labor support."

The strikebreaking bill itself was broken in the Senate on the rock-ribbed principles of Senator Robert A. Taft, "Mr. Republican." Taft, the author of the Taft-Hartley bill, said the proposal "offends not only the Constitution but every basic principle for which the American Republic was established. Strikes cannot be prohibited without interfering with the basic freedom essential to our form of government." The Truman bill quietly died. The Taft-Hartley bill, dubbed "the slave-labor bill" by the unions, passed in 1948. The bill not only outlawed the closed shop, but also made unions liable for damages if they broke contracts. It also allowed for sixty-day cooling-off periods in strikes affecting the national interest, put some restrictions on union contributions to politicians, and required union officials to swear they weren't Communists. The bill was passed by two-thirds majorities despite cries of "fascism" from unions and Truman's veto. Truman's veto mended fences with labor sufficiently to help him win another term in the White House.

But before Taft-Hartley passed, Truman had to take on and break a man whose power was greater than any political leader. Only the public humiliation of John L. Lewis by Truman would make possible reform of a labor movement that had become grossly irresponsible. Again, it would not have been possible if the nation's veterans had not been sitting on the sidelines.

In April 1946, while Truman and Congress were preoccupied by the railroad strike, Lewis and 400,000 coal miners marched out of the mines. Dimouts of electricity were ordered in twenty-two states, the railroads laid off 51,000 workers and Ford another 110,000. Lewis called a two-week truce when a state of emergency was declared in New Jersey, but negotiations with management quickly broke down. Truman avoided another head-on clash with labor by empowering Julius A. Krug, his secretary of the interior, to negotiate for the mine owners. The negotiations stalled again, and this time Truman ordered Krug to seize the mines. "Let Truman dig coal with his bayonets," Lewis sneered, and his members ignored Krug's orders to return to work. Nine days later, Krug caved in to Lewis's demands for a five-cent levy on every ton of coal mined for the miners' welfare and pension plan.

The miners went back to work, but that fall, the irascible Lewis demanded negotiations be reopened. This time he was rebuffed by Krug, so he ordered yet another strike. "No contract, no work" was the word spread from Lewis's mansion in Alexandria, Virginia, across the Potomac from Washington, D.C., to the miners. Lewis, whose picture was often displayed in homes next to religious statues, was obeyed religiously by miners who revered him as a living saint. Truman, who had privately referred to Lewis as a racketeer during the strike he led in 1943, was nonetheless leery of another labor clash. But as the days passed and the nation's activities ground down, Truman came to see the strike "as something much greater than a quarrel over wages, hours and working conditions," Goulden wrote in *The Best Years*. "He believed the sovereignty of the United States was at stake. . . . The miner's strike was not so much a strike, as an insurrection, a blow at every man, woman and child in the United States. The time had come to find out which was stronger, Lewis or the government; and whether the one element of American society could penalize the entire country and get away with it."

To meet that challenge, Truman resorted to a stratagem normally anathema to liberals: a court injunction. Such injunctions had been the principal instrument management had used to break strikes—and unions—for decades. Indeed, they had been outlawed by the Wagner and Norris–La Guardia Acts in the 1930s. But Truman told his government lawyers the laws didn't apply because the strike was against the government, since the Interior Department still controlled the mines—not their *private* owners. The argument was enough to haul Lewis before federal judge T. Alan Goldsborough on November 21, 1946. Lewis, who had perfected a "war of nerves" strategy to wear down his opponents, was about to find himself on the defensive. Truman, having come up with an effective strategy, stepped aside and let the lawyers do battle. He flew to Florida to swim and fish while Lewis blustered around Washington, denouncing a "yellow dog labor-hating administration." On November 22, Judge Goldsborough ruled that Lewis and the union had "beyond a reasonable doubt committed

and continue to commit a civil and criminal contempt of the court."
Sentencing was set for December 4, and a somewhat chastened Lewis
tried to telephone Truman. Truman, tanned and cheerfully ensconced
once again at the White House, had secretaries tell Lewis the matter
was out of his hands.

When December 4 came, Lewis denounced the "ugly recrudescence
of government by injunction" outside the court as government lawyers
inside asked for a $3.5 million fine. His lawyer denounced the gov-
ernment for placing a "crown of thorns" on Lewis merely to satisfy the
political program of an administration. An unimpressed Judge Goldsborough asked Lewis to describe his finances and threatened an additional contempt citation when Lewis flippantly told him not to be
deterred from levying any amount the judge wished.

Lewis then sat while Goldsborough delivered a withering denunciation: "This is not the act of a low law-breaker, but it is an evil,
demonic, monstrous thing that means hunger and cold and unemployment and destitution and disorganization of the social fabric. . . .
It is proper for me to say . . . that if actions of this kind can be successfully persisted in, the government will be overthrown." The fine
requested by the government, $3.5 million, was imposed. Since Lewis
still had $13.5 million in the union treasury, he considered an ap-
peals strategy all the way to the Supreme Court. That could take
months while the mines remained closed as winter and economic
devastation approached. It was the fifth anniversary of Pearl Harbor,
and Truman decided to broadcast an appeal to the miners to ignore
the chief they adored and return to work to avoid a Pearl Harbor of
peace.

It was a desperate gamble by a president whose popularity ratings
had plummeted. It paid off. That Friday afternoon at four o'clock,
Lewis called a press conference. The appeal up to the Supreme Court
"should be free from public pressure superinduced by the hysteria of
an economic crisis," he said. Therefore, he directed all mines in all
districts to resume production immediately. The crisis was over—
and it was all due to one man, Harry S Truman. "Let's be fair,"
Philip Porter wrote in *The (Cleveland) Plain Dealer* several days
after the strike ended, "It was the forgotten man, Harry S Truman,
who faced down John L. Lewis and made him call off his coal strike.
It was Truman who had the guts to bring the porkiest of labor
monopolists to heel. It was Truman who forced Lewis to admit the
government was bigger than Lewis."

The confrontation was the making of Truman, enabling him for the first time to emerge from the shadow of FDR. "I tell you there was a big difference in the Old Man from then on," Clark Clifford told *The New York Times*. "He was his own man at last." A White House aide was more graphic. "When Harry walked back to the mansion, you could hear his balls clank." Saul Alinsky, Lewis's biographer and a "community organization" strategist who emulated the CIO in creating coalitions of poor people in the 1960s, had an observation that revealed more about liberal attitudes than history. Lewis had failed, Alinsky believed, because he was "so accustomed to dealing with the subtle, brilliant, wary Roosevelt that he could not anticipate the directness of a politically insensitive Truman."[37]

In fact, Lewis hadn't anticipated, and Alinsky didn't realize thirty years later, that the real forgotten men who had swung the balance in this confrontation were those who stayed out of it, the veterans. A sense of class difference, never too strong to begin with, was, if not disappearing, going underground. Henceforth, most of the sixteen million veterans of World War II could never be persuaded to think of themselves as comrades in a class struggle with the bosses. Too many of them wanted to become bosses themselves—and now, for the first time, they had the opportunity to become white-collar workers, if not professionals and managers. Even those who went to a technical training school rather than college wanted, one day, to become more than working stiffs. Those from working-class backgrounds wouldn't feel comfortable about crossing a picket line, but even those who had been union members wouldn't be caught dead singing "Solidarity Forever." The old left was dying, and even though the new left enjoyed a resurgence in the '60s largely led by "red diaper babies," the passion would be spent as soon as the Vietnam War was over, lingering only as "radical chic." Those who could have been expected to become leaders of the Marxist-Leninist revolution were instead becoming both the rank and file and occasional luminaries of a middle-class revolution. They were men like Joe Valentich, another Turtle Creek alumnus, who wanted to be a mathematician-electrician rather than follow his father into a steel alloy plant. Another was an ex-army sergeant who had his mind expanded working in the military government in Germany. Harvard offered greater opportunities for Henry Kissinger than the accounting course he had been taking at the City College of New York before being drafted.

The almost one million ex-veterans enrolled in college in 1946 and the one and a half million in 1947 were too busy to take sides in labor strikes. These young men, obviously the most able and ambitious of their generation, weren't interested in becoming shop stewards looking to advance themselves in John L. Lewis's union or anyone else's. Neither were they forced to become strikebreakers determined to dig coal with bayonets, if necessary, to feed and clothe themselves and their families. They were busy instead taking, as Joe Valentich did, up to twenty-three credit hours a semester in courses to graduate from college as quickly as possible and get on with a professional life. Valentich was a Croatian-American, member of a group respected before the war only for their strong backs. Many, however, also had strong minds, strong enough to produce books, as Valentich did, with titles such as *Short Range Radio Telemetry for Rotating Instrumentation*. For men like Valentich, strikes would become something to be read about in newspapers, not to participate in. As the son of a union member, he and many other up-and-coming executives and professionals might not cross picket lines if they could avoid them. But they would never become members of picket lines.[38]

Obviously many of those who went to college after World War II would have done so even if there hadn't been a GI Bill. Even if just 25 percent of those who attended had not done so, the country would have had 110,000 fewer engineers, 60,000 fewer accountants, 59,000 fewer teachers, 22,700 fewer scientists, and 16,750 fewer doctors.

The GI Bill made trained minds, rather than land or minerals, America's most important resource. It began the shift to the knowledge society that was, as Drucker wrote, the most important event of the twentieth century, a transformation that may not be completed until 2010 or 2020.[39]

CHAPTER **8**

STORMING THE CAMPUS

N OW, GODS, STAND up for bastards!"
"When massed choruses of veterans who weren't even my
Shakespeare students began shouting the soliloquy of Edmund
the Bastard from *King Lear* in the University of Wisconsin quadran-
gle, I knew college life had changed."

P. Albert Duhamel, an English professor later at Boston College,
used to tell that story in the '50s and '60s to illustrate the fundamental change that took place on campuses when combat boots
replaced saddle shoes and battle jackets became more ubiquitous
than blazers. The poor, suffering bastards of the battlefield were
storming the campuses.

It was a change, or more accurately, a series of changes, welcomed
by most faculty, but like all changes, feared by others. The great
majority of faculty members quickly came to appreciate the adult
intensity veteran students brought to their studies. Others saw a
threat to the established social order coming from students whose
ancestry or religion had made them, until then, not quite accepted in
society. They feared these veterans were determined to "top th' legitimate. I grow; I prosper. Now, gods, stand up for bastards!"

Some even saw in this exuberant determination to succeed the
looming shadows of socialism. "We must not be surprised [if] this
great experiment in socialized education, sponsored and financed by a
paternal government, in an area heretofore traditionally and jealously
a state preserve" could "overturn the social and economic structure

as it exists." So wrote Byron Atkinson, coordinator of veterans' affairs at the University of California at Los Angeles (UCLA) in the journal *School and Society* in 1948. "This *social experiment* [emphasis in the original] has gone too far or not far enough," Atkinson concluded in one of the few contemporary efforts to assess the effectiveness of the GI Bill published in the social science literature at the high point of veteran enrollment. The program, "educationally, seems an unqualified success," he observed. But he worried that it was producing far more qualified graduates than the market could absorb. "The engineering faculty tells us that we are training three times as many engineers as the market can absorb," he wrote. "There are two-and-a-half times as many students in our College of Business Administration than there were in 1940. Along with this, there are 65,000 unemployed *veterans—veterans only*—in Los Angeles County, *now!* [emphasis his]. What shall we do with these people when they graduate?"

He disagreed with those who assumed that with or without the GI Bill the veterans would be unemployed anyway. Atkinson argued that the GIs gave up job opportunities to seize what seemed to them to be the greater opportunity. If they were deceived and no prize awaited them, he wrote, the country would find that having tampered with one foundation stone of our economic arch, it was also dislocating, if not disrupting, its opposite foundation stone.[1]

Atkinson had the temerity to say in public what unquestionably many more prominently placed people than he were thinking. The GI Bill of Rights was indeed a social experiment, the biggest in the history of the country, but it was an experiment without a guiding principle, a stated hypothesis, a test without any presumption of a governing law or an anticipated effect. Far from being socialized education, its sponsors just modestly thought it would help veterans make up for whatever opportunities they lost through their time in the service. Yet, in fact, it was doing far more. The GI Bill was overturning the social and economic structure, if only by shattering forever the idea that those who were not already members of the middle class could go to college.

At the same time, it was also reshaping what was being taught in college as veterans demanded that course material be more realistic. That didn't mean that veterans weren't interested in liberal arts or the values and traditions of the civilization they had fought for and some of their buddies had died for. Indeed, they wanted to know whether what they had been told was worth dying for was worth living for. But they were skeptical as well as passionate. At George Washington University, where Lehman Young Sr., a former pilot instructor, went, courses in the history of Western civilization were the most popular on campus, as at many other colleges. "I think the room held one thousand students, and it was *packed,*" Young remembered in an interview for a documentary on the GI Bill. The veterans weren't there just to listen. They insisted on comparing and evaluating their personal experience with—and against—the academic knowledge of the professors. "A college campus was an exciting place to be then," Edward Markey, who was teaching at Princeton, recalled. "I wasn't much older than the students. I can't remember a more stimulating group of students. They were serious about their studies. And they all brought this important life experience to the campus. I remember one of the professors complaining about a vet in his World History class who challenged him on some point, saying, 'Don't tell me about China. I've *been* to China.'"[2]

Faculties divided between those who sympathized with the veterans and those whose standards—and sensitivities—were offended by requests for more realistic courses. A veteran who had become a teacher, S. N. Vinocour of the University of Nevada, set off a monumental brouhaha in the normally sedate pages of *School and Society* in 1947 by observing: "If pedagogic desks were reversed and the veteran now in college were given the opportunity to grade his professor, he would give him a big red 'F' as insipid, antiquated and ineffectual." After touring colleges all over the country, Vinocour wrote that veterans, fearing another depression, were afraid the traditional college atmosphere was "not only stupid, but a definite hindrance to acquiring an education." Other educators responded vehemently that veterans really wanted credentials, not an educated mind. Bayard Quincy Morgan of Stanford accused veterans of wanting a degree, "oh, yes, but about as a man buys a railroad ticket or secures a passport. . . . Anything that doesn't contribute directly and demonstrably to the quickest acquisition of a degree is not only not wanted, but resented." The veterans wanted training rather than education, he wrote, and their attitude was, "Never mind the theory; that takes too long and we won't understand it anyway; all we want is the know-how." On the other hand, Morgan was also perceptive enough to see the veterans' demands were partially a result of the training they had undergone in the military. "The armed forces were always intent on 'getting the job done,' and always in a hurry. They rushed the recruits through 'just enough' of everything, trusting to the exigencies of actual fighting to augment the scanty education of the trainee. It is not surprising if the veteran thinks all education is like that, and expects the college to give him the same kind of training he got in the army or navy."[3]

To a large extent, that is exactly what the veterans got. Certainly, they crowded the engineering programs and colleges of business administration, as Atkinson complained, despite warnings that the jobs they were looking for wouldn't be there when they graduated. What Atkinson didn't anticipate was that the rapid demobilization of the armed services encouraged Joseph Stalin to precipitate the Berlin crisis of 1948, starting the cold war. The Soviet Union's attempt to block access to the city was defeated by a massive airlift, and it put the United States back on a war footing. "America has saved the world," Winston Churchill declared grandiloquently after 277,264 flights of air force planes carrying 2.3 million tons of food, fuel, medicine, and clothing kept the beleaguered city alive between June 24, 1948, and May 2, 1949. The cold war called for more scientifically trained warriors carrying slide rules and fewer toting rifles. The military-industrial complex was created, and at the time, the booming domestic economy needed as many accountants, marketing specialists, and managers as the schools of business administration could turn out. Teachers began to incorporate more and more practical elements into their courses without eliminating theory. In many respects, undergraduate classes became more like graduate programs as teachers began to appreciate that the veterans' practical experience provided soil out of which theoretical understanding could grow. Relationships between teachers and students became more like those of journeyman and master craftsman, rather than pupil and master. The initial fears turned to mutual respect. By the time the flood of veterans poured through the colleges, the attitudes of even the most skeptical faculty members had become respectful, laudatory, even nostalgic.

"The mature student body which filled our colleges in 1946 and 1947 was a delight to all who were then teaching undergraduates," James Conant of Harvard recalled almost a quarter of a century later in his 1970 autobiography, *My Several Lives,* subtitled *Memoir of a Social Inventor.* The GI Bill, which Conant had warned could flood the college campuses with the least capable of the war generation, had, instead, raised college performance levels. The bill had also overcome what Conant had described in 1940 as the greatest defect in the nation's educational system. The system was, he said, "in spite of universal schooling, perpetuating, more than we realize, a *hereditary class* [emphasis Conant's] of highly educated people." The bill he had denigrated had been the greatest social invention of the century, enabling many outside that hereditary class to obtain high-quality education.[4]

Evidence of the change was anecdotal and impressionistic, however, rather than objectively proven. Such studies as were done during and immediately after 1945–52 were ambiguous, if not contradictory. For example, the Education Testing Service (ETS) found in the late '40s that the grade difference between 10,000 veterans and nonveterans on sixteen campuses was "no more than the difference between a C and a C plus." But at the University of Minnesota during 1947, only 35 out of 6,010 veterans flunked out, one half of 1 percent compared with the normal civilian rate of 10 percent. Classmates certainly thought the veterans were doing well; nonveterans at Stanford called them DARs—"Damned Average Raisers." At the same time, ETS observed an apparent anomaly: Veterans "on the whole . . . attached less importance to college grades and to college education than nonveterans."[5] Education was seen as a means to an end, getting a job paying enough to support their baby-boom families. The veteran who had laid down his M-1 rifle and picked up a book in one hand and a baby in his other apparently felt the degree was important, but not the dean's list.

No one, including the veterans, really knew what was going on; the world everyone was living in had changed utterly. The Depression, chronologically, had lasted twelve years, from October 23, 1929, "Black Friday" when the stock market crashed, to December 7, 1941, when the United States went to war. But it lingered, psychologically, for another generation. In the three and a half years between the bombing of Pearl Harbor and August 14, 1945, the economy had experienced the most sustained—and widely distributed—boom in history. The gross national product had shot up from $90 billion in 1939 to $213 billion in 1945, and the income of the average worker had doubled to $3,000. The wealthiest 5 percent of the population still controlled a substantial portion of the national wealth, 16.8 percent, but that was considerably less than their 23.7 percent in 1939.[6]

The GI Bill turned veterans and their families into a privileged group, as Geoffrey Perrett wrote in *Days of Sadness, Years of Tri-*

umph. "Veterans' benefits were a type of Socialism that, counting the 16,000,000 veterans and their families, by 1950 embraced approximately one-third of the population." *Time,* in 1954, estimated the total of all veterans to be one half of the nation, including sixteen million from 1944 through 1946—twelve million were in service at the end of the war—three million from World War I and another two million from Korea. Yet, as Perrett noted, the GI Bill was "social welfare without Socialism," primarily because the recipients did not see themselves as the recipients of welfare programs. They had the "assertive, self-respecting attitudes of people whose claims are based on having earned, not just deserved, what they received" without any of the "sullen, self-destroying agonies of welfare clients. . . . It was a very middle-class program, all the more effective for the disguise it wore."[7]

The numbers of college degrees conferred provide the most unambiguous evidence that a silent revolution was occurring. In 1942, 213,491 were earned; in 1946, 157,349; in 1948, 317,607; in 1950, 496,874; and in 1951, 454,960. In less than a decade the number of college graduates being turned out had more than doubled. In addition, new colleges and universities had been established, as large as the State University of New York (SUNY) and as small as Marlboro College in Vermont, whose first graduating class consisted of one student in 1948. The number of two- and four-year colleges in the country went from 1,708 to 1,863, an increase of almost 10 percent. Of the 15.6 million veterans eligible, 7.8 million took advantage of the education and training provisions before the World War II bill benefits ended on July 25, 1956—2.2 million attending two- and four-year colleges. The total education costs of the World War II bill were $14.5 billion with the per capita expenditure running $1,858. The Labor Department estimated the government actually made a profit because veterans earned more and therefore paid higher taxes. The department estimated a male college graduate could be expected to make $250,000 more in a working lifetime than a high school graduate and, of course, pay taxes on the extra. "The federal tax on this added income alone," the Veterans Administration commented, "will be several times the cost of G.I. education."[8]

Educators wondered at the time how many additional degrees conferred in the postwar years were due primarily to the GI Bill. The ETS study comparing 10,000 veterans and nonveterans suggested about 20 percent. The study, conducted by Norman Fredericksen and William B. Schrader, concluded that about 446,400 of the 2,232,000

World War II veterans who attended college did so solely because of the GI Bill. The study was fraught with uncertainties, however. The least troublesome was how many veterans who had started college before entering the service completed their studies under the GI Bill. Frederickson and Schrader calculated that 1,785,000 veterans who had been enrolled in college returned under the bill. The next question was, How many of those 1,785,000 would have returned to the classroom if the GI Bill had not been available? Eighty percent of those asked said they would have completed college without the GI Bill. How many would have done so, however, if they had to pay for tuition, books, and fees as well as earn all their own living expenses? The sacrifice involved, especially for married veterans with children, undoubtedly would have been daunting. Even with the government paying all tuition up to $500 a year plus fees, the $65 monthly stipend for single veterans and $90 for those with dependents quickly proved inadequate. It was raised in 1948 to $75 a month for an individual, $105 for couples, and $120 for families. Even then, chicken soup was on the menu much more than roast chicken.[9]

Even if the GI Bill didn't substantially increase the numbers of those who attended college, it indisputably was responsible for a much higher percentage of veterans attending institutions with high academic standards and reputations. Most of those institutions were private and a lot more expensive than state colleges. Indeed, the veterans' two-to-one preference for the better-quality, and usually higher-tuition, schools was so pronounced that the Korean War bill deliberately eliminated the market advantage private schools enjoyed. Korean veterans had to pay their own tuition and fees out of a monthly stipend rather than have it paid separately and entirely. By contrast, the World War II veterans could use their entire stipends for living expenses. Veterans flocked to Ivy League schools, the state universities, and the better known liberal arts and technical schools, Keith Olson documented in the only book on the bill's impact on higher education. They enrolled only as a last resort in junior colleges, teachers' colleges, and lesser known, small, liberal arts colleges. Central College in Fayette, Missouri, for example, reported that enrollment was actually 250 fewer than peacetime levels of 600. At DePauw in Indiana, enrollment was only 80 percent of the 1,500 registered during peacetime. As *Time* magazine asked in its March 18, 1946, issue, "Why go to Podunk College, when the Government will send you to Yale?"

Why not, and the result at Harvard, for example, were veteran students who "for seriousness, perceptiveness, steadiness and all the other undergraduate virtues . . . were the best in Harvard's history," according to an article in the June 1946 *Life*. The Ivy League continued to set the standard of excellence in college education in the postwar years, but from 1945 through 1950, it might have been more appropriately called the Khaki League. Moreover, the top performance levels were set by many students who, until they were admitted, weren't even sure where Yale or Princeton was.[10] Bill Norris and Layman Allen, for example, had no idea they would ever go to college, never mind Princeton, when they entered Turtle Creek High School in 1941. No one in either Norris's or Allen's family had gone to college, so they signed up for the commercial course in high school, typing and secretarial skills. "We didn't expect college," Norris said, "but we didn't want to get our hands dirty in the mill. The plant had this nice big building full of offices, and we thought it would be nice to wear clean shirts and flirt with all the secretaries." The boys' biology teacher, however, saw greater intelligence and potential in the boys. One day she made them go with her to see the principal. "What kind of a school are you running?" she demanded. "These boys shouldn't be in a commercial course. They could get scholarships to college." She insisted the two transfer to the academic track, and they did, although as Norris noted, "We had a lot of credits to make up. But we did it." The two took first- and second-place honors in the graduating class of 1944, but the draft took precedence over college plans until V-J Day. Then Allen, who was stationed at Treasure Island, California, and Norris, who was in San Diego, met at Santa Barbara to discuss their future. "I told Bill a Navy friend had suggested we try Princeton," Allen recalled. "We were small town boys, what did we know? Bill said, 'Where's Princeton?'" The two not only got into Princeton and graduated, but Allen went on to Harvard Law while Norris went to Stanford Law. Allen became both a professor of law and a research scientist at the University of Michigan, establishing himself as a nationally known authority on the application of mathematical logic to legal problems. Norris clerked for Supreme Court Justice William O. Douglas, practiced law in Los Angeles, ran for California attorney general, and was appointed a U.S. circuit court judge in 1980. "Princeton opened all those doors for us," said Norris, who is also the founding president of the Institute of Contemporary Art in Los Angeles, "but the GI Bill opened the doors to Princeton."[11]

All the private and, at the time, most prestigious educational institutions began admitting not only working-class Anglo-Americans with names like Norris and Allen but also Irish-Americans, Italian-Americans, Polish-Americans, Hungarian-Americans, and Jews, all of whose names just a few years before would have been found only on the rosters of the maintenance and housekeeping staffs. Enrollments were also up at prestigious public colleges in Ann Arbor, Berkeley, and Madison—and down in teachers' colleges. Colleges and universities were crowded far beyond capacity, averaging a 50 percent increase over their peacetime records, Benjamin Fine, the education editor for *The New York Times,* reported on February 16, 1947. Even those figures were misleading; many of the 150,000 enrolled in teachers' colleges were veterans who either couldn't get accepted at other colleges or were diverted to the teachers' college campuses from the institutions of their choice. Pennsylvania State College and the University of Michigan, for example, farmed out several thousand freshmen to teachers' colleges until space could be found for them in sophomore or junior classes. Forty-one percent of all veterans were enrolled in 38 of the country's most prestigious 750 fully accredited four-year colleges in the spring of 1946. The other 59 percent were scattered among the remaining 712 schools.

Fine, the education editor for *The New York Times,* after touring college campuses in the East and Middle West in the autumn of 1947, reported "the most astonishing fact in the history of American higher education. . . . Far from being an educational problem, the veteran has become an asset to higher education."[12] The reasons for the educational prowess of the veterans weren't clear. The greater age of the veterans was the most plausible explanation, but it couldn't be demonstrated through social science data collected by Fredericksen and Schrader. Although the veterans were unquestionably older than their nonveteran peers in the classroom, when the researchers made adjustments in the data to compensate for relative age differences, they concluded that any correlation between age and performance had been virtually destroyed. The statistical wisdom, however, was often contradicted by personal stories of individual veterans.

Chesterfield Smith signed up for pre-law at the University of Florida back in 1935, but as his wife, Vivian Parker, recalled years later, "He was just a poker-playing, crap-shooting boy who couldn't settle down." By his own account, Smith "chose the easy life in college. I'd go to school a semester and then drop out for a semester to earn enough money to return"—in style. "I'd rather drop out and

work than skimp in school." He worked as a clerk in the Florida legislature, a soda jerk, a debt collector, and a candy and tobacco vendor.
By the time he was drafted in 1940, though, he had managed to complete three and a half years of college. Commissioned in the National
Guard, he was assigned to a field artillery unit in France beginning
"about D day plus 45" and served through the Battle of the Bulge
before returning to the University of Florida in 1946.

By the standards of the day, Smith had done well financially, saving $5,000 from his pay and winning another $3,000 in craps on the
long voyage home. But the man who had married Vivian in 1944
before shipping out for Europe had changed when he came back in
1945. She recalled, "He was a serious man when he returned." Smith
didn't give up the good life entirely; he found time to golf five days a
week through law school. Financially, his carefully budgeted savings
and a teaching job obtained in his second year at law school meant
the couple "had more than most." But he also budgeted his time as
carefully as his money. "I didn't go drink coffee or sit out on the
bench and bull it all the time. I never missed a day of class. I kept a
work schedule just like I had a job. If I had a paper due in three
weeks, I started it right away and finished a week early. Hell, here I
was, almost thirty years of age—I wanted to get that law license and
get into practice and make myself some money. The idea of playing
around a university for unnecessary months or years had no appeal
to me whatsoever."

Twenty years later, Smith was the president of the American Bar
Association and the principal partner in a Tampa-Orlando law firm.
"The way I was going before the war," Smith said, "I don't think I
would ever have made it through law school. But after the war, I felt
I had something invested in my country—five years of my life. I said
to myself, 'Boy, you've got to settle down and make something of yourself, otherwise you ain't going to 'mount to nothing.' My classmates
in the '40s, after the war, we wanted to get on with our lives. We were
men, not kids, and we had the maturity to recognize that we had to
go get what we wanted, and not just wait for things to happen to us."[13]

The GI Bill not only provided enormous stimulus for the expansion of private and public colleges, but it also literally created new
ones. For example, New York didn't even have a state university at
the time the bill was passed, and the justly famous City College of
New York City was only a college. With the end of the war, enrollment at the state's teachers' colleges was running 132 percent higher

than 1941 levels. Moreover, the Mayor's Committee on Unity in New York City released in early 1946 a report documenting discrimination against Catholics, Jews, and Negroes in private college admissions. With hundreds of thousands of veterans knocking on college doors seeking admission, discrimination could no longer be tolerated, if only for the practical reason that those applicants came prepared to pay with checks drawn on the U.S. Treasury. At the same time, the big private colleges in upstate New York didn't want competition from a state university. Syracuse, Cornell, Colgate, and Hobart, consequently, formed a consortium that was granted a temporary charter by the legislature on May 17, 1946, as the Association of Colleges of New York (ACUNY). That September, Champlain College, the first ACUNY campus, was opened for 1,101 students, 90 percent veterans and 99 percent male, in the brick barracks of the former Plattsburgh Military Base built in 1814. In October, Mohawk College was established on the grounds of the army's former Rhoads Hospital in Utica. "Let's get them in this year even though you will have to sacrifice some of your standards," Governor Thomas E. Dewey told the presidents of the associated colleges. Four years later, in June of 1950 when most colleges were experiencing a sharp decline in veteran enrollments, ACUNY still had fifteen thousand students, 88 percent veterans, scattered among Champlain College, Mohawk College, and Sampson College. However, the private colleges' hope that ACUNY could prevent gestation of "an embryo of a state university," in the awkward but vivid words of Chancellor George D. Stoddard of Syracuse, had been frustrated.

Almost every other state had a state university, and New York citizens felt it only fitting the Empire State have one also. Consequently, the legislature passed on February 16, 1948, and Governor Dewey signed into law six weeks later, a bill creating the State University of New York (SUNY), placing under a central administration all the state's teachers' colleges, the two-year technical and agricultural institutions, the Maritime Academy, and contract colleges at Alfred, Cornell, and Syracuse Universities. By that time the bulk of veteran enrollment was passing through the colleges, so Dewey and his successor, Averell Harriman, only modestly expanded the system, resisting the establishment of engineering, law, and fine art schools. However, when Nelson Rockefeller became governor in 1958, anticipated demands in the '60s as the children of World War II veterans reached college age couldn't be ignored. In the next few years, Rockefeller created four universities and two medical schools and turned teachers' colleges all over the state into liberal arts institutions. "The presence of veteran students in 1946–1950 clearly was the decisive catalyst . . . for a state college and university system that would rival that of any state in the country," Olson observed.[14] Today, in fact, with sixty-four campuses, SUNY is the largest public university system in the country, and New York City University, the old CCNY with twenty campuses, is the third largest.

By contrast and not far away in Vermont, Marlboro College was being built in converted barns by veterans for veterans on an old farmstead. Students literally built the classrooms they studied in and dormitories they lived in, mixing plaster, hammering nails, laying down flagstones. They even boiled maple sap for syrup to supplement the GI Bill benefits that were the college's sole source of income. The college was still tiny fifty years later, with only 250 students, but in 1948, it was so small the entire graduating class consisted of one person, Hugh Mulligan, later a top writer for the Associated Press. Marlboro was the brain child of Walter Hendricks, a graduate of Amherst who had been chairman of the English Department at the Illinois Institute of Technology, but the military was the midwife. Hendricks had been recruited by the army immediately after Germany's surrender to run an experimental education program for GIs who didn't have enough service time to be mustered out. In running an impromptu university for the army in Biarritz, France, Hendricks had been touched deeply, as Mulligan wrote later, by "the lust for learning that so many G.I.'s exhibited after months and years of murderous fighting. He talked about turning his 600-acre farm into a small college where students and faculty could live together as a community of scholars. Informal, like Biarritz, where a private like me could be elevated to English instructor in the second term and wind up flunking an Air Force major caught cribbing on an exam in Irish drama."

When Hendricks came back home, he started his new college on the family farm in the town of Marlboro in southern Vermont. A promoter as well as a visionary, Hendricks took advantage of the fact that his Marlboro neighbors included many prominent writers whose endorsements could provide the publicity needed to lure students to a new college without an endowment or reputation. The most prominent of the resident writers was Robert Frost, the poet, and Hendricks inveigled him into providing a national magazine with an appropriate "down home" quote. The September 8, 1947, issue of *Time* magazine related how Hendricks told Frost, "You know, Bob, I've got this idea to start a college." "I'll be durned," Frost replied. "I always wanted to myself." So successful were Hendricks's public relations efforts that presidents of many of New England's most prominent colleges, among them Conant of Harvard, turned out in full regalia to watch the sole member of the first graduating class receive his degree.

The GI Bill was also having a profound impact on social culture, tearing down assumptions of ethnic, religious, and racial superiority that were, if possible, even more deeply embedded in the minds of academics than ordinary citizens. Indeed, this piece of legislation, which had been first championed and then almost sabotaged by one of the notorious bigots in Congress, stimulated the formation of Jewish pressure groups determined to stamp out legally sanctioned prejudice against not only Jews, but also blacks. The bill's success in altering the social climate was accomplished so quietly, however, so unobtrusively, that pressure groups came to believe their efforts were responsible for the changes. During the 1920s, all the elite colleges and universities in the country, with the exceptions of Cornell, Brown, and the University of Pennsylvania, had imposed quotas on admissions of Jewish students. At the same time, "restrictive covenants" made the purchase of homes in wealthy communities very difficult, if not impossible, for Jews and for those few blacks who could afford it. Jews were also excluded from many private clubs and hotels at public resorts.

"At the turn of the century," Benjamin Ginsberg wrote in *The Fatal Embrace: Jews and the State,* "the intellectual defenders and spokesmen of the emerging American ruling stratum sought to blend liberalism with racism to demonstrate that a true elite class was marked by both success and breeding." The intellectual justification came from social Darwinists and practitioners of the new social science of eugenics, which presumably proved Anglo-Saxons occupied the top of the evolutionary tree with lesser breeds of Germans, Irish, and Italians in the lower branches, and Jews and blacks barely clinging to the trunk. The federal government, of course, didn't begin to challenge legal discrimination—against any group—until 1941 when FDR created the Committee on Fair Employment Practices in response to a threat of a black protest march in Washington on Independence Day. After World War II, discrimination against blacks remained legal in many states and even under some federal laws.

The army, for example, was officially segregated until 1948. While Jews and Catholics were exempt from legal forms of discrimination and not segregated in public facilities, more subtle forms of prejudice limited occupational and housing opportunities in the private market. Catholics, being more politically powerful—and Christian—were often able to push their way forward more readily than Jews. They were also sufficiently numerous to develop their own educational system, from grade school through universities. Jews, often more upwardly mobile in economic terms, felt the restrictions on admissions to elite colleges more keenly than Catholics. The hobbles placed on them, however, were often relatively difficult to pinpoint and attack. Consequently, by identifying themselves with blacks, who were obvious victims of prejudice, Jews could advance their own cause. "In mounting an attack on discriminatory admission practices," Ginsberg wrote, "Jewish organizations found it useful to link themselves to blacks. The number of blacks seeking admission to elite universities in the 1940s was very small. By speaking on behalf of blacks as well as Jews, however, Jewish groups were able to present themselves as fighting for the abstract and quintessential American principles of fair play and equal justice rather than the selfish interests of Jews alone. This would not be the last time that Jewish organizations found that helping blacks could serve their own interests."

The assault on anti-Jewish quotas in colleges and universities, according to Ginsberg, began with a legal challenge of Columbia University's tax-exempt status in the late '40s by the American Jewish Conference's Commission on Law and Social Justice (CLSJ). At the time, Lionel Trilling, the literary critic, was perhaps the only Jew on the faculty. "The CLSJ and other Jewish groups were also active in securing the enactment of state laws . . . prohibiting colleges from discriminating against any applicant on the basis of race, religion, creed, color, or national origin," Ginsberg observed. He then contended CLSJ and other Jewish groups also played a major role in persuading Governor Thomas Dewey to create the commission whose work led to the creation of New York's state university system in 1948.

Undoubtedly they did, but the existence of the GI Bill made the lawsuit against Columbia and the formation of the State University of New York possible in the first place. The walls of prejudice were already crumbling even before the lawsuits were filed and the New

York Assembly was asked to consider the establishment of SUNY. Veterans of the war against fascism were being paid to go to college by the government whether they were WASPs or Jews, Irish-Catholics or Negroes. No college could long deny them entrance because of prejudiced rules and regulations that were outdated and discredited vestiges of an era almost everyone wanted to put behind. The only substantive question the educators and legislators faced, given the fact that there weren't enough seats for veterans in existing institutions, was whether public or private facilities should be expanded. The issue was means, not ends. When it became obvious the number of students would be even greater in the '60s than the '40s, the associated colleges' objections to a public university faded. At the same time, revulsion over the Holocaust made it difficult, if not impossible, for Columbia University and other private colleges to justify racial and religious prejudice. Some faculty members may have clung tenaciously to now-discredited theories of social Darwinism or the natural superiority of the white Anglo-Saxon Protestant. But the prejudices not only couldn't be justified, sociologically or ethically, they made no sense financially. Veterans' bills for tuition and fees, up to $9.65 for every credit hour, were paid as promptly by Uncle Sam as by the parents of students admitted primarily because of old school ties. What's more, the veterans usually had better grades and caused administrators far fewer problems. In the final analysis, the GI Bill so completely altered the market for educational services that fringe benefits offered earlier customers, such as ethnic and religious exclusiveness, simply weren't affordable, or desirable, any more.

Prejudice—literally prejudgment—was more difficult, if not impossible to sustain when the veterans who were the overwhelming majority of students had learned, through experience, to literally depend on others regardless of their race, religion, or culture. Military life, of course, didn't automatically equip veterans who were Jewish, Catholic, or black to accept—or be accepted in—their new roles as students, so different from anything they or their families had expected for them. That was especially true in the Ivy League colleges that had been full of wealthy WASPs before the war.

At Cornell, for example, Jews were admitted as students but not accepted socially, as Charles Katz remembered. "There was no way if you were Jewish you were going to be invited to join a fraternity."[15] Nevertheless, social change on a seismic scale was happening and nowhere more so than at Harvard. Harvard was the oldest elite institution traditionally preparing the sons of America's WASP families to take their places as the economic and social leaders of the country. Yet it helped pioneer the new meritocratic society that Conant had called for but that the GI Bill made possible. Harvard had taken the lead a generation before under President A. Lawrence Lowell in restricting the percentage of Jewish students. But under President Conant after the war, the university began vigorously recruiting students from every ethnic and religious background and section of the country, often to the discomfort of alumni who assumed admission of their sons into Harvard Yard was part of the family patrimony. For the veterans who were unexpectedly within the walls of the Yard, it was both a disconcerting and liberating experience.

Frank O'Hara, for example, who was to become a leading literary and art figure of New York in the 1950s and 1960s, wasn't even sure the GI Bill of Rights was a good idea. He had been an enlisted man working as a sonar operator in San Pedro, California, in 1946 when a conversation with a bunkmate, Douglas "Diddy" Starr, turned to the GI Bill. O'Hara, unlike most of his fellow sailors who were singularly pleased with the windfall, was wary, according to his biographer, Brad Gooch. O'Hara had read and been impressed with an article by President Hutchins of the University of Chicago in *Collier's* arguing the bill would turn the nation's colleges into "educational hobo jungles." He was also suspicious of a bandwagon mood that assumed education was the answer to all problems. Nonetheless, O'Hara, whose father graduated from the College of the Holy Cross in Worcester, Massachusetts, applied for and was accepted at Harvard—and so far as living arrangements were concerned, might as well have been back in the navy. "In 1946, you might as well have been living in an American Legion post as in one of the Houses," a graduating senior reminisced in the 1950 *Harvard Yearbook*. Four thousand veterans were among the record 5,435 students enrolled at Harvard in 1946, filing through registration points in Memorial Hall at the rate of 3 a minute. The spectacle of seventeen-year-old beardless youths in white buck shoes, unloading Vuitton bags from their convertibles outside the "Gold Coast" houses along the Charles River was overshadowed by the sea of older faces surging into the red brick dormitories reserved for veterans on the north side of the Yard. Double-deck bunk beds had to be moved into some dorms, and cots were set up in the Indoor Athletic Building's basketball court to accommodate latecomers.

The words "invasion" and "siege" were predictably and incessantly used by *The Harvard Crimson* as lines formed everywhere—to register, eat, get books, cash checks. The more popular lecturers spoke in classrooms where students arrived early to claim seats on windowsills. The old rules still applied. Jackets and ties were required in the Union, the dining hall, but manufacturers had stopped making blazers and white shirts during the war, and veterans couldn't afford them even if they were available at the Coop, the university's cooperative store. So military coats were cut to hip length, service-issue trousers given a quick press, and insignia cut off old khaki shirts.

O'Hara found it amazing that he was at Harvard at all, Gooch wrote. A mere three months before he had been an enlisted man on the U.S.S. *Nicholas* who, without the GI Bill, would never have been able to afford Harvard's stiff fees. Yet not all of the nuances of Harvard pleased him. He couldn't help feel the pressure of elitism, and he wasn't sure if being at Harvard meant anything to anybody except snobs. He also felt pigeonholed by being Irish even though Irish-Catholics had been the first minority admitted to Harvard back in the 1870s. There had always been a subtle rivalry between Protestants and Catholics, Gooch wrote, although it usually didn't take any more serious form than drinking contests. O'Hara was also unlike relatively sophisticated big-city and wealthy Irish-Catholics like the Kennedys. He was from a small Massachusetts farm town, Grafton near Athol, and a graduate of a parochial high school. Almost another twenty years would pass before graduates of public and parochial high schools outnumbered the products of select private schools among the undergraduates at Harvard. One acquaintance described O'Hara at the time as looking "potato Irish, lower class, with pasty skin." He was often kidded as coming from "Asshole" and told a boyhood friend from Grafton, Phil Charron, "I'm going to Harvard; they say it's the death knell of all Catholics." O'Hara reacted to the social fencing, Gooch wrote, as did many others, by developing a personal style of speech using "arch Angloisms" to both blend in and subtly mock the accents and manners of WASP culture.[16]

Arch Angolisms weren't any part of the style of another member of the class of 1950, although his potato face did go well with the Germanic accent he has retained. Henry Kissinger, before being drafted into the army, had enrolled as a college student in what was often called the Jewish Harvard, CCNY. The German-Jewish immigrant had planned on becoming an accountant, like his father. "My horizons were never that great when I was in City College," Kissinger said,

according to his biographer, Walter Isaacson. Kissinger, who had fled
Nazi persecution in Germany with his parents, became an American
citizen in the army. The naturalization ceremony at dusty Camp Croft
in South Carolina had been just another event in the daily process of,
as Kissinger wrote to his brother, "being pushed around and inocu-
lated, counted and stood to attention." The erstwhile accountant
returned to Germany, Isaacson wrote, as part of a

> vast democratizing force, one that transformed how Americans
> lived. Soldiers from small towns in South Carolina and Louisiana
> for the first time saw places like Paris and Berlin, turning all-
> American boys with hardscrabble heritages into cosmopolitan
> conquerors. And, on a smaller scale, the army took young refugees
> from Nuremburg and Furth, put them into places such as Camp
> Croft and Camp Claiborne, then marched them off to war in melt-
> ing pot platoons, thus turning cosmopolitan allies into accultur-
> ated American citizens. For immigrant boys, such as Kissinger,
> serving in the war made citizenship more than a gift merely
> bestowed; it was an honor they had earned. Having defended the
> United States, they now had as much claim as any Winthrop or
> Lowell to feel it was their nation, their country, their home. They
> were outsiders no more.

Lowells and Cabots mingled quite freely with O'Haras and Kissingers
and the other provincial young men tossed up on the banks of the
Charles River by the GI Bill. The war, after all, had given all of them
the same veneer. Kissinger himself liked to say later that his experience with "the real middle American boys" in his regiment from Wisconsin, Illinois, and Indiana "made me feel like an American." He
quoted Helmut Sonnenfeld, a national security adviser, as observing,
"The Army made the melting pot melt faster." Indeed, the melting-
pot experience young men had undergone in the military was much
more readily replicated on college campuses than in established
multigenerational and ethnically dominated cities such as Boston,
where veterans were sometimes suspected of getting above themselves. That was particularly true of Harvard in comparison to the
Boston-Cambridge community where racial, ethnic, and religious
tensions would plague the community long after they had subsided
on the Harvard campus. Boston, in the late '40s, wasn't quite the city
made famous by the doggerel toast of an Irish-Catholic alumnus of
Boston College at the turn of the century: "Here's to Boston, the home
of the bean and the cod, where the Lowells speak only to the Cabots

and the Cabots speak only to God." Nevertheless, it was still a community in which the Yankees spoke rarely to the Irish; the Irish avoided conversation with their fellow Catholics, the Italians; and Jews talked with the Yankees, Irish, and Italians only on business. At the time, in fact, the Cabots were, according to a widely circulated story, suing a Jewish family named Cabotsky. The Cabotskys had changed their name so they could advertise their pharmacy as "Cabot's Drugs." Presumably the old toast had been changed to: "Here's to the home of the bean and the cod, where the Lowells speak to no one, for the Cabots speak Yiddish, by God!"

Kissinger's Germanic accent no doubt stood him in good stead on the Harvard campus and unquestionably helped him in his determination to avoid assimilation into democratic anonymity. His Teutonic tonalities served the same purpose as O'Hara's arch Anglo-isms. The difference was intriguing and enticing for insiders who not only accepted, but thought more highly of them for being outsiders. Kissinger had listened carefully to his first mentor, Fritz Gustave Anton Kraemer, a German refugee of Prussian background, who was his boss in the American military government of Germany. Kraemer advised him: "Go to a fine college. A gentleman does not go to the College of the City of New York." Kissinger was admitted to Harvard, however, only because the college was willing to take students whose papers were filed late, unlike Princeton and Columbia where he also applied. Isaacson attributed that to the fact that Conant, whom he incorrectly described as a driving force behind the GI Bill, had appointed an outreach counselor to make sure veterans had access to his university.[17]

Once the bill was passed, Conant added his own support to the bill's influence in breaking down the ethnic, religious, and especially anti-Semitic prejudices on campus, although Jews entering Harvard in 1947 were usually assigned other Jews as roommates. The college administration did caution residential housemasters not to take more Jews "than the traffic will allow," for several years after the war, but the practice was discontinued by the end of the decade. So, too, was the custom of designating the names of Jews on college records with asterisks. Actual enrollment of Jews in the late '40s was about 17 percent, slightly lower than the level in the 1920s when President Lowell imposed quotas. The difference wasn't in the numbers so much as the degree of acceptance. "Harvard welcomed us with open arms," remembered Henry Rosovsky, who served with Kissinger in Germany and later became an economics professor, dean of the faculty, and the first Jewish member of the Harvard Corporation. Discrimination was a reality in some departments of the university, Isaacson observed, but it was least evident in government where Louis Hartz, a Jew, was professor of political theory and onetime chairman.

Hartz might have found it amusing that the veterans in his classes were there largely because of an editor, Walter Howey, whose newspaper, *The Boston Record-American,* was read publicly on campus only by kitchen workers, maids, and groundskeepers. What he or anyone else at Harvard might have thought about the fact that the GI Bill was largely a product of one of the most notorious bigots in the country can only be speculated on. Yet Rankin's attitudes were not that far out of the mainstream at the time. This was still an era in which a Rankin was deplored, not so much because of his bigotry but because of his crudity. Indeed, the very blatancy of his bigotry held a certain fascination. Rankin "holds the same fascination for me that a big fire does," a northern member of the House confessed. "I hate to think of the waste and destruction, but I can't resist the entertainment."[18]

Unlike Rankin, refined people didn't use vulgar racial or ethnic epithets; they didn't have to. In 1939, Mrs. Rogers, Rankin's cosponsor of the GI Bill, cosponsored another bill with Senator Robert Wagner of New York to admit some 20,000 German refugee children to the United States. The bill was defeated, primarily because of reservations harbored by people like Laura Delano Houghteling, a cousin of FDR as well as the wife of immigration commissioner James Houghteling. "Her principal reserve on the bill was that 20,000 charming children would all too soon grow into 20,000 ugly adults," Alan M. Kraut observed in a book whose title sums up the fears of many of the nation's "best" people at the time about hyphenated Americans, *Silent Travelers: Germs, Genes, and the Immigrant Menace.*[19]

Experience even then indicated that those 20,000 children, whatever their ethnic or religious background, would probably grow up pretty much like other American kids. American kids back then, however, weren't nearly as much like one another as they are now. The economic and social divisions were wider and bigger, both in collective and individual terms. A higher percentage of people were poor, ill fed, unhealthy, and considerably less educated—even dumber. After the Depression, wartime prosperity as well as medical services and better diets improved the physical and mental condition of Americans. Nevertheless, much more had to be done before both the intellectual and physical standard of the Depression-era generation began to approach today's. The overall rejection rate for induction into the services had been 50 percent in 1941, mostly because of bad teeth and bad eyes attributable to malnutrition. Only one in four Americans had finished high school then; most hadn't finished elementary school. Ten million Americans were functionally illiterate. *The New York Times* created an uproar with surveys in 1942 and 1943 that showed most high school and college freshmen to be almost completely ignorant of American history. Progressive and traditional educators debated whether education should be "for college" or "for life." However, Harvard had produced a report, *General Education for a Free Society,* that, following on similar studies produced by the National Education Association and the American Association of Colleges, produced general agreement on a core curriculum. Acting on these recommendation, Harvard, Yale, and Princeton led the other colleges, and ultimately the high schools, in adopting a common core of studies in the humanities, the social sciences, and the physical sciences. Every student, whether going to college or not, was to be educated in the literary, scientific, and political traditions of Western civilization and the United States. Everyone was also expected to be, in the phrase of the time, "well rounded," able to change the spark plugs in a car as well as hold his or her own in a discussion about politics or books. The curriculum change was considered the most profound in American education since the adoption of the German method of objective research in the late nineteenth century with the introduction of Ph.D. programs at the graduate level and free electives among undergraduates.

If a new American cultural breed was being created in the colleges after the war, the Selective Service system had been a form of social Darwinism, screening in those best suited to take advantage of the GI Bill. Those who had been inducted or enlisted in the military were the nation's healthiest and most intelligent young men. The most muscular and well developed came from the New England, Pacific, and Mountain states with the South having the greatest number of rejects, white as well as black. On average, the World War II veteran was one inch taller, 5'8", and eight pounds heavier, 144 pounds, than the doughboy of World War I. After thirteen weeks training, he had usually gained six or seven pounds of muscle and added an inch to his preinduction 33½-inch chest. Intelligence was measured by the 150-question Army General Classification Test (AGCT) putting everyone into five classes based on scores. A score of 110 was needed to get into officer candidate school. Initially the army air corps siphoned off the brightest, but beginning in 1943, under orders from General Marshall, the chief of staff, the most intelligent eighteen- to twenty-year-olds were assigned to the infantry. Once in, the GIs were the beneficiaries of a short-term program of socialized medicine that provided millions with glasses and corrective surgery while also saving many more millions of teeth and providing hundreds of thousands of dental plates. Most were also being fed better than they ever had been in civilian life and, of course, at least during boot camp, were exercising enough to remain fit despite consuming as much as forty-three hundred calories a day.[20] The armed forces could and did train radar experts and pilots as well as paratroops and cooks. But they also needed engineers and accountants and managers, for whom they turned to the nation's top colleges, which also produced medical doctors in three years and lawyers in two. More than one million servicemen were enrolled in such college programs during the war years, all the more noticeable for being dressed in active-duty uniforms.

The virtual takeover of the colleges by the military during the war could have produced profoundly undemocratic results. College could have become a monopoly preserve of those selected by the army and navy to become officers. Even before the passage of the GI Bill, Congress had also begun to offer loans and scholarships to students taking courses of study considered in the national interest. That overarching concept of matching people to centrally determined national needs had guided the New Deal planners who devised the various administration alternatives to the GI Bill and had influenced Conant and other critics of the GI Bill as well. Government retraining and education programs for veterans could have been turned into a vehicle for simply turning out well-trained managers of an increasingly hierarchical state dominated by big government, business, and labor, the kind of Big Brother state described in George Orwell's novel *1984*. Indeed, many thought that was happening—and what's more, should happen. That was the central thesis of James Burnham's international best-seller, *The Managerial Revolution: What Is Happening in the World*. The ultimate reality is "the permanence of oligarchical rule," declared Burnham, a former disciple of Leon Trotsky. Both under capitalism and communism, everyone was working for "the power and the privilege of the managers and the building of a new class," he wrote. Any and all accomplishments of every society were the accomplishments of its elite.[21]

After he turned into a dedicated ex-Communist, Burnham continued to believe in the need for a New Class, just as long as it was capitalistic rather than communist. In a 1947 book, *The Struggle for the World,* he urged that the United States become an American Empire. But the American soldiers, sailors, and airmen who took advantage of the GI Bill showed few signs of considering themselves to be a New Class destined to rule the world. They just wanted to finish school, get a job, and buy a house for their families. Nevertheless, over the next thirty years their generation did shoulder the demands of being the world's greatest superpower without aspiring to become the American Empire. That was left to an elite largely educated before the war, such as former Secretary of Defense Robert S. McNamara, who became the best-known representative of the American mandarins dubbed "the best and the brightest" by writer David Halberstam. Members of the World War II generation switched back and forth in their attitudes toward foreign affairs. General Eisenhower as president warned them against the dangers of the military-industrial complex. Jack Kennedy summoned them to invigorated opposition to "those nations who would make themselves our adversary." Kennedy's fears, however, for "the slow undoing of those human rights to which this country has always been committed" weren't realized. Instead, the most remarkable postwar achievement of the World War II generation was the fulfillment of those rights, at least in part, for those Americans who had been kept outside the community of citizenship for hundreds of years, the blacks. It wasn't a neat process, and it was always a contentious one.

Nevertheless, the process began with the war and was continued through the GI Bill. It was not unlike the American GI of World War II: obedient but idiosyncratic, willing but not too enthusiastic. General Joseph Stilwell noted, "The GI is superbly equipped, but happiest when in fatigues with a dirty baseball cap." That attitude could be observed most closely in their marching. "It was not that the men marched out of step, or that they could not move about in bodies with ease and dispatch," Lee Kennett wrote in *GI: The American Soldier in World War II.* "It was that each man stepped out or swung his arms in his own way, giving European observers an impression of incipient discordance in any body of marching GIs. No amount of close order drill could completely erase that impression, for the GI never made that ultimate, intimate surrender of the individual to the mass. . . . A Czech villager remarked to an American officer as they both watched American soldiers swing by, 'They walk like free men.'" [22]

Blacks especially came back from the war walking—and feeling—like free men. They took advantage of the GI Bill in the same way whites did, as individuals, not as members of a group except insofar as membership in the American Legion, the VFW, or the DAV might be helpful in negotiating red tape. Of course, blacks weren't free in the same way whites were, and it seems probable they didn't take advantage of the education benefits in the same percentages as whites. No authoritative numerical estimates of black beneficiaries are available other than an assertion, without documentation, in the *Encyclopedia of the Second World War* that 250,000 blacks were given the opportunity to go to college for the first time under the GI Bill.[23] The percentage of those who wouldn't otherwise have gone to college was certainly much higher than whites, according to Reginald Wilson, senior scholar at the American Council on Education, citing a study that "approximately 20 percent of veterans could not have gone to college without the GI Bill. I would conjecture the figure was much higher for African-American veterans. Besides, having come from families that were disproportionately poorer, most had been subjected to underfunded, segregated schools. However, when special accommodations were made and relatively open admissions policies were put in place, black veterans flocked to the colleges and universities and did well academically." At his own alma mater, Wayne State University in Detroit, Wilson recalled, "it is estimated that nearly a third of the veterans enrolled between 1946 and 1950 were African-Americans, and during those years, veterans were almost a majority of the school's students."

The northern and western colleges many blacks attended didn't keep racial census figures, at least not in any systematic fashion. Statistics for black colleges are the best indices for determining the numbers of Negroes who took advantage of the bill. In 1940, enrollment in black colleges was 1.08 percent of the U.S. college enrollment. By 1950, in a greatly expanded student population, it had almost tripled, to 3.6 percent. Overall enrollment in the Negro Land-Grant colleges after the war was 50 percent higher than before. More significantly, the number of veterans in the black colleges was double the entire 1937–38 enrollment. Partially because black colleges had been traditionally shortchanged in funding for building purposes, another federal bill, the Lanham Act of 1946, actually made proportionately more money available for construction and repair at black institutions. Acting under the law, the officers of the Commission of Education recognized the relatively large need of the Negro institutions, according to Wilson. Consequently, funds were distributed to institutions on the assumption that 33.4 square feet of construction was needed for veterans in black colleges as compared with 17.4 square feet in white schools. Nevertheless, despite the additional money for construction, black colleges had to turn away twenty thousand veterans for lack of space.

The shortage of seats was more than made up by colleges and universities in the North and West. "Black veterans with vouchers in hand, paid for by the federal government, were an attractive commodity to many institutions in the North that would not have welcomed them in vast numbers (nor could many have afforded to go before the war)," Wilson wrote. "The white colleges welcomed them and made special provisions to accommodate all of the veterans; they were given additional points on admission tests; in some instances, admission requirements were waived; they were given credit for special training received in the military; tutors were provided in recognition of the veterans being three to five years out of school; and, despite sometimes mediocre high school records, they were welcomed."[24]

The special provisions, it should be noted, applied to many white veterans, not just blacks. As early as February 9, 1942, for example, the University of Wisconsin approved granting ten elective college credits to former enlisted men and fifteen to ex-officers. Wisconsin made other concessions, too. In March 1944, a veteran could even apply four special war credits to the sixteen high school credits needed for admission. If that wasn't enough to meet the admission requirements, a veteran could take an oral or written examination proving he was capable of college work. Credit was also given for college-level work completed in service schools and military training schools, and veterans were exempted from taking the physical education courses compulsory for other students. Wisconsin's medical school lowered admission requirements from three to two years of premed training. Refresher courses were offered in mathematics and English; a full-semester summer school was created; the engineering college operated on a trimester schedule with classes starting in March, July, and November.

The innovations and accommodations pleased some veteran students and didn't appeal to others. A navy officer, responding to a survey sent to former students by Columbia University, had mixed feelings about accelerated courses. "Education is too important to me to be rushed through," he wrote. "I want to have the feeling of leisure to do an honest job with the most valuable time of my life." A year-round trimester program would turn college into a factory, he thought. But a P-51 fighter pilot had a different attitude: "I remember how we used to think that a full year would be a tough grind, but it was probably laziness that prompted that feeling."[25]

Robert A. Eubanks was a black veteran who wasn't the least bothered about going to college full time; he thrived on it. He was bright enough to have graduated in 1942 from high school at the age of fifteen. But he couldn't get a job because he was black and couldn't take advantage of a tuition-only scholarship to Howard University in Washington, D.C., because he didn't have enough money to live on. So he joined the army, and he heard about the GI Bill through word-of-mouth—as most veterans did—when he mustered out in 1946. Eubanks got into a year-round program at the Illinois Institute of Technology (ITT) and earned a degree in theoretical and applied mechanical engineering in 1950. Once again, his job-hunting forays ran up against whites-only hiring policies, so he stayed on at ITT, earning a master's and then a doctoral degree in 1953, all on the GI Bill. With the changing social climate after the *Brown* decision, he was able to get high-paying work in industry. Later, he was lured back to academia, first as a visiting professor at the University of Illinois. After six months, he was offered a tenured full professorship and stayed on until retirement in 1986, teaching and conducting research. "It's very hard to explain now how things were during the 1940s," Eubanks said in reflecting on this life. "The restrictions on blacks then were rough. The GI Bill gave me my start on being a professional instead of a stock clerk."[26]

The story of Dovey J. Roundtree personified the enormous changes the war, and then the GI Bill, made in the lives of hundred of thousands of blacks, women as well as men. A member of the first class of black women admitted to officer candidate school in the Women's Auxiliary Army Corps (WAAC) in 1942, she was promoted to captain before being discharged and going to work for A. Philip Randolph.

With Randolph, she helped transform the Fair Employment Prac-
tices Commission from a temporary wartime agency under an execu-
tive order of FDR's into a permanent body under a law passed by
Congress. Later, Pauli Murray, the first black woman ordained as an
Episcopalian priest, encouraged her to enter Howard Law School.
Subsequently, Roundtree became a lawyer in private practice in
Washington, D.C., as well as an ordained minister after attending
Howard University Divinity School.

When Roundtree, all dressed up in red, white, and blue for the
occasion, had applied for the WAACs in 1942, there were no black
women in the army. Black officers numbered fewer than a dozen, and
the total of black enlisted men fewer than ten thousand, all of them
in service units, none of them fighting men. Roundtree was refused
even an application form in her first try at a recruiting office in
Charlotte, North Carolina. She tried again, farther north in Rich-
mond, Virginia, only at the urging of Mary McLeod Bethune, the
educator and founder of the National Council of Negro Women. She
was finally accepted. But only the desperate need for replacements
during the Battle of the Bulge forced the army to form fighting units
of black soldiers.

The Battle of the Bulge, which began on December 16, 1944, and
continued until the middle of January 1945, counted 19,000 killed
and 48,000 wounded among the Americans as contrasted to 120,000
Germans lost to death, wounding, and capture. The army needed
anyone who could shoulder a rifle or throw a grenade, no matter what
his color. The 90 percent of all black soldiers who had been assigned
to the rear lines as truck drivers, stevedores, longshoremen, and construction workers finally got a chance at combat duty with whites.
Until then, only three Negro divisions had been established, and
only one, the 92nd, had seen combat, in Italy. The 93rd was used only
in a few firefights in the Pacific, and the Second Calvary had been
broken into service units in North Africa.

Twenty-five hundred black ground troops assembled in Noynes,
France, in early January in response to a call for volunteers in the
Battle of the Bulge. After six weeks' training, they were sent into
battle as all-black platoons within white units, rather than as individuals in integrated units. In the melee of war, however, blacks and
whites fought, slept, showered, and played together and soon saw
themselves as the same as everyone else. "When I heard about it," a
sergeant from South Carolina said, "I said I'd be damned if I would

wear the same patch they did. After the first day I saw how they fought I changed my mind. They're just like any other boys to us." The sergeant's opinion was far from universal, but it did reflect a growing consensus. Sixty-four percent of white troops polled when the black platoons were introduced were skeptical; three months later, 77 percent approved.

In the army air corps, the 99th Pursuit Squadron, the famed Tuskegee Airmen, had been formed in March 1941 only in response to a lawsuit filed by Yancey Williams, a black pilot denied admission to the all-white air corps. By the spring of 1943, the squadron had produced more than one thousand pilots but had no combat assignment. "We were undoubtedly the most highly trained squadron in the U.S.," Louis Purnell, one member of the squadron, later wrote—and the most useless. Finally, in March 1943, Frederick Patterson, the director of the program, complained to Eleanor Roosevelt that the unit was virtually idle. She in turn wrote to Secretary Stimson about this "crucial situation." The 99th was finally shipped out for North Africa the next month, April 1943, and proved, in the words of a Defense Department study, that "blacks could fly in combat with the best pilots of any nation." Over the next two years, the squadron was credited with shooting down 111 enemy aircraft and destroying 150 on the ground in the course of 1,578 missions over North Africa, Italy, and Germany.

The navy, whose record on race was far worse than the army's before the war began, was fully integrated by war's end. Before 1941, blacks were employed in the navy only as mess stewards. In 1942, the general-service ranks had been opened up, but that had led only to work loading ships. On May 20, 1944, James Forrestal, the former Wall Street financier who was secretary of the navy and would later become the first secretary of defense, wrote FDR saying many Negroes felt they had simply swapped the waiter's apron for the stevedore's grappling hook. Forrestal felt the navy was wasting energy and resources in maintaining segregation and consequently issued orders to expand the use of Negro personnel by assigning them to general sea duty. As an initial experiment, Forrestal required no less than 10 percent of the crews of twenty-five large auxiliary ships be composed of Negroes. Soon the experiment was expanded to smaller ships where men lived and worked in even closer quarters. The experiment was successfully under way when an explosion in the hold of the S.S. *Bryan* in Port Chicago, a seaport in northern California, on July 17, 1944, killed 202 blacks and injured 233 in an almost all-black loading crew. The death and injury toll amounted to almost 15 percent of all black naval casualties in World War II and was the worst disaster to occur on the home front during the war. The loss of so many blacks at once, and the resulting public attention, convinced Forrestal integration was a practical as well as a moral necessity. He abolished all separate facilities and quotas for Negroes and opened admission to all promotion opportunities. A "Guide to Command of Negro Naval Personnel," issued at Forrestal's directive, flatly rejected, for the first time in the history of the U.S. government, "any theories of racial differences in inborn abilities, but expects every man wearing its uniform be trained and used in accord with his maximum individual capacity determined on the basis of individual performance." The black, once considered by the navy good enough only to be a servant, was now fully accepted as a sailor. Within three years, President Truman accorded equality of status to army soldiers through an executive order.

Declaring people equal was one thing; finding them, in fact, to be capable of mastering the techniques of modern warfare, in Secretary Stimson's words, was another. "It so happens," Stimson wrote in a letter to Representative Hamilton Fish of New York, FDR's congressman from Hyde Park and his devoted political enemy, "that a relatively large number of Negroes inducted in the Army have fallen within the lower educational classifications"—too low to be effectively trained. Approximately three-quarters of the blacks tested were, in fact, classified as slow learners. Those facts, however, don't tell the whole story. Only 17 percent of all blacks who had registered for the draft were high school graduates, compared with 41 percent of the whites. Moreover, almost 75 percent of the Negroes registered for the draft came from southern and border states where expenditures for public schools were so low only four out of five blacks had completed the fourth grade—and the percentage wasn't much better among whites. The military itself remedied many of those shortcomings, turning blacks as well as whites into artillerymen, tankers, pilots, paratroopers, even doctors. The number of blacks in uniform increased from 5,000 before the war to 920,000 by V-J Day. The proportion was roughly equal to the more than 10 percent of blacks in the general population. Seven thousand were officers.[27]

After World War II, history did not repeat the brutal episodes following World War I, when 350,000 black veterans came home and found themselves in the midst of twenty-five race riots, most in the North. In 1919 alone, more than 70 blacks were lynched, many of them veterans still wearing their uniforms. By contrast, only one black man, a laborer accused of raping a little girl in Madison, Florida, was lynched in the United States during 1945, according to the semi-official annual report compiled by the Tuskegee Institute. In 1946, however, Birmingham, Alabama, police officers commanded by Commissioner Eugene "Bull" Connor, later notorious for siccing dogs on civil rights protesters, killed five black men, all veterans, in the first six weeks of the year. In Walton County near Atlanta, two black men and their wives were lined up and shot by two dozen white men. An eleven-year-old white boy, who had helped one of the black men, an ex-GI, with chores, witnessed the murders but kept quiet. Persuaded to leave home at twenty-one because he "made people nervous," he asked the ringleader of the killers twenty years later why the four had been killed, especially the ex-GI. "Let me tell you something about them you don't know," the murderer told him. "Up until George went into the Army, he was a good nigger. But when he came out, he thought they were as good as any white folk."[28]

That attitude, inculcated in blacks in their military service, was reinforced by the GI Bill. Blacks getting the same veterans' benefits as whites began to believe they were entitled to other rights as well. Something was happening, and not just among blacks. "Our Negro fellow citizens are taking seriously the propaganda and preachments of two world wars," Frank Graham, president of the University of North Carolina, wrote in 1948: "With advancing education, the ideas of the Declaration of Independence, the Bill of Rights, Lincoln's Gettysburg Address . . . and the four freedoms of Franklin Delano Roosevelt are bearing fruit in the minds and aspirations of the present generation, white and colored. . . . The majority of students in a large number of Southern colleges and universities are quite ready for the admission of Negroes in the colleges, especially in the graduate and professional schools for which no provision is made by the state for Negro students. However, boards of trustees are just now more adamant in their resistance to such attitudes. . . . There is, of course, always an ebb and flow in human movements, but the democratic currents . . . move eventually onward to the larger sea."

Politically, there was little evidence that a new democratic order was in the making. Perhaps the most notable congressional election in the South that year was one in which Representative Rankin tried to succeed Theodore G. Bilbo in the Senate. Bilbo was a Populist who had been a genuine reform governor, but by 1939 he was introducing legislation in Congress calling for the expenditure of a billion dollars to deport twelve million blacks back to Africa. He was completely incapable of understanding—as was Rankin, who lost the race to John C. Stennis—the bonds of respect, even friendship that could be formed across racial lines by war. Bilbo asked a returning lieutenant from the state, Van T. Barfoot of Carthage, who had won the Congressional Medal of Honor, "Did you have much trouble with nigras over there?" Barfoot, who had initially appeared shy meeting Bilbo and other members of the state's congressional delegation, stiffened and drawled deliberately, "I found out after I did some fighting in this war that the colored boys fought just as good as the white boys. I've changed my ideas a lot about colored people since I've got into this war and so have a lot of other boys from the South."

The nineteenth-century Whigs would have argued democracy isn't dramatic, but deliberative and those who participate in a democracy should do so with the light of knowledge. The candle of the classroom illuminates better than the torchlight parade. No one knew that better than black veterans, and it was they who lit the way to the ballot box through the schools. "It was as if some universal message had reached the great mass of Negroes," Howard W. Odum, the South's most respected sociologist, wrote in 1949, "urging them to dream new dreams and to protest against the old order." The time had come for the South to move forward, the sociologist wrote, and "stop being afraid of democracy."[29] The South and the rest of the nation would move forward largely because of black veterans who, having learned to stop being afraid of whites in the military, used the GI Bill of Rights to get the education, middle-class occupations, and status as home owners that made challenging the system realistic.

The first great victory in the struggle against segregation was won through a lawsuit filed by a veteran in Topeka, Kansas. The lawsuit, *Brown vs. the Board of Education,* which produced the Supreme Court decision outlawing segregation in primary and secondary schools, was named after Oliver Brown, a World War II veteran acting on behalf of his daughter Linda. Two veterans were also responsible for overcoming segregation at the University of Mississippi, "Ole Miss," the one college that no one, least of all John Rankin, ever thought would surrender to the forces of integration. The victory was won by two blacks whom Rankin assumed would "not want to go to

the University of Mississippi or Harvard . . . [preferring] to go down
to this training shop where this man is teaching the boys how to be
automobile mechanics." However, Medgar Evers, a veteran of D day,
and James Meredith, a former air force enlisted man, wanted to go
to Ole Miss. Evers was unable to get admitted in 1954, partially because the recently decided *Brown* case had stiffened white resistance
to any other efforts to cross the color line. In 1962, Evers was able,
however, to orchestrate Meredith's acceptance into Ole Miss, with the
help of 123 deputy federal marshals, 315 border patrolmen, and 97
federal prison guards. When Meredith was awarded a bachelor's
degree in political science in 1963, he wore a "Never" button on his
gown—turned upside down. The legal strategy that culminated
in these victories and the overturn of official segregation was developed by a World War I officer determined that the veterans of World
War II shouldn't have to endure the hardships his generation was
subjected to. The march through the courts that led to *Brown vs. the
Board of Education* and James Meredith's one-man integration of
Ole Miss began with a precedent-setting case at a southern university where a black applicant's principal supporters were white
students led by an ex-GI. From the end of the World War II into the
early '60s, separate cases involving primary school pupils and college
students were argued at different times and places, usually by lawyers who were veterans. The resolution of each case established precedents that influenced the resolution of others. It wasn't very neat or
orderly—or even always logical—but it was the law. The one consistent element behind all these cases, however, was the presence of
human beings whose involvement was intricately connected with military service and the catalytic workings of the GI Bill.

    When the war ended with more than 920,000 black veterans eligi-
ble for GI Bill benefits, both black and northern institutions were
overwhelmed by applicants, especially in graduate and professional
schools. The Howard University Medical School, for example, had
places for only seventy new students, but more than one thousand
applied. There just weren't enough colleges providing enough seats
for qualified black students. Southern colleges and universities had
to be desegregated, if only as a practical matter, because so many
blacks wanted a professional education and could pay for it through
the GI Bill. Before the war, Charles Houston, the dean of the Howard
University Law School, had started to pry open access to graduate
schools in the South with the help of one of his former students,

Thurgood Marshall. He and Marshall would now use World War II veterans to help batter down the slightly ajar doors. Houston had served as a lieutenant in the District of Columbia's "1st Separate Battalion" during World War I. A graduate of Amherst as well as a member of Phi Beta Kappa, he was assigned to the judge advocate's office, where he quickly found defense lawyers weren't supposed to be too zealous in defending black soldiers. He decided that if he got through the war, he would study law and use his time fighting for men who could not strike back. After going to Harvard Law School and earning a doctorate in civil law, he became the dean of the Howard University Law School, vastly improving standards and winning accreditation from the American Bar Association and the Association of American Law Schools.

In the 1930s, Houston, along with Marshall and several other lawyers he had trained, began the series of legal cases that would culminate in *Brown vs. the Board of Education*. The practical difficulty, if not moral absurdity, of segregated schools, became manifest in the case of Heman Sweatt, an ex-GI who applied to the law school of the University of Texas at Austin in 1946. Two thousand white students, many of them veterans, rallied in Sweatt's behalf, demanding that the democratic rights he had fought for overseas as a GI be respected at home. The president of the student body, also an ex-GI, told the rally Christianity ought to be practiced as well as preached at the university. Ten campus organizations, including an all-white campus chapter of the NAACP, supported Sweatt and offered financial support for his lawsuit. When the case was appealed to the Supreme Court, eleven southern states filed an *amicus curiae* brief in support of Texas. An *amicus* brief filed by 187 law professors from leading schools argued for Sweatt: "Laws which give equal protection are those which make no *discrimination* because of race in the sense that they make no *distinction* because of race . . . for the Equal Protection Clause makes racial classification unreasonable per se." The U.S. Justice Department also agreed with the NAACP on the basis of a 1942 case in which it had argued that blacks should not be forced to eat separately in railroad dining cars. That case was, in many respects, a replay of the original *Plessy* case in which Homer Plessy, a white known to have a black grandmother, was taken off a train in which he tried to sit in a car reserved for whites.

That 1942 case, however, relied on federal law governing interstate transportation, not state education law. So Marshall and the NAACP took a more cautious approach in *Sweatt* than either the law professors or the Justice Department. They decided not to target segregation itself as the heart of the case, Richard Kluger explained in *Simple Justice*. Marshall was still clinging to the organization's tried-and-true formula used in previous cases: "Segregation was illegal because, as practiced, it never produced equality for Negroes." However, during the original *Sweatt* trial in 1947, Marshall did get on the record, for the first time, expert sociological opinion that state-imposed racial separation was scientifically unjustifiable and socially destructive—although the evidence didn't impress the Supreme Court justices. Robert Redfield, an anthropologist who had been dean of social sciences at the University of Chicago and a lawyer, observed that scholars had started with a rather general assumption: that there were inherent differences in intellectual ability or capacity to learn between Negroes and whites. But they "slowly, and I think convincingly, have been compelled to come to the opposite conclusion," he said. The conclusion stemmed primarily from studies of Negro performance in the military during the war. Segregation, Redfield argued, "intensifies suspicion and distrust between Negroes and whites, and suspicion and distrust are not favorable conditions either for the acquisition and conduct of an education, or the discharge of the duties of a citizen."

While the case was on appeal to the Supreme Court after being decided in the state's behalf, Texas tried to accommodate Sweatt by providing a separate but equal Texas State University Law School for Negroes in three basement rooms of an office building near the university campus in Austin. Sweatt, as the only student, would be taught by three part-time first-year instructors. He refused to attend, saying during his trial, "I don't believe equality can be given on the basis of segregation." Three years later, in 1950, when the Supreme Court handed down its decision, the law school for Negroes had twenty-three students and five full-time professors. Nevertheless, in a unanimous decision read by Chief Justice Fred M. Vinson, the court ruled, "We cannot find substantial equality in the educational opportunities offered white and Negro law students by the state." The issue raised by Sweatt, Vinson wrote, was whether he was being offered "a legal education equivalent to that offered by the state to students of other races. Such education is not available to him in a separate school as offered by the state. We cannot, therefore, agree with the respondents [Texas] that the doctrine of *Plessy vs. Ferguson* . . . requires affirmation of the judgment below."

Texas was ordered to admit Sweatt to the University of Texas Law School. The court's decision made it clear that a school established exclusively for blacks couldn't provide equal educational opportunity. As Vinson wrote, "The University of Texas Law School possesses to a far greater degree those qualities which are incapable of objective measurement but which make for greatness in a law school . . . reputation of faculty . . . position and influence of alumni . . . standing in the community, traditions and prestige. It is difficult to believe that one who had a free choice between these law schools would consider the question close."[30] It was an important victory, but a limited one. The Supreme Court had decided a specific law school set up exclusively for blacks was unequal, not that all segregated schools were inherently unequal. It opened doors only at the University of Texas Law School.

A different legal approach was needed. James M. Nabrit, later to be president of Howard, came to see Houston, who was confined to a Washington hospital by a heart attack while the Supreme Court was still considering *Sweatt*. He wanted to discuss a case brought by Washington, D.C., black parents protesting overcrowded conditions, which was the first involving children rather than college-age adults. "You know, for the past three years, Charlie," Nabrit said, "I have been trying to get you all to agree that you would take these cases and fight them on the grounds that segregation itself is unconstitutional. If I take these cases I am telling you now I am going to abandon this separate but equal theory you have, and I am going to draft a new theory. I am going to try these cases on the theory that segregation *per se* is unconstitutional." Houston agreed, saying, "I'm glad to hear you say that because I've about come to that position myself." On April 20, 1950, Houston died at the age of fifty-four; the Supreme Court handed down its decision in *Sweatt* two months later, on June 5, 1950.[31] That month, Marshall called an NAACP conference in New York; the organization decided to attack *Plessey* directly, arguing segregated schools were inherently unequal and, therefore, unconstitutional.

The first case in which the new doctrine was argued, *Briggs vs. Clarendon Country, S.C.,* was one in which the plaintiff was, once again, a veteran. Harry Briggs, a thirty-four-year-old navy veteran of the South Pacific, was acting on behalf of his son, Harry Jr., in a class action suit. Briggs was a service station attendant who wasn't allowed by his boss to be a mechanic, but who had been able to take out a loan under the GI Bill to build a small house. Briggs was fired from his service station job after he'd signed the complaint; "Harry, I want me a *boy,*" his boss told him. Briggs and his family eked out a living farming twelve rented acres while the case made its way through the courts.

Briggs was the first case in which "contemporary knowledge" was used to prove segregation was inherently unequal. Kenneth Clark of City College of New York testified on the results of tests in which Negro children were asked to choose between brown and white dolls. Their overwhelming preference for the white dolls was interpreted as evidence of a lack of personal esteem due to the pervasive effects of racism. The tests failed to distinguish between psychological damage cased by segregated education and that caused by segregated living conditions and were the subject of considerable derision, according to Kluger in *Simple Justice,* even among some NAACP lawyers.

The federal district court decided that Clark's psychological data were irrelevant because the problem of segregation at the common school level is a very different one than the graduate school situation presented in *Sweatt.* The court did find school facilities for black children in Clarendon County unequal and instructed the county to correct the differences promptly. However, the dissenting voice on the three-judge panel, that of Judge J. Waities Waring, would be upheld in the end.[32] Waring's viewpoint had been shaped by a case involving a black veteran that so horrified Negroes and many whites that actor and singer Harry Belafonte remembered it clearly fifty years later when interviewed for a documentary on the GI Bill.

"The GI Bill was extremely critical for all of us," he recalled. "Those of us who returned from the war had hoped that we would return to a more welcoming society, a society more prepared to look past race. We returned to a nation where the Ku Klux Klan was on the rise. Many of us were devastated that, after all we had done, America was still that way. Do you know the story of Isaac Woodward? He was the great black hero, highly decorated. When he came back they gouged out his eyes because he wouldn't sit in the back of the bus. All the doors which should have been open to us weren't. Had it not been for the GI Bill, we would have been severely shut out."[33]

Waring was the judge in the case in which the police officer who had gouged out Woodward's eyes was tried. He was far from being liberal, describing himself as a descendant of "fine, decent slaveholders" who loved their Negroes and were good to them. "We didn't give them any rights, but they didn't ask for any." He was horrified, however, when federal prosecutors presented as their only witness the bus driver who insisted Woodward was drunk and disorderly. None of the passengers on the crowded bus was called. "I was shocked at the hypocrisy of my government . . . in submitting that disgraceful case," Waring said later. The police officer was acquitted, the people in the courtroom cheered, and the resulting scandal encouraged President Truman to demand civil rights reforms. Waring went on to dissent in *Briggs,* writing: "There is absolutely no reasonable explanation for racial prejudice. It is all caused by unreasoning emotional reactions and those are gained in early childhood. . . . Segregation in education can never produce equality and . . . is an evil that must be eradicated. *Segregation is per se inequality* [emphasis Waring's]."

In *Brown vs. the Board of Education,* the Supreme Court agreed with Waring. Black veterans as individuals and sociological evidence, based on World War II military experience, would be crucial in that case. Brown's local lawyer in Kansas was Elisha Scott, a flamboyant black attorney helped by two of his three sons. All three sons had gone to law school under the GI Bill. Elisha Scott Jr. and his brother Charles had served in Europe, and John had been on an aircraft carrier in the Pacific. Both Charles and John were active in the American Veterans Committee (AVC), composed largely of blacks, some Jews from the nearby Menninger Foundation for psychiatric treatment, and a few homegrown "radicals." The NAACP lawyer in the case, Robert Lee Carter, was another veteran, as was Brown himself.

Carter, who had done some graduate work at Columbia in sociology, argued segregation damaged black children psychologically, using Horace B. English of Ohio State University as his principal expert. English had been a full professor of psychology for thirty years who had also served as a morale analyst for the American occupation forces in Japan. He came to the stand with specific evidence of the effect that expectations had on learning capacity, based on military experience. "If we din it into a person that he is incapable of learning, then he is less likely to be able to learn . . . and there is a tendency for us to live up to—or perhaps I should say down to—social expectations and to learn what people say we learn, and legal segregation definitely depresses the Negro's capacity and therefore is definitely prejudicial to his learning." As an example of what can happen when expectations are increased, English cited his own work during World War II with a group of illiterate soldiers. Put into school to be brought up to fourth-grade literacy standards, 84 percent of the whites and 87 percent of the blacks met the test.[34]

That was the contemporary knowledge introduced in *Brown vs.*

the Topeka Board of Education, sociological and psychological evidence based on extensive military experience, not tests with dolls. Indeed, Chief Justice Earl Warren prefaced the announcement of the decision Monday, May 17, 1954, with an observation citing education in connection with military service: "Today, education is perhaps the most important function of state and local governments. . . . it is required in the performance of our most basic public responsibilities, even service in the armed forces. It is the very foundation of good citizenship. . . . In these days, it is doubtful if any child may reasonably be expected to succeed in life if he is denied the opportunity for an education." Having said that, Warren addressed the central question: "We conclude, unanimously, that in the field of public education, the doctrine of 'separate but equal' has no place. Separate educational facilities are inherently unequal."

Unfortunately, Warren just dismissed "whatever may have been the state of psychological knowledge at the time of *Plessy vs. Ferguson*" by simply invoking "amply supported modern knowledge." No supporting evidence was given other than a list of seven sociological studies the NAACP had cited in its litigation. The list happened to be headed by Clark's *Effect of Prejudice and Discrimination on Personality Development,* based on his doll studies. "Invoking Kenneth Clark was a mistake because of the vulnerability of the doll tests," Alexander Bickel of Yale, a constitutional scholar who was a law clerk for Justice Felix Frankfurter at the time, observed later.

That criticism, in far less measured tones and far more vicious words, was to haunt and often frustrate all the subsequent efforts by the courts to implement *Brown.* Had the court cited the testimony of Redfield in *Briggs* and English in *Brown,* demonstrating the educational success achieved by blacks in the military in World War II, public support for the Court decision might have been much greater, and the indirect appeal to patriotism might have muted the subsequent attacks on integration orders.

A case in which the Supreme Court ruled it was wrong to bus a black child out of her neighborhood in order to maintain a segregated school system became the grounds for ordering millions of black and white children bused out of their neighborhoods to establish integrated school systems. One set of rules imposed arbitrarily by institutions governed by elected officials was replaced by a set of rules imposed arbitrarily by institutions governed by appointed judges. There was something illogical and certainly not persuasive in terms of shared human values and social goals about the coercive methods used to induce people to believe forced integration was morally preferable to forced segregation.

By contrast, there was nothing coercive about the GI Bill. Resources were placed directly in the hands of individuals to use as they saw fit rather than being made available to individuals to use only as a bureaucracy saw fit. Whether a comparable program using vouchers for private and public schools of their choice would work is another question. As a practical matter, that is a matter of speculation because such programs never have been tried. Efforts that have been made to help minorities, notably the Great Society, have drawn their inspiration from the bureaucratic New Deal rather than the GI Bill. Great Society programs, although presumably created in response to the needs of their beneficiaries, Ginsberg charges in *The Fatal Embrace,* were really established "at the behest of professional reformers, public policy intellectuals, and representatives for service providers such as educators and mental health professionals. The reform efforts turned out to be full employment—or welfare—programs for the professional reformers. This, in fact, has been the great differences between the American and European welfare states," in Ginsberg's opinion. "The European welfare state rests fairly securely on the broad base of support created by the organized recipients of services (the working-class and Social Democratic parties). The American welfare state, by contrast, teeters on a narrow base of support provided by the organized providers of support."[35]

As a matter of reality, with the great exception of the GI Bill of Rights, government programs to help people haven't directly given people the resources to help themselves. That was the GI Bill's greatest characteristic and accomplishment. It didn't have to appeal to shared human values and social goals by persuading people that institutions knew what was best for them. It gave the individuals the power to decide for themselves what was best for themselves and, at the same time, freed educational institutions to do what they did best, teach. It caused a silent revolution, not by the force of the state, but by using the resources of the state to encourage what George Mason spelled out in the Virginia Declaration much more explicitly than Thomas Jefferson did in the Declaration of Independence: the means of acquiring and possessing property for pursuing and obtaining happiness and safety. The GI Bill gave people the economic resources to train their minds, their most important property, and they went out and used it to pursue happiness and safety.

When Harry Briggs and Oliver Brown were able to walk into

a bank and get loans to build their homes for their families just on the strength of their military service and their own signatures, that wasn't enlightened reform. It was working reality. That gave them houses of their own and unquestionably helped turn them into men who would no longer accept second-class citizenship, who wanted to be whole men. When the U.S. government paid the tuition of the O'Haras and Kissingers at Harvard, those checks for Irish-Catholics and German Jews didn't take anything away from their most WASPish classmates or even cause enlightened reformers a twinge of agony. No one, including the Briggses, the Browns, the O'Haras, and the Kissingers, had to take orders from overweening bureaucrats or judges conferring those benefits. Neither individuals nor institutions had to bow to organized group demands. Inner conscience did not have to be dictated by "social uplifters," in the scornful phrase of Rankin and other members of Congress who passed the GI Bill. Personal morality become public morality because it made sense personally and publicly.

CHAPTER 9

MAKING MODERN
AMERICA

T HE FOUNDING Fathers believed in pursuing happiness, but many Americans after World War II had good reason to think they could make it or buy it.

The feeling wasn't new, but never before had it been so widely shared. A new society was being created while everyone thought he was just going about his business. An entire generation of entrepreneurs took advantage of a vastly expanded market created by the GI Bill of Rights, government-insured investment capital, mass production economies, and local service outlets to create new ways of living, working, and shopping. We call it "suburbia," but that word is so familiar now its very use obscures the fact that it refers to living, school, working, and social arrangements that were virtually unknown a half century ago. Another name, one reflecting suburbia's origins in both World War II and the GI Bill of Rights, provides a little perspective: "The Big PX."

Large department stores on military bases overseas during the '40s, '50s, and '60s were called big PXs, post exchanges. The phrase was also the nickname American foreign service workers gave the affluent oases they lived in amid the economies of Europe and Asia slowly being rebuilt after World War II. Post exchanges with an attached commissary (supermarket) were, for several decades, everything Americans abroad associated with America—convenience, cleanliness, efficiency, discount prices, guaranteed service, and delivery—all in contrast to what they often found outside the post gates.

In America, the GI Bill, coupled with social and economic trends already under way and an instinctive preference by Americans for semirural living, gave rise to mass-produced housing, stores, schools, and transportation, delivered and serviced locally and led to the dominance of supermarkets and chain enterprises and franchises offering everything from fast food and overnight accommodations to religious services.

What people do and make and build and, above all, buy—not what politicians say—changes America. America had become an urban society in the '20s in which middle-class standing was defined by the consumer goods people chose. By buying the right brand of cigarettes and toothpaste, wearing ready-made clothing, reading newspapers, seeing movies, and listening to radio programs, both hayseeds and greenhorns were reshaped into regular Americans. Although the Depression sharpened class antagonisms, workers, particularly union members, were even more eager to become fully assimilated Americans. Those workers, largely the sons and daughters of the immigrants who had poured into American between 1900 and 1917, were different from their parents. They spoke English both at home and at work, and English was the language of collective bargaining. Union membership brought not only bigger paychecks, but also a growing sense of self-worth and identity as Americans. Then the fires of World War II burned away many prejudices associated with hyphenated identities. After the war, old roots were ignored in the suburbs, if not forgotten. Irish, Italians, Poles, and Jews lived contentedly next to one another. Hostile feelings rarely emerged except when children considered marriage across ethnic lines, a hostility that wasn't muted even when their religion was the same, such as Italian-Irish matings. But Europe itself was largely ignored, Asia was only a place to spend a couple of years as a draftee, but who cared, anyway? The old U.S. urban neighborhoods, with their links to the past, were old and tired and worn down. Suburbia was the bright new world of the present and future.

People wanted new things, and the first new things they bought were automobiles. With gas no longer rationed, they drove out to the country just a few miles from the cities and, when they found new homes being built there, bought them with VA and Federal Home Administration mortgages. Now living in new homes outside the cities, they commuted on new roads, even an entire interstate highway system, obligingly built by politicians aware that a new constituency had been created: suburbanites. They no longer had to endure the inconvenience, dirt, and crowding of streetcars, trains, and buses. Soon, new stores came out to the suburbs so people wouldn't have to go into the city to shop. Those stores came with parking lots and carts on wheels so people could transport their food and clothes and other purchases out to the automobiles. Both large and small stores stopped making deliveries; it was easier and cheaper for customers to take things home in their own cars. When people went out to eat, they didn't walk to neighborhood restaurants, but with unlimited cheap gasoline available, went wherever good—and inexpensive—food was to be found. Since more people had young families, that meant restaurants that gave children what they liked: hot dogs, french fries, ice cream, and above all, hamburgers. The kids were happy with the food, and their parents were happy with the prices charged by franchise operations. Of course, when the family went on vacation, the scenery and people were different, but the rooms in chain motels where they stayed were as reassuringly the same as if Mom and Dad and Sis and Buddy were back home.

Everything was new: new homes, new cars, new appliances, new markets, new foods, new friends, new ways of entertaining (barbecues instead of sit-down dinners), new schools, even new churches. And most of it was a chain operation, a franchise. Rarely in the history of the world had more people enjoyed so many new things so quickly. At the same time, those people were making themselves into a new people in a social culture defined, above all, by home ownership in the suburbs. That was America's real New Frontier, settled fifty-five years after the old frontier was closed in 1890 and begun fifteen years before John Fitzgerald Kennedy coined the phrase. It was in the suburbs where the bountiful harvest of the bloodiest war in history was reaped. It was in the post–World War II suburbs where almost five million of the sixteen million veterans bought homes under the GI Bill. It was there that post–World War II families moved so their children would have a backyard of their own to play in. It is where present-day America was born and lives today. The fundamental changes, which took place in those suburbs and backyards, only superficially noted at the time and not studied since, were on such a scale that only the word "revolution" can suggest their sweep and depth. Yet only another term, "middle class," conveys how extraordinarily normal it all seemed.

The civilian counterpart of the Big PX could be called the Big

Franchise. The franchise or chain enterprise had originated before World War II with the dawning of chain supermarkets, a string of stores usually owned and operated by the same company, and franchise restaurants, which were usually licensed by local entrepreneurs and provided standardized food and service. After the war, franchises would spring up across the nation in the wake of the suburban homes—which their owners could afford because the GI Bill offered them mortgage money assured through the VA.

David Halberstam summed it up in his book *The Fifties:* "If the first great business figure of the 20th century was Henry Ford, the second, arguably, was William J. Levitt." But Levitt wasn't an inventive genius like Ford. He didn't develop a device or a process that could be patented. He didn't come up with a franchise concept he could sell to others. As a builder, he did introduce the slab foundation in suburban home construction, but the concept was as old as the Romans. He also introduced the use of preassembled housing sections and employed rotating crews of workmen to install floors, walls, and roofs in successive operations. But those were methods he had learned in the navy's Seabees. Levitt's great contribution was taking those construction methods, wedding that to an understanding of the needs and desires of America's first great demographic market, families booming with babies, and using the "no money down, twenty to thirty years to pay" mortgage program offered by the GI Bill of Rights to create the modern suburb. Out of those suburbs came all the other chain and franchise operations that now dominate the American social and economic landscape. Levitt, as both conduit and catalyst for the swirling forces that swept through the American housing market after World War II, was, more than any other person, responsible for making modern America—helping turn what might have been a violent revolution into a silent one instead. Ford put America on wheels; Levitt built a new nation called "suburbia"—but the catalyst was the GI Bill.

And what Levitt and the country had to start with was pretty decrepit. When the war ended, about half of the 37.3 million housing units in the country, 18.2 million, either needed major repairs to make them safe for occupancy or lacked private bathrooms. Almost 30 percent (10.9 million) lacked refrigerators; 22 percent (8.2 million) had no gas or electricity; and 7 percent (4.3 million) had neither central heating nor stoves. The National Housing Agency (NHA) estimated in 1944 that approximately 12.4 million new homes—or 1.25

million each and every year—would be needed in the next decade. Given 1944 income levels, the agency also estimated 22 percent, or 2.7 million, of those 12.4 million homes would have to be either public housing or subsidized rentals. Almost a quarter of the population to be housed in the next decade, in other words, could not be expected to earn enough to pay for the roofs over their heads.

The NHA itself had been created by Franklin Delano Roosevelt in 1942 under his war powers authority and incorporated, under one roof, the Federal Housing Administration (FHA), the Home Loan Mortgage Corporation (HOLC), the Federal Public Housing Administration, and another dozen agencies. The agency was the domestic equivalent of the War Production Board (WPB), also created in 1942, to mobilize government, industry, and workers for a total war in which victory would go to the side that produced the most weapons. Both were established under the command of single administrators with the powers of czars, the WPB under William S. Knudson of General Motors and the NHA under the direction of John B. Blandford Jr., former general manager of the Tennessee Valley Authority (TVA).

The WPB was, despite the inevitable confusion, foul-ups, and corruption, a tremendous success. Between the fall of France in 1940 and the Japanese surrender in 1945, America spent $186 billion for 296,000 airplanes, 86,000 tanks, 64,000 landing craft, 6,500 navy ships, 5,400 merchant ships, 15 million rifles, pistols, and machine guns, 4 million tons of artillery shells, and 40 billion bullets. The WPB was a bureaucracy, but contrary to conventional wisdom, bureaucracies work well in a crisis that subordinates everything to an ultimate goal: fighting wars, going to the moon, even putting people in concentration camps. In war, taxes could be raised, wages frozen, food rationed, people of both sexes and all races effectively drafted, while natural resources were plundered, all with little or no complaint.[1]

Bureaucracies, however, are not very good at solving social problems. People, as individuals and families, can't be made to behave in the same way as an army, a space program, or a police force, a reality FDR's planners weren't prepared to accept, despite the limited successes of the New Deal's economic initiatives, such as the National Recovery Administration. Nevertheless, the planners were confident that a bureaucracy such as the NHA could solve the housing crisis that the war was exacerbating. Moreover, NHA could presumably do so in the same orderly, coherent way that produced so many tanks and airplanes and bullets. In 1943, Blandford told the contractors, bank officers, architects, materials producers, and public policy administrators who were the readers of *Architectural Forum:* "In my judgment, the advantages secured in wartime from a unified approach to housing apply with equal force to the postwar period, if we are to achieve a really adequate postwar housing program. There is increasing realization that housing is one, broad, interrelated problem rather than a series of unrelated problems which can be neatly segregated into separate compartments . . . a reflection partly of the experience we have all gathered through a unified attack on war housing. . . . I therefore believe teamwork and a unified approach to housing should be preserved in the postwar period."[2]

The NHA's record in building new housing during the war wasn't much to boast about, however. About 1.6 million units were constructed throughout the four years of the war. By comparison, the private sector built 715,000 homes—almost half that number—in 1941 alone. Nevertheless, as the war ended, politicians, along with allies in labor, academia, and some industries, firmly believed the government could build new housing as efficiently as airplanes, tanks, and trucks. They were also convinced the public housing program begun under the Housing Act of 1937 needed to be expanded to accommodate the estimated one quarter of the nation that couldn't afford adequate shelter. Most, if not all, the units built under the public housing program would, of course, be rentals, separate from the FHA mortgage program that was providing federal guarantees on mortgages for 40 percent of all housing starts by 1940. Such public housing construction had been very limited before the war. Only 413 projects had been built, with a total of 145,646 units. In addition, 20,000 units had gone up in 164 rural projects, including experimental new towns such as Greenbelt in suburban Washington, D.C. In the postwar program envisioned by the NHA proposal, wherein low-rent units would make up 22 percent of an estimated 1.25 million housing starts a year, a massive construction program was called for. To meet that goal, 275,000 public housing units would have to be built each year between 1945 and 1954—100,000 more than the entire stock of public housing units before the war.[3]

Regardless of the math, everyone agreed with Blandford, from Harry Truman in the White House to Robert A. Taft in the Senate, from Walter Gropius, head of the school of architecture at Harvard, to Walter Reuther, the president of the United Auto Workers. To all of them only the unified attack Blandford called for would produce an adequate postwar housing program—and a massive program of public housing was essential. That meant traditional housing construction techniques would no longer do the job, they believed. Housing, like airplanes, tanks, and ships, could and should be prefabricated on assembly lines and erected on foundations in much the same way as trailers. The fact that the availability of lumber was restricted by military requirements provided additional justification for prefabricated housing. If there wasn't enough lumber, the new and modified materials pressed into service for the duration—concrete, steel, aluminum, even plastic-impregnated paper—could be substituted using assembly-line methods. Any concern over the practicality—or even desirability from the standpoint of the prospective occupants—of such unconventional methods was outweighed by the enormous need for new homes, a need intensified by the clamor of returning veterans. Such an unconventional job, however, called for an unconventional leader, and Blandford lacked the color and sex appeal to exert effective political leadership in the veterans' housing crisis.[4]

Consequently, Truman reached out to the new and flamboyant face of Wilson W. Wyatt, a lawyer and former mayor of Louisville, Kentucky. The voluble and frequently eloquent Wyatt "quickly aligned himself with the aggressively liberal forces in the Truman Administration," wrote Nathaniel Keith, a former *Wall Street Journal* reporter who was Blandford's speechwriter and congressional liaison officer. Wyatt was appointed by Truman's executive order of January 28, 1946, to the position of housing expeditor. With the moral and public relations authority conferred by the title, Wyatt called for a national housing program marked by "the same daring, determination and hard-hitting teamwork" with which the nation had tackled the emergency job of building the world's most powerful war machine. Five weeks after his appointment, following hectic brainstorming sessions, Wyatt unveiled with great fanfare a plan calling for 2.7 million houses to be built by the end of 1947, almost all of them prefabricated.

Under the bill, standardized prefabricated housing would be rolled off the assembly lines of surplus war plants and then erected, sold, and occupied as efficiently as the military had thrown up barracks during the war. A price ceiling, extending wartime controls, would keep already-low-cost prefabricated homes even more affordable. During the ensuing congressional debate, however, right-wing Republicans attacked the bill as a "dictatorship bill," according to Keith. The bill was also considered anathema by the National Association of Real Estate Boards (NAREB) because the price ceiling applied to existing homes as well as new homes and building lots. In return, Wyatt charged that the association wanted to perpetuate the housing shortage in order to gain speculative profits from inflationary real estate prices.

Nevertheless, the bill was enacted May 22, 1946, without the price ceilings, by votes in which Republicans heavily opposed the legislation in the House but were evenly divided in the Senate. Senate opposition was led by Senator Taft from Ohio and signaled more serious disagreement down the line.

Six months before Wyatt was appointed, the Senate Subcommittee on Housing and Urban Redevelopment, of which Taft was a member, issued a long-awaited report that represented a major victory for the National Housing Agency and its allies and a major setback for its enemies. The committee praised the NHA for its performance and recommended that it be made permanent. In addition, the committee called for a low-rent public housing program at the rate of 125,000 dwellings per year. The committee also rejected the real estate lobby's proposal for giving low-income families rent certificates rather than building public housing. The committee argued that rent certificates would be likely to maintain the profitability of slums. Much of the opposition to rent certificates came from the usually conservative Taft. He felt capitalist society had an obligation to provide a minimum standard of decent shelter along with subsistence, medical care, and education to every family. Taft particularly objected to the "hand-me-down theory" in housing, a phrase critics used to criticize rent certificates.

"The hand-me-down theory works, but it works to provide indecent housing for those who get it on the last hand-me-down," Taft wrote in *Modern Industry* of October 15, 1946, shortly before the congressional elections that year. Acting on his beliefs, Taft, after the subcommittee issued its August 1945 report, signed on to what became known as the Wagner-Ellender-Taft (WET) Act. The other authors of the bill were Robert Wagner of New York, who wrote the Wagner Act of 1936, which would be superseded in 1948 by the Taft-Hartley Act; and Senator Allen J. Ellender, a conservative Democrat from Louisiana. WET's opponents were stigmatized later because one of their leaders was a freshman senator from Wisconsin, Joseph McCarthy. Whether because of McCarthy or for other reasons, WET took four years to pass. When it finally did, the public housing provision was approved by a margin of four votes in the House, 209–204. The narrow margin provided "a classic illustration of the informal coalition of conservative Republicans and conservative or reactionary Democrats which was a threat to all progressive legislation," wrote Keith, "and a forecast of the political troubles in store for liberal housing legislation."[5] Such an informal congressional coalition, of course, had also been responsible for passage of the GI Bill of Rights. The big difference was that the WET failed and the VA mortgage program under the GI Bill succeeded incredibly.

The WET provided for the construction of between 135,000 and 200,000 public housing units a year, even more than the 125,000 called for, or some 2 million by 1960. Planners believed the act would prove a great social lesson had been learned from World War II: that government could do what capitalism couldn't, that is, provide decent, affordable housing for everyone. It didn't. By 1962, there were about 646,000 federally aided public housing units in the country, about 30 percent of those called for in the 1949 law. But in the next three decades many of those would be abandoned or, in some instances, literally blown up, eradicated from the face of the earth by the government itself. The grand dream of those who believed the government could build and run a better society, rather than more modestly finance and guide its development as accomplished through the GI Bill, was reduced to rubble.

For a time, however, the dream burned brightly. The manifesto of the believers was written by Reuther, the president of the UAW, in an article published in *The New York Times Magazine* shortly after V-J Day entitled "Our Fear of Abundance." Reuther contended that the productive genius of the United States had always been stalemated at the distributive end.[6] Reuther wanted to remedy what he saw as the central flaw in the economy by creating a Peace Production Board, comparable to the War Production Board. The board would lease war production plants to manufacturers who would (1) produce civilian goods determined by social priorities and (2) maintain uniform wage standards and employment levels while (3) selling their products at fair prices. War Production Board officials agreed with Reuther and went him one better. They also wanted the government to run a public corporation, using private patent rights taken over during the war to promote new technologies, inventions, ideas and keep them out of the hands of business.⁷ Government would control and run the economy.

There was more to Reuther's vision—industrywide wage agreements, regardless of geographic area, and the introduction of guaranteed annual wage systems through collective bargaining. He wanted to convert war plants to the mass production of modern railroad equipment as well as low-cost housing. Housing would become, like the TVA, a public utility but nationwide in scope, a public works program on an immense scale.

It was a wonderful dream, and the designers of that dream were architects, planners in steel and stone whose work after the war captivated the imagination of both the left, in the persons of Frank Lloyd Wright and Buckminster Fuller, and the right in the fictitious personage of Howard Roark, the hero of Ayn Rand's book *The Fountainhead*. The nation's leading schools of architecture at the time, particularly Harvard under Gropius, were led by German refugees, who in fleeing Hitler, had brought to the New World blueprints for new worker housing. They were disciples of the Bauhaus School started by Gropius—called the "Silver Prince" by his admirers—amid the rubble of the First World War in Berlin. The school originated what was to become the International style of twentieth-century architecture, using glass, flat roofs, exposed structural beams, and "honest" materials, such as streaked or stained beige stucco, rather than "luxurious" granite, marble, or wood. The school's leaders, which included other famous architects such as Le Corbusier and Mies van der Rohe, felt they had a special mission to design housing for workers, "machines for living," in Le Corbusier's phrase. They would become "engineers of the workers' souls," in Joseph Stalin's admiring words.

The first such worker housing project was built in Stuttgart, Germany, in 1927 and called the Radiant City by its designers. Unfortunately, its inhabitants hated it and tried to "beautify" its bare, uncompromising lines with upholstered furniture, rugs, carpets, and drapery. The architects sadly concluded the intellectually undeveloped workers would have to be reeducated. Before that happened, however, Hitler came to power, and members of the Bauhaus School fled to the United States, where, with Gropius installed at Harvard, they and their American disciples became the architects of most of the glass buildings, factories, and schools built after the war. They also designed many of the luxury high-rise apartments that housed the wealthy in American cities and the housing projects for the poor.

But the projects simply didn't meet the needs and satisfy the desires of the working-class men and women the Bauhaus architects thought they were designing housing for. Neither did the prefabricated veterans housing called for by Wyatt. That vision lost its luster far more quickly than public housing. Wyatt and his second-in-command, Joseph L. Rauh, a *éminence grise* in Democratic politics for many years thereafter, proposed 100 percent federal loans to producers of industrialized housing. That idea was politically unacceptable to both Truman and the 1946 Republican Congress. Only 37,000 prefabricated housing units for veterans were built in 1946, and no more than 50,000 were built in the next three years. What Reuther had called "the creative assignment of building homes and rebuilding cities" using prefabricated housing had proven to be beyond Washington's capabilities.

Between 1945 and 1954, more than 13 million houses were built, just slightly more than the 12.4 million called for by the NHA in 1944. Most of the homes were privately built and privately owned, and a substantial percentage were financed through VA-backed mortgages. In other words, the private market, supported by federally insured mortgages, supplied all the housing needs projected by the NHA, including 2.7 million units the agency thought people could only rent rather than buy. The profound effect the VA mortgage program had on the entire market is clear from the statistics: Of the 324,900 homes built in 1945, only 43,000 were sold on VA mortgages (7.5 percent), but in 1946, when housing starts almost tripled (to 1,015,200), 412,000 (40.5 percent) were VA. In 1947, VA mortgages accounted for 542,000 of the 1,265,100 total (42.8 percent). The numbers and percentages dropped to 498,000 (26 percent) of 1,908,100 in 1950, but by that time, the forces propelling the suburban development in America were inexorable.[8]

Although the United States had a set of housing policies for the postwar period, only the GI Bill helped solve the housing problem. Even then, the bill might not have worked as effectively as it did without William J. Levitt. His grasp of modern building methods and the financial incentives the GI Bill provided enabled him to turn housing into a mass market instead of a cottage industry. VA mortgages were never a majority of those issued, but Levitt realized that veterans clearly constituted an identifiable market, both in demographic and financial terms, which he could build marketing plans around. As a veteran, Levitt understood the needs and hopes of other veterans. He knew what these twenty-five- to thirty-year-olds with two or three children wanted. He decided to build entire communities for them, making little effort to accommodate older couples with adolescent children, for example, or the retired or young singles. Segmenting the marketing into target groups started with Levitt and rippled through American society as the baby boomers became Yuppies in the '70s and '80s and are still a potent economic and social force in America.

Levitt had critics, but their concerns underlined, rather than undermined, the scope of his accomplishments. His most severe critic was Lewis Mumford, the nation's most influential architectural writer and a fervent believer in planning, who, faced with the choice in 1932 between FDR and Herbert Hoover, declared, "If I vote at all it will be for the Communists. It is Communism which desires to save civilization."[9] Mumford thought Levitt's suburban development was uncivilized. In 1961, he described the first Levittown as "a multitude of uniform, unidentifiable houses, lined up inflexibly, at uniform distances on uniform roads, in a treeless common waste, inhabited by people of the same class, the same incomes, the same age group, witnessing the same television performances, eating the same tasteless prefabricated foods from the same freezers, conforming in every outward and inward respect to a common mold manufactured in the same central metropolis. Thus the ultimate effect of the suburban escape in our time is, ironically, a low-grade uniform environment from which escape was impossible."[10]

Mumford was an advocate of garden cities, utopias that had been on the drawing boards of New Deal planners for years. Only three had been built of wood and stone in the '30s under the auspices of the government, Greenbelt in suburban Washington, D.C.; Green Hills, Ohio, outside Cincinnati; and Greendale, Wisconsin, near Milwaukee. The fifteen thousand units in these communities were clustered in villages, separated by belts of trees and grass. They were unlike both World War II suburbs and suburban neighborhoods developed in the '20s. The '20s suburbs were built a few houses at a time. Foundations were dug out with simple earth movers. Adjacent trees remained undisturbed, and almost every house had a porch overlooking large lawns or backyards. Neighborhoods evolved slowly: schools, churches, libraries, and markets were filled in as houses and residents proliferated.

Mumford and other planners liked such communities, except for their large lots. They wanted much more land devoted to common uses in the European pattern through networks of greens and small parks. They also wanted to integrate small apartment houses and town-houses among single-family homes. Improved production methods to control costs were advocated, as were basic house plans using pre-assembly techniques built on a small scale in the 1910s and 1920s by groups as diverse as the American Public Health Service and the National Forest Products Laboratory. In the '30s, the FHA adopted as a "minimal house" a plan for a square, four-room house with a bath and without a basement. Several thousand such houses were sold and erected on site by Sears Roebuck in the '20s. Mumford and a colleague, Henry Wright, called for mass production of such houses after World War II, but implementing these ideas would have required a convergence of defense-related government policy with the objectives of community builders.[11]

That convergence was not forthcoming, although industry and labor leaders alike thought "miracle" materials they had developed for the war could revolutionize housing. Even before Pearl Harbor, model homes at the Century of Progress in Chicago and the World's Fair in New York showed off bright new metals such as stainless steel and aluminum for kitchens and bathrooms; and Bakelite, artificial resins, used in countertops, tables, and cabinets. It was a vista called "Dreamworld," a Buck Rogers society in which people would not only live in futuristic homes but also commute to work in airplanes. Richard T. Frankensteen, a UAW vice president who ran against Reuther for the union presidency, advocated light, mass-produced commuter airplanes selling for less than $1,000. Frankensteen predicted sales as high as a million units a year for such a creation, according to *Businessweek,* and he advocated that Washington should underwrite the light plane program if private industry did not.[12]

Most of these miracle products were mirages conjured up by advertisers. During the war, companies flush with profits poured money into magazines to create expectations for cars, appliances, and furnishings everyone was looking forward to buying after the war. Two aircraft manufacturers, Beech and Consolidated Vultee, commissioned Buckminster Fuller to design a single-family home version of his dome-shaped Dynamaxion structure, ultimately used only to house personnel and electronic equipment for the DEW line in Alaska to detect atomic attacks. Houses to be made of aluminum-sandwiched paper panels produced in factories were designed by Henry Dreyfuss and Edward Larrabee Barnes. Shiny machine-tooled Dynamaxion, Tournalayer, and various solar homes would presumably roll off assembly lines by the millions and spring up like mushrooms—which most resembled—in new neighborhoods behind traditional picket fences, looking twenty-first centuryish but homey nonetheless. The Lustron Company leased part of Ford's huge Willow Run plant and commissioned Senator McCarthy to write an article urging government subsidies for prefabricated home builders. His fee was $10,000, the annual salary for a member of Congress. McCarthy's endorsement resulted in a total of $22.5 million in government loans to Lustron over the next three years, but only a few Lustron houses were built. What Levitt offered the public, unlike Lustron or Buckminster Fuller or Mumford or the government or the advertisements, was reality.

Mumford complained that Levitt was using new methods but a backward design. What Levitt was doing, however, was the culmination of a two-decade-old process in which private real estate developers, rather than planners, had been learning how to create entire suburban communities. Following legally enforceable deed restrictions as well as zoning laws, subdividers had created entire communities at the high end of the income scale in many states, notably California, as far back as the 1920s. Previously, developers had simply cut up land into building lots and sold them without any concern about street layout, the kinds and types of houses to be constructed, common uses, parks and recreational amenities, and so forth. A new pattern of private innovation preceding public action initially was led by the National Association of Real Estate Boards, according to Marc A. Weiss, author of *The Rise of the Community Builders*. Later, the pattern was institutionalized through the FHA created by the Federal Housing Act of 1934. Like the HOLC, the FHA was a mortgage insurer, not a planning agency. However, to ensure the economic soundness of its insurance system, it created a risk-rating system that not only evaluated the ability of people to pay for houses, but also made sure the property itself could be expected to appreciate in value. Appraisal of the property, neighborhood, and location within the community became an indirect planning tool. It was already beginning to make housing more affordable for the moderate middle class during the early 1940s. This was an intentional cooperative effort, as an FHA publication made clear: "The Administration does not propose to regulate subdividing throughout the country, nor does it intend to stereotype patterns of land development. It does, however, insist upon the observance of rational principles of development in those areas in which insured mortgages are desired." And, in fact, by 1940, about 70 percent of the new homes built with FHA financing were in subdevelopments, using neighborhood planning principles.

The tool used was a financial carrot that was much more powerful than a planning stick. "The genius of the FHA system . . . is that mortgage insurance fit the American image of voluntarism," wrote Weiss, a Columbia University professor who as a special assistant to HUD Secretary Henry Cisneros helped develop the department's 1995 plan for abandoning high-rise public housing. "Unlike direct government police power regulations, FHA always appeared to be noncoercive to the private sector," he added. Weiss noted that FHA officials were always careful to cultivate and preserve the image of voluntarism. Therefore, the FHA had already cast the die for post–World War II suburban development a good five years before Levitt, as he was going into the navy, had bought options on the Long Island potato fields from which Levittown would spring.

Up until then, the one great barrier to bringing single-family home ownership within the financial range of young couples was technology. However, in the 1940s, the housing construction industry was experiencing a radical break with old-fashioned traditions. The war produced more efficient dwelling designs, materials, and building processes. Fulfilling government orders also enabled builders to bypass the work rules of the construction unions. Consequently, all the elements that would create what many have referred to as "postwar suburbanization" were firmly in place by prewar 1940. Levitt, in particular, was extremely well positioned to take advantage of all the elements that would go into developments after the war.[13]

Two other elements were needed, however, to make postwar suburbanization possible. One was institutional—the GI Bill, whose housing provisions the FHA was originally asked to administer but relinquished to the VA. The other was an individual—Levitt. Even before the guns stopped, wartime prosperity was producing a remarkable change in the most basic of demographic and social indicators: birth rates. Babies, which had been born at rates as low as 2,315 per 10,000 of population in 1936 were being heard from at a rate of 3,104 by 1943 and 3,817 in 1947. After the first rush, the number slacked off slightly to 3,637 in 1948, climbed back to 3,823 in 1952, and reached an all-time peak of 4,308 in 1957, almost double the number exactly one generation earlier.[14]

As the war roared toward V-E and V-J Day, the quintessential

model for the surroundings in which these baby boomers would grow
up was a 1,500-acre potato field in Long Island, twenty miles from
Manhattan in New York City. Levitt had kept payments up on his
options to the land during the war while piecing together in his mind
the elements that would go into his massive, almost completely self-
contained suburban community. First, he had to learn from failure.
He and his brother, Alfred, had won a government contract in 1941 to
build 2,350 workers' homes in Norfolk, Virginia, but couldn't make a
profit because, faced with union demands, they could not complete the
work on time. The two brothers began to study the entire construction
process, breaking it down into twenty-seven steps. Each step could
be assigned to a separate team, and all twenty-seven teams, working
one after another, could be held to preset norms of performance. The
teams could increase their earnings by cooperatively finishing each
step faster than prescribed by the norms, rather than by accumulat-
ing overtime. Having refined the techniques while building airfields
with the Seabees, Levitt came home determined to build and sell
housing for a "real market." He defined that as the equivalent of an
ordinary mass-produced suit of clothes, rather than one made to
measure.

The potato farm outside Manhattan soon became the largest housing project in the country. "This is Levittown," the first advertisement in *The New York Times* proclaimed in the fall of 1946. "All
yours for $58"—presumably the amount needed for closing costs.
The ad ran on a Monday. Thirty people were waiting when Levitt
arrived to open the door, and by Tuesday night, fourteen hundred
sales agreements were signed. By Wednesday, the line had become so
long the ex-GIs figured out a system so that people could go to the
bathroom and eat without losing their place.

What the prospective owners were waiting for as they stood in line
was something unique in the history of home construction—and in
the way in which people would live. Not only the actual houses, which
were familiar designs, but the way they were built, positioned on their
lots, and related to one another were distinct from other middle-class
housing built in the affluent sections of cities and towns before the
war. The basic styles weren't that different, the traditional Colonials
mixed with more modern ranches and split-levels. But the houses
lacked one thing houses in New York had been thought to need just
to stand erect: a basement. Perhaps Levitt's most distinctive contribution to home building was the slab foundation made of concrete laid

on top of terrain flattened by a bulldozer. Levitt modestly attributed the invention of slab foundations to the Romans. A local bureaucrat in Hempstead took umbrage at the construction method on historical grounds. Long Island at the time was the bailiwick of old stock Yankee farmers and fishermen who were distant descendants of the Anglo-Saxon lords who forced King John to agree every man's home is his castle. The bureaucrat was no doubt convinced that castles, no matter how humble, ought to have basements. Where else would householders put the coal needed to heat their houses in the winter? The logical answer was nowhere, since oil or gas was going to be used for heating, not coal. Logic, of course, isn't a strong point of bureaucrats, so consequently, Levitt was denied a building permit "on general principles." The bureaucrat, however, was effectively overruled by a protesting editorial in *The New York Herald-Tribune.* The newspaper was the voice at the time of those direct descendants of Anglo-Saxon aristocracy who actually lived in castles and respected a higher law, transmuting potato fields into prime real estate.

Some seventeen thousand homes were soon built in the original Levittown along with seventeen swimming pools, one to serve every thousand families. The county built five schools on land contributed by Levitt, despite grumbling of earlier settlers about the cost. The county officials were satisfied that the tax revenues from the new houses would pay for construction and the salaries of teachers. Churches and schools went up on land donated by Levitt, as well. As for gardens in this garden community, they were in the individual backyards of individual home owners, not in common areas and greens along the European model advocated by Mumford. The traditional pattern of land use in America, rooted in the old pioneer and yeoman custom of each family settling on its own land rather than clustering in villages, had been confirmed in the new suburban settlements that would become the residences of most Americans in the late twentieth century. Each home owner would be lord and master, or lady and mistress, of his or her own plot of land as well as house.

The American dream house is, as Herbert J. Gans, a sociologist, observed, "a tiny farm (not to be farmed) with all the conveniences of urban and suburban living, including easy access to social life. This dream residence is not of recent origin, but is rooted in the culture of most Americans, Protestant and Catholic, middle class and working class alike. Among middle-class Protestants, the home-ownership aspiration can be traced back to the rural and small-town heritage of eighteenth and nineteenth century England and America; among working class Catholics, to the peasant settlements of continental Europe. Only the Jews do not share this rural heritage . . . although acculturation has persuaded many to accept it."[15] In Levittown the tiny farm occupied a 60-by-100-foot lot, and Levitt was proud of the fact that the house took up only 12 percent of the lot. Levitt had to change one thing in his original plans, however. The kitchen had to be redesigned so that mothers could look out at their children at play in their backyards. Having grown up in the streets, without supervision other than an occasional admonition yelled down from two- or three-story apartment buildings, these young mothers and fathers knew how much mischief children could get into if not closely observed. It was a lesson the architects of three- to fifty-story Radiant Cities never learned; the children of the city streets who became GIs and their wives were determined their children would have backyards of their own.

That pattern of land use persists today, although house sizes have grown in the vastly expanded suburbs where more than half of Americans live and work. "The people in the United States are not going to live the way people in Paris do," Jack Linville, the former head of the research foundation of the American Planning Association, told Joel Garreau, the author of *Edge City,* a 1991 book about today's suburbs beyond the beltways. Americans "will not live in a thousand-square foot apartment and raise a family and go out and get the jug of vine and a loaf of bread and walk down the street and live their whole life in one square mile," Linville said. "That is not the way Americans live. They have a different level of freedom, a different level of expectations. There is still a lot of Daniel Boone left in America. I don't know what the people of Paris want. What they have is a very small amount of space that is theirs, and a lot of public amenities. What we have is a [larger] amount of space that is ours and we control, and very little in amenities. We have very much more individual life styles. We have our own excellent interior spaces. We have our *own* park. It's right out in back. The yard."[16]

That personal park was particularly important to the veterans who had, in some instances, spent years living, sleeping, eating, washing, and fighting no more than inches away from others, every moment of every day, in barracks, shipboard berths, foxholes, and hospitals. Neither did they have any quarrel with the fact that Levitt's building methods weren't those of old-world craftsmen admired by Mumford and the planners. Not too long before, the most comfortable places most veterans had slept in were stateside barracks that were painted only because Mrs. Roosevelt had insisted on it. The military had regarded paint as an unnecessary indulgence. Levitt's new mass-produced homes weren't prefabricated on assembly lines but, rather, assembled on the sites. Just a few feet from the sales office and the few model homes clustered around it, paved roads were the only visible evidence that a community of seventeen thousand homes was rising on potato fields. The ex-Seabee had learned that what is now called infrastructure comes first. Once built, the roads enabled trucks to drop off largely preassembled building materials at precise intervals of sixty feet. Sheetrock walls, complete with electrical wiring and piping, went upon asphalt floors, and cabinets and appliances rolled in on Levitt-owned trucks straight from wholly owned Levitt subsidiaries, cutting out middlemen. Semiskilled workers, often paid more than union craftsmen, laid floors, put up siding, painted, and put down tiles to Levitt specifications on a Levitt timetable. Thirty-six houses were built each and every day on the clockwork timetables Levitt had first developed as a Seabee. "Eighteen houses completed on the shift from 8 to noon," Levitt noted to himself one day, "and 19 more houses finished on the shift from 12:20 to 4:30."

The first Levitt basic Cape Cod sold for $7,900 with two bedrooms and one bathroom. For the first buyers—all veterans—a free television set and Bendix washing machine were thrown in. Later, three other models became available, a Cape Cod with two bedrooms selling for $11,500, a three-bedroom "Rancher" for $13,000. For the slightly more affluent with incomes above the $6,000 to $7,000 a year most buyers were making at the time, a two-story "Colonial" provided three bedrooms for $14,000. Four bedrooms cost $14,500. Such houses, of course, now sell for ten to fifteen times as much as the original $7,900 Cape Cods. Of course, additional rooms often have been added on the side or by converting the attic. Levitt had carefully provided for such additions. Perhaps the greatest selling point for those houses, outside of price, was the fact that no lawyers or real estate agents were needed. The buying process was simplified; there was no down payment, no closing costs—and, above all, no extras that mysteriously materialized only when the contracts were ready to sign.[17]

By 1955, Levitt-style subdivisions accounted for 75 percent of all

housing starts. Almost all of those houses were being built by 10 percent of the builders, assembly-line builders like Levitt rather than
the old-time small operators. In California, August W. Wynne Jr.
built homes for $10,000 with air-conditioning, "an innovation for
Southwestern homes," as his ads proclaimed. Admittedly, the revolution in house building often came with a price people didn't want
to pay: lowered quality. While building methods became more cost-
efficient, quality often declined; glue replaced nails, and screws gave
way to automatically punched nails. Linoleum was substituted for
tile in bathrooms; plywood replaced pine; one coat of sprayed paint
had to do where three had been customary, and Levitt used asphalt
tile rather than hardwoods in living rooms. An investigation by Representative Olin Teague of Texas found horror stories in more than
twenty-six cities. Driveways and paved roads promised by developers
mysteriously failed to materialize; lawns washed away in the rain;
water and sewer pipes weren't even connected to drains. The "inferior type of small house being provided by speculative builders to
meet the veterans' demands [were] doll houses that out-slum the
slummiest of our pre-war slums," Dr. Charles Winslow, professor
emeritus of public health at Yale University, told an American Institute of Architects forum.[18]

Regardless of the quality of the workmanship in the suburbs,
people were leaving the cities to find a better life. They were also
fleeing them to avoid the dark shadows cast by urban blight—and
people of darker skin. Levitt's own family history illustrated that
experience, and his own attitudes helped prolong it. Abraham Levitt,
his father, had prospered enough in the '20s to buy a handsome
brownstone in the Bedford Stuyvesant area. The family lived there
happily until the father heard a local black attorney was moving into
the neighborhood. Levitt's father gathered the family and, according
to writer Halberstam, told them: "If this man moves in, the neighborhood will soon be black, and then the only question is whether we'll
be able to sell our house and for how much. The longer we wait, the
lower the price will go."

William Levitt himself refused to sell his houses to blacks for
almost two decades. He explained his policy in the '50s this way:
"The Negroes in America are trying to do in 400 years what the Jews
in the world have not wholly accomplished in 600 years. As a Jew I
have no room in my heart or mind for racial prejudice. But . . . I have
come to know that if we sell one house to a Negro family, then 90 to

95 percent of our white customers will not buy into the community. That is their attitude, not ours. . . . As a company, our position is simply this: We can solve a housing problem, or we can try to solve a racial problem, but we cannot combine the two."[19]

Nevertheless, in 1958, blacks did come to Levittown and were welcomed, warily, fearfully, but nevertheless welcomed. Integration was accomplished, says sociologist Gans, "through nonpolitical means, enforcing a decision made outside the community" without "the approval of the community's majority." Gans lived in the West End of Boston for two years while researching his book *The Urban Villagers*. The book has been widely quoted by critics of federal urban renewal programs for more than a quarter of a century. Subsequently, Gans spent two years in Levitt's third Levittown, twenty miles from Philadelphia in New Jersey, and published *The Levittowners*, which is less often cited, perhaps because he concluded that post–World War II government housing policy putting suburbia within reach of the urban lower-middle and working classes—unlike "poor removal" in the cities—was a success. The "elected officials who decide to subsidize suburbia were aware of their constituents' aspirations," Gans concluded, although critics such as Mumford deplored them.[20]

That some blacks not only aspired but were poised to take advantage of suburban housing opportunities in the '40s and '50s is evident from the statistics. The number of blacks in college more than quadrupled from some 27,000 in 1930 to more than 113,000 in 1950, according to Harvard Sitkoff, author of *The Struggle for Black Equality*. Between 1940 and 1952, the percentage of blacks engaged in professional, white-collar, skilled, and semiskilled work doubled to 40 percent of the total. Despite the dual-wage scales that prevailed, not only in the South but in much of the North as well, black earnings, as a percentage of median white income, jumped from 41 percent to 51 percent in 1949 and 57 percent in 1952. Meanwhile, the proportion of five- to nineteen-year-old blacks in schools increased from 60 percent in 1930 to 68.4 percent in 1940 to 74.8 percent in 1950. Life expectancy rates also leaped, from 53.1 years for blacks in 1940 (compared with 64.2 for whites) to 60.1 years for blacks in 1953 (69.4 years for whites). The home ownership rate among blacks went from 25 percent to 30 percent while it went for whites from 43.6 percent in 1940 to 55 percent in 1950, a proportionate increase.[21]

Unquestionably, some of the homes blacks bought during the 1940s were acquired under the hand-me-down theory deplored by Senator Taft. However, many of those houses were acceptable housing. Although most were bought from whites leaving the cities, many were obtained through FHA and VA-backed loans, requiring appraisals that attested the house was structurally sound enough to warrant a twenty-year mortgage. Moreover, many such houses may well have been sold by owners who, rather than wanting to get rid of a run-down house, were both eager to join the exodus to the suburbs and flee people "taking over the neighborhoods." Without a doubt, the GI Bill was also accelerating "white flight." More and more blue-collar workers were becoming white-collar workers with better educations, but they were also migrating to the suburbs to avoid people with darker skins, not just for better houses and better schools. That migration should, however, be placed in perspective. In Boston, for example, the number of blacks counted in the 1950 census was twenty thousand in 1950 and sixty thousand in 1960, even as the total population declined from more than eight hundred thousand to less than seven hundred thousand. The net inward migration of blacks into new neighborhoods tripled, in other words, while the outward migration of whites to new communities was probably less than 17 percent. And by the '60s, African-Americans would be joining the migration.

Economic and social realities as well as legal compulsion ultimately forced Levitt to bow to demands for desegregation. His conduct throughout the process was guided by pragmatic considerations: how to allow blacks to buy into Levittown without scaring whites away. He accomplished both without social disruption and minimal economic loss to the firm. Levitt himself anticipated the desegregation issue would arise before any prospective purchasers arrived at the site of a new community he was building in Willingboro Township in New Jersey in 1958—the one Gans was studying. He announced at a press conference proclaiming the start of construction that he wouldn't sell to blacks. The company's position was explained to Gans by a Levitt executive who said: "Our firm is liberal and progressive, but we don't want to be singled out or used as the firm which should start the other builders off. If there is no other builder who can keep Negroes out, we will not do so either; we will go with the group if the state makes us, but we don't want to lose millions by being the first. . . . we could not afford to take such losses."

Two Negroes who were turned away from the new community complained to the State Division of Antidiscrimination (SDAD) that the use of VA and FHA mortgage insurance to buy homes in Levittown constituted government support of discrimination. Levitt began a series of drawn-out appeals in courts to prevent hearings by SDAD, "hoping to sell an all-white community to as many people as possible before a higher court finally ruled for integration," according to Gans. When that strategy failed, he agreed to desegregate and hired an outside expert, a recently retired executive director of SDAD. Levitt wanted to head off a repetition of an earlier racial disturbance in a Levittown built in Pennsylvania. A Negro family moving in without any notification to the community had been confronted by five hundred angry whites. Local police had been unable or unwilling to maintain order. State police had to be called in, and although only two rocks were thrown and no one was hurt, the older Levittown had acquired a worldwide reputation as a riot-torn community. Fearing another disturbance that would scare away more buyers than integration would, Levitt decided to take a public rather than a surreptitious approach to integration. The expert he had hired enlisted support from the community's religious leaders and briefed the police, government officials, the press, and Levitt's own sales force. The outside expert also formed a task force to head off anti-integration activities, "Operation Hothead," and carefully screened the first Negro applicants to make sure they were "our kind" of middle-class people.

The most ingenious element in the plan was suggested by Levitt's salesmen. They were aware that many whites were willing to live in an integrated community but wary of living next door to blacks. So the salesmen gave the first choice in lots to Negroes. They, like other sensible purchasers, preferred private lots adjacent to woods, water, or open space rather than next door to other houses. Consequently, Negro families located themselves at the edges rather than the middle of neighborhoods. Whites had to choose between open space near blacks or being surrounded by fellow whites. "Most white buyers preferred privacy with Negro neighbors to interior lots," Gans wrote. Few houses next to ones owned by Negroes went without buyers.

Gans gave considerable credit for the integration to the consultant. "He did not attempt to change community attitudes," Gans wrote; "rather, he helped people to adjust to the inevitable situation that conditions and the law imposed." Hearts and minds might not have been won initially, but people did conduct themselves civilly. However, neither the "invisible hand" of the market nor the whispered wisdom of consultants was primarily responsible for the integration of Levittown. If the courts hadn't interpreted the VA's and the FHA's mortgage insurance as government support of housing, Levittown might still be an all-white community today. At the same time, if a law cosponsored by one of the most notorious racists ever to serve in Congress hadn't provided the catalyst for a middle-class way of life for working-class whites, middle-class blacks might very well have been unable to find suburbs to integrate.

A brand new world was being created through the encouraging hand of government, one filled with shiny cars parked by returning husbands in the driveways of homes still smelling of freshly sawn wood and recently applied paint. Young mothers preparing dinner in kitchens filled with gleaming new appliances kept an eye on toddlers playing in the backyard through picture windows until it was time for them to come in and watch *Howdy Doody* on the ten-inch television bought for $50 down and $20 a month for twelve months. That was a strain on a typical monthly budget on which $80 a month went for principal and interest on a twenty-year mortgage at 4½ percent, $20 for real estate taxes, and another $35 a month for the new Studebaker. There was still enough left over, however, on an income of $400 a month after taxes to eagerly consider new monthly installments on bedroom and living room sets advertised in the paper while watching *Uncle Miltie* and *Dragnet* after the kids had gone to bed. It was a new world, a brand new world.

The war and the Depression were over, although far from forgotten, and "Happy Days Are Here Again" wasn't just an election day song. The needs and desires accumulated over almost an entire generation were being satisfied, the social chasm dividing the haves and the have-nots being forgotten. A mixed economy, rather than a welfare state such as England's, was being created. The New Deal had helped build the foundation of this modern society through Social Security and unemployment compensation; the minimum wage; bank and stock market regulation; and substantial participation of ethnic minorities, blacks, and women in the national political coalition previously dominated by male WASPs. The GI Bill, coming on top of those reforms, provided people with resources to take care of themselves, rather than having to depend on the government to take care of them. It was monumental, massive change, but perhaps because it was in the American grain, its premises and guiding principles were never clearly articulated. FDR's greatest accomplishment, looking backward through the prism of the GI Bill, may have been that, as a hereditary aristocrat, he helped forge a community between the upper- and working-class extremes comparable to what Benjamin Disraeli and Otto von Bismarck accomplished in England and Germany in the late nineteenth and early twentieth centuries. But the Tory democracy FDR forged gave way to a real, working democracy that was primarily the work of his philosophical and political opponents.

The HOLC, a New Deal measure, had been one of the basic building blocks of this society as a precursor of the GI Bill. Created by Congress in June 1931, as a "salvage operation," it refinanced and saved the homes of 1,018,390 families while creating the current mortgage system making home purchase possible for millions. Before HOLC, borrowers needed to have most of the money to buy a house outright or had to obtain both first and second mortgages. Lending institutions would risk about 60 percent of the value of a piece of real estate on a first mortgage, Gertrude Fish of the University of Maryland and editor of the university text, *The Story of Housing*, explained. "The buyer then had to have the cash to complete the transaction or find someone willing to lend him the balance on a second, or junior mortgage, so called because that lender's claim on the property was subordinate to the holder of the first mortgage." The mortgages were short term, usually no more than five years, and both the first and junior mortgage holders could institute foreclosure proceedings. That meant, even when times were relatively good, borrowers often had to refinance or renew several times before the debt was paid off. With most home owners vulnerable to foreclosure even in the best of times, the Depression set off wave after wave of evictions. The banks, unable to borrow enough money to carry them through the crisis, felt obligated to foreclose to protect their depositors. But with so many properties being offered at auction and so little money offered to buy, more often than not sales failed to produce enough to pay off the principal. Junior mortgage holders usually lost their entire investment. The HOLC, by contrast, offered fifteen-year mortgages on loans of $14,000 or more. When the GI Bill was enacted in 1944, the VA was only authorized to guarantee a portion of a house loan, $2,000 in principal with twenty-year terms, but in 1945, the guarantee portion was raised to $4,000 and twenty-five years. In 1950, Congress raised the guarantee to $7,500, or 60 percent of the total mortgage, whichever was less, with a maximum maturity of thirty years. That was when the program really became attractive to private lenders.[22]

The mortgage system was strengthened further by the establishment of the Federal National Mortgage Association (FNMA, or Fannie Mae) in 1939 as a secondary market to stimulate bank lending in economically depressed areas. Local banks as well as savings and loans sold most of their mortgages off to Fannie Mae, reducing their own risks and the need to foreclose if local economic conditions worsened. The system created stable, predictable conditions encouraging the banks and the savings and loans to make even more mortgage money available, especially with the added stimulus of VA guarantees. But none of the house programs or any of the other "alphabet soup" employment efforts of the New Deal put enough money in the pockets of enough people to make the United States a nation of home owners. That took a war, a total war.

And after the war, the GI Bill brought a total relandscaping of America with the growth of the suburbs. Making the masses into home owners changed their objective conditions, in Marxist terminology. It also opened up unprecedented opportunities for entrepreneurs like Levitt, who could think of new—but standardized and replicable—ways of giving the masses, now increasingly the middle class, what they wanted, even if that conflicted with what intellectuals thought they really needed. What Mumford decried as a multitude of uniform, unidentifiable houses by people who were all the same was also a market for an enormous variety of services and products. Indeed, many of the products and services that would become available had been unheard of just a few years before. Soon social critics would wonder who needed so many choices. The baby boomers and their parents needed them, that's who.

Television, frozen dinners, rock-and-roll, and the pill would change America as much as Henry Ford's development and marketing of the Model T automobile two generations before. The transformations, in both instances, were first physical and then social; first the landscape changed and then the people. And the automobile also encouraged chain and franchising operations. In 1923, the first transcontinental road in the world, the Lincoln Highway between New York and San Francisco, was opened, the brainchild of Carl Graham Fisher, a highly successful businessman and founder of the Indianapolis Speedway. It was followed three years later by the storied Route 66, stretching from Chicago to Santa Monica, California. Soon the Dixie Highway from Bay City, Michigan, to Florida, the William Penn Turnpike across Pennsylvania, the Merritt Parkway in Connecticut, and Route One along the Atlantic Coast, "America's Main Street," followed, as did outlets for food, lodging, and thrills—all cheap.

Franchising and chain-store operations would provide uniform, predictable products at a price calculated to be as affordable for as many as possible. But to make this modern system of distribution dominant in the economy actually required a huge government program, although it's not what Walter Reuther had in mind. It wasn't a program of factory-built housing carried to building sites on new trains also built in former war plants, as he advocated. Instead, an interstate highway system would vastly expand the Lincoln Highways and the William Penn Turnpikes of the '20s and '30s largely to serve the suburban communities springing up outside cities, great and small. The automobile, truck, suburban airport, and shopping mall would replace the railroad, mine, and factory as the symbols and engines of the American economy. The great strikes of 1946 broken by Harry Truman had already speeded up the obsolescence of railroads, with their steam engines fueled by coal. Even before then, FDR had thought of a national highway program as the ultimate public works project. That's what it became, in the end, costing $186 billion between 1956 and 1981. By comparison, total public works had been $2.39 billion in 1929, which slumped to less than $1 billion in 1933. Total private investment fell from $7.52 billion in 1929 to $1.22 billion in 1933 and only climbed back up to $3.62 billion in 1939. Fittingly, the interstate highway program began under President Eisenhower, who as a young officer had led a truck convoy across the country in 1919. But Eisenhower, who wanted the interstate highway system mainly to enhance the country's military capabilities, was in a real sense only its godfather. The real parents were the authors of the GI Bill who, in passing a law to help the returning veterans of the nation's greatest war, had helped create a new nation, building on earlier marketing innovations.

The basic marketing principles that flowered to serve the suburbs after World War II had their origins in World War I with a new kind of store. Charles Saunders of Memphis, Tennessee, came up with an idea in 1916 for a food store that could get around the shortage of clerks anticipated with the draft. He opened, and actually patented, the first supermarket. By the outbreak of World War II, Saunders had several hundred of his Piggly-Wiggly self-serving stores operating. Saunders had chosen the name because it made people curious, but once customers had come in, they came back because of the convenient shopping arrangement. Instead of telling a clerk what they wanted, waiting for the clerk to fetch each item, and going through the even more time-consuming toting-up process, customers simply entered through a turnstile, picked up a basket, chose their selections from conveniently laid-out aisles and paid at a checkout counter with an automatic cash register. The result was one of the most profound changes in retailing in centuries, but it took a while to catch on.

Piggly-Wiggly and other chain stores such as Safeway were tiny by today's standards. They had no more than fifteen hundred square feet, about the size of a large two-bedroom apartment and with only three or four aisles. Before supermarkets would become America's primary food source, two other developments would be necessary: the marketing of frozen foods and the invention of the shopping cart. And it took the buying public a couple of decades to accept both. Sylvan Goldman, a store owner in Oklahoma City, put a shopping basket on wheels in 1936 and called it a basket carrier. Customers, however, eyed the contraption suspiciously. Goldman had to hire people to browse through the aisle all day pushing a cart before customers warily began to imitate them.

Self-service innovations, however, didn't work well until merchandisers greatly expanded the number and variety of products for sale and the space in which to display them—as well as parking lots to accommodate shoppers' cars. As late as 1955, 95 percent of all grocery stores in America were either corner operations or superettes (which were less than 1,500 square feet). By that time, however, vastly expanded state and county road systems, soon to be linked by interstate highways, were already drawing millions of customers to sprawling new supermarkets. These new supermarkets, defined as selling more than $2 million annually, accounted for only 5 percent of all grocery stores, but they were selling half the meat, vegetables, produce, and other foods bought. And new, more convenient, and tastier—in comparison to canned—food was drawing the customers in droves: frozen dinners.

The idea of freezing food came to Clarence Birdseye, a naturalist from Gloucester, Massachusetts, while ice fishing. He noticed fish he had caught and thrown on the ice would stiffen as though dead but immediately revive when put in a bucket of water. Intrigued, he experimented with fast flash-freezing and found the process preserved both texture and flavor. The "frosted" foods he sold during the '30s and the war years were separately packaged meats, vegetables, and fruits, which had limited appeal as convenience foods. The breakthrough in consumer acceptance came when complete frozen dinners were produced, first for the army in 1945 and then for the public under the names of Strato Meals and Frigidinners. But it wasn't until 1954 that C. A. Swanson Sons of Omaha, Nebraska, marketed TV Brand Dinners, and America was changed forever.[23]

Roadside franchise operations began with restaurants. Royce Hailey is credited with being the operator of the first modern drive-in restaurant, the Pig Stand. This barbecue pit, located between Dallas and Fort Worth, opened in 1921, and the idea quickly spread to the southern states and California. A&W Root Beer stands, named for a Mr. Allen and a Mr. White, and featuring tray girls who brought food to the customers' cars, followed in 1924. Harland Sanders, an Indiana farm boy, started a Servistation Cafe in Corbin, Kentucky, in 1929, which became Kentucky Fried Chicken in 1946 about the time Sanders was becoming the most famous honorary Kentucky colonel in history. The real developer of the franchise restaurant, however, was Howard Johnson, a drugstore owner who opened in 1929 an ice cream stand on Wollaston Beach, Massachusetts, then a summertime resort area south of Boston where Joseph Kennedy maintained a home. Johnson lured in children with promises of "29 delicious flavors" of ice cream and courted their parents with coffee, hot dogs, and clam rolls. Seafood fanciers complained the clams were just quahog strips rather than Ipswich bellies, but city workers taking the family out for a day on the beach didn't know any better and they tasted good. Johnson also quickly realized neo-Colonial style furnishings and decor gave customers, who were often of immigrant stock, a sense of homey reassurance. He made a rooftop cupola with weather vane, dormer windows, and a distinctive orange roof the trademarks of his rapidly expanding empire. By 1940, he had 125 restaurants along the East Coast, two thirds owned by franchisees.[24]

Charles, Saunders, Sylvan Goldman, Clarence Birdseye, C. A. Swanson, Carl Graham Fisher, Royce Hailey, Mr. Allen and Mr. White, Col. Harland Sanders, and Howard Johnson were all pioneers in the development of the Big Franchise. So, too, had been William Chrysler, John F. and Howard E. Dodge, David D. Buick, Ransom Olds, and William C. Durant; they pioneered the development of the automobile and the locally owned franchises through which they sold cars.

But the man who was probably the first to sense and exploit the potential of the market created by home-buying veterans was Eugene Ferkauf, a World War II army veteran who had run one of his father's two luggage stores in midtown Manhattan before the war. A lousy salesman, Eugene observed that discounters, who sold for small markups over wholesale rather than full retail prices, didn't have to talk customers into buying. Cards offering discounts distributed throughout nearby office buildings brought in the customers; prices clinched the sales. Stationed in the Philippines while waiting for the invasion of Japan that never came, he talked with a high school friend, Joe Swillenberg, about the potential in selling not only suitcases but pens, watches, gloves, even small appliances on discount.

Back in Manhattan, Ferkauf added those items to the inventory of his store and was soon grossing $500 a day, in contrast to the $50 daily taken in by his father. Initial success convinced Ferkauf the formula for success was selling more by charging less. Eugene gradually worked up the nerve to go out on his own, although he was afraid of falling behind other veterans who were doing something with their lives. His mixture of trepidation and determination, flexibility and willingness to try something new was typical of the World War II generation, whether in business, careers, or marriage across hitherto sacrosanct ethnic and religious lines. He spent $1,500 of his $4,000 in savings to start his first store near Grand Central Station. Offering 33⅓ percent discounts on everything in the store, Ferkauf cleared $3,000 his first day. That Christmas, sales averaged $13,000 daily. In 1951, he opened two more stores, also in Manhattan, and two more followed in the suburbs—White Plains and Hempstead, Long Island. In 1953, Ferkauf, who by this time had moved out of a tiny, $75-a-month apartment in Brooklyn for a $75,000 mansion in Queens, was driving through Westbury, Long Island. The still-rural area was near the suburban migration Levitt had touched off several years before. Developers were already referring to such open countryside as "fertile acres." That wasn't because of the crops already under cultivation but because of those that would be planted soon, houses and children.

Ferkauf knew the young couples who bought those homes would also be buying furniture and appliances and, unlike their parents, wouldn't be afraid to go into debt. He also knew they would prefer not to schlep all the way into the city to comparison shop around the department stores and then wait days, even weeks, to have the sofa or washing machine they bought shipped out by truck. Having a store, a giant one with a variety of substores stocking appliances, toys, clothing, and so on right in the area would mean wives could look around at leisure during the week, actually buy on the weekend with their husbands, and have the purchases shipped out the next day. The sixth store in Ferkauf's chain and the first one to be dubbed E. J. Korvette's opened in Westbury on December 2, 1953, and until Christmas, salespeople weren't allowed to leave for lunch. They might not have been able to get back in, the crowds were so big. Instead, coffee and sandwiches were brought in to be gulped in hasty, ten-minute breaks. Since the E. J. Korvette stores had become successful during and after the Korean War, the legend grew that the name stood for (E)ight (J)ewish (Kor)ean (Vet)erans. Actually the store's name had come for Ferkauf's first initial, "E," and that of his friend and partner, "J" for Joe Swillenberg, and a line of clothes, Corvette's. A few years later, Ferkauf had only one regret when he looked over another chain, Toys 'R' Us. He hadn't thought of having the customers pick up and carry their purchase to the cash register as if they were in a supermarket.

In December 1954, Ferkauf took E. J. Korvette's public. By the end of the decade, almost fifty Korvette stores were bringing in annual sales of $157.7 million. It was, however, the way Ferkauf financed his first new stores through banks that was the key to his success and that of other chain operators and franchisers who followed in the path he blazed. Ferkauf had, of course, a successful track record, and banks by this time were realizing huge suburban developments such as those Levitt was building had, in effect, guaranteed government backing. That didn't guarantee that enterprises essentially piggybacking on the home building—furnishing the new homes, for example—would be equally successful, but it did provide a mental framework to demonstrate how such spinoffs could make money. The market for housing, furniture, and appliances was also clearly defined demographically and presumably could be replicated. In other words, if Ferkauf's store in suburban Hempstead made a profit, a loan officer could be more easily persuaded that another store in New Jersey where there were more potential buyers in the same age, economic, and family brackets could make even more money.

Markets are like scientific experiments: how they work can be defined only by trial and error. If a first experiment succeeds and is followed by another that replicates the first, explanations for why and how the experiment worked can be deduced from observation. To use another analogy, franchisers were playing variations on a theme written for the piano by the National Association of Real Estate Boards and the FHA and arranged for full orchestra by the GI Bill. The process is the opposite of the deductive, top-down method used by theoreticians and planners.

Even before the interstate highway was authorized, however, the motel became another symbol of a new age and an economy dominated by the automobile and the suburb rather than the railroad, the city, and the downtown hotel. Tourist camps and motor courts, as they were called, sprang up after the war, although the first one actually called a motel was the Milestone Mo-Tel in San Luis Obispo, California, in 1925. By the 1940s, "motel" had become the preferred generic name for Kozy Kourts, Sleepy Hollows, and Bide-a-Wees.

The motel as another franchise operation was created by a veteran who was also a home builder. Kemmon Wilson of Memphis, Tennessee, on a 1951 trip to Washington, D.C., with his wife, Dorothy, and their five children, discovered hotels in cities and roadside motels rarely catered to families, often charging extra for each child even though they brought their own bedrolls. Wilson was a high school dropout who borrowed $6,500 on a house he built for his mother for $3,700 and parlayed it into a successful home construction business before Pearl Harbor.

After the war, he profitably sold $7,500 to $12,000 houses by making them bigger—but no more expensive than his competitors' houses. He realized the real expense in home building is in plumbing and electrical wiring in kitchens and bathrooms. Making living rooms and bedrooms bigger increases cost marginally but sales prices substantially. Knowing that, Wilson calculated that the optimal size of a motel room for customer convenience and construction efficiency was twelve feet by thirty. Driving back to Memphis from Washington, he told his wife he was going into the hotel business. When she asked how many motels he intended to build, he answered, "About four hundred; that should cover the country. And if I never do anything else, children are going to stay for free at my motels."

The first 120-room Holiday Inn, whose name was inspired by the Bing Crosby movie, complete with restaurant, gift shop, swimming pool, air-conditioning, and free—as opposed to $1 a night—television was opened in Memphis in August 1952, exactly one year after Wilson had taken his trip to Washington. Wilson had estimated it would cost $325,000. But he brought the job in at $280,000 and used the extra funds raised on a bank loan to parlay additional capital to build three more motels on the main roads in and out of Memphis. When his wife pointed out he was still 396 short of his goal of 400 motels, he offered franchises to local lawyers, doctors, and businessmen at $500 for rights to the Holiday Inn name plus five cents royalty out of the $4-a-night single and $6 double rate then being charged. In 1954, eleven more Holiday Inns opened, and two years later, Eisenhower signed the National Highway Act. By the early '70s, Holiday Inns had 208,939 rooms, triple that of his competitors. Hundreds of requests for franchise agreements were also coming in from people who, like Wilson himself, saw revolutionary prospects—and the fulfillment of the American dream—in their own backyards.[25]

The physical infrastructure of forty-one thousand miles of high-speed, limited-access, nonstop highways linked the social infrastructure of housing started by Levitt with a marketing infrastructure begun by Victor Gruen, a Viennese immigrant who had fled Hitler's Anschluss with $8 in his pocket. Becoming a planner whose ideas appealed more to business investors than government bureaucrats, Gruen began to advocate the construction of what he called "shopping towns," but others began to refer to as shopping malls. He didn't fulfill his dream of replicating the colorful, stimulating, and commercially busy urban scenes in the market squares of Central European cities. But with the opening of his Southdale Center in the Minneapolis, Minnesota, suburb of Edina in 1956, he began a new way of buying and working, as office complexes began to locate near shopping malls. Within twenty-five years, America had twenty thousand shopping centers accounting for 60 percent of all retail trade, employing nine million people (8 percent of the workforce) and generating 13 percent of gross national sales. By 1992, twice as many malls were operating as in 1982.[26] The shopping malls and the office building parks that joined them, as well as high-tech factories adjoining the highways, transformed not only the landscape but much of the economy. The highways both generated new wealth and condemned old economic bastions in the urban centers to limbo and sometimes death. Massive new shopping malls sprang up outside every population center of size while old downtown centers declined and decayed. The trucking industry boomed, and a feisty fireplug of a labor leader by the name of James Riddle Hoffa was worshipped, for a time, as much by his Teamsters—and equally detested by many in the public—as the beetle-browed John L. Lewis.

By the 1960s, however, not only had the American economy and society been transformed, but its psyche as well. Hoffa, like Lewis, could dream of shutting down the entire economy through a national trucking strike. That was only a dream, though, because even Hoffa realized neither the public nor the government thought strikers were the heroic figures of the '30s. Between V-J Day and 1962, the number of blue-collar workers had declined by four million while the number of professionals, managers, salespeople, and other white-collar workers had grown by ten million. Union membership was also rapidly declining. At the same time, the weekly pay for the average production worker was $100, four times the comparable wage during the Depression. Murray Kempton, a liberal writer, was talking about the twilight of the labor union movement. Even more significantly, ten times as much money was being spent on education as in 1929. In 1957, three years before John Kennedy took office, the percentage of high school graduates in college was 37 percent. Those students were the children born in the middle of the Depression, the lowest demographic ebb in modern history. When Kennedy took office in 1960, the first baby boomers were fourteen and freshmen in high school, and the percentage of eligible Americans in college was 40 percent. When Kennedy died three years later, the first baby boomers were entering college, and the percentage in college had soared ten points, to 50 percent. Statisticians calculated between 60 and 70 percent of all Americans belonged to the middle class. This middle class was, in fact, becoming the dominant class, the values of which were those that had once belonged to a small, highly educated, upper middle class.[27]

CHAPTER 10

CAN DREAMS COME TRUE AGAIN?

T HE GROWTH OF the middle class and the suburbs, stimulated by the war and the education and housing provisions of the GI Bill, would reshape American society and politics—even though the politicians didn't always see this clearly.

"All middle-class citizens of education have a common belief that the tendencies toward centralization and paternalism must be halted and reversed. No one who voices these opinions can be elected." So observed Dwight Eisenhower in July 1949 after meeting Thomas Dewey, who was still smarting over his humiliating defeat by Harry Truman. "Consequently we must look around for someone of great popularity and who has not frittered his political assets. . . . Elect such a man to the Presidency, *after which* [italics Ike's] he must lead us back to safe channels and paths."[1] The two men agreed no Republican could win by directly attacking planning.

Dewey and Eisenhower were looking at political patterns, the alignments of power among government, business, and labor and didn't see the economic and social changes that had been wrought by the war and were currently changing the shape of society. America was fulfilling Jefferson's idea of a yeoman's republic by becoming an overwhelmingly middle-class nation, where more people than ever had their own land, even if it was only a backyard. Suburbia wasn't paradise, but it was most assuredly better housing than any home the parents of the new home owners had ever lived in, usually rented apartments. Above all, the veteran and his wife, and the neighbors who followed, owned their own home, on their own lot of land. They weren't renters dependent on a parsimonious landlord; neither were they stacked up over picturesque but littered and dangerous streets.

The New Deal had good intentions, but the war produced better results. *Time* dismissed the National Resource Planning Board's overall postwar conversion plans announced in 1943 as "480,000 words of foggy good-will." The report's most striking characteristic was its "essential conservatism," *The Saturday Evening Post* commented. Stuart Chase, whose 1931 *The New Deal,* provided FDR with the name for his new administration, wrote that the war provided "a better break for the common man than liberals in 1938 could have expected for a generation."[2]

Fortunately, thanks to the American Legion, there wasn't any need to seek a better society. Like Candide, the veterans could tend to their own gardens. The GI Bill gave rise to a backyard revolution. Perhaps it was fortunate both the government and the observers of government were almost entirely unaware of the impetus and guidance the bill was giving individuals, the economy, and the society. If they had known, they probably would have tried to improve on what the bill was accomplishing and would have turned the encouraging hand of government into a regulatory bureaucratic one. Instead, this law was quietly delivering far more than the politicians had promised, without any political rhetoric about what was being done. Instead, the rhetoricians kept calling on people to wake up to the terrible dangers confronting them. But the people didn't see them because the dangers weren't there. Even the specter of class warfare was diminishing.

As a direct consequence of the confiscatory taxes during the war, which automatically allowed the government to plow capital into industry, and leaving aside economic and social arguments about whether such progressive taxation is appropriate in peacetime conditions, the distribution of wealth in the country was more equitable than at any time since. Suddenly, there weren't that many poor people around any more, and perhaps even more remarkably, the rich weren't that much richer than anyone else. Between 1919 and 1939, the top 5 percent in the population had siphoned off 30 percent of the national income. By 1946, however, their share of the national wealth had dropped to 18 percent. In 1935–36, families making less than $2,000 a year accounted for 77.7 percent of the population. In 1945–46, those making $2,000 or less amounted to 26.4 percent. Those making $5,000 or more had only been 1.7 percent of the population in 1936;

in 1945–46, they were 21.1 percent. Part of the difference was attributable to inflation, but that was relatively modest. A rising economic tide was lifting more small boats much higher than it was lifting luxury cruisers, as shown by the increase in family incomes between 1941 and 1945.

> Lowest fifth: +68 percent
> Second fifth: +59 percent
> Third fifth: +36 percent
> Fourth fifth: +30 percent
> Top fifth: +21.1 percent

Conditions were such that in the wartime United States, the rich got relatively less and the poor got relatively more. The number of poor declined; almost none of the 16.5 million who were on some form of relief in 1939 needed help by 1945. Family incomes would rise another 50 percent during the next twenty years, but during that time, income distribution would remain roughly the same. Only after the Great Society programs of 1965 would the number and percentage of poor swell and the old structure return.

Unemployment had disappeared during World War II, and it stayed away during most of the remaining decade. As early as 1942, Jeff Davies, president of Hoboes of America, reported all two million members were "off the road." The few men still out there were "just bums," Davies sneered. Being handicapped was no handicap in getting work. Deaf-mutes were eagerly recruited to work in factories where the noise level was intolerable for those with normal hearing. Midgets were indispensable as inspectors to crawl into aircraft wings or the plumbing of ships. Ten percent of Ford's workforce were blind, deaf, or missing a limb. The approximately four million Okies and other poor, white farmers who had been set adrift as migrants by the dust storms and crop failures of the '30s were settling into new communities near urban factories, acquiring bank accounts, homes, and a determination to get the best possible education for their children. Women made up one third of the wartime workforce; and along with a paycheck, they acquired a sense of independence. With war's end, many surrendered their jobs with great reluctance. Other desires were uppermost, however, as women looked forward to the lights coming on all over the world. If being Rosie the Riveter had a certain appeal, so did being Harriet the Housewife; their daughters and granddaughters weren't the first women who wanted it all.

At war's end, husbands and wives had the resources to get it all, both in accumulated savings and in the no-money-down mortgages available through the GI Bill. If they already had children, that reinforced their desire for homes of their own with backyards. Care for preschool children was an enormous and largely unsolved problem during the war; regulated nurseries were almost nonexistent. The veterans and their wives wanted to raise their children in a safe, happy environment—and that was their own home.

And these young Americans establishing their own homes after World War II had another advantage to enjoy and offer their children—health, better health than their parents and better than they had experienced as children and adolescents. The principal basis for that good health was more and better food, despite rationing. A year after Pearl Harbor, eight million people were still dependent on a federal food stamp program; a school lunch program was feeding nine million children. By 1944, both were being severely cut back under a conservative onslaught in Congress on New Deal programs. But no one really cared, not even the farmers who benefited from the programs as much as the recipients, not even the farmers who were driven off their farms. Many were delighted to go, happily selling out to bigger farmers and emerging agribusiness interests, carrying away checks big enough to ease their way into urban jobs and lives. Not just city folk were flocking to the suburbs; their country cousins were too. No figures are available, but no doubt a substantial percentage of veterans buying suburban homes under VA mortgages were fleeing rural rather than urban slums. At the turn of the century, more than 40 percent of the nation's people lived on farms and another 20 percent in rural small towns. By the end of World War II, the farm population was probably less than 30 million, and the 1950 census found only 23 million, 15 percent of the total population, down on the farm. The latest census released in 1993 showed only 4.6 million living on farms, down from 6 million in 1980. That total, 1.9 percent of the population, was so small that the Department of Agriculture and Census Bureau announced no more farm surveys would be conducted; the cost wasn't worth the information gained.[3]

Americans began to benefit from greatly improved medical care. The initial beneficiaries were those in the military. By 1943, the ratio of doctors to servicemen was one to one hundred, compared with one for every thirty-five hundred civilians. At the same time, more doctors were being trained under the military's "V" program in the colleges. So many were turned out that, by war's end, the number of doctors greatly exceeded the demand. Consequently, many returned to school for further specialized training under the GI bill. The family doctor was about to become a relic; the age of the specialist was coming due largely to wartime needs and the GI Bill.

The most fundamental change in medical care for civilians—insurance—was both pioneered and resisted by doctors. Before the war, Blue Cross–Blue Shield had been started by Texas doctors and slowly spread, mostly under their control. The first health maintenance organization (HMO), controlled by an employer, was started by a hard-nosed builder of Liberty ships, Henry J. Kaiser, despite determined opposition from the American Medical Association (AMA). Doctors who joined Kaiser group practices affiliated with his wartime shipyards were denounced by the AMA for engaging in contract medicine and threatened with expulsion from the association. Kaiser persisted, and in the end, the AMA desisted under a Justice Department antitrust suit.[4] Both forms of prepaid medical insurance became widely available as a fringe benefit of the Taft-Hartley Act. Although Taft-Hartley had stripped the union movement of what seemed its most powerful weapon, the closed shop, it inadvertently provided it with one almost as valuable. An unanticipated Supreme Court interpretation of the law gave unions the right to bargain for fringe benefits.[5]

Reuther and the UAW, in particular, took adroit advantage of the decision. Since news reports of agreements focused only on wage increases, Reuther persuaded management that providing benefits wouldn't upset stockholders unaware of the full cost of the settlement. Other large employers, unionized or not, felt obliged to also provide health care. Within six years, the number of workers with health insurance multiplied from three million to thirty million. Within another ten years, as health insurance became an integral element in the compensation package offered by most large employers, the government began to seek ways to cover small-business employees, the elderly, and the indigent. Medicare and Medicaid were born, but Lyndon Johnson was the grandfather; the AMA and Henry J. Kaiser were the quarreling parents; and Senator Taft was an unwitting midwife.

Over the years, the GI Bill subtly has worked to change the face of America. The influence of this omnibus bill, put in place largely by a middle-of-the-road coalition, produced a middle-class nation. By giving veterans the wherewithal to make their dreams come true, the

GI Bill of Rights was built upon a rock-solid philosophy whose enactment has had a ripple effect throughout the lives of millions of Americans. Education became a necessity; mortgage lending was altered
to the point that home ownership is a national goal—not just a benefit for the monied few. As suburbs sprang up, so did an interconnect-
ing highway system, and a different way of working, shopping, and
living. The ground was laid for a high-technology information age
and for blacks, hardened by the war and educated by the GI Bill, to
demand equal treatment under the law.

The cumulative effects of the GI Bill's approach may finally be
dawning on a few in the government. In 1995 HUD released a "reinvention" report on public housing. The department had done enough
surveys to discover the obvious: 86 percent of all adults prefer to own
a home, and two thirds of all renters would buy a house if they could
afford one. HUD was also concerned by studies showing a discourag-
ing trend in home ownership. The percentage of Americans owning
their own homes had peaked in 1980 at 65.6 percent, after climbing
from 43.6 percent in 1940 to 55 percent in 1950, then 61.9 percent in
1960 and 62.9 percent in 1970. Reacting to the evidence, the Clinton
administration committed itself to "an all-out effort to restore home-
ownership to its previous peaks—and to exceed those rates—by the
year 2000." The administration's reinvention of public housing may
well produce better housing for the poor by the simple expedient of
allowing them to obtain shelter in the private market using vouchers.
Fifty years before, a key Senate committee, with Senator Taft's bless-
ing, had rejected the real estate lobby's proposal for rent certificates
on the grounds that this approach would promote slums. In 1995,
HUD declared, "Where the current system funds bureaucracies, we
will fund people," encapsulating the same basic philosophy as the GI
Bill. The reinvention report declares: "Where the current system gives
public housing agencies capital and operating subsidies to maintain
projects, we will give families rental certificates—modeled on the Section 8 program and pegged to the local cost of decent housing—that
could be used in public housing or a private apartment of their own
choice. Where the current system relies on a complex, complicated
array of rules and regulations to oversee the performance of agencies, HUD will now rely on families to decide whether management
will perform well."[6] That language could have been written by Representative Rankin, while the Section 8 program the Clinton administration's plan relies upon was sponsored in Congress by Senator

Edward W. Brooke, a Republican from Massachusetts, the first black elected to the Senate since Reconstruction, who earned his law degree from Boston University after army service with the Partisans in Italy.

The GI Bill of Rights was the law that worked, the law that paid for itself and reaped dividends because it made the American dream come true for so many. It enabled millions of working-class people to make a middle-class way of life for themselves. It did it by giving them an educational grubstake and a homesteader's claim on the New Frontier—but left the rest to them. They had to make the dream work for themselves, and if for some reason, it didn't, they had no grounds for complaints. Pursuit of happiness is guaranteed—not the obtaining.

That's what the American dream is, after all: the promise and often prosaic reality of a middle-class way of life. It isn't about crusading in a great war to end all wars. It isn't about dying to save the world for democracy or free markets or humanity. The veterans of World War I had enough of that, and they made sure their children had something better, a decent life after the fighting was over. The dream is about living in a system that rewards being an honest citizen and a hard worker. Only that makes the ultimate sacrifice, if needed, worthwhile. That's not very dramatic or uplifting, but it rewards people with lives in which they are as secure as possible, in a world always fraught with danger, in their liberties and opportunities, both of person and property. And that's been the best hope of this world for more than two hundred years.

American life is still a struggle in a society filled with conflict and sometimes with injustice. But it's also life in a society in which liberties and opportunities have expanded dramatically over the past fifty years, in large part because of the GI Bill. These liberties and opportunities should expand further. The nation where the American Legion was formed in 1918 to combat the rule of the classes or the masses is now an overwhelmingly middle-class nation that can hope that becoming an almost exclusively middle-class nation is not a wild-eyed dream. Doing that will, of course, be difficult and contentious, needing men and women of great knowledge and sophistication to make it work. But the job will never be done by turning control over to one group or government or markets alone.

In 1932, FDR in his first campaign for president, said of government: "Our task now is not discovery or exploitation of natural resources, nor necessarily producing more goods. It is the soberer, less dramatic business of administering resources and plants already in hand; of adjusting production to consumption; of distributing wealth and products equitably; of adapting existing economic organizations to the service of the people. . . . The day of the manager has come."[7]

America has proved, however, that it is just too big for managers or the government or the market or anything other than its people to run. America can always be made better, but only if a lot of citizens do the job, in and out of government, trying to find out what works, what is rooted in us as a people and making that, rather than any ideology, work better. Sergeant William Patterson wanted to go home and "start a veterans' association . . . to get the whole job done." He died on a battlefield in France instead. But he had passed on his dream.

The world war that began in 1914 and ended in 1989 is over, but the whole job isn't done yet. It will never be done. But as long as Americans believe the job can be done, dreams will always come true.

NOTES

CHAPTER 1

1. William Manchester, *The Glory and the Dream: A Narrative History of America* (Boston: Little, Brown & Co., 1973), 453–54.

2. Chalmers M. Roberts, "Peace at Last! Cheers Erupt in Washington," *The Washington Post,* World War II special section, July 26, 1995.

3. Stanley Weintraub, *The Last Great Victory: The End of World War II, July-August 1945* (New York: Penguin Books, 1995), 617, 639–40.

4. Naomi Bliven, "V-J Night: The Way It Was," *The New Yorker,* August 14, 1995.

5. W. A. Swanberg, *Citizen Hearst* (New York: Charles Scribners Co., 1961), 175–76.

6. Peter F. Drucker, *Post-Capitalist Society* (New York: Harper-Business, 1993), 3.

7. Joseph C. Goulden, *The Best Years: 1945–1950* (New York: Atheneum, 1976), 93.

8. Doris Kearns Goodwin, *No Ordinary Time: Franklin and Eleanor Roosevelt: The Home Front in World War II* (New York: Simon & Schuster, 1994), 469, 608.

9. Bruce Catton, *The War Lords of Washington* (New York: Harcourt, Brace & Co., 1948), 306 and charts.

10. Telephone interview with author. Also, Paul H. Weaver, *News and the Culture of Lying: How Journalism Really Works* (New York: The Free Press, 1994), 146–47.

11. Manchester, *The Glory and the Dream,* 488–89.

12. Robert H. Ferrell, *Harry S Truman: A Life* (Columbia, Mo.: University of Missouri, 1994), 229–30.

13. David R. B. Ross, *Preparing for Ulysses: Politics and Veterans During*

World War II (New York: Columbia University, 1969), 238–39, 265–66.

14. U.S. Bureau of the Census, *Colonial Times to the Present: Historical Statistics of the United States* (Washington, D.C.: Government Printing Office, 1976), 379.

15. Department of Veterans Affairs, *A Very Nice Thing: Fifty Years of the G.I. Bill,* audiovisual tape, 1994.

16. Manchester, *The Glory and the Dream,* 490–97.

17. Keith W. Olson, *The G.I. Bill, the Veterans and the Colleges* (Louisville, Ky.: University Press of Kentucky, 1974), 20.

18. Ibid., 40–44.

19. Sar A. Levitan and Joyce K. Zickler, *Swords Into Plowshares: Our G.I. Bill* (Santa Barbara, Calif.: Olympus Publishing Co., 1973), 42.

20. Charles J. V. Murphy, "GIs at Harvard: They Are the Best Students in College's History," *Life,* June 17, 1946.

21. Edith Efron, "Two Joes Meet: Joe College, Joe Veteran," *The New York Times Magazine,* June 16, 1946.

22. Art Buchwald, *Leaving Home* (New York: G. P. Putnam's Sons, 1993), 201–2.

23. Olson, *The G.I. Bill, the Veterans and the Colleges,* 52–53.

24. U.S. Census Bureau, *Historical Statistics,* 49.

25. Ibid., 639–41.

26. David Halberstam, *The Fifties* (New York: Villard Books, 1993), 132–43.

27. Marc A. Weiss, *The Rise of the Community Builders: The American Real Estate Industry and Urban Land Planning* (New York: Columbia University Press, 1987), 2–3.

28. "What G.I.s Are Doing Now," *U.S. News & World Report,* September 20, 1946.

29. Geoffery Perrett, *Days of Sadness, Years of Triumph: The American People 1939–1945* (New York: Coward, McCann & Geoghagan, 1973), 10–11.

CHAPTER 2

1. Richard Severo and Lewis Milford, *The Wages of War: When America's Soldiers Came Home: From Valley Forge to Vietnam* (New York: Simon & Schuster, 1989), 65–71.

2. John C. Miller, *Triumph of Freedom 1775–1783* (Boston: Atlantic Monthly Press, 1948), 653–57.

3. Samuel Eliot Morison, *The Oxford History of the American People* (New York: Oxford University Press, 1965), 300–304.

4. John Dos Passos, *Men Who Made the Nation* (New York: Doubleday & Company, 1957), 122–23.

5. Severo and Milford, *The Wages of War,* 44–50, 101–2.

6. Morison, *The Oxford History of the American People,* 666–67.

7. Severo and Milford, *The Wages of War,* 176–86.

8. Morison, *The Oxford History of the American People,* 867, reference to W. L. Wanger, *Encyclopedia of World History,* 960.

9. Dixon Wecter, *When Johnny Comes Marching Home* (New York: n.p., 1944), cited in David R. B. Ross, *Preparing for Ulysses,* 13.

10. Ralph Henry Gabriel, *The Course of American Democratic Thought* (New York: The Ronald Press Co., 1940), 402.

11. U.S. Bureau of the Census, *Historical Statistics,* 8, 14.

12. Raymond Moley Jr., *The American Legion Story* (New York: Duell, Sloan and Pearce, 1966), 91–92.

13. Robert E. Park, *The Immigrant Press and Its Control* (New York: Harper & Brothers, 1922), 252–302.

14. Frances Fitzgerald, *America Revised: History School Books in the 20th Century* (Boston: Little, Brown, 1979), 78.

15. Gabriel, *The Course of American Democratic Thought,* 356–58.

16. Howard Zinn, *A People's History of the United States* (New York: Harper & Row, 1980), 363–64.

17. Oscar Theodore Barcke and Nelson Manfred Blake, *Since 1900: A History of the United States in Our Times* (New York: Macmillan, 1965), 231.

18. Zinn, *A People's History,* 339–40.

19. Eleanor Roosevelt, *Day Before Yesterday* (New York: Doubleday & Co., 1959), 101–2.

20. Kurt Snow, "My General, Theodore Roosevelt, Jr.," *American Legion Magazine,* May 1945. Reference to *Story of the American Legion,* by George S. Wheat (New York: Putnam, 1918).

21. Theodore Roosevelt Jr. to his wife, Eleanor, Theodore Roosevelt Jr. Collection, Library of Congress.

22. Goulden, *The Best Years,* 54–55.

23. Eleanor Roosevelt, *Day Before Yesterday,* 119, quoting from George S. Wheat, *Story of the American Legion* (New York: Putnam, 1918).

24. Eleanor Roosevelt, *Day Before Yesterday,* 120.

25. Williams Slavens McNutt, "America First: The Story of the American Legion Caucus in St. Louis," *Collier's Magazine,* June 7, 1919.

26. Peter Collier with David Horowitz, *The Roosevelts: An American Saga* (New York: Simon & Schuster, 1994), 211.

27. Moley, *The American Legion Story,* 65–66.

28. Ferrell, *Harry S Truman,* 69.

29. Frederick Lewis Allen, *Only Yesterday* (New York: Harper's, 1931), 40–44.

30. "Dementia Praecox," *The Freeman,* June 21, 1922, reprinted in Leon Baritz, *The Culture of the Twenties* (Indianapolis: Bobbs-Merrill, 1970), 28–40.

31. Moley, *The American Legion Story,* 91.

32. Barcke and Blake, *Since 1900,* 353–55.

33. Moley, *The American Legion Story,* 109, 145–6.

34. Manchester, *The Glory and the Dream,* 12.
35. Barcke and Blake, *Since 1900,* 300–302.
36. Ross, *Preparing for Ulysses,* 13.
37. Barcke and Blake, *Since 1900,* 290–92.
38. Moley, *The American Legion Story,* 195–98.
39. Manchester, *The Glory and the Dream,* 10, 18–19.
40. Ross, *Preparing for Ulysses,* 21.
41. Manchester, *The Glory and the Dream,* 12–19.
42. Severo and Milford, *The Wages of War,* 274–76.
43. Moley, *The American Legion Story,* 197–201.
44. Barcke and Blake, *Since 1900,* 484.
45. Ross, *Preparing for Ulysses,* 25–26.
46. Moley, *The American Legion Story,* 206.
47. Ross, *Preparing for Ulysses,* 18.
48. Ibid., 27.
49. Moley, *The American Legion Story,* 206.
50. Barcke and Blake, *Since 1900,* 485.
51. James MacGregor Burns, *The Crosswinds of Freedom: The American Experiment* (New York: Alfred A. Knopf, 1989), 105–6.
52. Nathaniel S. Keith, *Politics and the Housing Crisis Since 1930* (New York: Universe Books, 1973), 24–25, 38.
53. Bill Bryson, *Made in America: An Informal History of the English Language in the United States* (New York: William Morrow and Co., 1944), 41–42.
54. Eleanor Roosevelt, *Day Before Yesterday,* 418–21.
55. Burns, *The Crosswinds of Freedom,* 130–31.
56. Severo and Milford, *The Wages of War,* 288–89.
57. Gary Dorrien, *The New Conservative Mind* (Philadelphia: Temple University Press, 1993), 42–43.
58. Morison, *The Oxford History of the American People,* 986.
59. Drucker, *Post-Capitalist Society,* 135–36.

CHAPTER 3
1. Severo and Milford, *The Wages of War,* 289.
2. David Camelon, "I Saw the GI Bill Written," parts 1–3, *American Legion Magazine* (September, October, November 1949). Part 1 is titled "The Fight for Mustering Out Pay"; part 2 is "A Surprise Attack"; and part 3, "The Wild Ride from Georgia."
3. Camelon, "The Fight for Mustering Out Pay" and "A Surprise Attack."
4. Alan Drury, *A Senate Journal: 1943–1945* (New York: McGraw-Hill Company, 1963), 135–36, 189.
5. Ross, *Preparing for Ulysses,* 39–42.
6. Olson, *The GI Bill, the Veterans and the Colleges,* 5.
7. Ross, *Preparing for Ulysses,* 40–50.

8. Ibid., 51–58.

9. Ibid., 59–60.

10. Olson, *The GI Bill, the Veterans and the Colleges,* 7.

11. Ross, *Preparing for Ulysses,* 61–63.

12. Olson, *The GI Bill, the Veterans and the Colleges,* 12.

13. Ross, *Preparing for Ulysses,* 51, 64–66.

14. Drury, *A Senate Journal,* 25.

15. Olson, *The GI Bill, the Veterans and the Colleges,* 10–15.

16. Earle Cocke Jr., interview by author, June 1995.

17. *Dictionary of American Biography,* s.v. "Andrew Jackson May."

18. Camelon, "The Fight for Mustering Out Pay."

19. Paul H. Stevens, "Walter Howey: Fort Dodge's Most Famous Journalist," *The Palimpest,* January-February 1975.

20. Joe Guillotti, former employee of *The Boston Record-American,* interview by author, December 1993.

21. Camelon, "The Fight for Mustering Out Pay."

22. Ross, *Preparing for Ulysses,* 64–66.

23. Ibid., 51, 81.

24. Perrett, *Days of Sadness, Years of Triumph,* 280–81.

25. Richard J. Whalen, *The Founding Father* (New York: New American Library, 1964), 66–68.

26. W. A. Swanberg, *Citizen Hearst* (New York: Charles Scribners Sons, 1961), 524–26.

27. Ibid., 59, 162.

28. Ibid., 483.

29. Ibid., 168, 212–13, 222, 278–79.

30. *Dictionary of American Biography,* s.v. "William Randolph Hearst."

31. Swanberg, *Citizen Hearst,* 168, 212–13, 222, 278–279.

32. "GI Bill of Rights Passed by Senate," *The New York Times,* March 25, 1944.

33. McCullough, David G., *Just Truman* (New York: Simon & Schuster, 1992), 317–18.

34. General Roosevelt, correspondence file, Library of Congress.

35. *Dictionary of American Politics,* s.v. "Bennett Champ Clark."

36. McCullough, *Truman,* 124, 206–7, 223, 228–29, 235–37.

37. Cocke, interview.

38. Zinn, *A People's History,* 283–84.

39. Russell Whelan, "Rankin of Mississippi," *The Nation,* July 1944.

40. Morison, *The Oxford History of the American People,* 790–93.

41. Robert Caro, *Means of Ascent* (New York: Alfred Knopf, 1990), 251–52.

42. *Dictionary of American Biography,* s.v. "John Rankin."

43. Ross, *Preparing for Ulysses,* 86.

44. Barbara Sicherman and Carol Hurd Gich, *Notable American Women* (Cambridge, Mass.: Belknap Press of Harvard University, 1980), 587–89.

45. Zinn, *A People's History,* 223–25.
46. *Dictionary of American Biography,* s.v. "Edith Nourse Rogers."
47. Zinn, *A People's History,* 409.
48. Hope Chamberlain, *A Minority of Members: Women in the U.S. House* (Westport, Conn.: Praeger Publishers, 1973), 56–60.
49. Perrett, *Days of Sadness, Years of Triumph,* 338–59, 671.
50. Burns, *The Crosswinds of Freedom,* 125, 671.

CHAPTER 4
1. Veto record from "Presidential Vetoes," quoted in "Clinton Breaks the Ice," *The Washington Post,* June 8, 1995.
2. Drury, *A Senate Journal,* 93.
3. Ross, *Preparing for Ulysses,* 91.
4. Drury, *A Senate Journal,* 86, 96–97.
5. Kearns Goodwin, *No Ordinary Time,* 484–90.
6. Drury, *A Senate Journal,* 96–97.
7. Ibid., 53.
8. Ibid., 179.
9. Ibid., 114, 171–72.
10. Olson, *The GI Bill, the Veterans and the Colleges,* 20–21.
11. Severo and Milford, *The Wages of War,* 283.
12. Drury, *A Senate Journal,* 194.
13. Burns, *The Crosswinds of Freedom,* 186–88.
14. Goulden, *The Best Years,* 112.
15. Ross, *Preparing for Ulysses,* 91.
16. Drury, *A Senate Journal,* 26.
17. Ross, *Preparing for Ulysses,* 95–97.
18. *Report of the President,* Harvard University, January 22, 1944.
19. Olson, *The GI Bill, the Veterans and the Colleges,* 18.
20. Camelon, "The Fight for Mustering Out Pay."
21. "Legion Bill Asks Wide Veteran Aid; Legion-Sponsored Bill World War II Veteran Aid Discussed," *The New York Times,* January 9, 1944, 28, col. 2.
22. Camelon, "A Surprise Attack."
23. Ross, *Preparing for Ulysses,* 98.
24. "Rep. Rankin Offers Skeleton Bill," *The New York Times,* January 11, 1944, 17, col. 3.
25. "O. B. Ketchum Testifies," *The New York Times,* January 13, 1944, 11, col. 1.
26. "Conf. with Roosevelt," *The New York Times,* January 15, 1944, 4, col. 7.
27. Camelon, "A Surprise Attack."
28. *Congressional Record,* March 24, 1944, S3076–77.
29. "Atherton Lauds House Mustering-Out Pay Bill Approval, *The New York Times,* January 20, 1944, 7, col. 5.

30. Olson, *The GI Bill, the Veterans and the Colleges,* 22–23.

31. Camelon, "A Surprise Attack."

32. "Cmdr. Atherton Announces Drive for Signatures Veteran Rehabilitation Bill," *The New York Times,* March 7, 1944, 10, col. 5.

33. R. B. Pitkin, "How the First GI Bill Was Written," *The American Legion Magazine* (January, February, and May 1969). This series of articles provides details about the Ketchum memo and the role of Kearney not found in the original Camelon series.

34. Ross, *Preparing for Ulysses,* 104.

35. Ibid., 108–9.

36. Olson, *The GI Bill, the Veterans and the Colleges,* 18–19.

37. The latter observation is in the Pitkin, rather than the Camelon, version of the American Legion series. The quote is directly attributed to Camelon.

CHAPTER 5

1. *Congressional Record,* May 12, 1944, H4449.

2. Geoffrey Perrett, *There's a War to Be Won: The United States Army in World War II* (New York: Random House, 1991), 28.

3. Clark Kerr, "Expanding Access and Changing Missions: The Federal Role in U.S. Higher Education," *Educational Record,* Fall 1994.

4. *Congressional Record,* May 12, 1944, H4435.

5. Ross, *Preparing for Ulysses,* 92.

6. Ibid., 81, 108. This cartoon appeared February 17, 1944.

7. Ibid., 110 and footnote 67.

8. Ibid., 105, 110.

9. Ibid., 112–15.

10. *Congressional Record,* May 11, 1944, H4340.

11. "House Is Divided on Veterans' Bill," *The New York Times,* May 12, 1944, 10, col. 3.

12. *Congressional Record,* May 12, 1944, H4515.

13. *Congressional Record,* May 11, 1944, H4352.

14. Severo and Milford, *The Wages of War,* 304, 309.

15. Merchant seamen, particularly, were excluded from coverage under the bill until 1933. The casualty rates among seamen were comparable to servicemen in actual combat, but they were excluded from coverage as civilians drawing higher pay than those in the military. Also excluded were the Women's Army Auxiliary Corps (WAAC) and WASPs, Women's Air Service Pilots who ferried planes for the army air corps. Most of those who enlisted in the WAACs were, however, included if they served in the Women's Army Corps, which replaced the WAACs as a full-fledged rather than an auxiliary part of the army.

16. *Congressional Record,* May 11, 1944, H4346.

17. Ibid., H4361.

18. *Congressional Record,* May 15, 1944, H4505.
19. Ibid.
20. Ibid., H4507.
21. Ibid., H4511.
22. Ibid., H4512.
23. *Congressional Record,* May 12, 1944, H4439.
24. *Congressional Record,* May 15, 1944, H4506.
25. Ibid., H4517.
26. *Congressional Record,* May 11, 1944, H4346.
27. *Congressional Record,* May 12, 1944, H4439.
28. *Congressional Record,* May 11, 1944, H4360.
29. *Congressional Record,* May 17, 1944, H4620.
30. Ross, *Preparing for Ulysses,* 75–76.
31. Ibid., 24, 74–78.
32. *Congressional Record,* May 16, H4546.
33. Ibid., H4545.
34. "G.I. Education Plan Could Cost $20,000,000,000 More," *The Saturday Evening Post,* July 8, 1950.
35. *Congressional Record,* May 16, 1944, H4543–44.
36. Ibid., H4554.
37. *Dictionary of American Biography,* s.v. "Vito Marcantonio."
38. *Congressional Record,* May 18, 1994, H4675–76.
39. "House by 387 to 0 Approves GI Bill," *The New York Times,* May 19, 1944, 20, col. 2.
40. *Congressional Record,* May 18, 1944, H4672–74.
41. "The Battle of Washington's Birthday," *Time,* March 5, 1945.
42. *Congressional Record,* May 16, 1944, H4639–40.

CHAPTER 6
1. Collier, *The Roosevelts,* 393.
2. Cornelius Ryan, *The Longest Day* (New York: Simon & Schuster, 1959), 233.
3. Eleanor Roosevelt, *Day Before Yesterday,* 452–53.
4. Marvin Gibson, interview by author, February 20, 1993. Dr. Gibson, an orthopedic surgeon, is apparently the only living person with personal memories of the events associated with the passage of the bill, at least from a congressional perspective.
5. "Coffee County Attorneys Lankford, Gibson Served 20 Years in United States Congress," *Douglas (Georgia) Enterprise,* September 20, 1963.
6. Sol M. Linowitz and Martin Mayer, *The Betrayed Profession; Lawyering at the End of the Twentieth Century* (New York: C. Scribners Sons, 1994), 6.
7. Ross, *Preparing for Ulysses,* 117.

8. Stephen Ambrose, *D-Day, June 6, 1944: The Climactic Battle of World War II* (New York: Simon & Schuster, 1994), 258.

9. Ryan, *The Longest Day,* 231–33, 285–86.

10. Bernard deVoto, "Easy Chair: GOP Candidates and Policies," *Harper's,* June 1944.

CHAPTER 7

1. Ross, *Preparing for Ulysses,* 3, 35–36; and Severo and Milford, *The Wages of War,* 284–85.

2. Edwin Keister Jr., "The GI Bill May Have Been the Best Deal Made by Uncle Sam," *Smithsonian Magazine,* November 1994.

3. Morison, *The Oxford History of the American People,* 1053.

4. Drucker, *Post-Capitalist Society,* 2–3, 5, 22.

5. Severo and Milford, *The Wages of War,* 293; and Bureau of Labor Statistics, *1993 Annual Census of Occupational Deaths* (Washington, D.C.: U.S. Department of Labor).

6. *Historical Statistics,* 126–28.

7. Olson, *The GI Bill, the Veterans and the Colleges,* 44.

8. *Historical Statistics,* 126–38.

9. *Minorities in Higher Education,* 51, table 4.

10. Manchester, *The Glory and the Dream,* 486.

11. Severo and Milford, *The Wages of War,* 294.

12. Ibid., 291–92.

13. Goulden, *The Best Years,* 31.

14. Perrett, *There's a War to Be Won,* 533–34.

15. Goulden, *The Best Years,* 23–24, 28.

16. Ross, *Preparing for Ulysses,* 185.

17. Goulden, *The Best Years,* 501.

18. Ibid., 26–30.

19. Ross, *Preparing for Ulysses,* 174.

20. Goulden, *The Best Years,* 26.

21. Ross, *Preparing for Ulysses,* 174.

22. Manchester, *The Glory and the Dream,* 497.

23. Goulden, *The Best Years,* 24.

24. Ibid., 30.

25. Manchester, *The Glory and the Dream,* 498–500; and Goulden, *The Best Years,* 30–33.

26. Ross, *Preparing for Ulysses,* 183–86; and Goulden, *The Best Years,* 33–34.

27. Goulden, *The Best Years,* 34–35.

28. Manchester, *The Glory and the Dream,* 504–8.

29. Ross, *Preparing for Ulysses,* 189.

30. Morison, *The Oxford History of the American People,* 1052.

31. Manchester, *The Glory and the Dream*, 487.

32. Goulden, *The Best Years*, 110–18.

33. Ibid.

34. *Twentieth Century America: Selected Readings*, ed. E. David Cronon, vol. 2 (University of Wisconsin, 1966), 362–63.

35. Severo and Milford, *The Wages of War*, 294–95.

36. "Veterans, Unions and Jobs," *The New Republic*, October 23, 1944.

37. Manchester, *The Glory and the Dream*, 496; and Goulden, *The Best Years*, 125–27.

38. Keister, "The GI Bill May Have Been the Best Deal Made by Uncle Sam."

39. Drucker, *Post-Capitalist Society*, 135–36.

CHAPTER 8

1. Byron Atkinson, "Waltzing Me Around Again, Willie," *School and Society*, July 17, 1948.

2. Karen Thomas, *The GI Bill of Rights: The Law That Changed America* (Washington, D.C.), unpublished manuscript for television documentary.

3. Goulden, *The Best Years*, 79–80.

4. James Conant, *My Several Lives: Memoir of a Social Inventor* (New York: Harper & Row, 1970), 373, 622–23, 663.

5. Goulden, *The Best Years*, 71.

6. Severo and Milford, *The Wages of War*, 294.

7. Perrett, *Days of Sadness, Years of Glory* 341–42; and "One-Half of a Nation," *Time*, September 13, 1954.

8. Goulden, *The Best Years*, 157.

9. Olson, *The GI Bill, the Veterans and the Colleges*, 45–49.

10. Goulden, *The Best Years*, 75–77.

11. Keister, "The GI Bill May Have Been the Best Deal Made by Uncle Sam."

12. Olson, *The GI Bill, the Veterans and the Colleges*, 42–50.

13. Goulden, *The Best Years*, 66–70.

14. Olson, *The GI Bill, the Veterans and the Colleges*, 71–72.

15. Thomas, *The GI Bill of Rights*.

16. Brad Gooch, *City Poet: The Life and Times of Frank O'Hara* (New York, Alfred A. Knopf, 1993), 92–99.

17. Walter Isaacson, *Kissinger* (New York: Simon & Schuster, 1992), 38–40.

18. John Egerton, *Speak Now Against the Day: The Generation Before the Civil Rights Movement in the South* (New York: Alfred A. Knopf, 1994), 221.

19. Alan Kraut, *Silent Travelers: Germans, Genes, and the Immigrant Menace* (New York: Basic Books, 1994), 252.

20. Perrett, *Days of Sadness, Years of Glory*, 375–77.

21. Dorrien, *The New Conservative Mind*, 42–49.

22. Lee Kennett, *GI: The American Soldier in World War II* (New York: Charles Scribners, Inc., 1987), 82–83.

23. Elizabeth Anne Wheal, Stephen Pope, and James Taylor, *Encyclopedia of the Second World War* (New York: P. Bedrick Books, 1989), 182.

24. Wilson, "GI Bill Expands Access for African-American," *Educational Record,* Fall, 1944.

25. Goulden, *The Best Years,* 68–71.

26. Wilson, *Educational Record.*

27. Kearns Goodwin, *No Ordinary Time,* 425, 523–24, 567, 626–28.

28. Egerton, *Speak Now Against the Day,* 326–27, 364–69, 514.

29. Juan Williams, *Eyes on the Prize: America's Civil Rights Years 1954–1965* (New York: Viking Books, 1987), 2–18.

30. Ibid., 17–18, 208–9.

31. Ibid.

32. Kluger, *Simple Justice,* 23–24, 295–305, 328–29, 354–55, 366.

33. Thomas, *The GI Bill of Rights.*

34. Kluger, *Simple Justice,* 23–24, 272, 395–423, 407–10, 415–16.

35. Ginsberg, *The Fatal Embrace,* 150.

CHAPTER 9

1. Perrett, *There's a War to Be Won,* 399.

2. Nathaniel S. Keith, *Politics and the Housing Crisis Since 1930* (New York: Universe Books, 1973), 41–57, 59.

3. Gertrude S. Fish, ed., *The Story of Housing* (New York: Macmillan, 1979), 248–49.

4. Ibid., 61–62, 72, 76, 100.

5. Ibid.

6. Walter Reuther, "Walter Reuther Challenges 'Our Fear of Abundance,'" *The New York Times Magazine,* September 16, 1945.

7. Catton, *The War Lords of Washington,* 131.

8. *Historical Statistics,* 639–41.

9. Manchester, *The Glory and the Dream,* 59.

10. Halberstam, *The Fifties,* 139–40.

11. Donald Albrect, ed., *World War II and the American Dream: How Wartime Building Changed a Nation* (Washington, D.C.: National Building Museum, 1995).

12. *Businessweek,* January 1, 1944.

13. Weiss, *The Rise of Community Builders,* 2, 145–46, 152, 155–56, 160.

14. *Historical Statistics,* 49.

15. Herbert J. Gans, *The Levittowners: Ways of Life and Politics in a New Suburban Community* (New York: Pantheon Books, 1967), 287.

16. Joel Garreau, *Edge City: Life on the New Frontier* (New York: Doubleday, 1991), 233–34.

17. Halberstam, *The Fifties,* 132–37.

18. Goulden, *The Best Years,* 140–41.

19. Halberstam, *The Fifties,* 141.

20. Gans, *The Levittowners,* 287–88, 371–84.

21. Harvard Sitkoff, *The Struggle for Black Equality* (New York: Hill & Wang, 1993), 18.

22. Fish, *The Story of Housing,* 183–94, 253, 207–9, 473.

23. Bill Bryson, *Made in America: An Informal History of the English Language in the United States* (New York: William Morrow and Co., 1994), 142–43.

24. Ibid.

25. Halberstam, *The Fifties,* 173–79.

26. Bryson, *Made in America,* 216–17.

27. Manchester, *The Glory and the Dream,* 928–29, 1225–26.

CHAPTER 10

1. Halberstam, *The Fifties,* 4.

2. Perrett, *Days of Sadness, Years of Triumph,* 326–29, 355; Manchester, *The Glory and the Dream,* 57, 67.

3. "Farm Census Dropped by Department of Agriculture," *The Washington Post,* October 9, 1993.

4. Perrett, *Days of Sadness, Years of Triumph,* 234–35, 332–36, 405–7.

5. Joseph A. Califano Jr., *Radical Surgery: What's Next for American Medical Care* (New York: Time Books, 1994), 7.

6. U.S. Department of Housing and Urban Development, *HUD Reinvention: From Blueprint to Action,* March 1995.

7. Thomas Langston, *With Reverence and Contempt: How Americans Think About Their Presidents* (Baltimore, Md.: Johns Hopkins University Press, 1994), 111–13.

INDEX

ABOUT THE AUTHOR

FORMERLY A reporter for the *Boston Herald,* MICHAEL J. BENNETT is a veteran journalist and author who resides in Washington, D.C. His reporting at the *Detroit News* was nominated for a Pulitzer Prize.